CARLO ROSSELLI

CARLO ROSSELLI

Socialist Heretic and
Antifascist Exile

. . . .

Stanislao G. Pugliese

HARVARD UNIVERSITY PRESS

Cambridge, Massachusetts

London, England · 1999

Library of Congress Cataloging-in-Publication Data

Pugliese, Stanislao G., 1965–
Carlo Rosselli : socialist heretic and antifascist exile / Stanislao G. Pugliese.
p.   cm.
Includes bibliographical references and index.
ISBN 0-674-00053-6 (cloth : alk. paper)
1. Rosselli, Carlo, 1899–1937—Views on socialism.   2. Socialists—Italy.
3. Fascism—Italy.   4. Liberalism—Italy.   I. Title.
HX289.7.R67P84   1999
335′.0092—dc21
99-31395

To Jennifer
for the past

• • • •

To Alessandro
for the future

. . . .
Contents

· · · ·
Illustrations

. . . .
Acknowledgments

After nearly a decade of work on Italian antifascism, I have accumulated numerous debts and would like to acknowledge them here.

The Ph.D. Program in History at the CUNY Graduate School made it possible for the son of immigrants to pursue a life of the mind and a teaching career. I wish to thank Professors Abraham Ascher, Paul Avrich, John Cammett, Philip Cannistraro, Daniel Gasman, Mary Gibson, David Nasaw, Stuart Prall, Bernard Semmel, and John Weiss for their intellectual guidance and personal interest in my work. Frank Rosengarten supported this project from its inception with his friendship and scholarship.

My thanks to Charles F. Delzell, whose classic *Mussolini's Enemies: The Italian Antifascist Resistance* was the first book I read as a graduate student in the magnificent Reading Room of the New York Public Library. John Patrick Diggins and the participants in a Summer 1995 Mellon Seminar gave useful advice on an earlier draft of the manuscript, as did Joel Blatt, Alexander De Grand, Roy Domenico, Abbott Gleason, William McCuaig, Nadia Urbinati, David Ward, and Dan S. White. Giulia Melucci and Rosemary Ahern also read the manuscript and offered excellent suggestions. I am grateful to the Society for Italian Historical Studies, which granted this work the SIHS Award for Best Unpublished Manuscript in 1996.

I would like to express my appreciation to the University Seminars at Columbia University for assistance in the preparation of the manuscript for publication. Material drawn from this work was presented to the Columbia University Seminar on Studies in Modern Italy, whose members made insightful comments

My research in Italy was facilitated and encouraged by the Bianchino family, who always had an open door for a wandering American cousin. In

Italy I received gracious assistance from Lidia Amendola, the late Costanzo Casucci, Aldo Garosci, Pietro Polito, Giorgio Spini, the Honorable Valdo Spini, as well as the directors and staff of the Istituto Storico della Resistenza in Toscana, the Istituto Nazionale per la Storia del Movimento di Liberazione in Italia, and the Archivio Centrale dello Stato in Rome. For their gracious hospitality and encouragement, I am indebted to John Rosselli, Lisa Sarfatti, and Silvia Rosselli.

The Hofstra College of Liberal Arts and Sciences supported my work with two Faculty Research and Development Grants and a Presidential Research Award; I wish to thank Dean Bernard J. Firestone and my colleagues in the Department of History for their collegial support. I owe a special debt of gratitude to my former teachers at Hofstra University, especially John T. Marcus, Pellegrino D'Acierno, and the late Thomas V. Belmonte.

At Harvard University Press, I was most fortunate in working with Jeff Kehoe, Assistant Editor for History and Social Science, whose professionalism, encouragement, and sound advice have made this a better book. Carolyn Ingalls improved the manuscript with her meticulous editing. The anonymous scholars who read and offered useful criticism will, I hope, recognize some of their suggestions here.

For their moral support, I am indebted to the Romanello family, especially *consigliere* Salvatore Romanello. The Murphy family proved to be a source of grace over the years. Carman Pugliese was patient in guiding me through the (still) complex world of computer technology and rescuing parts of the manuscript from cyberspace oblivion. This work could not have been completed without the sustenance provided by my parents, Angelo and Lena Pugliese, who passed on to me a love of learning and teaching, inspiring by quiet example.

Finally, this book is dedicated to Jennifer Romanello and to our son Alessandro Antonio Pugliese in the hope that one day he may come to understand why his father dedicated years to such a study and why his parents named him "defender of men."

CARLO ROSSELLI

. . . .

Introduction

A man lives not only his personal life as an individual, but also, consciously or unconsciously, the life of his epoch and contemporaries.

THOMAS MANN, *THE MAGIC MOUNTAIN* (1924)

Who am I?
I am a socialist . . .
A young socialist—a new and dangerous kind.

CARLO ROSSELLI, *LIBERAL SOCIALISM* (1930)

In the late spring of 1937, two brothers were brutally assassinated on a lonely stretch of road in the tranquil French countryside. Both men were Italian antifascists, but with different temperaments and ideological positions. Nello Rosselli, the younger of the two, was a liberal democrat and a respected historian of the Risorgimento, who represented a quiet yet unwavering moral opposition to the fascist regime. Nello's scholarly works, although dealing with the nineteenth century, stand as an explicit condemnation of fascism. His older brother, Carlo, was a heretical socialist who prided himself on being the enfant terrible of Italian antifascism; he was intransigent in his harsh criticism not only of fascism but also of the culture of liberal Italy that produced such a monstrous political animal.

A tolerant revolutionary, a humane fighter, and a skeptical prophet, Carlo Rosselli was a crucial protagonist of Italian antifascism, but the complexity and richness of his thought have led to varying interpretations of his role in the antifascist movement. Rosselli has been called both the "Mazzini of the twentieth century" and the "critical conscience of Commu-

1

nism."[1] He is a figure known to some in America as "a hero of the Italian resistance to fascism . . . a larger-than-life figure."[2] For many he was "a prophet of the Italian Republic."[3] Michael Walzer has called him "the Italian Camus."[4] H. Stuart Hughes notes that Rosselli was the organizer of "the most dynamic wing of anti-Fascism in exile." Another scholar cites him as "one of the greatest Italian socialists, one of the greatest twentieth-century Italians, and one of the greatest European antifascists."[5] With Antonio Gramsci in prison and leading intellectuals such as Piero Gobetti, Giacomo Matteotti, and Giovanni Amendola murdered by the fascist regime, Carlo Rosselli was the most influential antifascist in the 1930s. No one else personified the ideals, potential, and problems of Italian antifascism as did Rosselli; he was the very incarnation of the Resistance. After his death, his ideas continued to shape both the theoretical and practical dimensions of Italian antifascism, bearing fruit in the Action Party and Rosselli Brigades during the armed Resistance. After the war, his liberal socialism remained a powerful subterranean current, always challenging the dominant hegemonic ideologies of the Italian Communist Party (PCI) and the Christian Democrats (DC).

Abandoning a promising career as a professor of political economy in the 1920s, Rosselli threw himself into the antifascist struggle. After several years of clandestine activity, including the publication of two important underground newspapers, he was instrumental in assisting Filippo Turati, the "grand old man" of Italian socialism, to flee the country in the face of fascist violence. For his role in Turati's escape, Rosselli was arrested; he defended himself in a dramatic trial but was imprisoned. In 1929, after a daring escape worthy of a nineteenth-century novel, he made his way to Paris, where he founded Justice and Liberty, the largest and most influential non-Marxist antifascist group in Italy and in exile. For Rosselli, the task of Justice and Liberty was nothing less than reconciling the political and social potential of the Russian Revolution with the scientific, humanistic, liberal legacy of the West. It is not surprising that the fascist regime considered Rosselli its most dangerous opponent both for his theoretical elaborations as well as for his political intransigence. The fascist Chief of Police, Arturo Bocchini, felt that Justice and Liberty represented a danger "potentially equal to that of the PCI."[6] For the Director of the Ecole Normale Supérieure in Paris, where Rosselli occasionally made inquiries for his studies, "No man was so dangerous for fascism as he with his wide culture, his finely tempered character, his rare mixture of coolness and audacity."[7]

Justice and Liberty was the only antifascist movement to arise after the victory of fascism and therefore was not tied to prefascist ideology. Characterized by an intellectual restlessness and creative heterogeneousness, it attracted some of the best minds in Italy: historians Gaetano Salvemini, Franco Venturi, Luigi Salvatorelli, Enzo Tagliacozzo, and Max Salvadori; writers Augusto Monti, Carlo Levi, Cesare Pavese, Leone Ginzburg, and Nicola Chiaromonte; Sardinian radical Emilio Lussu; juridical philosophers Silvio Trentin and Piero Calamandrei; and political philosopher Norberto Bobbio. During the armed Resistance against fascism and national socialism (1943–1945), Justice and Liberty was the inspiration behind the Action Party, second only to the PCI in its effectiveness and daring. A close reading of postwar Italy reveals that Rosselli's ideas remained a powerful current, attracting individuals who were repelled by the conservatism of the Christian Democrats but uncomfortable with the rigid orthodoxies of the PCI or the PSI, the Italian Socialist Party. These included Ferruccio Parri, Italy's first postwar prime minister; Sandro Pertini, president of the Republic; Giovanni Spadolini, the first non-Christian Democrat prime minister; and scores of other politicians, union leaders, and intellectuals. Rosselli worked feverishly to unify the disparate elements of Italian antifascism. On the theoretical plane, he never wavered in his insistence that socialism, far from opposing liberalism, was its natural heir, hence his heretical formulation of a "liberal socialism." At first glance, Rosselli might seem to be part of a long and noble tradition in European socialism, characterized as "between Marxism and anarchism" or "between reform and revolution" and personified by Benôit Malon and Jean Jaurès in France, Filippo Turati in Italy, Emile Vandervelde in Belgium, and Eduard Bernstein and Rudolf Hilferding in Germany. The fate of European democratic socialism has usually been described as a "dilemma" or a "tragedy"; but a recent work has argued that European democratic socialists were more creative, flexible, and original in their response to fascism than their communist brethren, and that they were responsible for the "genesis and articulation of novel socialist strategies" and the "driving force" for social change.[8]

Although Rosselli was deeply influenced by his social democratic colleagues in Italy and the rest of Europe, his liberal socialism was neither another attempt at socialist revisionism nor a variant of social democracy. Rather, Rosselli held that the revisionists were too timid theoretically, while the social democrats wished to repudiate nineteenth-century liberalism.

Liberal socialism did not identify socialism with liberalism, nor did it disavow classical political liberalism. Although it sounded like an impossible intellectual and political hybrid in Rosselli's day, liberal socialism has, in the words of one political scientist, "acquired modernity with the passage of time."[9] Liberal socialism is here understood to be a way of organizing society in which the state—as an expression of the community—seeks to defend and expand social rights as vigorously as it defends liberal rights. Rosselli would no doubt revel in the historical irony that the Democratici di Sinistra (DS), the latest incarnation of the Partito Democratico di Sinistra (PDS—itself the political heir of the Italian Communist Party) is the ideological heir of Justice and Liberty.[10]

Rosselli has also been associated with the recent turn to "market socialism." First coined as early as 1922 and developed during the interwar period, market socialism was a response to the contention that a rational economics and freedom were incompatible with socialism. Market socialism does not object to the market per se, but instead to *capitalist* markets, and it proposes a system in which markets are combined with social ownership of capital and production with the goal of greater economic efficiency, individual liberty, increased democracy, and social justice.[11] The ideology of the market may appear all-pervasive in ways that Karl Marx never imagined, yet to paraphrase Mark Twain, the recent reports of the "death of socialism" and the "end of history" have been greatly exaggerated.[12]

With the outbreak of the Spanish Civil War in 1936, Rosselli left Paris and was among the first to arrive in Barcelona in defense of the Republic. In Spain he commanded a volunteer column comprising anarchists, socialists, republicans, and members of Justice and Liberty (known as *giellisti* by the initials of the movement, Giustizia e Libertà). His radio broadcasts from Barcelona, beamed into Italy, probably sealed his fate. Since the early 1930s, Rosselli had been considered the regime's most dangerous enemy both for his founding of Justice and Liberty and his reported attempts to organize the assassination of Mussolini. His constant demand for a "preventive revolution" was read (correctly) by the fascist police as a thinly veiled call for assassination. The regime responded in kind: OVRA (the fascist secret police) called GL "the most dangerous of the conspiratorial movements," while an anonymous spy reported from Paris that "the greatest danger comes from Rosselli, and, in my view, it is absolutely necessary that he be suppressed."[13]

With his dramatic life, unbounded enthusiasm, and forceful charisma, Rosselli is a rich source for the biographer. Through his life and ideas, we can unravel some of the more complicated episodes of twentieth-century Italian history and can address some of the more important philosophical issues of modern society: totalitarianism and the character of the modern state; the role of intellectuals in forging contemporary culture; and the moral necessity of resistance to oppression. This work, the first English-language study of Rosselli, situates him in the wider context of Italian antifascism.[14] American readers might recognize themes treated by the democratic socialist tradition of Michael Harrington or Irving Howe. Some might discern philosophical questions addressed by Richard Rorty and John Rawls. Rosselli and Justice and Liberty attracted the attention and support of independent thinkers in the United States: Supreme Court Justice Felix Frankfurter; the founder of the American Civil Liberties Union, Roger Baldwin; cultural critic Lewis Mumford; Alvin Johnson of the New School for Social Research; Norman Thomas; Dorothy Thompson; and writers at *The Nation, The New Republic,* and *Foreign Affairs.*[15] In Europe Rosselli could count on the support of Raymond Aron, Élie Halévy, André Malraux, G. D. H. Cole, R. H. Tawney, John Maynard Keynes, George Macaulay Trevelyan, Lady Nancy Astor, Geoffrey Dawson and Henry Wickham Steed (both editors of the London *Times*), G. P. Gooch, Thomas and Heinrich Mann, Harold Laski, Aldous Huxley, and Sidney and Beatrice Webb.

Rosselli was a more sophisticated theorist than has been acknowledged, though his political activism and clandestine work hindered him from elaborating a unified system of thought. Even if he had been given the time and opportunity, it is unlikely that he would have constructed a unified, closed, abstract ideology. Such a thought system would have contradicted his belief that political and social realities were in a constant state of transformation. His deeply felt humanism and historicism[16] were better expressed in the essay form, which he mastered. Those essays, together with his intransigent political activity, combined to produce a profound critique of Italian liberalism, socialism, and Marxism while elaborating a unique strain of Italian antifascism. Rosselli was to Italian antifascism what Benedetto Croce was to Italian philosophy. Croce spent a lifetime expanding the vistas of an Italian philosophical tradition that had once been in the forefront of European culture but that had become isolated and therefore ossified. Rosselli brought Italian liberalism and socialism closer to their European counterparts: the "utopian socialism" of John Stuart Mill and

Keynesian economics; the sincere idealism of Benôit Malon and the moral fervor of Jean Jaurès; the liberalism of Élie Halévy and Thomas Mann; the voluntarism of Henri Bergson and Georges Sorel; and always there was the great example of European anarchists: the demonic Mikhail Bakunin, the angelic Pietr Kropotkin, and the saintly Errico Malatesta.

In many ways, it may be more appropriate to think of Rosselli as a "public moralist" rather than as a political theorist (except for the puritanical vision that this phrase confers for the English reader). Public moralists seek to be both more ambitious and less alienated than the critic as "double agent." They are neither "mere rationalizers" nor "publicists of given ideologies," but seek to "deploy their distinctive voice in public intellectual debate." Ira Katznelson identifies England's T. H. Green, Germany's Walter Rauschenbusch, France's Jean Jaurès, and America's John Dewey as those who "sought to make liberalism more social and socialism more compatible with liberal democracy while tempering both with a large dose of civic virtue." [17] In the Italian tradition, we might think of the moral intensity of Savonarola railing against the despotism of the De Medici; the classic tyrannicide of a Brutus assassinating Caesar; Giordano Bruno or Galileo insisting on scientific truth in the face of Church dogma; Garibaldi's innate sense of justice; during fascism, Piero Gobetti or Antonio Gramsci suffering death at the hands of the regime; in our own time, Primo Levi being witness to the Holocaust. It was Gobetti who lamented the lack of a Protestant Revolution as the reason for Italy's political immaturity. We might think of Rosselli both as being a Hebrew prophet and as fostering a "revolution of the saints." [18] Rosselli as public moralist is most evident when he depicted fascist dictatorship and the betrayal of socialism in Stalin's Russia as two sides of the same coin of moral crisis in the West. He found fascism and Stalinism *morally offensive.* Rosselli refused to divorce politics, morality, and culture. Taking another road, we may find it fruitful (and controversial) to read Rosselli—notwithstanding the many differences—as an Italian variant on the Frankfurt School. [19]

Rosselli's heretical ideas of the 1920s and 1930s are today so commonplace that it is only with difficulty that we can grasp their originality. Together with a few other independent Italian thinkers, such as Benedetto Croce, Piero Gobetti, Giovanni Amendola, and Guido De Ruggiero, he defended a liberalism under attack from both the Left and the Right. Rosselli's critique of the established Italian political parties is all the more prescient after the massive corruption scandals of the 1990s; his analysis of the ontology of political parties is still a fruitful avenue for study; his differentiation between economic and political liberalism, which was greeted with scorn in his time, is nonetheless accepted by many today; his distinction between liberalism as a method and liberalism as a system was provocative; his study of fascism (flexible enough to change after 1933) has outlasted both the rigid class-based formulations of the communists and the flaccid explanation of the classic liberals; his defense of "bourgeois" values was bitterly attacked by his enemies; his idea of an ethical socialism countered the arguments of the "scientific" socialists; contrary to the legions of thinkers who had proclaimed the death of Marxism in order to bury socialism, Rosselli argued that it was necessary to bury Marx for socialism to be resurrected; and his argument of a preemptive, revolutionary war against fascism and nazism strikes us as bold and daring at a time when most European leaders were timid and fearful. Rosselli was among the first to recognize that fascism was the central fact of his time, neither the irrational parenthesis described by Benedetto Croce nor simply the brutal class reaction of an embattled bourgeoisie. Trained as a political economist, he was acutely conscious of the continuing power and importance of the bourgeoisie, while sensitive to the importance of bringing the proletariat, artisans, and peasants onto the stage of history. Before the era of the Popular Front, he argued that the appeal of fascism cut across class lines and that a revolutionary alliance of the proletariat, the peasants, and the bourgeoisie would be necessary to defeat fascism and thus usher in a second, and truly popular, Risorgimento. In forging a vital link between liberalism and socialism, he suggested a new politics by reexamining the role of the state and the function of political parties. His critique of the state recalls the great anarchist thinkers, while his insistence that the political party transform itself into a microcosm of the future socialist society rather than a replica of the oppressive state was provocative.

Rosselli was not without his defects. An unflattering portrait comes from no less than his own cousin, the noted writer Alberto Moravia. At age eleven, Moravia had received from Carlo a French copy of Dostoyevsky's *Crime and Punishment*. Moravia was close to both Carlo and Nello but critical of the "strongly bourgeoise atmosphere" in which they lived. The character of the antifascist Professor Quadri in Moravia's *The Conformist* is loosely based on Carlo:

> Quadri . . . had fled to Paris and had become one of the principal anti-Fascist leaders—perhaps the cleverest, the most wily, the most aggressive of all. His speciality, it seemed, was proselytism. Benefitting by his teach-

ing experience and his knowledge of the youthful mind, he was often successful in converting young men who were indifferent, or even of contrary opinions, and then urging them to bold and dangerous undertakings which were almost always disastrous, if not to him, their inspirer, at any rate to their artless executants. He did not appear, however, as he flung these initiates into the conspiratorial struggle, to feel any of the humane anxieties that, in view of his character, one might have been tempted to expect of him. On the contrary, he sacrificed them quite coolly in desperate actions that could be justified only as part of an extremely long-term plan and that, indeed, necessarily involved a cruel indifference to the value of human life.[20]

Unwittingly, Moravia replicated the image in the minds of the fascists themselves. A police report described Rosselli as "the most terrible [of the antifascists] . . . ambitious to excess, cold, calculating, ready to risk when it appeared to him that there was even a lone possibility of success."[21]

One may argue that Justice and Liberty had a fatal flaw. Even though it attracted some of the best minds in Italy and in exile, it was accused of being elitist and never managed to transform itself into a mass party. Although Rosselli devoted considerable attention to the peasants, artisans, and industrial workers, Justice and Liberty soon became known as the "party of intellectuals" and never achieved the mass support of its main ideological competitor, the PCI. Even the middle class failed to gravitate toward the movement, despite his insistence that fascism could not be defeated without bourgeois support. Instead, Justice and Liberty was the refuge of independent Leftist intellectuals. Its ideological heterogeneousness generated some of the most important discussions within the antifascist camp but proved in the end to be a political weakness. Rosselli was impatient with formal abstract theorizing and enamored of action, prompting some to compare him with the early stages of fascism itself. And although he excelled as a charismatic leader of an intransigent, underground, revolutionary movement, it is highly unlikely that he would have been successful as a postwar politician; he may not have had the skills necessary to compete with a wily Togliatti or a cunning De Gasperi. The political heir to Justice and Liberty—the Action Party—gave Italy her first postwar prime minister but could not challenge the mass parties of the PCI and the Christian Democrats. Yet a close examination of the larger political canvas during the fascist epoch as well as the immediate postwar period might lead to another conclusion: that Rosselli and Justice and Liberty were ultimately and tragically defeated less by their own shortcomings than by the inherent problems of antifascism and the ideological constraints of the Cold War. It is no coincidence that more than fifty years after the Second World War, Justice and Liberty finds itself to be at the center of an intellectual debate that bears more than a passing similarity to the notorious German *Historikerstreit* of the 1980s.

As a multifaceted re-creation of a worldview that some fear to be lost, this work employs a strategy of close reading of Rosselli's personal letters, journalism, and theoretical essays. The portrait that emerges is of an intellectual and activist ideologically positioned (not trapped) between Antonio Gramsci and Piero Gobetti. According to Marcel Cachin, editor of the French communist daily *L'Humanité*, Rosselli possessed a "perfect consciousness of Gramsci's social philosophy."[22] He was not only a remarkable and charismatic figure but also an original theorist of Italian antifascism. No one else was daring to make the same arguments, hence Rosselli's universally acknowledged status as a maverick, heretic, and the enfant terrible of Italian antifascism, even by those who were his ideological critics. Born into wealth and privilege, he renounced the subtle seductions of a comfortable bourgeois academic life. "We are the outlaws," he once wrote in defiance, "the traitors of the fascist nation and even of the old nation *tout court*."[23] A controversial reading of Rosselli might even position him in some sense as Mussolini's doppelgänger; with their common heretical positions, with their incessant thirst for action, with their charismatic personalities, Rosselli and Mussolini both reflected—each in a very different way—the failure of traditional political theories and politics.

An understanding of Rosselli and the movement is critical for a fuller comprehension of Italian antifascism and illuminates some of the darker corners in the labyrinth of twentieth-century Italian history. Italian historiography still lacks a tradition of biography; ironically, it is English-speaking scholars who have turned their attention to this genre.[24] I have tried to be aware of my own ideological position and hope that the worst defects of an uncritical reconstruction have been avoided. This work makes no claim to scientific objectivity; such a claim must be viewed with suspicion, especially in the realm of biography. Instead, this work is closer to Gaetano Salvemini's belief that "impartiality is a dream, honesty is a duty." My hope is that an inherent subjectivity and admiration for the subject have been tempered by a critical consciousness. If it is true that every work of writing is in some sense autobiographical, then the writing of biography must be even more so.

This reconstruction of Rosselli's life and thought is informed by the tropes of heresy, exile, and tragedy. I did not begin with this profane trinity in mind; rather, it seemed to impose itself in the course of writing. The triad might remind some of Stephen Dedalus's recourse to "silence, exile, and cunning."[25] Whereas James Joyce's own history—and the history of the Irish and countless millions—demanded cunning as an answer to the silence imposed by exile, Rosselli refused to be silenced by exile; his heresy was both cause and effect of that exile, ultimately ending in tragedy. He first earned a reputation as a heretic in the early 1920s by criticizing the "intellectual paralysis" of the Italian Socialist Party and insisted on an unrelenting "self-critique." Rosselli was adamant that socialism was not a "science" but rather a faith, and he infuriated his colleagues when he linked nineteenth-century liberalism to twentieth-century socialism. Simultaneously, he earned the wrath of contemporary liberals when he castigated them for not following liberalism through to its logical conclusion—socialism. Attacked by liberals on his right and orthodox socialists and Marxists on his left, he stubbornly carved out and defended a unique political space. In his analysis of fascism, he roundly condemned the legalitarian, pacific tactics of the traditional political parties and called for an illegal, revolutionary movement to fight totalitarianism with force.

That heretical stance would cast him into exile. In a perceptive essay, cultural critic Edward Said has revealed the essential nature of the exile experience that explains much of Rosselli's subsequent thinking and actions:

> Exile is strangely compelling to think about but terrible to experience. It is the unhealable rift between a human being and a native place, between the self and its true home: its essential sadness can never be surmounted. And while it is true that literature and history contain heroic, romantic, glorious, even triumphant episodes in an exile's life, these are no more than efforts meant to overcome the crippling sorrow of estrangement. The achievements of exile are permanently undermined by the loss of something left behind forever.[26]

Nothing could better illustrate Said's thesis than the collection of letters between Carlo and his wife, Marion Cave, appropriately titled *Dall'esilio*

(From Exile). Moments of "heroic, romantic, glorious, even triumphant" elation are overshadowed by a bitter sorrow and deep melancholy.[27] The Italian political philosopher Norberto Bobbio, himself profoundly affected by participation in the Action Party, once wrote that those who have committed themselves to the ideal of a liberal socialism have always experienced a condition of exile: for its founders, during the fascist regime, it was a political exile; for its followers, during the decades of the Cold War, it was a moral exile in their own country.[28]

Related to the reality of exile, the concept of the tragic hero is especially apt in aiding our understanding of Rosselli's life and death. "His gaze was fixed on a goal with a steadfastness that none of the rest of us could equal," Alberto Tarchiani wrote after the assassination. "He went forward to meet the future. It seemed as if an irresistible force drove him toward the Golgotha which he was one day to tread."[29] Rosselli first laid eyes on his firstborn son only from within the walls of a prison, several months after the baby's birth; his other two children were born in exile. His wife suffered not only from ill health but from depression as well, an affliction that would haunt his daughter and ultimately contribute to her suicide. "It is fate," Carlo once wrote to his wife, "that our children are born in tragedy." [30]

From the moment that he took up the antifascist struggle, Rosselli seemed to prefigure his own death. In his writings, images of sacrifice and death are ever present. "One sometimes has the impression," he wrote from exile, "that the journey must overwhelm everything according to an inevitability that appears almost inexorable." It appears that he was acutely aware of how his life would end: "This destiny of ours is not the fruit of chance but of a free and extremely conscious choice [*consapevolissima elezione*]; I couldn't conceive of it any other way."[31] Rosselli was at his most eloquent when commemorating the deaths of antifascist martyrs: the reform socialist member of Parliament, Giacomo Matteotti; the precocious "liberal revolutionary" Piero Gobetti; the resolute democrat Giovanni Amendola; and the brilliant communist Antonio Gramsci. Apparently Rosselli was fully conscious of the destiny that lay before him when he wrote of "the sad death in exile that appears almost inevitable for the finest sons of Italy."[32]

Rosselli personified an antithetical and possibly irreconcilable intellectual position: a sincere belief in the Enlightenment with its stress on the dignity of the individual, its faith in progress, and its optimism for the future, along with an ancient belief that the human condition is—in the end—profoundly tragic. Through the prism of Rosselli, we can see the contradictory, conflicted, paradoxical, and ironic position of the twentieth-century intellectual. He was a thinker always conscious of his own icono-clastic position, refusing to occupy the traditional space of the intellectual and resisting the temptation to forge another, competing hegemonic ide-ology. Instead, his thought is ideology in a minor key, always painfully aware of its own shortcomings, marked by a "critical demon" and a "virile doubt." Imprisoned, exiled, and finally murdered by the fascist regime, Rosselli is a crucial figure in the socialist and antifascist tradition. In him we might recognize our better natures. This work attempts to capture some faint echo of that heretical voice banished into exile and silenced by assassi-nation.

CHAPTER ONE

. . . .

Younger Brothers

Young men outraged by the corruption of the age and burning
with zeal for justice . . .

PIERRE-JOSEPH PROUDHON, *LA JUSTICE DANS
LA REVOLUTION ET DANS L'EGLISE* (1858)

There is a new system of life to put into place. At first we will have
bitter disillusions; but we must succeed. If not, one must arrive at
the sad conclusion that love among the Italians arises only during
war. And that would be a sad and painful paradox.

CARLO ROSSELLI, "NEW TASK" (1919)

Carlo Rosselli was born in Rome on 16 November 1899 to Giuseppe
Rosselli, a musicologist, and Amelia Pincherle, a noted author. Both the
Rosselli and Pincherle families had been actively involved in the Risorgi-
mento, the movement for national unification in nineteenth-century Italy.
The two families were part of an urbane, cosmopolitan, and polyglot "cultural aristocracy," secure in its social position and confident in its abilities.
As secular Jews and members of the upper bourgeoisie, the Rosselli and
Pincherle families fully participated in the commercial, political, and cultural life of the new nation. They saw their emancipation directly tied to
the Risorgimento and the Enlightenment, liberating Italy and her Jews
from the rule of both the Austrians and the papal authorities. Amelia
recalled that her parents "belonged to that period which still remained
aware of the benefits of the liberation from the ghettos."[1] Accordingly, like
almost all of their fellow Italian Jews, they supported the constitutional
monarchy as it was formed in 1861. Scholars as diverse as Antonio Gramsci
and Arnaldo Momigliano have noted that the full assimilation of Italian
Jews proceeded apace after unification. Two Italian Jews, Luigi Luzzatti and
Sidney Sonnino, became prime ministers, and Jews were promoted and

13

decorated in all ranks of the military, in stark contrast to countries like Germany or the France of Dreyfus.[2]

In 1841 members of the Rosselli family in London met the exiled hero of the Risorgimento, Giuseppe Mazzini. Not only did they become passionate Anglophiles (Giuseppe Rosselli was called "Joe" at home, and Carlo would eventually marry an Englishwoman), but the encounter with Mazzini transformed them into active participants in the struggle for Italian independence. The Rosselli family kept—almost as a sacred relic—a note from Mazzini to Sabatino Rosselli, asking the latter to purchase "fifty sacks of the usual merchandise" (arms and weapons for the unification movement). Mazzini was to pass the last days of his life with the family of Pellegrino Rosselli in Pisa, dying in their home on 10 March 1872 under the assumed name Joseph Brown.[3]

Madre

After an intense courtship of several years,[4] Joe Rosselli and Amelia Pincherle were married on 3 April 1892 and moved to Vienna, where Joe continued his studies and career as a musicologist. In July 1895, Aldo, their first son, was born in the Austrian capital. Amelia's 1898 play *Anima* was first staged in Turin, garnering national acclaim and winning a literary prize. The famed writer Alberto Moravia, a first cousin of the Rosselli brothers, recalled his aunt Amelia as "severe and sentimental," whereas his uncle Joe was an artist, "a weak man" who may have encouraged Amelia's identification of him with Franz Liszt.[5] Amelia could view the world with a stark, brutal honesty. Her letters to Joe reveal an extremely intelligent, strong-willed, and independent woman, serious and assertive and yet sometimes insecure and uncertain, with a trace of puritanism, inflexibility, and calculating shrewdness. For his part, Joe often sought refuge from the demands of their relationship in the complexities of his favorite composers, Liszt, Beethoven, and Brahms. He seemed to revel in the role of the seemingly carefree yet tormented artist, constantly fleeing Rome or Florence but always sending Amelia flowers from wherever he might happen to be. Revealingly, whereas Amelia preferred Tolstoy, Joe favored Zola.

Joe, Amelia, and Aldo returned to Rome, where Carlo was born; a year later, the third son and last child, Sabatino (Nello), was born in Florence. These were momentous years for the young country: in 1896 Italy suffered a humiliating defeat at Adowa in an ill-conceived attempt to acquire an

African "empire"; in 1898 the military fired on unarmed workers as political repression set in; yet the next year—in the very month of Carlo's birth—Filippo Turati of the Italian Socialist Party was elected to Parliament.

In 1901 Joe and Amelia separated, ending what their grandson Aldo intuited as a great love and leaving indissoluble traces of bitterness that remained until Joe's premature death a decade later. Amelia and the three boys enjoyed considerable wealth from their shares in Siele, one of Europe's largest mining concerns. A temporary but serious financial setback in 1903 forced them to move to more "modest" quarters in Florence. Still, the Rosselli brothers had a privileged childhood, living in a house with Biedermeyer furniture, Ming vases, a Steinway piano, and Bokhara carpets. Marital separation and Joe's early death meant that Amelia was charged with the upbringing of her three young sons, becoming the dominant force in their moral and intellectual development. The president of the Italian Republic, Sandro Pertini, a colleague of Carlo's in the antifascist struggle, recalled that Amelia was "always an exemplary wife, mother, grandmother; a very fine writer, truly worthy to be remembered among the great Italians of this century."[6] Writing from prison years later and meditating on the relationship with his mother, Carlo wrote to her what was at once both a homage and a not-so-subtle declaration of his independence:

> In real life—like the fictional one of subjects in a novel or the theater— there is always an inevitable separation between the creator and the creation. And the more worthy, noble, and pure the labor of the creator, the more so will be the autonomous capacity of the creation for life and original development. The great artist is distinguished precisely by the rare privilege of being able to provide for the creation its own initiative and unmistakable life which allows it to evolve on paths other than those marked for it.[7]

Carlo spent much of his life in an intellectual and emotional tug-of-war with his formidable mother. An illuminating episode concerning Aldo reveals something of her character: noticing that her eldest had developed a streak of social vanity, snobbery, and overweening pride, Amelia sent him to work as an apprentice in the humble shop of a local Florentine carpenter. The incident became the basis for her short story of 1909 in which a wealthy young boy embarks on a personal odyssey, discovering the privations, sacrifices, and dignity of another stratum of society. The paternalistic moral of the tale—that wealth and privilege impose social responsibilities—was not lost on the three brothers. Family letters reveal a continuous dialogue concerning politics, culture, and society, demonstrating that the Rosselli brothers developed a strong social conscience at an early age.[8]

Amelia's writings were to be reflected in the character, thought, and actions of her three sons. A recurring motif of her work was the seemingly intractable problem of poverty and the conflict between different social classes trapped in the defense of their respective interests. In her 1903 collection of novellas, *Gente oscura* (Obscure People), the protagonists were the working and nonworking poor who were portrayed in a way that received a sympathetic review in the Socialist daily *Avanti!*; the reviewer declared that such a depiction of the laboring classes had to have been written by a socialist.[9] Although Amelia was close to several members of the Italian Socialist Party, she, like most other members of the upper bourgeoisie, supported the conservative-liberal parliamentary state. Before 1922 she was a fervent nationalist in her politics and a follower of D'Annunzio in her aesthetics. Yet her writings would create an active interest in social problems and a sense of duty, obligation, and responsibility in all three brothers. The ideals that she passed on to them were the imperative of moral freedom; a heroic modern sensibility reminiscent of Ibsen, whom she admired; the emancipation of men and women from the hypocritical dictates of convention; and a submission to the dictates of conscience—of the free will striving for, but never actually achieving, perfection.[10] She was active in the cultural life of Florence and familiar with contemporary political debates.[11] Among the founders of the Lyceum of Florence, Amelia Rosselli counted some of the most important politicians of Italy among her acquaintances. At the Rosselli house in Florence, the family paper was not *La Nazione* of that city (which supported neutrality in 1914), but *Il Corriere della Sera* of Milan, which advocated intervention in the First World War on the side of France and Britain. It was in this liberal, nationalist, interventionist milieu that the Rosselli brothers first became immersed in politics.[12]

Carlo was a vivacious child, with a lively temperament, naturally generous and extroverted. His character could not be tamed by a classical education. He found Latin and the humanities to be especially difficult and was proficient only in mathematics. Amelia, aware of his nature, made the courageous decision to withdraw him from the classical *ginnasio* and enroll him in a local technical school. This was no small decision, considering that the *ginnasio* (middle school) traditionally led to the university and eventually a "proper" bourgeois career, whereas the technical schools implied a certain social and intellectual inferiority. Consequently, Rosselli did not receive the classical, literary, humanist education that formed his contemporaries in the antifascist struggle but was trained in a more pragmatic and practical tradition. This orientation would inform his later thinking and make him wary of elaborate, sophisticated "systems" of thought with their obtuse abstractions. Carlo acquired "culture" only through an intense immersion in the classical humanist tradition after the war; he felt that his position as a leader of antifascism required a command of that intellectual and cultural legacy.

Carlo and Nello were often inseparable, but they were a study in contrasts. Carlo was animated, passionate in his convictions, anxious to transform thought into action, eager to argue for hours, willing and able to command others. Nello was more the scholar, quiet yet passionate about his historical studies.[13] Also, he was well liked by everyone who met him, in marked contrast to Carlo, who sometimes provoked highly emotional reactions—both positive and negative—in the people he met. The two would often argue about questions of the day, with Carlo building in enthusiasm to a conclusion until Nello would cry out in exasperation, "Enough, I can't take it any more!"[14] Carlo's overflowing vitality needed to express itself in unceasing activity. Nello was of a gentle, serene, contemplative disposition. Whereas Carlo's immediate desire was to act, Nello considered all aspects of a problem before deciding on a course of action. Carlo was willing to change course if he felt mistaken, but Nello—once his mind was made up—never wavered.

Judaism

Italian Judaism was a "rare and exquisite flower" that bloomed during the mid-nineteenth century, only to wilt with the racial laws of fascist Italy in 1938.[15] Carlo Rosselli experienced a brief yet acute religious crisis at the tender age of twelve after the death of his father. As Passover approached, he made it known to his mother that he wished to attend the religious ceremonies. Amelia accordingly brought the children to the magnificent synagogue in Florence, where, from the women's gallery, she sent down her sons to stand under the *taleb* of their uncle Pellegrino for the family blessing.[16]

Carlo Rosselli was never a practicing Jew, yet in his writings, one can find traces of the ethical impulse of the ancient Hebrew prophets. In the Preface to his *Liberal Socialism,* he explicitly claims that socialists are "the disciples of the prophets." Socialism derived from the "messianism of Israel," which demanded "terrestrial justice" and spurred a "myth of equality." So strong was this "spiritual torment" that it "forbids all indulgence."[17] Rosselli's famous radio broadcast from Barcelona in 1936, "Today in Spain, tomorrow in Italy," bears an unmistakable resemblance to the traditional Hebrew Passover Haggadah, "This year in exile; next year in the land of Israel."[18]

Amelia Rosselli once explained that she and most other Italian Jews supported the liberal monarchy because the new nation-state had opened the gates of the ghetto and permitted Jews to participate in the life of the country. The reactionary binds of the Austrians and the Papal States were replaced by a tolerance that other Jews in Europe rarely enjoyed. In her unpublished memoir, *Memoriale,* she proudly revealed the position of her fellow Jews: "[We are] Jews, but *first and foremost* Italians. I, too, born and raised in that profoundly Italian and liberal atmosphere, preserved only the purest essence of my religion, in my heart. These were religious elements of a solely *moral* character; and this was the only religious education I gave my children."[19] Amelia could even be an unsparing critic of Judaism, as in a letter to Carlo regretting the distinction that Judaism made among men. She recognized that Judaism's "great characteristic" (monotheism) had not been superseded by any other religion but that Christianity had added something fundamental: equality among men.[20]

In London during the autumn of 1924, as the English were preparing for national elections, Carlo met Emilio and Enzo Sereni, the former a communist, the latter an ardent Zionist. Although he did not support Zionism, Carlo found much to admire in Enzo Sereni; no doubt—like Primo Levi—he recognized a spiritual affinity with young men and women who were willing to "sacrifice their intellectual and material life for the attainment of an ideal that seems unattainable to me."[21]

If Carlo can best be described as a "modernist Jew," Nello was more sensitive to his religious heritage, joining the Federazione Giovanile Ebraica Italiana. It was Nello who best articulated how the Rosselli brothers related to their Jewish heritage. In a speech at a Zionist conference in November 1924, he explained their ambiguous ties to Judaism. Confessing that he did not attend the synagogue on Saturday, that he was ignorant of Hebrew, that he did not support the Zionist cause, and that he did not observe any of the religious practices demanded by his religion, Nello asked, "How can I call myself a Jew?"

> I call myself a Jew . . . because . . . the monotheistic conscience is inde-structible in me . . . because every form of idolatry repels me . . . because I regard with Jewish severity the duties of our lives on earth, and with Jewish serenity the mystery of life beyond the tomb—because I love all men as in Israel it was commanded . . . and I have therefore that social conception which seems to me descends from our best traditions.[22]

Although Carlo would later write that "there is only one ethic . . . the ethic of Socrates, Christ, and Kant," clearly their Jewish heritage remained a subtle component of the Rosselli brothers' private and public personae.[23] Carlo's later eclectic religiosity was a mixture of Judaism's ethical impulse toward social justice and equality, Kant's categorical imperative, and a humanistic socialism. Consequently, one might disagree with H. Stuart Hughes's description of him as "the greatest of Jewish oppositionists" to the fascist regime, but at least three scholars have intuited that the Hebraic legacy may have had more of an influence on Rosselli than he himself admitted.[24]

War

In 1911 Liberal prime minister Giovanni Giolitti guided an Italy inflamed by nationalist passion into a war with Libya as part of a colonial policy to acquire an African "Empire." The right wing of the PSI supported the war effort; it was subsequently expelled, and the party swung to the left, under the charismatic leadership of Benito Mussolini. Anna Kuliscioff, the fiery Russian revolutionary who was mistress first to Andrea Costa and then to Filippo Turati, was devastating in her assessment: Mussolini was "nothing of a Marxist, nor is he really a socialist at all," she quipped, "he is a sentimental poetaster who has read Nietzsche." Angelica Balabanoff was to write that Mussolini was, after Grigori Zinoviev (first secretary-general of the Comintern), the most despicable person she had ever met.[25] By June 1914, the country was on the verge of civil war, which almost exploded during the events of the *settimana rossa* (Red Week). When the First World War broke out two months later, Carlo was not quite fifteen years old, yet the correspondence with his mother reveals a young man already familiar with international politics. Florence in 1914 was experiencing a cultural renaissance through the work of Giuseppe Prezzolini, Ardengo Soffici, Giovanni Papini, and others. The country as a whole was witnessing a new type of nationalism created by Enrico Corradini, former editor of the political review *Il Regno* (1903–1906). Corradini had forged an ideology of reactionary and radical nationalism that aimed to incorporate the emerging proletariat, thus defusing its revolutionary potential. His particular strain of nationalism featured state sovereignty, strong executive leadership, social cohesion, enlistment of the working class, the disciplinary function of hierarchy, reconciliation between church and state, irredentism, militarism, the corporate state and colonial empire[26]—a program taken over in its entirety by Mussolini. Corradini had also been cofounder and director of the art periodical *Germinal* and director of the literary review *Marzocco,* clearly illustrating the nexus between art, literature, and the politics of nationalism.

The Rosselli family instead espoused a cosmopolitan, culture-oriented nationalism. They were also convinced interventionists. In her 1921 work *Fratelli minori* (Younger Brothers), Amelia Rosselli painted a poignant image of her family on that night in May 1915 when Italy entered the war:

> It was an unforgettable sight . . . The older brother was in the void of the gaping door, hair in the wind, face lit up, almost hidden beneath the cloth of the tricolor . . . there was an open window, with fresh and sweet air bursting in and the pealing of bells . . . Her heart strained. Behind them, straight and rigid on the threshold, the mother watched with a fixed stare that saw nothing. They threw themselves upon her, yelling with happiness. The mother wept . . . .[27]

When Carlo returned from his summer vacation in 1914 at the beach resort of Viareggio, his mother, who had been vacationing in the mountains for her health, noted a marked change in her son: he was "another person," taking up his studies with a vengeance and returning to his beloved piano. Meanwhile, Aldo had refused the privilege as a medical student and as the eldest son of a widow of being assigned to the Red Cross, volunteering instead for the infantry, where he soon rose to the rank of lieutenant. Since his sector was relatively quiet, he requested a transfer to the front. Aldo, who had been born in Vienna, was killed by the Austrians in battle on 27 March 1916.[28] The death of her eldest (and by all accounts her favorite) son left an indelible impression on Amelia Rosselli. *Fratelli minori* was both a memorial to Aldo as well as a moral challenge to Carlo and Nello to live up to her idealized vision of the martyred son, and the work was also symbolic of the intersection of the private, the public, and the political that was to characterize the Rosselli family. It was a narrative about the "older brothers" (such as Aldo), who had died in the war and the "fratelli minori" or younger brothers (such as Carlo, Nello, and their colleagues), who returned from the front or had not fought at all. There was, perhaps, a note of reproach in the work that did not escape the younger brothers.

Carlo, influenced by his mother's fervent nationalism and by Gaetano Salvemini's paper *L'Unità*, was a "democratic interventionist"—believing that the war was a moral, ethical, and political struggle between the reactionary forces of Austria-Hungary and Germany against the liberal, democratic traditions of France and Britain. Participating in the war left an indelible mark on Rosselli, as it did on countless others of the "war generation."[29] For many participants, this experience and the resulting demoralizing return to civilian life led to fascism, whereas for Rosselli the war worked to crystallize certain vague ideas regarding the social problems of modern Italy. In his own words, it was the war experience that, at least in part, liberated him from "the isolation of class" and made him feel the necessity for political and social renewal. The upheaval of the war was to be found not only in things but also in the souls and consciences of all those who had fought. Its ruins had been sown in the young and the old, those who had fought and those who had remained behind.[30]

In June 1917, Carlo was called to arms and four months later was enrolled in a course for military officials at Caserta. He passed the winter of 1917–18 at the front in the mountains of northeastern Italy. War for Rosselli was "a great school of life," an incubator of ideas, a revealer of false idols; "I left a boy and returned a man," he wrote years later.[31] As a lieutenant in the crack mountain troops of the Alpini, he experienced an epiphany via contact with ordinary soldiers, most of whom were simple peasants from the South. While many intellectuals were scornful of the "masses," Rosselli was struck by their profound sense of justice and equality, their "remarkable *virtù*." The daily contact with death and unimaginable suffering—the "small and eternal tragedies"—cured nationalistic youth of their inebriated folly. The war forced them to "understand many things that certainly would have escaped them in their isolation of class."[32]

A great and bitter irony of the war was that it was fought by many as the last battle of the Risorgimento to bring about the final unification, this time in spirit, of the new nation. Instead, the war revealed and exacerbated the social tensions created by unification and fostered an atmosphere that contributed to the rise and appeal of fascism. The government, by promising both land and glory during the war that it knew it would not and could not provide, brought upon itself the wrath of the returning soldiers. Wilson's postwar orchestration of the peace made moot the secret clauses of the Treaty of London and contributed to the creation of the myth of the "mutilated victory." In the concept of war as a force of moral and spiritual renewal, Rosselli recognized an affinity between revolutionary syndicalism and nationalism (he could have added futurism and fascism as well).[33]

By the end of the war, Rosselli began to feel the hindrance of his sparse education. He lamented his placement in a technical school instead of in the more traditional *liceo* (classical school) which would have allowed him entry to university. During the first two decades of the twentieth century, Italian cultural and intellectual life was a smoldering cauldron of irrationalists and mystics (Giuseppe Prezzolini, Giovanni Papini); antidemocrats (Vilfredo Pareto, Gaetano Mosca); decadents (Gabriele D'Annunzio); positivists (Cesare Lombroso, Roberto Ardigò, Enrico Ferri); nationalists (Enrico Corradini), Marxists (Labriola, Gramsci); and idealists (Gentile, Croce). Rosselli read them all and rejected most of what they had to offer. During the last months of the war, he was increasingly interested in social and political problems and studied the works of the Neapolitan historian Pasquale Villari and the political philosophy of Giuseppe Mazzini. Rosselli was drawn to Alfredo Oriani's *La rivolta ideale* (The Ideal Revolt) published in 1908, which tried to resurrect the lost dimension of a heroic, popular, and democratic Risorgimento, but he rejected Oriani's imperialism, nationalism, and authoritarianism. This concern with social and political problems—derived from Gaetano Salvemini, Piero Gobetti, and Leo Ferrero—was evident in his earliest essays. "Compito nuovo" (New Task) is evidence of a new vitality among Italy's youth, tempered by the experience of the war that was "destroyer and creator, dissolver and evolver, brake and catalyst for every passion, hate and love together." The war, Rosselli wrote, had the power of stripping man of all his lying vestments; his soul then appears in all its fierce dignity or its cowardice. Perhaps thinking of his own privileged background, he proposed abolishing all the private schools, since "it is not proper that because of the stupid fear of retrograde parents, the child of the wealthy does not know the child of the poor, and therefore grows up in the most perfect ignorance of the life of the people, nourished only by unjust and evil prejudice." He closed the essay with a poignant plea: "We want to know and be known . . . There is before us a new system of life to put into place. At first we will have bitter disillusions; but we must succeed. If not, one must arrive at the sad conclusion that love among the Italians arises only during war. And that would be a sad and painful paradox."[34] Rosselli believed that the war generation and its experience would pave the way for a rebirth and moral regeneration of political, social, and cultural life in Italy. The war changed the perception of politics in all social classes. Between 1915, when Italy entered the war, and 1920, a potential social revolution was brewing in the country. The Russian Revolutions of 1917, the occupation of the factories by the workers' councils in Turin, D'Annunzio's expedition to Fiume, and the rise of fascism all contributed to a new obsession with politics. In Milan on 23 March 1919, Mussolini laid the foundations of the fascist party in organizing the fascio di combattimento, composed mostly of ex-soldiers. A month later, they destroyed the printing press of the PSI daily organ, *Avanti!*. Intimidation, beatings, arson, and murder were to be their weapons of choice as a veritable civil war enflamed northern and central Italy. The internecine warfare within the PSI did little to combat the new movement. When the revolutionaries declared the moment ripe for insurrection, Turati witheringly remarked that a party that could not protect its own printing presses could hardly make a revolution.[35] The Second Congress of the Communist International a year later laid down twenty-one conditions for membership in an attempt by Lenin to control the various national parties. In January 1921, the communist faction (itself divided between Amadeo Bordiga's soviet strategy and Antonio Gramsci's worker-council movement) broke off to form the PCd'I (PCI). Another split (the endemic disease of Italian socialism) occurred in October 1922 when Giacomo Matteotti formed the Italian Socialist Unitary Party (PSU), just as Mussolini was organizing his "March on Rome." When a wave of strikes in 1920 led to the occupation of factories in the North, it seemed as though the revolution was at hand; but it was not to be. Giolitti skillfully defused the revolutionary situation, and stability returned, but the industrialists and large landowners were not convinced. As the anarchist Errico Malatesta prophetically lamented, "If we let this favorable moment pass, we shall later pay with tears of blood for the fear we have instilled in the bourgeoisie."[36]

The war pushed Rosselli into a vague, humanitarian socialism. He and Nello wrote several novellas, all with the same theme: a young idealistic youth gives up all his worldly possessions and devotes his life to the *popolo;* in essence, the youth is a modern-day St. Francis of Assisi. After the war, they approached their mother and proposed the following: "What would you think if we abandoned our house and our inheritance? If we asked you to come live with us, a poor life based only on what we earned?" Amelia Rosselli, realizing that her sons were in earnest and feeling that their sincerity merited a respectful reply, responded that there was nothing intrinsically wrong with their proposal but that she could not see any use in it. Would it not be better to use their wealth and position to achieve their noble goals? The two brothers looked at each other and then said, "We thought you would answer like that. We were sure that you would not ridicule or deride our ideas." Yet from that moment on, Amelia recalled, she felt distanced from her two surviving sons, separated from another world that she could neither participate in nor understand.[37]

After his return from military duty, Carlo began to frequent socialist circles in Florence after Alessandro Levi, a family member, introduced him to Filippo Turati, leader of the PSI, and to Claudio Treves. Turati and Treves had been appointed by prime minister Orlando to a postwar commission to address the problems raised by the conflict. Both had to resign under pressure from the maximalist forces in the PSI. By August 1918, the PSI had returned to a revolutionary program and could not accept any compromise with the Liberal regime. Rosselli was drawn to Turati's good humor, paternalism, and human sympathy. The PSI could boast of a glorious but fractured past: founded in 1892 by including the Italian Workers' Party and expelling the anarchists, it was always riven by an internal split. A maximalist wing insisted on an orthodox Marxism and cultivated the rhetoric, if not the reality, of violent social revolution. The revolutionaries propounded a synthesis of Marxism and positivism; Enrico Ferri, Arturo Labriola, and Enrico Leone put forth Darwin, Spencer, and Marx as prophets for the new age. A reformist wing, revolving around Turati, Treves, and Modigliani, was willing to acknowledge the benefits of the parliamentary system and the possibility, if not the necessity, of achieving a socialist society through peaceful alternatives. This perpetual division would continue to be the fatal flaw of the PSI, even after the left wing broke off to form the PCI in January 1921. Turati's political and cultural review, *Critica Sociale,* was the intellectual anchor, and a party newspaper, *Avanti!,* was born on Christmas Day 1896. Repression soon followed, but the PSI became, along with the Catholic Popular Party (PPI), the largest mass party in Italy.

In the fall of 1919, Rosselli enrolled in the Istituto di Studi Scienze Sociali "Cesare Alfieri" in Florence, receiving his *liceo* diploma. He once recounted a telling incident involving the future fascist Italo Balbo that took place at the school:

> One must return to 1920. The [future] Quadrumvir of the Revolution [Italo Balbo], today in disgrace [1936] had to take an exam in international law . . . he didn't have a clue, but as a good *squadrista* [fascist thug] he didn't forget that force always prevails over law, above all in that nebulous jurisdiction that is international law. He took the exam with a frail and timid professor. At the end of the exam, confronted with total disaster, Italo Balbo crashed a big fist on the table, making the professor turn pale with fright:
>
> "Either you pass me or it will end badly."
>
> "I can't, you don't know anything. You have no right to be promoted."
>
> "Either you pass me or it will end badly."
>
> The professor left the hall in haste, but Balbo was right behind him in a "punitive expedition." A tram saved the professor. But Balbo passed the exam in international law.[38]

Balbo later gained fame for his exploits as an aviator, and few seemed to remember that he was implicated in the murder of an antifascist priest, Father Giuseppe Minzoni, in August 1923. (When he sued a newspaper for libel in linking his name with the murder, he lost the case and was forced to pay damages.)

By the time Carlo was discharged and returned to his studies, he was already beginning to question the ideas, assumptions, and presuppositions of democratic interventionism. His reading of the French pacifist writers Henri Barbusse and Romain Rolland forced him to reconsider the war and to forge a deeper understanding of the motives of democratic interventionism and of the neutralism of the PSI. By December 1920, the veteran Rosselli was a very different person from the interventionist of 1915. Carlo must have realized that his new perception of the war was a blow to his mother, who clung to an heroic illusion of the conflict to console her for the loss of her eldest son.

Trade Unionism

Rosselli continued his studies, completing his work for a degree in social science with a thesis on revolutionary syndicalism, which he defended in

June 1921. The thesis reflects his concern with the political, social, and economic events taking place in Italy and Europe after the war. In August and September 1920, the FIAT factories of Turin were occupied by workers under the influence of Gramsci's *L'Ordine Nuovo* movement, while the relationship between the Confederazione Generale di Lavoro (CGL) and the PSI was reaching crisis levels concerning the role and function of the workers' union in the modern state. The thesis, which demonstrates an easy familiarity with the economic and political theories currently evolving in Britain, Germany, and France, begins with a historical review of workers' associations in ancient Rome and sketches various types of unions from the revolutionary brand to the reformist and even Christian workers' unions. In attempting to define trade unionism, Rosselli cited Bernstein ("organized free-trade"); Arturo Labriola ("free-trade of class"); and the Belgian economist Griffuelhes ("le mouvement de la classe ouvrière qui veut parvenir à la pleine possession de ses droits sur l'usine et sur l'atelier"). But for Rosselli, trade unionism is "the theory that aims, by means of the union of producers, for the social revolution that installs a federalist and socialist regime, in which the unions themselves must constitute the fundamental nuclei." Echoing Bernstein, Rosselli insisted that trade unionism, "whether of the revolutionary or reformist variety, is a movement for the elevation of the proletariat; like revolutionary and reformist socialism, the importance of the movement is precisely in the activity of the movement itself; the ends are almost secondary." Socialism is, in a historical and theoretical sense, the "father" of modern trade unionism. Yet revolutionary trade unionism rebels against the father. Revolutionary syndicalism rests on four elements: class struggle; the union of producers; a critique of the state; and federalism. From these precepts flow the antimilitarism, antipatriotism, anti-intellectualism, and antiparliamentarianism of the movement, along with its condemnation of democracy and its conception of violence. Rosselli's conception of class struggle was idiosyncratic, reflecting his own struggle to reconcile the privileges of his family's social position with his political beliefs: class struggle was "historically inevitable," but not all members of the bourgeoisie were exploiters.[39]

Reformist socialism and syndicalism should focus their attention on the daily problems of the workers: the organization of the factory; contracts for land tenure; the role and function of the artisan in an age of increasing industrialization. Consequently, Rosselli singled out the English tradition of guild socialism, which was little known in Italy, as a model for the future ordering of society. "After the recent experience in Russia and other countries, the concept of a collectivist socialism, which makes the State the great centralizing power with an immense bureaucracy, will be superseded." The workers' movement, the syndicalist tradition, and the workers' cooperatives that were evolving were, for Rosselli, fulfilling a positive, creative, liberal, and liberating function.[40]

In a passage that foreshadows his heretical stance as a socialist, Rosselli declared that it was "useless" to deny the religious character of socialism or to assert that its essential trait was economic. "The true socialist is a religious man; socialism is faith," which in its present form "is not sufficient to satisfy a spiritual thirst."[41] Rosselli was advocating a closer relationship between the ideal of socialism and the practical work of the trade unions, modeled on the working class parties of England and Belgium, in which the trade unions, in their daily, practical activity, shaped the theory of the political party and not vice versa. In his early writings, he even went so far as to view trade unionism as a panacea for modern society, but after a trip to England in 1924, he realized the limitations of this concept, concluding that in modern capitalist society, workers' unions could achieve only certain limited goals. Rosselli agreed with Lenin that the unions were inadequate to the task of a radical transformation of social and political relations.

While crediting Sorel with being the chief theorist of the revolutionary syndicalists, Rosselli charged the French thinker and his followers with falling into the trap of supporting a theory even in the face of a contradictory reality. From Sorel, Rosselli stressed the necessity of the moral education of the working classes and agreed with Bernstein that "socialism might come about, and yet it might not." At the same time, Rosselli was careful to criticize Sorel's fascination with violence, his myth of the general strike, his denigration of democracy, and the corresponding insistence on an audacious minority to lead the masses (although Rosselli himself was later to insist on this last point). What Rosselli took from Sorel—and Mazzini— was the stress on "voluntarism" against the crude determinism that had shaped Marxism in Italy for several decades.[42] Antonio Gramsci was making the same argument within the ranks of the newly created PCI.

On the question of violence, different countries, with different historical experiences, could make use of revolutionary methods. Echoing Croce's concept of historicism but arriving at a different conclusion, Rosselli defended "the victory of socialism through the reformist method," yet he would not deny the value of "the revolutionary method," which might be necessary in certain historical periods as a means to reach a desired end. The great historical example was Russia, where revolution could not have been achieved except by violence. "We had a mistaken conception of Russia," Rosselli confessed in 1917. The Russians were a people who "spoke a language of blood that we, free and independent, could not understand."[43] Violence in Russia was "painful, yet necessary and inevitable given the conditions of the old regime." Yet other countries (such as Italy), where conditions were fundamentally different, could afford the luxury of peaceful change.[44] Rosselli acknowledged that the revolutionary brands of socialism and syndicalism were more attractive; they had an "élan vital," a "mystique," a "myth" in the Sorelian sense that inspired faith in the movement, hope for the future, and action for the present. The reformist method, which was concerned with more mundane matters, seemed pallid and bland in comparison. Yet the latter had a greater chance of success in societies with strong civil and political institutions. Rosselli emphatically defended an idea that would inform all his subsequent work, both political and theoretical: "It is in the forge of reality, in daily practice, that the power of a theory is measured."[45]

The thesis was approved with highest honors, and the dean of the school offered Rosselli a position as his assistant. Carlo, however, recognizing the antiquated methods of the school, declined. It was after completing the thesis, in his attempt to recast it in book form, that Rosselli sought out the advice of Gaetano Salvemini, who at the time was teaching at the University of Florence and advising Nello, thus beginning a strong relationship that ended only with the Rossellis' deaths in 1937.[46] Salvemini had been born (1873) in the *Mezzogiorno* and had broken with the PSI over the Libyan War of 1911. He was "generous and impetuous, incisive in his speech and penetrating gaze, inhabited by the demon of sincerity to the point of rudeness."[47] Rosselli undoubtedly thought Salvemini rude when he criticized the thesis as "a volcanic eruption, a statement of faith" rather than a work of historical or critical scholarship. Despite the socialist framework, Salvemini noted that "the liberal-democratic roots remained intact."[48] For Salvemini what was needed were more facts and fewer "professions of faith." The historical reconstructions that Rosselli depicted— although valid—were then marred by "personal affirmations, declarations of faith and prophecies." The manuscript that Salvemini returned to Rosselli was covered with corrections and criticisms on every page, and the work remained unpublished. But the historian did see a fundamental idea embodied in the work: "the search for a socialism that incorporated liberalism and did not repudiate it."[49] Reminding twentieth-century socialists of their nineteenth-century liberal heritage was an essential facet of Rosselli's heresy.

Rosselli's unorthodox positions had not yet estranged him from the PSI. In January 1921, he participated in the Seventeenth National Congress of the PSI and foretold the coming split within the party that would lead to the birth of the PCI.[50] Despite his familiarity with the leaders of the political parties, he was more attracted to the formations and organizations outside the sphere of party politics. Most of these groups were forming around political-literary journals like *Il Caffè* of Milan, in the tradition of the eighteenth-century Enlightenment journal of that name. Another important center was Turin, which could boast of having both the precocious Piero Gobetti with his journals *Energie Nuove* and *La Rivoluzione Liberale,* along with Antonio Gramsci's *L'Ordine Nuovo* movement. What these various enterprises had in common was the attempt to forge an alliance of intellectuals to fight fascism on the ethical-cultural plane. The model— whether to follow or reject—was Croce.[51] These intellectual groups could trace their lineage back to the cells that formed during the Risorgimento in the nineteenth century. This attraction to people and ideas outside the traditional structure of the political parties is critical to an understanding of Rosselli's ideas and actions later in the antifascist cause.

After the successful defense of his first thesis Rosselli continued his studies, which were now in jurisprudence, at the University of Siena, completing another degree there in 1923. He also conducted research at the London School of Economics. In a bitter letter, he railed against the politicians in the Italian Parliament who refused to act in the face of increasing fascist violence because of their hypocrisy and self-interest. He was drawn into examining the political situation as it was evolving in 1923 with the Pact of Union when the Italian Nationalist Association formerly merged with the National Fascist Party (PNF). In February he was realistic enough to concede that the Right had been victorious. "I am happy because all this will open the eyes of many people that deluded themselves on the content and motives of fascism."[52]

Circolo di Cultura

As fascism was coming to power, Rosselli became active in the Circolo di Cultura that was established in the winter of 1920–21 by students at the

University of Florence. Carlo worked with Gaetano Salvemini, Ernesto Rossi, Piero Calamandrei, and others in creating a forum for debate on social and cultural issues. Their intention was to create "an apolitical Circolo di Cultura, open to all the free currents of modern thought."[53] First meeting in the private homes of various members, including the Rosselli house on via Giusti, the Circolo moved to permanent quarters in February 1923 in Piazza Santa Trinità and gained legal status as a formal association. Carlo, in keeping with his character, threw himself with great energy into the activities of the Circolo. "I remember Carlo's almost infinite joy when we received the locale for the Circolo," Calamandrei wrote in 1945; "he bought the furniture, the bookshelves, the books, the foreign journals. In that expansive vitality of his, he could bring a spiritual significance even to these small practical matters."[54] Although the Circolo di Cultura began as "an apolitical association," it was soon drawn into the vortex of Florentine politics. For its members, resistance against fascism was first and foremost a moral impulse: it was an insurrection of human reason against bestiality and embodied "the last expression of democratic life in Florence."[55]

The members of the Circolo thought of it as "a form of intellectual cooperative," an initiative with a long tradition. Salvemini, Rossi, and Rosselli may have had the Rainbow Circle—a group of British New Liberals gathering in London's Rainbow Pub during the 1890s—as a model. Some topics that were debated included the following: the "Southern Question"; university reform; the "Roman Question"; the state budget; workers' organizations; the problem of the *latifundia* (large estates); land reform; and Italian foreign policy. There were also presentations on various political parties and movements: socialism; liberalism; fascism; revolutionary and reform syndicalism; anarchism and federalism. Rosselli led a discussion on syndicalism and political representation in the spring of 1923 and another on the English elections in November of that year.[56]

The driving force of the Circolo was Gaetano Salvemini, who encouraged the students to adopt a critical method in analyzing the various positions of the political parties. The eldest of nine brothers and sisters, Salvemini had been born in the *Mezzogiorno* and knew its history and tragedies firsthand: during the great earthquake of 1908, he lost his sister, wife, and five children. (He himself was saved by the architrave of a window.) In a letter to the idealist philosopher Giovanni Gentile, he wrote: "I move ahead, work, give lectures, prepare conferences, and throw stones at those who do not seem honest or sincere to me. People think me strong . . .

In truth I am a miserable wretch, without home or hearth, who has seen the happiness of eleven years destroyed in two minutes. I have here on my table a few letters from my poor wife, my sister and the children. I read them little by little. I seem to hear their voices. And after having read a few, I stop, because a desperate sadness overwhelms me, and I want to die."[57]

As a historian, Salvemini made his mark with works on medieval Florence, the French Revolution, and Mazzini. Like Croce, he had a brief flirtation with Marxism; unlike Croce, he gravitated to the PSI, joining in 1893, but was especially critical of its passivity. Later the critique of its passivity was taken up by Rosselli. In 1911 Salvemini founded a radical and independent newspaper, *L'Unità*, which he used to attack the policies of Giolitti, whom he called "il ministero della malavita" (minister of the underworld). He had been a democratic interventionist in 1914 and 1915 and was elected to Parliament as an independent in 1919. Salvemini's position as professor at the University of Florence, his "delight and his pride," gave him, in the eyes of the young intellectuals, an immeasurable status. That prestige was particularly strong at a moment in which the intellectual and ideal foundations of politics were being reexamined. As Nello explained: "The truth is that Salvemini did not sow for the satisfaction of picking the fruit. He planted the tree, in the hope that it would not be uprooted by the storm, and that one day men who came after him would rest in its shade."[58] Salvemini was not afraid to cut himself off from formal parties and organizations; often he struck out on his own, daring to instigate arguments. In an essay on the significance of culture, he ended with an appeal for intellectuals to consider justice their social duty. From 1923 to 1925, antifascism in Florence was synonymous with the name Salvemini and, by extension, with his students Carlo Rosselli and Ernesto Rossi and with the Circolo di Cultura.[59] Rossi compared him to Socrates as "an obstetrician who helps bring the truth to light."[60] Eschewing all dogmatism and abstract systems, Salvemini became known for his *concretismo*. Between the eagles of idealistic theology and the sparrows of empiricism, he placed himself among the sparrows.[61] More than Croce, more than Gobetti, it was Salvemini who shaped Rosselli's intellectual formation.

Rosselli and Salvemini shared more than an intellectual propensity toward independence. Both had an eye for the ladies. Gossiping in a letter to Ernesto Rossi, Salvemini confessed about an incident that occurred when both he and Carlo were in England:

Rosselli was a great success in the feminine world, and I, poor old man as I am, have no complaints. A Junoesque widow, between 35 and 45 years old, waited on us at table. Well, Rosselli admired that lady very much; and so did I. Rosselli, with youthful energy, launched his attack; I stumbled in the background. On the last evening she asked us both for a moonlight walk. Rosselli was aggressive, I silent. In the end the fair lady said she liked me best. Irreparable disaster! Rosselli went off on his own. I remained the sole master of the situation. What happened then, in the presence only of the moon, I cannot say . . . because nothing happened.[62]

Salvemini introduced an intelligent and beautiful young Englishwoman to the Circolo di Cultura. Marion Cave had developed into a passionate Italophile during her studies in England and in 1919 she arrived in Florence to teach at the British Institute. Born in December 1896 to Ernest Cave and Mary Russell, the Circolo group took to calling her "Biancafiore" (Whiteflower); Filippo Turati's longtime companion, Anna Kuliscioff, said she was "a ray of sunshine" in that serious group of antifascists.[63] Marion Cave once confided that she had come to Italy to participate in what she thought was an imminent socialist revolution, ready, if necessary to "die on the barricades."[64] Carlo was immediately taken by her fiery idealism, beauty, and intelligence; they married on 24 July 1926.

The Circolo di Cultura was an elite group of middle-class intellectuals with no workers, artisans, or peasants among its members. (Radical workers in Florence attended the Università Popolare and the "Giubbe Rosse" [Redcoat] Club, where writers and artists convened for discussion.) The Circolo did not support any particular ideology or political party. An experiment in open-mindedness clearly shows the character of the club. In the interest of "fair play" and curiosity, two fascists, Giacomo Lumbroso (who later joined the antifascists and was killed by the Nazis in 1945) and Alberto Luchini, were invited to present their case before the Circolo. It was the latter who made the stronger impression on the group. Luchini was a writer in the decadent style, translator of the Russian Jewish writer Leon Koshnitsky and a veteran of D'Annunzio's Fiume adventure. His presentation glorifying irrationalism and an "intellectualized violence" came as a rude shock to the students of the group, who shared a common humanist intellectual framework. Luchini made it abundantly clear that the fascists scorned those values such as tolerance and the distrust of absolutism that the students considered the patrimony of civil society. As Marion Cave succinctly put it, "At that moment, we understood, indeed we deeply felt that there was an abyss between them and us, and nothing could bring us together, not even language."[65] On New Year's Eve 1924, the fascists moved against the society.

> During the holiday afternoon, a squad of fascists entered the hall [of the Circolo] and destroyed it. From the windows that opened onto the Piazza della Trinità, they threw all the furniture, books and journals; and at the foot of the statue of Justice [in the piazza], they made a great bonfire. Passers-by stared with curiosity, and a sanitation truck, conveniently sent earlier by the diligent mayor, waited on the side for the bonfire to end, to whisk away the burnt remains. Several days later, the prefect ordered the dissolution of the Circolo di Cultura, because its activity "provoked the just resentment of the dominant party," and could incite "grave disruptions of public order."[66]

The timing and coordination of the attack, along with other "punitive expeditions" in Florence and the decree issued only days later legally dissolving the Circolo, left no doubt that the entire episode was planned in advance by the civil, political, and military authorities.

In a satirical commentary on the entire episode, an article appeared shortly afterwards in one of the first antifascist newspapers:

> This Circolo was a real and true association to commit crime, worthy of much more severe repression than the clandestine bomb factory, since these conspirators were concerned with manipulating that explosive which is much more potent than nitroglycerine—culture . . . we are pleased to inform the Illustrious Prefect that the evening of 31 December was a very edifying spectacle for every person who loves civil life to see the wicked ingredients with which the conspirators used to prepare their betrayals burning in that beautiful bonfire in Piazza della Trinità . . . we can in fact confide in the Illustrious Prefect that all the components of that Circolo, foreseeing the just destruction of their venue, were able to hide in their cranial boxes, with the hope that the Authorities will not notice, a supply of that explosive, whose evil power we mentioned above; and with that contraband cleverly hidden under their hats, they circulate undisturbed in the streets of Florence, among the conformists that do not suspect, alas!, their perverse intentions.[67]

The Circolo di Cultura was not the only association that was destroyed in Florence during the early days of fascist rule. Squads of blackshirts assaulted and destroyed the British Institute, the Università Popolare, and its library. As a final injustice and with bitter irony, the hall of the Circolo was turned over by the authorities of the city to the "Circolo di Cultura Fascista."

Reformist Politics

By early 1924, beginning his university career as a professor of political economy in Milan, Rosselli was frequenting the reformist circles of the PSU, cultivating personal and political relationships with Turati, Treves, Modigliani, and Matteotti, among others. Characteristically, he also developed ties to antifascists who were not in the socialist camp, such as the journalist Carlo Silvestri (later a fascist) and the republicans Cipriano Facchinetti and Raffaele Rossetti, founder of the important journal *Viribus Unitis*. What was important to Rosselli was not so much one's party affiliation (usually based on an abstract ideology) as one's visceral opposition to fascism. His association with Luigi Einaudi and Attilio Cabiati at Bocconi University in Milan led to several articles and book reviews on political economy that appeared in the journal *Riforma Sociale* between 1924 and 1926. The rector of the university, Angelo Sraffa, recognizing Rosselli's vitality and intellectual rigor, proposed several projects on which they would collaborate, such as a law and economics review. Carlo was also able to meet Angelo's son Piero Sraffa, who was teaching economics at the University of Perugia and would return to Milan on the weekends. The younger Sraffa, at first close to the *L'Ordine Nuovo* group in Turin but later attracted to the PSU, would be instrumental in preserving the prison notebooks of Antonio Gramsci, remaining a "spiritual" communist and confidant of Palmiro Togliatti. Piero and Carlo, both interested in classical British economics, became friends and passed many evenings in discussion. Sraffa's work eloquently challenged classical theories of competition and had a profound effect on Rosselli's own economic thinking.[68]

Rosselli's university lectures were well received by faculty and students. While teaching at Bocconi University in Milan, he was asked by the leaders of the PSU and the CGL to give ten lectures for the Università Proletaria, and he enthusiastically accepted their invitation. He welcomed the challenge of speaking to workers and party members, which would require a language different from that of the university lecture hall. In February 1924, he wrote to his mother in Florence that his classes, which included lectures on protectionism and free trade, were going well. Other topics of his lectures included the influence of trade unions, the history of economics, methodology, pure and applied economics, and economic stability and crises.[69]

Meanwhile, Mussolini, who had at first sought to preserve a façade of democratic government, began to show his true colors. In July 1923, the regime passed the Acerbo Law, which stipulated that any party that received the largest number of votes (if this was more than 25 percent of the votes cast) would be granted two-thirds of the 535 seats in Parliament; the remaining seats would be divided proportionally among the other parties. This "electoral reform" was passed with the support of the Liberals and the right-wing Catholics. The Acerbo Law led to a fierce debate as to whether the democratic parties should participate in the 1924 elections or abstain. By early 1924, clearly the Left could not reconcile its differences to form an electoral alliance: the PCI and the PSU refused to moderate their positions, and the PSI, in the middle, would side with neither the PSU on its right nor the PCI on its left.[70] From Milan, Rosselli wrote to his mother that he did not foresee a legal solution to the political predicament, since the opposition had failed to act effectively while the bourgeois elite distanced itself from the crisis to protect its own narrow interests.

A Genealogy of Intellectuals

In an apocryphal scene conjured up by Aldo Rosselli, his father, Nello, confesses to Carlo that "the persons dearest to me, the ones I have studied the most, were all great losers" Carlo, with a smile, replies, "Yet you love them because of that. Isn't that a bit decadent?"[71] At the time of his death in 1937, Nello had completed a study of Carlo Pisacane[72] and was contemplating his magnum opus: a massive biography of Mazzini. In truth, Carlo also loved the great "defeated" intellectuals of Italian history and saw himself as an heir to their noble tradition. In a letter to the anarchist Luigi Fabbri, he once described his brother's book on Pisacane as helping to "keep alive that small flame in the middle of a desert of ashes."[73] For Rosselli, men like Filippo Turati, Piero Gobetti, Giovanni Amendola, and Giacomo Matteotti were the direct descendants of Giuseppe Mazzini, Giuseppe Garibaldi, Carlo Cattaneo, Carlo Pisacane, and Giuseppe Ferrari. In an essay commemorating the death of Turati in 1932, Rosselli called the old man's struggle for a new social Risorgimento "temporarily defeated" and placed him in the older Risorgimento tradition.[74]

This legacy did not rest on consensus; rather, like the French Revolution, its meaning has been continuously contested in Italian politics and society. Not only did fascists and antifascists clash over "inheriting" the Risorgimento tradition, but also within the Italian Left itself, there were bitter disputes over its meaning. Was the resistance to fascism to be a "second Risorgimento" as Rosselli and others insisted, or was the Risorgimento tradition to be condemned as a bourgeois, failed revolution, as the communists held? Even Gobetti had eloquently written of a "Risorgimento without heroes."[75] The Risorgimento triumvirate of Cavour, Mazzini, and Garibaldi could not have been more disparate in spirit and goals: the idealist Mazzini and the heroic Garibaldi were no match for the wily Cavour, whose only equal in realpolitik was the Prussian Bismarck. The failures of Mazzini, Garibaldi, Pisacane, and Cattaneo were not due to any inherent deficiencies or a lack of skill; instead, Italian unification failed to produce a united, democratic nation because of larger social, economic, and political factors. But their legacy, what one American scholar has called the three principles of Risorgimento democracy—secularism, political equality, and the concern for social justice—"have been for over a century and are still today the foundation for whatever unity of thought and action exists between the Marxist and non-Marxists groups on the Left." Yet if we examine their goals of national independence, unity, liberty, and equality (in descending order of importance), then we can say that they were successful only in obtaining the first.[76]

Mazzini was the great "prophet of the religion of humanity,"[77] anticipating a united Europe marked by a cosmopolitan nationalism and enlightened humanism; his colleagues were the Hungarian Kossuth and the Pole Mickiewicz. Once Mazzini described his secret revolutionary movement, Giovane Italia, in words that Rosselli could have used to describe Justice and Liberty: "Neither a sect nor a party; but rather a faith and a mission. Precursor of Italy's rebirth." Mazzini's self-perception as a prophet crying out in the wilderness must have had a strong appeal for Rosselli: "I have renounced even a semblance of happiness on this earth. Far from my mother, from my sisters, from everything that I hold dear, I lost in prison the best friends of my youth . . . I despaired of what an individual can accomplish . . . and I told myself: 'Persecuted and misunderstood, you shall die midway.'"[78]

Mazzini, Pisacane, Cattaneo, Ferrari, and Garibaldi were representatives of a "truer, greater Italy," comprising peasants, workers, and intellectuals who had not "prostituted" themselves.[79] They were representative in another way as well: many of these thinkers had spent time in exile. Garibaldi had been in the Americas, Mazzini in England, Pisacane in France. A radical anticlericalism bound them together. The firebrand Giuseppe Ferrari had written (before Nietzsche) that God was dead and that "the religion of the revolution is that which deifies man."[80] If Mazzini and Pisacane believed that the new nation should have a strong central government, Rosselli was closer to Cattaneo and Ferarri, who insisted that only federalism could protect the fertile yet disparate cultural traditions in the new state. Their models were the independent, republican city-states of the late Middle Ages or the cantons of the Swiss Confederation.

If Rosselli inherited Mazzini's ethical conception of revolution, he also inherited Garibaldi's charisma. Garibaldi was the modern *condottiere*, the "knight of liberty" who generated one of the most potent myths in modern Italian history; he was a veritable icon with his red neckerchief and cigar.[81] This almost obsessive desire for action was to be found in much of Rosselli's "front generation." Bergson, Sorel, and D'Annunzio combined to create the *arditismo* (shock-troop movement) of the First World War and the immediate postwar period. This desire for action is what Rosselli recognized in Mussolini: the dictator had correctly gauged the mood of a younger generation that could not be satisfied with the idealism of Croce or the positivism of Ardigò.

Once the nation had been unified, a concerted effort was made to deny the revolutionary potential inherent in the thought of Mazzini and Garibaldi. They were dutifully inducted into the hagiography, but only in a way that was not threatening to the new state. These dissidents[82] of the Risorgimento refused to reconcile themselves to the new nation-state, which they felt was born out of moral compromises and expediency rather than true principles of liberty, equality, and social justice. Although they had failed to fashion the new nation as they had wished, they gave birth to a long tradition of intellectuals such as the Rosselli brothers, Piero Gobetti, Giovanni Amendola, and Giacomo Matteotti. It can hardly be a coincidence that it was precisely these men whom the fascist regime destroyed.

Matteotti

Giacomo Matteotti, who was from a prosperous family near Rovigo, graduated from the University of Bologna with a degree in law and then traveled extensively throughout Europe, learning English at Oxford. After an apprenticeship in the Po Valley organizing agricultural workers and serving as mayor of Villamarzana, he was elected to Parliament in 1919 as a moderate socialist. An ardent pacifist, he was against Italy's participation in the First World War, but he served in the army and became the first secretary of the PSU in October 1922. The PSU attracted many of the most important members of reformist socialism, besides the leaders of the CGL. The party's weakness was precisely in this alliance of political antifascists with labor leaders who were willing to make compromises with fascism to protect their unions.[83]

The national elections of April 1924 were to be carried out under the provisions of the Acerbo Law. With the complicity of the police, voting took place under conditions of intimidation, violence, and widespread fraud; in fact, one socialist candidate was murdered. As it turned out, the PNF did not need the Acerbo Law; the national ticket brought 374 supporters of Mussolini to power, of whom 275 were fascists. The remaining seats were divided among the opposition, with the socialists winning 46, the PPI 39, smaller democratic groups 30, and the PCI 19.

On 30 May, Matteotti rose in the Chamber of Deputies and presented a scathing attack on voting "irregularities."[84] The Acerbo Law represented the end of true parliamentary rule in Italy; fraud and intimidation deprived Mussolini's government of any legitimacy. For an hour and a half, citing innumerable episodes from around the country, with a pile of handwritten notes before him and in a clear, unwavering voice, Matteotti documented the abuse of power by *squadristi* (blackshirt fascist squad members) and officials. Constantly interrupted by the fascist deputies waving daggers and threatening retaliation, the socialist deputy continued his denunciation as Mussolini, who was in attendance, listened without uttering a word. At the end of his speech, seeing Mussolini leave the Chamber and return to his office at Palazzo Chigi, Matteotti turned to a colleague and said, "You may now prepare my eulogy." Bursting into the office of Giovanni Marinelli, administrative secretary of the PNF, Mussolini exploded: "If you weren't all a pack of cowards, no one would have dared to make that speech . . . People like Matteotti, after having said certain things, should not be allowed to circulate."[85] On 10 June, while walking alongside the Tiber River in Rome, Matteotti was abducted by several men and forced into a black Lambda Lancia automobile. His body was found two months later in the countryside outside Rome.

The assassination of Matteotti created the most serious challenge yet to Mussolini's regime. Immediately denounced by Parliament and in the Italian and foreign press, fascism was on the brink of collapse. Those responsible for the assassination, sensing that they might be served up as scapegoats or fearing for their lives, began composing "testimonials" and "memoirs" incriminating Mussolini. These were then used to blackmail Mussolini into silence. Several documents would later be published by Rosselli and others in one of the first underground papers.[86]

One week after Matteotti's abduction, Mussolini met with King Victor Emmanuel III, who declined to remove his prime minister from office. Instead, Mussolini dismissed his undersecretary of the Interior, Aldo Finzi, an Italian Jew. (Twenty years later, with the Nazis in Rome, Finzi aided the antifascists, and then was arrested and executed in the notorious Ardeatine Caves massacre of 24 March 1944.) The King's refusal to act came as a severe blow to the opposition, who had hoped that since the King had appointed Mussolini, he now would have to ask for Il Duce's resignation. The Left would never forget this betrayal by the King, an event that lifted the veil from the eyes of many. For their part, both Benedetto Croce and Pope Pius XI refused to condemn Mussolini. In Britain, Winston Churchill defended Mussolini; he was later to praise the fascists in their "triumphant struggle against the bestial appetites and passions of Leninism." [87]

The Matteotti assassination forced the opposition to decide: would they continue their legalitarian methods, some still hoping for monarchical intervention, to depose Mussolini? Most refused to consider the use of violence or illegal methods to defeat fascism. The most important response to the assassination was the "Aventine Secession." Deputies from the communists and socialists to the republicans and Popolari withdrew from the Chamber and took the name of Gaius Gracchus's protest movement during the ancient Roman Republic when he withdrew to one of the seven hills of Rome (the Aventine). The most energetic and outspoken leaders of the modern Aventine Secession were Antonio Gramsci of the PCI (which later returned to Parliament), Filippo Turati of the PSU, and Giovanni Amendola of the Unione Democratica Nazionale. Amendola, an important journalist who had studied philosophy and was critical of the positivist tradition in Italy, had founded the journal *Il Mondo* in January 1922 to give voice to a moderate antifascist current in Italy. *Il Mondo* became the mouthpiece for the Aventine Secession and in December 1924 published Cesare Rossi's "Memoriale," which directly implicated Mussolini in Matteotti's assassination. On 1 May 1925 it also published Benedetto Croce's "Manifesto of Anti-Fascist Intellectuals" in response to Giovanni Gentile's "Manifesto of Fascist Intellectuals." Nello Rosselli, in his own defiant gesture against the regime, joined Amendola's Unione Democratica Nazionale along with the Venetian scholar of jurisprudence, Silvio Trentin. Amendola was destined to suffer the same fate as Matteotti and Gobetti: he was severely beaten by fascist thugs and fled to France, where he died of his wounds on 7 April 1926.

For Rosselli, Matteotti was a model in several ways. In recalling his first meeting with Matteotti, Rosselli wrote that both he and Piero Gobetti had noticed Matteotti's gravitas (*serietà*) and avoidance of rhetoric. And in words that revealed something about Rosselli himself: "Antifascism was for Matteotti an instinctive, intimate fact; more a moral imperative than a political one."[88] Their lives were similar: both having been born into the wealthy bourgeoisie, both being determined to change the conditions in Italy, both refusing to be seduced by the attraction of the revolutionary mystique and its rhetoric—hence Rosselli's description of Matteotti as a "prosaic hero." Unlike other bourgeois intellectuals, Matteotti's socialism was not a passing fancy of youth; or as Rosselli wrote in words that were obviously self-referential, it was not

> the romantic adventure of a bourgeois heretical youth who is a revolutionary at twenty, a radical at thirty (matrimony plus career), reactionary [*forcaiolo*—literally "a hangman"] at forty . . . Born rich, he had to overcome the difficulties that rightly oppose rich socialists. He did not overcome them with demagogic outbursts, with mystical renunciations, or squandering money on electoral banquets or in paternalistic cooperatives and unions, but by personally participating in the movement for proletarian emancipation, forming free workers' institutions, organizing the peasants.

And in these words of Rosselli that now seem eerily prophetic: "This type of antifascist, the prosaic hero, was destined to be killed. Just as Amendola and Gobetti had to die. As Rossi, Gramsci, Bauer, and many other Matteottis will die if we don't save them."[89]

The Matteotti assassination acted as the catalyst that pushed Rosselli into active participation in socialist politics and antifascism. In a letter to Piero Gobetti in early July 1924, he made clear his intention to join Matteotti's PSU, telling his friend in Turin that "the hour has come for all to assume their post in battle."[90] For Rosselli the Matteotti crisis was a turning point: either the regime would be brought down by the opposition, or it would survive and consolidate its power. Although he still felt that the political parties would be the vehicle for the overthrow of fascism, he was critical of their passivity and legalitarian tactics. Soon he would become disillusioned with their strategy and would force an irrevocable break with the traditional parties. He was correct in sensing the hesitancy of party leaders to act. Max Ascoli described the scene in Rome during the Matteotti crisis and the sense of paralysis that seemed to grip the opposition:

> We went almost every night to a restaurant behind the Pantheon with the leaders of the Socialist Party: Turati, Treves, Canepa and others. For a week or ten days there was no sign of the fascists on the streets of Rome. It was known that the people of Trastevere, all republicans, were ready to march with their clubs and revolvers. They only awaited the orders of the Aventine leaders. Carlo and I wasted our breath in asking: "Why don't you make them come? What other way is there to free ourselves?" But no one wanted to give the order. . . . .[91]

Italia Libera

Ascoli was not alone in lamenting the passivity of his fellow intellectuals. Although no one had wanted to give the order for a general uprising in Trastevere, not all antifascists had resigned themselves to inactivity. In mid-1923, a prototype antifascist organization had appeared, Italia Libera, which was dominated by republicans but comprising liberal and socialist war veterans who had broken with the Associazione Nazionale Combattenti because of that group's allegiance with fascism. On 24 June 1923, as Mussolini was addressing a crowd of war veterans in Piazza Venezia, he was interrupted by cries of "Viva l'Italia Libera; viva la libertà!" Turning to the listeners closest to him, the Duce muttered something about "melancholy imbeciles."[92] Raffaello Rossetti and Randolfo Pacciardi, both veterans and both members of the Partito Repubblicano Italiano (PRI), were the driving force. Others included some of the most prominent antifascists in later years: Piero Gobetti, Camillo Berneri, Leone Ginzburg, Carlo and Nello Rosselli, and Ascoli himself. Many members had been democratic interventionists in 1914–15. Italia Libera could boast two descendants of Giuseppe Garibaldi (one a general). The program called for the dissolution of the fascist militia to be replaced by a national guard not tied to any particular party; free and open elections; freedom of the press; an independent judiciary; and freedom of assembly and association.

A report filed by the Chief of Police on 4 January 1925 may have exaggerated the group's influence:

> [Italia Libera] is no longer a movement that agitates just for propaganda or freedom of association; but a movement that, thanks to ample means of obscure provenance, is seeking practical means to violently subvert appointed powers, arranging itself militarily, arming itself, instigating in a way to provoke riots, disorders, sedition, to destabilize the State domestically and abroad, and to damage its prestige and public credit.

Ernesto Rossi may have been both more modest and closer to the truth when he claimed that the goal of Italia Libera was to "give antifascists something to do as antifascists; to keep them in contact with each other."[93]

A Florentine section of Italia Libera appeared in the wake of the Matteotti assassination. Nello Rosselli was an active member, using his car to carry manifestos and propaganda around Florence, including one memorable night when they plastered flyers of the martyred Matteotti all over the city. Nello and Carlo were involved in another escapade in Florence. Arnaldo Mussolini, brother of the dictator, was scheduled to visit Florence on 7 December 1924. On the night of 6–7 December, Carlo, Nello, Ernesto and Paolo Rossi, and two others quietly arrived at one of the great walls lining the Arno River. While Nello waited in the getaway car, Carlo and Ernesto lowered Paolo over the wall, along with a pail of white paint. As Carlo and Ernesto calmly smoked cigarettes and exchanged pleasantries with the few unsuspecting passersby, Paolo painted *Viva l'Italia Libera!* along the wall. "It was no masterpiece of calligraphy," admitted Ernesto Rossi, "but it was legible." The next day, the entire city was abuzz, Arnaldo Mussolini was furious, and the fascist authorities in Florence were red-faced. Although these actions may seem a bit foolish in retrospect, Italia Libera performed an important function in the early years of fascism: it succeeded in "breaking the isolation of every antifascist before triumphant bestiality."[94]

Members such as Carlo Rosselli, Ernesto Rossi, Nello Traquandi, Tommaso Ramorino, Piero Calamandrei, and others would constitute the nucleus of *Non Mollare!*, the first underground antifascist newspaper. From the newspaper, many would find their way to Justice and Liberty after 1929; and in 1943 the same antifascists could be found in the Action Party. The connecting thread was an adamant demand for a republic, a tradition of insurrection tracing back to Mazzini, a federalism reminiscent of Carlo Cattaneo, and a democratic conception of socialism—in short, an ethical and moral revolt against fascism. Although never more than a handful of members in a few cities, which at no time amounted to more than a few hundred adherents, and formally dissolved by decree in January 1925, Italia Libera had planted the seeds of a radical antifascism in Florence and throughout central and northern Italy. For his part, Rosselli was ready to take the next step on the path to exile.

CHAPTER TWO

· · · ·

Autocritica

History is always self-critique.

IGNAZIO SILONE, *DER FASCISMUS* (1935)

The liberal state of mind of a socialist is precisely in this doubt
that urgently impels action; in this relativism that induces respect
of adversaries . . . ; in this critical demon that accompanies and
forces one not to be estranged from reality but rather to continuously re-vision—in the light of new experiences—theory and
practice.

CARLO ROSSELLI, "LIBERALISMO SOCIALISTA" (1924)

If "fascism" has been the political term that has bedeviled historians, political scientists, and philosophers for much of the twentieth century, much as
"socialism" occupied those of the nineteenth century, "liberalism" has generated a similar debate for several centuries. Liberty, according to historian
Guido De Ruggiero, has "a tendency to return to its own source, to criticize
and reflect upon its own identity."[1] This self-consciousness and reflexivity
led Rosselli to a trenchant critique of Italian liberalism while defending
unorthodox liberals such as Piero Gobetti. From the European tradition,
he ignored German liberals and instead turned to Alexis de Tocqueville,
Élie Halévy, and the British tradition of John Stuart Mill, Matthew Arnold,
T. H. Green, and L. T. Hobhouse.

A Critique of Italian Liberalism and Socialism

Italian liberalism was dominated by the towering figure of Benedetto
Croce. From the pages of his cultural review, *La Critica,* and several works

of history published under the regime, the Neapolitan philosopher explicitly condemned fascism. In his unshakable belief that liberty constituted the fundamental explanatory principle of history as well as the highest moral ideal, Croce upheld a tradition under attack on all fronts. Fascists, conservatives, socialists and communists had united in an unholy alliance to destroy classic European liberalism. In the early 1920s, Croce refused to condemn fascism outright, hoping that the new movement might offer a solution to the intractable problems of Italian political life. Croce even voted for the regime in his capacity as senator in a no-confidence motion after the Matteotti assassination. But the Matteotti crisis, along with Mussolini's 3 January 1925 speech, belatedly convinced the philosopher that fascism was a threat to the liberal tradition. When Giovanni Gentile, Croce's former colleague in idealist philosophy and the most prestigious convert to fascism, published in April 1925 the infamous "Manifesto of Fascist Intellectuals," which was signed by such luminaries as the playwright Luigi Pirandello and the futurist poet Filippo Marinetti, Croce responded immediately with a countermanifesto of antifascist intellectuals, published on 1 May 1925 in the pages of Giovanni Amendola's *Il Mondo*. Signatories included De Ruggiero, Luigi Einaudi, Guglielmo Ferrero, Giustino Fortunato, Arturo Carlo Jemolo, and Luigi Salvatorelli. Subsequent editions of the manifesto carried new names: Gaetano Salvemini, Piero Calamandrei, Silvio Trentin, Adriano Tilgher, Gaetano Mosca, and others.

Croce represents the most famous example of what came to be called the "inner emigration." Antifascists who were not assassinated (as Gobetti, Amendola, and Matteotti were), imprisoned (as Gramsci was), or exiled (as Rosselli, Nenni, Pertini, and Saragat were) could remain in Italy in a tacit understanding with the regime. They could continue their work if it did not entail an explicit criticism of fascism. Croce was a special case: his international prestige protected him from punishment or reprisals, allowing the regime to claim that "culture flourishes under fascism." More common was the experience of Nello, who sought solace and resistance in his scholarly historical works, or Cesare Pavese, who found refuge from the bombastic rhetoric of the regime by translating American literature.

Carlo Rosselli's intellectual relationship with Croce was marked by both respect and rebellion, as it was for many others of his generation. Norberto Bobbio, a member of Justice and Liberty and later the Action Party, recalled that Croce—"the voice of his time"—was the "spiritual guide" who had shown the "straight path to antifascism" for himself and other young thinkers such as Piero Gobetti and Leone Ginzburg. Following Croce's conception of liberty meant being "in the course of history." Another Action Party member, Ugo La Malfa, who would later become the leader of the highly respected PRI, called Croce the "greatest and highest spiritual and intellectual guide of the entire generation whose civil conscience was formed in the struggle against fascism."[2] Croce's influence extended even to Antonio Gramsci of the PCI; indeed, some commentators have argued that Gramsci's *Prison Notebooks* are an extended dialogue with Croce.

Croce was not alone in his defense of classical liberalism. The Sicilian Giuseppe Antonio Borgese had been strongly influenced by Croce's philosophy and aesthetic criticism. A university professor of Germanic literature and literary criticism in Milan, Borgese is best known for his first book in English, *Goliath: The March of Fascism,* in which he traced the historical roots of fascism back to the fourteenth-century "tragic farce" of Cola di Rienzo, the "real model of the Duce."[3] In 1931 Borgese refused—along with only a dozen other university professors—to swear an oath of allegiance to the regime. He fled to America, where he taught at the University of California, the New School for Social Research, Smith College, and the University of Chicago.

Borgese was unsparing in his criticism of Croce and the tradition of Machiavelli: "All the books and essays of Croce played into the hand of Mussolini, and no substantial objection to fascism and nationalism was visible in a theory idolizing the state as the embodiment of the divine . . . If fascism is wrong even in the years of its triumphs, then all Machiavellian and Crocean philosophy is wrong." Borgese was equally critical of socialism, sounding, in 1937, much like Rosselli in 1927: socialism was "numerically a giant and practically a cripple." Orthodox Marxism could not defeat fascism because it rested on a flawed premise: "As economic class warfare had not been the essential source of fascism, so could not class insurrection be its final issue. The sin had been in the mind; and from the mind should have come redemption."[4]

In New York City, as a member of the Mazzini Society, which was inspired by Justice and Liberty, Borgese worked to refute the propaganda of the fascist regime in the United States. Another liberal colleague took the opposite road. Giuseppe Prezzolini was a major protagonist in the "revolt against positivism" that occurred in Italy around the time of Carlo Rosselli's birth. With Giovanni Papini, he edited the Florentine cultural reviews *Leonardo* (1903 to 1907) and then *La Voce* (1908 to 1916). A fervent nationalist, antisocialist, and antirationalist, he also worked with Enrico Corradini's review *Il Regno*. Prezzolini existed uneasily between a deep admiration for Croce and a profound ambivalence toward fascism. He admired Mussolini and Gobetti simultaneously and attempted to solve this moral dilemma by moving to Paris in 1925 and then to New York in 1929. As professor of Italian literature and director of the Casa Italiana at Columbia University, Prezzolini used his position to praise fascism and to garner the support of the large Italian-American community in New York.[5]

Rosselli was not extraneous to this continuing debate over how to define liberalism. For several decades liberalism had been derided as a utilitarian, individualistic, and materialistic excrescence of the eighteenth and nineteenth centuries. The official philosopher of the fascist regime, Giovanni Gentile, had even developed the thesis that liberty could be understood only within the state, not against it. The ethical state as Gentile conceived it was highest form of freedom. In *Che cosa è il fascismo* (What Is Fascism) of 1925, Gentile held that Italian liberalism and fascism were one and the same.[6] Rosselli was determined to counter such depravations.

In July 1923, after receiving his law degree, he traveled to Genoa to meet with Attilio Cabiati, professor of economics at Bocconi University in Milan. Cabiati, favorably impressed with the young scholar, named Rosselli his assistant for the 1923–24 academic year. It was Cabiati who shaped Rosselli's ideas regarding free trade and who caused a long-running debate with the liberal economist Luigi Einaudi. By publishing his critique of free trade, Rosselli was challenging Loria, Einaudi, and the other "big guns" of classic economic liberalism. He insisted, contrary to common assumptions, that there was no strict connection between the economic policies of free trade and the freedoms defended by political liberalism.[7] He echoed Croce in insisting on the distinction between *liberalismo* (liberalism) and *liberismo* (laissez-faire or free-market economics), while attacking the classic economic theorists and their modern counterparts who praised the "freedom to work." This was neither the free development of the individual nor freedom for all, but rather "freedom for a minority (capitalists) to oppress a majority."[8] While Rosselli was not the first thinker to delineate this difference, he was perhaps the only socialist seriously to engage it rather than simply to dismiss it on the basis of abstract theory. "The fundamental dogma of the [liberal] school is 'the free play of economic forces,'" Rosselli wrote in his first article for Gobetti's journal, *La Rivoluzione Liberale*.[9] From this came the liberal argument against workers' associations. As long as the capitalist system exists, there is only one hope for the workers: class struggle between the workers (grouped in unions that transcend national borders) and the capitalists. There were two essential facts that were ignored by most of the liberal economists: the workers are both producers and consumers, and the realities of the marketplace did not square with their theories of free trade. If it was true that a new oligarchy was arising that controlled the economic life of the world and the politics of Europe and America, then the only response for the workers was to organize, because their organization would be larger and more unified, since they are also consumers. "By a play of forces that appears dialectical, it can be stated that the best defense of the consumers can be reached only through their coalition as producers, that is to say, the positive side of human activity."[10]

Rosselli's public critique of the Italian socialist and liberal traditions continued in the summer of 1923 with "Liberalismo socialista."[11] A month earlier, Rosselli had written to Novello Papafava, a young intellectual who was working with Gobetti on *La Rivoluzione Liberale* in Turin. Papafava had contributed articles that sought an ideological renewal of liberalism, which attracted Rosselli's attention. The only possibility of a renaissance of liberalism, according to Rosselli's letter, was for the spirit of liberalism to inform the groups and parties that had the greatest contact with the masses, above all the socialists. "I, for the very little that I can do, will work for a revision—in a liberal sense—of the socialist methods."[12] The letter goes on to suggest a possible coalition against fascism, one that would span the political spectrum from liberal Catholics such as Don Luigi Sturzo, classical liberals like Luigi Albertini and Count Carlo Sforza (former Foreign Minister), to moderate socialists like Turati, democrats such as Amendola, and independent radicals like Salvemini. It would be a coalition based on antifascism as the unifying common denominator. After the defeat of Mussolini's regime, each group would then go its own way in a free political system.

"Liberalismo socialista" generated considerable interest among left-wing intellectuals. In a letter shortly after the publication of the article, Rosselli modestly noted that it had struck a chord with several leading figures of antifascism.[13] Gobetti was so impressed with the piece that he published a similar article with the same title by Rosselli a year later in his own journal preceded by an approving commentary. Gobetti noted that he and Rosselli shared a common belief in socialism as "the conquest on the part of the proletariat of a relative economic autonomy and the aspiration of the masses to affirm themselves in history."[14] If Gobetti agreed with Rosselli's definition of socialism, Rosselli assented to Gobetti's understanding of liberalism as an ethical conception of the world and human relations. To Gobetti, Rosselli was modest: "I don't believe I've said anything new or profound. It is a draft of an organic arrangement made from a point of view a little different from the usual." In a letter written home, though, Rossellini revealed his enthusiasm: "I believe it is destined to spark fierce polemics. But I am in a very strong position and above all, it seems to me, rather original."[15]

The essay begins with an examination of the history of liberalism to clarify an anomaly: how is it that in Italy, men as diverse as Antonio Salandra, Luigi Albertini, Luigi Einaudi, Giovanni Amendola, Mario Missiroli, and Filippo Turati can all call themselves "liberals"? Salandra, prime minister from March 1914 until June 1916, was instrumental in bringing Italy into World War I on the side of the Entente; he exalted national values, proclaimed the absolute authority of the State, and allied himself with reactionary currents in the Vatican. Salandra welcomed fascism because it restored the authority of the state even while sacrificing freedom; he believed that "the essential element of the State is authority not freedom."[16] Salandra, wrote Rosselli, was really a reactionary donning the euphemism "liberal" for electoral success. Luigi Albertini, editor of Italy's leading liberal daily, *Il Corriere della Sera* of Milan, defended the constitutional state and criticized prime minister Giovanni Giolitti, clericalism, and socialism in his paper. The Libyan War of 1911 and the First World War pushed his politics further to the right. At first ambivalent about fascism, Albertini eventually became one of the most outspoken critics of the regime, garnering the admiration of former enemies Gaetano Salvemini and Piero Gobetti. Because of his stance, Mussolini removed him as editor of *Il Corriere della Sera*, which fell to fascist control.

Einaudi, a collaborator of Albertini, supported classic liberal economic theories and taught at the University of Turin. From the pages of *La Riforma Sociale*, which he edited, Einaudi supported the creation of workers' organizations and trade unions. During the fascist period, he did not voice any opposition to Mussolini's regime. Giovanni Amendola, like Croce, was from Naples and was a philosopher in the antipositivist movement. His real influence, though, was as a journalist. He had been a nationalist member of the Liberal Party and had supported the Libyan War of 1911. Drafted into World War I, Amendola's experiences forced a reconsideration of his politics; he abandoned nationalism and berated the fascists in his cultural review, *Il Mondo*. He was one of the very few politicians who urged preemptive action against Mussolini's threatened "March on Rome." In the wake of the Matteotti assassination, he organized the Unione Democratica Nazionale, a party that tried to reconcile—as its name suggests—democracy and patriotism. It was this philosophical and political stance that attracted Nello to the party. For Carlo Rosselli, men like Albertini, Einaudi, and Amendola embodied the classical, or British, form of liberalism.

Another type of liberal would find it easy to make the transition to fascism. Mario Missiroli was editor of *Il Resto di Carlino* in his native city of Bologna. In 1921 he was forced to resign from the newspaper *Il Secolo* because of his antifascist articles, but in the 1930s he "converted" to fascism. Giovanni Ansaldo, a journalist from the famous steel-producing family, had written for the socialist paper *Il Lavoro* in his native Genoa, Salvatorelli's *La Stampa* in Turin, and Gobetti's *La Rivoluzione Liberale*, before joining the fascists. Aldo Borelli, too, had begun as a conservative liberal journalist in Naples and Florence, close to prime ministers Salandra and Sonnino. He eventually was named to Albertini's post as editor of *Il Corriere della Sera*, a position he held until Mussolini's downfall in 1943. To be fair, liberals were not the only ones to abandon their original political faith: socialists had their embarrassments with Piero Bolzon and Alberto Beneduce; the anarchists in their Leandro Arpinati; the syndicalists in their Michele Bianchi and Italo Bresciani; and even the PCI had members that "converted" to fascism, such as Nicola Bombacci. "The Catholic becomes a fascist because of reactionary, dogmatic, and hierarchical logic," Rosselli explained; "the demo-liberal to save order and bourgeois income; the socialist because of the reformist cult of the state; the communist (but more rarely) because of dictatorial technicality and opportunism."[17]

This confusion of terminology and labels did not exist when liberalism had to confront the absolutist ideology of Church and State two centuries ago. "After the French Revolution, the word liberalism indicated something very precise: Liberals were those who opposed the absolute authority of Church and State and saw freedom as the fundamental instrument for human progress." With the definitive defeat of absolutism, everyone declared themselves "liberals" and recognized a common set of freedoms: freedom of worship, of thought, of association, of the press. Yet many of these late nineteenth- and early twentieth-century liberals refused to countenance that liberal ideology might be historically conditioned, if not determined. For them liberalism had been defined and defended—it could not be something that evolved. Hence the oxymoron of "conservative-liberals" as defenders of the monarchical, constitutional state in Italy after unification.

Although Rosselli declared that liberalism was an "indispensable premise for all successive reasoning," he was nonetheless very clear on its historicist character: "Liberalism does not consist of a static ensemble of principles and norms. Instead, it must be considered as continual becoming, in perpetual renewal, a perennial overcoming of the positions already reached. The concrete content of liberalism changes through time; that which is fundamental is the spirit, the immortal function, the dynamic and progressive element inherent in it."[18] As Harold Laski was to write in 1940, liberalism had assumed that its principles were eternal. "It failed to understand that no procedures have that quality unless men who live by them accept the results to which they give birth."[19] Freedom alone—of all philosophical values—was absolute and eternal, an idea that surely would have Croce nodding in agreement. De Ruggiero, too, had defined liberalism as "an imperishable value." Even if the historical and contingent manifestations of liberalism change, "freedom can never lose the power of creating for itself new paths, new forms, and new institutions."[20]

What Rosselli brought to this debate on the nature and ideology of liberalism was a distinction between liberalism as a *system* and liberalism as a *method*. The supporters of liberalism as a system conceived of it as a collection of economic, social, and juridical principles that were immutable, that is, "bourgeois capitalism." Accepting freedom of religion, of speech, of the press, and of association, the system adds the freedom of owning unlimited private property, right of inheritance, right of free enterprise, right of free trade; and the conception of the State as an organ of the police (the "night-watchman"). Those who viewed liberalism as a method held that its fundamental premise was that the free persuasion of the majority is the best method of arriving at the truth. The method must be understood as a complex of norms that are the base of European civilization; they function as "a set of rules of the game," allowing progressive forces a legal method. In short, liberalism as method was "the minimum common denominator" for civil society. Yet liberalism as an ideology of liberation had failed its potential. Because the bourgeoisie came to see liberalism as a means to preserve its privileges, both the social class and the philosophy became complacent.[21]

What characterized liberals such as Albertini, Einaudi, and Amendola was their contradictory effort of trying to reconcile the system with the method. Although this reconciliation may have been possible, indeed necessary, in the middle of the nineteenth century, in the twentieth century, it was an anachronism. Their liberalism was one that was completely abstracted from daily practice, trapped in a "theoretical wall of China" and ultimately conservative. The drama and tragedy of Italian liberalism was that it first gave birth to a creature but then clipped its wings; it generated subversive currents, only then to deny those currents the possibility of overcoming the reality from which they had sprung, namely, capitalist society. Others, such as Croce, Missiroli, and Prezzolini, saw liberalism as the intellectual and political patrimony of an elite; they insisted that liberalism can never be extended to the masses, and that between the method and the masses there exists an unbridgeable chasm. Rosselli charged that this position, which was held by Missiroli and Prezzolini, led to "black skepticism" and a tacit admission of the bankruptcy of liberalism, because, as Rosselli wrote in a not-so-subtle criticism of Croce: "A liberalism that remains entrusted to the virgin and sovereign mind of some philosopher or historian, or historian-philosopher, a liberalism that is not grafted on to a practical mass movement, that does not gradually inform the spirit of the masses, that does not try to conquer the forces that express and fulfill— even unconsciously—a liberal function in society, is a pure abstraction."[22] Croce, for his part, was horrified that his beloved liberalism would be put to such utilitarian use.

The liberalism of the nineteenth century cannot be that of the twentieth, just as the liberalism of the nineteenth century was not that of the eighteenth century. It was universally denied that liberalism and democracy had anything in common, even to the point of opposing one against the other. But for Rosselli, "the second is nothing if not the logical development of the first, and the first does not exist in substance in a representative modern State without the second." How though, is liberalism to be established in those countries without the experience and tradition of an England? Citing Thomas Macaulay's famous essay on John Milton, Rosselli agreed that freedom is the only cure for the problems of a liberty that has only recently been attained. If the people had to wait until they were worthy of being granted freedom, in truth they might wait for eternity. But political liberty and freedom, in and of themselves, are not enough. Without some degree of economic autonomy, the individual is still denied the possibility of the full development of his or her personality, and society is still not fully evolved. "It is not a coincidence that the poorest peoples and the most backward economic societies are the easiest prey for dictatorship."[23] What does freedom of worship mean to someone who has no bread; what is political liberty for one who has no control over his or her own resources? Liberty and freedom have a different meaning in different historical and social contexts. For the bourgeoisie, "the concession and the conquest of political liberty constituted the sublimation and the coronation of its already affirmed economic and cultural power," whereas for the proletariat, liberalism represents "if not the beginning of the struggle for emancipation, the premise, the instrument for its rapid attainment."[24] Agreeing with De Ruggiero, Rosselli interpreted the bourgeois revolution as one that legitimized, consolidated, and consecrated its social position while refusing to extend liberalism to the masses. The socialists must take this task upon themselves: to bring liberalism, in the fullest sense of the word as conceived of by Gobetti (that is, complete personal autonomy), to the proletariat and the peasants.

If Rosselli challenged Croce, Einaudi, and the other classical liberals, he did not refrain from criticizing his friends in the socialist camp as well. Unlike his colleagues who conceived of socialism as a goal, Rosselli stressed its intangibility. Socialism—interpreted as the aspiration of the people to affirm themselves in history and to participate in the historical process as active protagonists—is a perennial becoming, something that is never achieved once and for all. Socialism is an ideal of life and action that propels society to surpass its own positive results; in short, socialism is the idea of an infinite progress, or more accurately, progression. A spirit of "incompleteness" and perpetual striving bound socialism and liberalism. This is precisely what the official Socialist parties in Europe had ignored or condemned at their own peril. And in a direct criticism of Stalin's Soviet Union, Rosselli charged: "The recent experiences, all the experiences of the past thirty years, have hopelessly condemned the primitive programs of the socialists. State socialism especially—collectivist, centralizing socialism— has been defeated."[25] The abolition of private property and the expropriation of the means of production were potent myths: increased productivity, decreased and enjoyable labor, humanity freed from material needs, and the elimination of class conflict were to be the results.[26] Instead, no one any longer believed in these "fairy tales," and many were wary of the enormous burden of the state bureaucracy, incompetence, and the invasion of personal liberties. Rather than imprison themselves in theoretical models, modern socialists must jettison their dogmatic baggage and have the courage to have no theory, model, or blueprint except experience. Only from experience can humanity grasp any indications for the future. Experience for Rosselli points to an indisputable premise: *Conditio sine qua non* is the conquest of economic autonomy; without this, nothing can be accomplished. Everything clashes against poverty—the great enemy.

This idea and ideal of autonomy was central to Rosselli's thought; both in practice and in theory, socialists must be guided by autonomy. "One must proceed not from above to below, not from the center to the periphery, but inversely. Socialism in all its aspects must not be the fruit of imposition, but of conquest, indeed of self-conquest; it must be an autonomous creation of the working classes." And in impassioned language, he offered his own "act of faith":

> I do not believe in the scientific proof of socialism; I do not claim to possess absolute truth; I don't intend to bow my head before dogmas, nor do I delude myself into thinking I have the key to the future . . . I am a socialist because of an ensemble of principles and experiences, by the conviction brought about by the study of the evolution of the society in which I live; I am a socialist by education, by reaction, but also . . . by faith and by sentiment. I do not believe socialism will come about and that the working class will affirm itself in history by the inevitable evolution of things, human will notwithstanding. To those who speak this language to me, I reply with Sorel, and in this is all my voluntarism: *"Socialism will be, but it might also not be."*[27]

This doubt and relativism—the "critical demon"—pushes the socialists into action rather than into passivity, induces a respect for their adversaries, and demands a continuous revision of their theoretical positions and practical actions; it is, in short, the liberal essence of socialism.

Rosselli continued his critique of Italian reform and revolutionary socialism in two other articles that together present a penetrating analysis of the recent history of socialism in Italy and the role of the PSI.[28] Since Turati characteristically remained above the fray, it fell to Claudio Treves to respond to Rosselli's criticism. For the next several years, the two debated Rosselli's main contention that socialism had become petrified in Italy and incapable of leading a mass revolution. Rosselli agreed with the former revolutionary socialist Mussolini and Georges Sorel that the proletariat, by itself, could not achieve the revolution; an intellectual and political elite would have to prepare the way. "La crisi intellettuale del Partito Socialista" appeared in *Critica Sociale* in November 1923, and it is revealing that both Turati and Treves permitted such a strong critique of their position to appear in the journal. The article was preceded by an editor's preface that noted its "noble passion and holy spiritual restlessness," while attesting that with the publication of Rosselli's essay, "we have thrown open the doors of our journal—as Rosselli recognizes and can attest—to the voices of the 'heretics.'"[29] The editors had requested Rodolfo Mondolfo to respond to Rosselli's criticism in an essay that appeared in the same issue.

As they stand, the articles are an echo of Gramsci's position in *L'Ordine Nuovo* and a clear indictment of the policies of the PSI over the last two decades. "La crisi intellettuale" begins with a startling declaration: "It has been at least fifteen years that the socialist movement in Italy has been struck by intellectual paralysis." Sixteen years earlier (1907) Ivanoe Bonomi had published his *Le vie nuove al socialismo,* which tried to counter an excessive dogmatism in the socialist camp and which was one of the few works of the time with any theoretical sweep. This was followed two years later by Rodolfo Mondolfo's work on the philosophy of Feurerbach, with which it seems that Rosselli may have been familiar. In 1908 the PSI Congress at Florence had ended with the victory of the reformist current which for Rosselli, symbolized the beginning of intellectual stagnation. If Rosselli's premise is assumed to be correct (and an argument can be made against it), what are the reasons for this state of affairs? Rosselli was convinced that this intellectual paralysis was the result of the nature of the diffusion of Marxism in Italy, in particular, the fact that the socialist movement had adopted Marxism as its official doctrine (even if the German revolutionary—in words that have haunted his followers ever since—once declared, "I am not a Marxist"). Socialism suffered paradoxically from both intellectual rigidity and an abundance of variants. Although this diversity of thought could be perceived as a sign of intellectual vitality and freedom, it has actually hindered the socialist movement in Italy. The problem began when the theorists and ideologues of the workers' movement sought to reconcile, utilize, and synthesize all the various Marxist currents in a practical, pragmatic program of everyday action. The result was "all the problems of a rigid, authoritarian codification entrusted in reality to the works of Marx, and all the problems of free interpretation."[30]

For several decades, there had been revisionists of Marx on the Left and on the Right, but no one, "with the possible exception of Bernstein," saw what remained of use from the original body of Marx's work. This outcome is what Rosselli called a theoretical judgment (*bilancio teorico*) of Marxist doctrine that can be summed up in Croce's famous phrase, "that which is living and that which is dead in Marxism." Rosselli, although he had read Croce's most important work on Marxism, *Materialismo storico ed economia marxista*, which first appeared in 1900, perhaps underestimated the Neapolitan philosopher. Croce's essay "Come nacque e come morì il marxismo teorico in Italia (1895–1900)," which appeared in 1937 (long after the philosopher's brief flirtation with Marxism), is a perceptive analysis of "how theoretical Marxism was born and died in Italy." Characteristically, Croce dates the "death" of Marxism in Italy at precisely the time when his own interest in Marx's work was waning. But Croce was to maintain, even many years later, that the introduction of Marxism into Italian intellectual and cultural life at the end of the nineteenth century was a positive force that acted as a catalyst for new thinking. Because he felt Marxism to be a "realistic reflection on history" and a "realistic historicism" (high praise indeed from the idealist philosopher), Croce had even written that "one could not not be a Marxist."[31] It was Croce's friend and mentor, Antonio Labriola, who had introduced Marxism into Italy and to Croce. Years later, Croce confessed that he was a better thinker and a better person for having gone through his Marxist phase.

Rosselli had studied not only Croce's work on Marx but also the influential book by Rodolfo Mondolfo, *Sulle orme di Marx*, that appeared in a new and expanded edition in 1923. Mondolfo, unlike Croce, did not pass through a Marxist "phase"; he became (and remained) one of the most important Marxist philosophers in Italy. Born into a Jewish family, he studied in Florence and taught at the Universities of Bologna and Padua. In 1908, with the reformist victory at the PSI Congress at Florence, Mondolfo, like Rosselli, detected an ideological and ethical paucity that he tried to address. He spent a lifetime defending socialism from its more authoritarian and deterministic variants. Rosselli praised Mondolfo for his originality and independence of thought in contributing to the formation of a humanistic socialism, to be held completely autonomous from the thought of Marx. This, though, was not Mondolfo's intention. Although Rosselli may have been mistaken in his criticism of Mondolfo, he was indebted to the philosopher, especially for the stress that Mondolfo placed on the importance of human will in history. Mondolfo agreed with Rosselli that socialism was not the antithesis of liberalism, but rather its historical fulfillment.

As a product of a certain time and place, Marxist doctrine could not explain all social and economic problems of the twentieth century. Through his training as an economist, Rosselli pointed out the flaws in Marx's labor theory of value. By the early decades of the twentieth century, many scholars were challenging Marx's ideas on the worsening business crises, increasing poverty of the proletariat, capitalist concentration of wealth, the disappearance of the middle class, and dictatorship of the proletariat. For Rosselli a distinction had to be made between Marx the social scientist and Marx the propagandist. The masses had embraced the most superficial aspects of Marx and Marxism, yet there remain two pillars in the Marxist pantheon that are still standing: historical materialism and the class struggle.[32] But as Rosselli was to write later, these were no longer the patrimony only of Marxists; the ideas have seeped into modern consciousness to such an extent that we are all, in a certain sense, "Marxists." From idealist philosophers like Croce to historians like Gioacchino Volpe and Gaetano Salvemini, Marx's ideas have been inserted into the modern frame of thinking. "The blood of Marx has silently been transfused into the hearts of even his most bitter enemies. What greater triumph could he have hoped for?"[33]

This realization led Rosselli to what seems to be a semantic paradox: "one can be a Marxist without being a socialist." He might have added that one must be a socialist without being a Marxist. Marxism had become more a methodological principle of interpreting history than a philosophy of action for the working classes. Democratic and reformist socialists were opposed to the authoritarian and dogmatic spirit that informed Marxism in its present shape. A sane empiricism in the British fashion would be a thousand times better than "this blind and tortuous dogmatism."[34]

The Marxist parties in Europe, including the PSI, were hindered by their rigid adherence to abstract theories. A political party needs the freedom to change with time and social conditions. Instead, the fatal error was to consider Marxism as the final destination rather than as a liberating method. The result was entrapment in a closed intellectual system. Rosselli pointed out that Marxism developed into a school, and more than a school, a sect: a new Church with its own logic, discipline, dialectic, prophets, and martyrs, its scholastic philosophers writing exegeses of the volumes of Marx and Engels. He could have added, from personal experience, that like any other religion, those who disagreed were branded as "heretics" and suffered the consequences. If the central project of socialism is to be defined as the extension of political freedom and social justice to the working classes based on the liberal method, then we can understand how Rosselli excludes Marxists (as he conceives them) from the ranks of the socialists. Dogmas, slogans, and "old formulas" must be abandoned; once a general line of theory and action had been accepted, each person would be allowed to think on his or her own. It was imperative that the Socialist Party make an appeal to the youth of Italy. It was necessary to reach out to these groups because "although limited in number, they constitute a great force in a country so lacking in elites like our own."[35] Both the reformists and the revolutionaries were to be condemned for their passivity; the former sought too little, and the latter felt that they were on the right side of history and had merely to wait. "They were to be destiny's children," writes Alexander De Grand, "agents of the inevitable. Little wonder they soon became history's orphans."[36]

Rosselli sought to pinpoint an exact meaning to the word "Marxism," working toward a theoretical judgment of the function that Marxism can and must exercise for his contemporaries.[37] But in the course of this endeavor, he contradicts himself: on the one hand, deploring the confusion arising from the various interpretations of Marx, all of which claim direct descent from the Master and all claiming to be "scientific"; but on the other hand, urging modern socialists not to be fearful of "doctrinal heresies." If this was not a contradiction, it was a paradox that Rosselli relished. A good deal of the ideological confusion arose from the equivocal use of language. Rosselli confessed to his own hesitation when using words such as "bourgeoisie," "proletariat," "class," and "capitalism," whose meanings change and that even acquire a plurality of meanings. Contrary to the accepted use of the words and in accordance with his own study of economic history, he insisted that "the bourgeoisie and the proletariat are no longer (and in an economic sense never were) two uniform blocks of forces."[38]

Another indictment leveled against modern socialists was their failed relationship with the working masses—both urban proletariat and rural peasantry. The one indisputable contribution of Marx—historical materialism—was completely unknown by the workers, who instead were fed a steady diet of the worst aspects of Marxism: the apocalyptic and inevitable triumph of socialism, the historical function of violence, and the labor theory of value. The socialist method and ideal must be taught and diffused among the masses (and also, Rosselli added, among the intellectuals) with simpler arguments, closer to life and practice. "A little more faith and a little less science. Today, it is especially important to return to that conception, to that religious sense of socialism that characterized the first blazing ideal. Scientific demonstrations can be believed only up to a certain point."[39] The enemy is not so much a particular social class as a regime composed of complex elements; these economic, ethical, moral, and juridical elements exist even within us, Rosselli pointed out. This being the case, a gradualist, liberal, and moral approach is the only logical alternative. Marxism must be given a more modest role in shaping the ideology and activities of the modern Socialist Party.

Socialism must abandon the class character of Marxism because of philosophical reasons, and antifascism must abandon the ideology of class conflict to defeat fascism. The bourgeoisie had been the central character on the stage of history for the last five hundred years; its role was not yet over. True, the bourgeoisie no longer functioned in a liberal sense, yet there were segments of the bourgeoisie that could and did act as catalysts for the development of liberty in history. Obviously, Rosselli had himself and his antifascist colleagues in mind, most of whom were from the humanistically educated middle classes. Even Antonio Gramsci was born to a father who worked in the state bureaucracy and a mother who was from a petit bourgeois family. Only the anarchists could truthfully claim to be led by workers and peasants, who were symbolized by the great figure of Errico Malatesta.

Mondolfo responded by insisting that Marxism was still the directing force, the "compass" of the workers' movement and that socialism could not be divorced from Marxism.[40] This was the most serious disagreement between the two thinkers and stemmed from a more basic philosophical dispute. Both agreed that human free will was the defining factor in history, but Rosselli saw Marxism as essentially a determinist philosophy; indeed, all the efforts of the revisionists from Bernstein onward, according to Rosselli, were precisely to reinsert the element of human will into the deterministic system of Marx. Mondolfo, on the other hand, read Marx, but perhaps not Marxism, as a philosophy that liberated human will and that was essentially a humanist vision of the world.[41] Giuseppe Saragat was attempting to make the same arguments, as is evident from his early study, *L'humanisme marxiste*. By the 1940s, though, Saragat had repudiated this work and had moved closer to Rosselli's position.

Rosselli, unlike most of his fellow socialists and antifascists, was well versed in the British political tradition from John Stuart Mill to the Fabians and the Labour Party. Although Mill's essay *On Liberty* was not published in Italy until 1925, Rosselli was familiar with the essay in the original English.[42] His Anglophilia was furthered by a trip to England in the summer of 1923, where he met G. D. H. Cole, R. H. Tawney, the Webbs, and members of the Fabian Society.

Rosselli also studied the nineteenth-century liberalism of de Tocqueville and De Ruggiero's classic work *History of European Liberalism.* De Ruggiero, like Croce, was from Naples and deeply immersed in Continental idealist philosophy. Impressed with the precocious Gobetti, he wrote several essays for *La Rivoluzione Liberale.* Along with Nello, he joined Giovanni Amendola's Unione Democratica Nazionale. When the *History of European Liberalism* first appeared in 1925, its diagnosis of a crisis of liberalism confirmed Rosselli's ideas. De Ruggiero criticized Marxism and was sympathetic to the role of the reformist socialists. Tellingly, after the Second World War, De Ruggiero joined the Action Party (successor of Justice and Liberty), whereas Croce refused to do so and remained in the Partito Liberale Italiano (PLI) which became increasingly conservative.

Rosselli was searching for an ideal synthesis between his liberal principles and the socialist movement, what would be a new formula that substituted not only the positivistic interpretation of Marxism but also the idealistic and neo-Kantian revisionism of Marx that was beginning to circulate in Italy.[43]

Non Mollare!

In January 1925, Rosselli began teaching political economy in Genoa. Carlo, who had not been born a great public speaker, acquired the skill only after much effort. "I felt a terrible and humbling impression," he wrote to his mother, "on hearing myself addressed as 'Professor.'" A few days earlier he had confessed, "The only thing that disturbs me a bit is the absolute solitude in which I find myself . . . give a thought to your exiled son." In a sarcastic postscript he wrote: "I think with horror of the publication of our correspondence. My place in history is in jeopardy."[44]

While Rosselli fulfilled his duties as a professor in Genoa, he was also involved in one of the most important enterprises against the fascist regime—the publication of an underground journal committed to exposing the crimes of Mussolini and his supporters. As a journalist (he was for a time editor of the Socialist Party organ *Avanti!* and continued to "supervise" the fascist newspapers), Mussolini had been particularly sensitive to the power of the press in shaping public opinion and influencing political policy. The press would no longer be a vehicle to inform the people, but rather an instrument to acquire and maintain power, forge a "consensus," and establish hegemony. Accordingly, some of the first decrees issued by the regime restricted freedom of the press. When on 17 October 1922 Mussolini met with the leaders of the fascist press, the soon-to-be prime minister declared ominously that "it is quite possible that at a certain point we may no longer feel like tolerating the survival of some prominent newspapers." Although freedom of the press had been considered sacrosanct for the functioning of a liberal, parliamentary state, there was a history of press censorship in Italy after unification in 1860. The most recent and disturbing episode was the harassment and censorship of the socialist daily *Avanti!* during the Great War when it upheld the cause of nonintervention. On 15 July 1923 and 10 July 1924, King Victor Emmanuel III signed two decrees that severely limited the freedom of the press; the first gave fascist prefects the power to suppress publications, and the second was in response to the frenzy of antifascist journalism in the wake of the Matteotti assassination. On 31 December 1924, a law was signed that effectively ended freedom of the press. By April 1927, all newspaper people who had been approved by the regime were required by law to register with the National Fascist Syndicate of Journalists. Mussolini, the former journalist, had "effectively reduced Italian journalists to the status of servants of the Fascist regime."[45]

This legal offensive against the press was taken after the physical and often violent assaults that the Blackshirts had carried out for several years. As early as 1919, fascist *squadristi* had undertaken punitive expeditions to intimidate Catholic, liberal, anarchist, and socialist writers. Often these expeditions ended with the destruction of printing presses and offices; physical violence against journalists was not uncommon. In April 1919, fascists destroyed the offices of *Avanti!* in Milan; in February 1921, Spartaco Lavagnini, editor of *L'Azione Comunista,* was murdered in Florence; during 1921 and 1922, the offices of Gramsci's *L'Ordine Nuovo* were repeatedly invaded by fascists.[46] A favorite method of the *squadristi* was to humiliate their opponents by forcing them to drink castor oil. More than a few people suffered the same fate as Lavagnini. The two most famous cases were the attacks on, and subsequent deaths of, Piero Gobetti and Giovanni Amendola.

In early January, hosting a group of students at his house in Florence,

Gaetano Salvemini predicted, "Now that freedom of the press has been suppressed, you will see a clandestine press arise."[47] When Salvemini returned two weeks later from a trip to Rome, Carlo Rosselli and Ernesto Rossi presented him with the first edition of *Non Mollare!* (*Don't Give In!*). The newspaper was born in the Rosselli house in Florence that was rapidly becoming a general headquarters for the young antifascists of that city; the name of the paper, which was suggested by Nello the historian, echoed Mazzini's battle cry. Rossi later wrote: "[Non Mollare] was exactly what we wanted to say: a reproach, an incitement, a command to all those who had a thousand reasons to prove that by now there was nothing left to do; to all those timid souls that accepted fascism as a *fait accompli,* adapting themselves to servitude for fear of something worse."[48] The paper, which appeared when it could, soon became a model for others in Italy, but it retained a diversity that was exceptional. Besides Salvemini, Ernesto Rossi, and the Rosselli brothers, there were Piero Calamandrei, student of law, Nello Traquandi, Dino Vanucci, and the anarchist Camillo Berneri. Tristano Codignola, from Assisi, was director and editor of the newspaper; later he would be among the founders of the Action Party and, after the war, director of La Nuova Italia, a major publishing house. Fascist authorities in Florence became obsessed with uncovering the operation and those responsible for it. The paper managed to exist only ten months, but in that short period, it published several devastating documents against the regime.

All sorts of subterfuge were employed to put out the newspaper. It was never printed more than twice in the same place for fear of betrayal by some worker. An elaborate system was established in which the paper would be printed in the late hours of the night and picked up in the early hours of the morning to be distributed throughout the city. Marion Cave, who acted as secretary, often had manuscripts, addresses, and recent editions hidden under her clothes as she went about Florence. One edition was just off the press when word arrived that the police were on their way. Several thousand copies were bundled into a large suitcase and whisked away as the police arrived. The entire run was hidden with the frozen cadavers in the hospital of Santa Maria Nuova.[49]

With Rosselli personally financing much of the printing costs of the newspaper, an extensive network of volunteers managed to bring the paper to other cities; the anarchist Camillo Berneri, student of Salvemini, was teaching in Umbria; Riccardo Bauer and Ferruccio Parri were in Milan;

Max Ascoli, Tullio Ascarelli, and Umberto Zanotti-Bianco were responsible for Rome. To those who felt that the enterprise was a waste of time, Rossi and Rosselli argued that it was important to make some gesture, some defiant act, an example of civil disobedience, to reclaim a hard-won right that existed in all free societies. The first issue, dated January 1925, printed a manifesto on the first page and forcefully declared: "Freedom of the word has not been granted us: we will take it."

The fifth number of *Non Mollare!* (February 1925) published the notorious "Filippelli memoir." Filippo Filippelli was the director of the fascist daily *Il Corriere Italiano* and was one of those responsible for the assassination of Matteotti. On 14 June 1924, threatened by arrest for the murder of the socialist deputy, Filippelli composed his "memoir" and let it be known that it implicated the highest levels of government in the Matteotti affair, including Mussolini. Another participant in the Matteotti murder, Cesare Rossi, director of Mussolini's press office, had also written a "memoir" on 14 June as insurance against being used as a scapegoat. Both the Rossi and the Filippelli memoirs ended in the hands of the Aventine leaders, who published only the former on 29 December 1924 in the nation's dailies. For some reason, the more damaging Filippelli memoir was not printed. The next day, the regime effectively ended any freedom of the press. The memoir made its way from the hands of Giuseppe Emanuele Modigliani, socialist member of Parliament and brother of the painter Amedeo, and then to Rosselli and Rossi, who published it in their paper. For a few days, *Non Mollare!* became more important than the nation's preeminent daily, *Il Corriere della Sera*.

> Dumini [Amerigo Dumini wielded the dagger that killed Matteotti] is a person *extremely well-known* to the President of the Council [of Ministers, i.e., Mussolini] . . . Dumini is a *friend* of Cesare Rossi and others in the government besides Mussolini . . . *Mussolini knew everything* . . . Mussolini received the papers and passport of the Honorable Matteotti to prove his disappearance.[50]

The publication of the Filippelli memoir was followed the next month (March 1925, no.7) by a similar document concerning the beating death of Giovanni Amendola. Vico Perrone, a member of the MVSN (Milizia Volontario per la Sicurezza Nazionale) wrote on 29 June 1924 of an order received from General De Bono, "Triumvir of the Fascist Revolution," to attack Amendola.[51] That same month, another issue appeared that printed a letter from Guido Narbona, former vice secretary of the Fascio of Turin, dated 24 November 1924, in which he recounts receiving instructions directly from Mussolini to "give Gobetti a severe lesson."[52] With biting sarcasm, Salvemini commented that "June of 1924 was the month of memoirs. Every fascist . . . was writing a memoir and consigned it to a friend to serve as a defense." Even Aldo Finzi, the undersecretary of the interior who was forced to resign to direct suspicion away from Mussolini, wrote his memoir.[53]

Gaetano Salvemini, betrayed by a typographer, was arrested on 8 June 1925, accused of complicity in the publication and diffusion of *Non Mollare!*. Rossi managed to escape to France; the police did not know of Rosselli's participation. In his memoirs, Salvemini recalled that the few weeks he spent in prison for this "crime" were "among the best times of my life." The enforced rest was welcome after months of frenetic clandestine activity. Someone loaned him a copy of Victor Hugo's *Les Misérables*, and his cellmate was a young communist who whispered to Salvemini as he was about to be transferred to Florence, "Let's hope that in Purgatory the holy soul of Lenin is praying for us." The historian, moved by this sincere display of affection, wondered: "Where could one find a more beautiful case of religious syncretism? Catholicism perpetuated itself in the Communist religion, just as centuries ago, paganism was perpetuated in Christianity."[54]

Salvemini's trial was scheduled for early July, with Ernesto Rossi to be tried in absentia. Because of a technicality, the trial was temporarily postponed, and Salvemini was granted provisional freedom, an outcome that infuriated the fascists waiting outside the courthouse. The defense team and its supporters were attacked on the streets, as Salvemini managed to make his way to the Rosselli house in Florence, where he spent the night. The family gardener, who was in the pay of the fascists, betrayed the historian, and two days later, a band of Blackshirts broke into the house. Finding neither Salvemini nor the Rosselli brothers, they proceeded to destroy the furniture (including a priceless sixteenth-century table) and Carlo's library.[55]

With Rossi in France and Salvemini in jail, Rosselli still managed to put out two issues of *Non Mollare!*. The paper directly attacked King Victor Emmanuel III for his complicity in allowing fascism to come to power. The King had sworn to uphold the *Statuto*, which guaranteed freedom of the press, yet signed into law those decrees that effectively ended freedom of the press in Italy. "After 4 January 1925, it is no longer possible to distinguish, unfortunately, the King from Mussolini," the paper asserted. "To applaud the King is to applaud Mussolini."[56]

Salvemini's trial began on 13 July. As the proceedings began, he was shocked to see Carlo Rosselli present in the courtroom—a tremendous risk for him to take. Carlo, in full view of the fascists, went up to his teacher and shook his hand. Salvemini, shaken and worried that Rosselli might be implicated, ordered him to leave. Temporarily freed on a legal technicality, Salvemini decided to flee Italy on 4 August.

During the summer of 1925, *Non Mollare!* continued to publish incriminating documents against the regime. In June the paper put together a special commemorative edition in honor of Giacomo Matteotti on the anniversary of his assassination, assembling the many pieces of evidence that directly tied Mussolini to the crime.[57] In July it republished a letter sent to the *Times* of London challenging Mussolini's claim that freedom of the press was still permitted in Italy: "Our paper is not legal according to fascist laws. It is one of the many clandestine newspapers that have risen in Italy following the suppression of freedom of the press. You have, therefore, in us the living proof of the lies that Mussolini has written to you . . . Already hundreds of persons have been arrested solely on the basis of possessing one of our newspapers; some have been tried and condemned to two years in prison."[58]

The fascists, convinced that the Masons were behind the newspaper, expended considerable time and effort in trying to track down those who were responsible. Rosselli, who was spending three days a week teaching in Genoa, managed to avoid suspicion. His decision in the fall to publish another document incriminating Mussolini in Matteotti's murder led to a veritable "Saint Bartholomew's Massacre" in Florence and thus to the painful decision to end publication of *Non Mollare!*. The 5 October edition of the paper carried Cesare Rossi's memoir written on 14 June 1924. *"All that has happened came about through the direct will and complicity of the Duce."*[59] The issue unleashed the full fury of the Blackshirts in Florence, and the contributors paid a heavy price: one committed suicide (Piero Burresi in Siena); another (Dino Vanucci) was forced into exile in Brazil, where he died; three were eventually condemned to prison: Riccardo Bauer, Ernesto Rossi, and Nello Traquandi all were sentenced to thirteen years; and three were murdered on the night of 3–4 October 1925: Giovanni Becciolini, Gustavo Consolo, and the war veteran and former socialist deputy Gaetano Pilati.[60] Consolo and Pilati were murdered in their homes in front of their families; Becciolini, seeing a group of fascists assaulting the house of a Mason, intervened and killed the *squadrista* Giovanni Luporini. The young Becciolini was lynched on the spot. Since the publication of *Non Mollare!* was now putting the lives of innocent people in jeopardy, Rosselli decided to cease publication. Antifascism in Florence was becoming too dangerous. It was time to work in Genoa and Milan.

Il Quarto Stato

By dividing his time between Florence, Milan, and Genoa, Rosselli had managed to avoid the attention of fascist thugs for some while. But an incident in Milan in the spring of 1926 proved that the Blackshirts were watching and not completely ignorant of his ideas:

> Tuesday I was leaving the Hotel Bavaria at nine when I was approached by three young men. One politely asked me: "may I have a word professor?" I raised my eyes and looked at him. "Yesterday in class you made a statement . . . " I interrupted him saying that I gave explanations about my scholastic work only at school and made to go on my way. The three jumped me from behind with punches. I defended myself very energetically and with success shouting that they didn't frighten me and landing a punch myself. Two light cudgels don't hold me down!
>
> After half a minute, aware that people were gathering and that things were not going well for them, the three heroes suspended their action while I continued to shout in a loud voice. The three, fearful, said in a low voice that I attacked them!!! In any event, after the scene cleared, I left tranquilly after only receiving one punch without consequence.
>
> At three in the afternoon I gave my lesson. When I entered, about eighty students greeted me with great applause. About fifteen fascists then appeared shouting "Viva l'Italia!" and "Viva il Fascismo!" but they were driven away with force. I made a short and measured speech and began the lesson.[61]

That Rosselli could teach at all was something of consequence. On 24 December 1925, the regime had passed a decree that deprived all civil servants of political and intellectual freedom. In protest, Gaetano Salvemini, Silvio Trentin, and former prime minister Francesco Saverio Nitti resigned their academic posts (the only three to do so). Bocconi being a private (and Catholic) university, Rosselli was not bound by the new decree. Salvemini and Nitti were already in exile; Trentin followed them to France. "I cannot remain in Italy," he responded to a request to stay. "If I were a professor of mathematics maybe I could stay, but as a professor of law, how can I remain here to teach when the present regime is contrary to all that I believe?"[62]

Early in 1926, a project took shape in Rosselli's mind that had roots in the political crisis after Matteotti's assassination. The idea was to create a theoretical journal that would address the shortcomings of the Socialist Party and that would contribute to a renewal of socialist vitality in Italy. The experience of *Non Mollare!* proved to be extremely important in showing the possibility, problems, and potential of an underground newspaper and network. But *Non Mollare!* was a popular organ, aimed at the widest possible audience; what Rosselli had in mind now was a more sophisticated journal that would kindle debate among intellectuals and party leaders. He was convinced that the younger generation was being lost by the socialists; they were attracted to the idealism of Croce and Gentile, the vitalism of Bergson, the myths of Sorel, and even Catholic modernism. Many were drawn to the avant-garde literary and cultural movements as they developed in Milan and Florence.

By 1926 Rosselli was grappling with a profound personal crisis. A career as a university professor may have been ideal in another time, but the reality of fascist Italy denied any such luxury to a person of moral conscience. His letters of 1926 hint at a certain impatience with teaching. Instead, he arrived at the conclusion that fighting fascism would demand all of his time, much of his fortune, and perhaps even greater sacrifices. It was in this context that *Il Quarto Stato* (The Fourth Estate) was born.[63]

It was not an easy birth. Rosselli traveled to Milan to convince the socialist Pietro Nenni to collaborate on the new journal. "One morning, I heard a knock at my door," wrote Nenni later. "When I opened the door, there was a young man with a smile on his face. He introduced himself as professor Carlo Rosselli."[64] Nenni had first written for *Avanti!* in 1921, and by the next year, he was appointed the paper's editor. In this position, he blocked the fusion of the socialist and communist parties demanded by the Bolsheviks in Russia. At this time, he believed instead in a more moderate alliance of democrats, reformists, and liberal members of the Catholic Popular Party as the most viable alternative to fascism. For his theoretical stance, Nenni was ousted as editor of *Avanti!*. Later, he fled into exile and arrived in Paris on 21 November 1926.

Rosselli recognized in Nenni some common characteristics: both had written severe critiques of the Aventine Secession; both had realized that the struggle against fascism would have to move beyond a purely legalitarian mode; both had the desire to create a wide antifascist coalition that would include everyone from the maximalists of the Socialist Party on the Left to the Liberals and Catholics on the Right, and from the proletariat to the artisans and peasants to that minority of the enlightened bourgeoisie. Perhaps of most importance, both Rosselli and Nenni were searching for a way to combat fascism while safeguarding democracy. Rosselli and Nenni were willing to concede that the victory of fascism meant the defeat of socialism. They understood—as did few others—that fascism, although it had its roots in Italian history and society, was a new political phenomenon, something not recognized by the older generation of the Left. Yet the two men were also very different. Nenni later commented on their differences:

> One—Rosselli—was a mystic, a romantic. The other was somewhat of a skeptic. One was an optimist who had a happy youth. The optimism of the other was tempered by that bit of pessimism that flows in the life of a man who has a youth without joy and without bread. One joined the battle with the absolute thirst that is particular to those youths raised with great moral and intellectual qualities. The other came from a very difficult battle, bitter and a little discouraged . . . Rosselli intuited things; the other knew them.[65]

In two important letters, one to Nenni and the other to Tommaso Fiore, Rosselli outlined his vision of the new journal and its potential. To Fiore he wrote on 11 March 1926 that the new journal would initiate "the revision of the socialist program and ideology, for now remaining, *et pour cause,* fundamentally in the cultural arena." It was to "redirect socialism in general and Italian socialism in particular, to a contact with reality, both economic and cultural . . . For too long the movement has drifted along in a state of intellectual paralysis and it is no coincidence that in the last twenty years it has completely lost favor with the best elements of the new generation."[66] Perhaps Rosselli was too harsh in his assessment of the recent history of the Italian Socialist Party; yet the fact that creative and original thinkers such as Piero Gobetti and Rosselli's cousin, the writer Alberto Moravia, were often to be found outside the Socialist Party—indeed outside any political party—lends force to his critique. Rosselli himself, though formally a member of Matteotti's reformist PSU, was never very active in the party.

Rosselli had first thought of Nenni as a possible colleague after the latter's open letter of 14 November 1925 to the PSI that warned that "we must prepare ourselves for a very long struggle" and "have the courage to begin from the beginning and with a new spirit."[67] Rosselli's letter to Nenni was instrumental in getting the former editor of *Avanti!* to join forces for *Il Quarto Stato*. It also foretold Rosselli's own tragic end:

> You spoke to me once and in a moving way of Matteotti; and you told me that it would please you to give your life for an idea, just as he had done; we find ourselves in agreement in lamenting the total absence of a spirit of sacrifice and the thirst for sacrifice among our friends. I also have often dreamed of usefully lending my life for such a great cause . . . it is the decisive hour . . . I put at the service of the initiative my money, believing that in doing so, I, a socialist and rich capitalist, fulfill a *strict duty* which no one has to acknowledge, because for me it is a liberation . . . I am young, and wealthy, and do not come from fifteen years of hard and tormented struggle; and I ask myself if I have the right to speak to you, a veteran, a similar language. But I am convinced, today, that I have that right.[68]

Nenni, although his relationship with the PSI was strained at the time, felt obligated to request permission to begin the project with Rosselli; the maximalist leaders of the party granted him authorization, and Nenni was free to work on the new journal. On 27 March 1926, the first of thirty issues of *Il Quarto Stato* appeared in Milan. There were no formal rules of association nor statutes; instead, those who worked for and contributed to *Il Quarto Stato* were all young writers, maintaining cordial contact with each other and exchanging ideas, information and assistance. The general tone of the new review was a critique of the positivism still dominant in certain intellectual circles and in the PSI; an attack against what was perceived as a socialism that was too accommodating; an awareness that the advances of the Giolittian era were given from above rather than won from below; and that the great ideals and passions of early socialism were not to be subservient to the politics of *trasformismo*. This position of Rosselli and the other "young Turks" of *Il Quarto Stato* led to a direct confrontation with the old guard of socialism on the editorial staff of Turati's *Critica Sociale*.

Another trait of *Il Quarto Stato* that would also define Justice and Liberty was its cosmopolitan character; in this regard, it followed and resembled Gobetti's group around *La Rivoluzione Liberale* in Turin. By calling on the exponents of various political tendencies, Rosselli and Nenni gave *Il Quarto Stato* a lively impetus. From the maximalist wing of the PSI, there were Lelio and Antonio Basso, Guido Mazzali, and Antonio Valeri; the reformist wing was represented by Giuseppe Saragat, Giuseppe Faravelli, Eugenio Passerini, Libero Lenti, Piero and Paolo Treves, Max Ascoli, and Nino Levi. There were liberals and followers of Gobetti and Salvemini, like Mario Vinciguerra, Mario Ferrara, Santino Caramella, Tommaso Fiore, and Tulio Ascarelli. What they all had in common was a general will to infuse socialism with a new vitality, an intransigent antifascism, and the desire to create a new coalition on the Left that transcended the constraints of political ideology. The journal defined itself as "a socialist review of political culture" and called for a complete revision of the socialist idea in the light of the fascist victory. The task, according to Rosselli and Nenni, was the political and cultural preparation of the Socialist Party of the future, with a mass base that would form a coalition with other parties fighting fascism, the monarchy, and the Church, to establish a democratic republic in Italy. The battle would have to be fought outside the legal political institutions, since fascism permitted no other option.

Rosselli envisioned *Il Quarto Stato* as a medium to diffuse the ideals of a more democratic socialism, one imbued with the vitality of voluntarism and avoiding the cruder aspects of Marxism, such as economic determinism and apocalyptic visions of the future. As could be expected, the journal drew criticism at the time and was not immune from attack even half a century later: the communist Giorgio Amendola declared in a 1976 interview that "now *Il Quarto Stato* is becoming a myth, when at the time only a few hundred copies circulated."[69] Yet there is evidence that several thousand copies were printed at the height of its activity and that it was widely read by the antifascists. Amendola failed to recognize that the PCI under the influence of Antonio Gramsci had made similar points in the fall of 1925, which were promulgated in the Lyons Theses of January 1926. Gramsci, too, had admitted that fascism was victorious and that the end of bourgeois capitalism was not imminent. He also insisted that fascism could be defeated only by an alliance of peasants, artisans, and the bourgeoisie that would effect both a political and a cultural revolution simultaneously.

To Tommaso Fiore on 11 March, Rosselli wrote that their problem was not in finding potential collaborators but in fostering a more serious conception of antifascism. In his detailed conception of *Il Quarto Stato,* he stressed that it would have the same format as Gobetti's *La Rivoluzione Liberale* and would address the many problems of southern agrarian practices. In addition, it would have regular columns on foreign politics, the work of the unions, and a "third page" of philosophy and literature. A month later, Rosselli again remarked on the difficulty of putting out the journal: "Since we wish, at least for the first issues, to avoid the old men, we are really a lonely bunch [*quattro gatti*] . . . We need patience and compassion. Besides, a newspaper, like a child, is not made in a single day." Fiore, for his part, agreed to assist the endeavor with articles on the "Southern Question." [70]

The first edition of *Il Quarto Stato* (27 March 1926) contained Rosselli's article "Il socialismo ha sofferto troppo poco" (Socialism has suffered too little), in which he claimed that the victories gained by socialism in the first decades of the twentieth century, such as universal suffrage, were granted from above by politicians like Giolitti in return for social peace. For socialism to regain the ethical fire that had once been its greatest asset, it must be prepared for even greater sacrifices. Here the religious component of Rosselli's thought seems evident: victories are worthy only if they are achieved by suffering and sacrifice. As could be expected, the old guard was quick to challenge this heretical analysis of recent socialist history.

The real polemic—and one that was to hound *Il Quarto Stato* for its entire existence over the next seven months—was Rosselli's lead editorial of 3 April 1926, "Autocritica." The essay would thrust Rosselli into the forefront of the debate raging on the character of fascism and the failure of the socialist response. It also went even deeper than this important discussion to an analysis of modern Italian history with all its defects and deficiencies. As such, it is at once a work of historical interpretation, cultural analysis, and political critique. In the space of a few short pages, Rosselli had shaken the complacency of the older reformists and had chartered a new direction for the younger generation of socialists. This editorial sharpened the heretical nature of Rosselli's critique of Italian socialism, in both its maximalist and reformist strains.

Rosselli opened the editorial by claiming that the true measure of men is taken in times of misfortune and that in defeat the Socialist Party would give the best proof of its force and vitality. This was neither the first nor the last time that Rosselli implied that fascism was almost a blessing in disguise for socialism. Mussolini's movement would force the socialist and workers' movement to regroup and to give an accounting of themselves in the face of adversity. What was called for was an examination of conscience, a self-critique that would spare no one and no idea. In a single essay, Rosselli presented an intellectual indictment against the reformists, the maximalists, and the five-year-old PCI. Those that flee to the refuge of "pseudo-marxist determinism" to justify their passivity and "supine resignation" show that they do not understand the spirit of Marx, which is a spirit of combativeness. Like the voluntarist that he was, Rosselli maintained that the answer to the defeat is not to be found "out there" but much closer to home. "The reasons for the defeat," he wrote, "are not to be found in the exterior events of the forces that by definition, elude our control, but in ourselves. We are the authors of our good and evil."[71]

Italy was a premodern country, and the Italian people were still too much the children, or perhaps the victims, of the past. The evolution of capitalism had been erratic and confined only to small areas of the north; hence the idea of creating a mass movement based on Marxist ideology was a case of putting the cart before the horse. The Italian people were politically immature and affected by a "congenital provincialism." Echoing Gobetti, Rosselli insisted that

> Italy is a country in which there was never the great religious struggles that everywhere constitute the great leaven of the liberal regimes and the surest guarantee of the principle of tolerance and of respect of a minimum common denominator of civilization; it is a country in which political liberties conquered in the Risorgimento by the work of a restricted bourgeois and patrician elite always remained the patrimony of a few. Unfortunately, the conquest in Italy of that which is correctly called and considered the highest good of the people of western civilization, is not tied to any mass movement capable of filling a mythical and admonishing role. The masses were absent from the battles for independence and political freedoms. Italian freedom is the daughter of compromises, adaptations and tacit accommodations.[72]

Since the proletariat did not gain its freedom through struggle but was granted these freedoms "from above" and since "one does not love and defend that which one did not struggle and sacrifice for," it was inevitable that the Italian working class did not fight to defend itself, its rights, and its liberties against fascism. This failure was in contrast to activities in countries like Britain and France, where the working classes were the most interested and vigilant party in defending the democratic method. In one of his most serious accusations, Rosselli charged that the "supreme values" of the democratic method were, unfortunately, foreign to the conscience of the Italian working class.

In the tradition of the critiques of Gaetano Salvemini and Arturo Labriola, Rosselli pointed out one of the critical errors of Italian socialism: its failure to adapt socialism and the workers' movement to the particular historical, social, cultural, and economic conditions in Italy. Instead, the PSI was overwhelmed by the victory of 1900, which affected only the "workers' aristocracy of the North," and it did not know how to carry on the struggle after 1900 for the fundamental political liberty of the entire working class, which also included artisans and peasants. The result was immobility and impotence as the Socialist Party lost itself in a wordy and abstract revolutionary ideal, allowing itself to be seduced by the *trasformismo* of Giolitti. Soon the gradualist and reformist conception of the socialist future came to be seen as something repugnant, which alienated many of the best minds in the socialist camp. What socialism had lost was "the sense of the heroic, the spirit of sacrifice, the consciousness of universal values." The socialists were forced to face the possibility that "perhaps this tragedy was necessary so that Italian Socialism places moral values once again in a position of honor, it re-adheres to reality and finally gains consciousness of the great political questions."[73]

Rosselli's essay sparked a debate within the socialist movement, one based on theoretical and philosophical concerns rather than on questions of tactics. He began this polemic from within the socialist movement, he criticized this world *as his own,* and he did not dissociate himself from the defeat.[74] The most important response to Rosselli's provocative editorial came from Claudio Treves, former editor of *Avanti!* and second only to Turati among the reform socialists. Under the pseudonym "Rabano Mauro," Treves used the pages of *Critica Sociale* to mount a defense against Rosselli's charges. His "Autocritica o demolizione?" was a trenchant piece that displayed the strengths and weaknesses of the Italian Left. By attacking Rosselli's critique of Italian socialism, Treves was attempting to refute his interpretation of Italian history. The working class was defeated because of a process that it was not able to control, not because of any deficiencies of the intellectual leadership or because of any underestimation of the political problem. Treves here was betraying the strict determinism that Rosselli felt hindered the socialists from taking action. Responding to Rosselli's query "Why were we defeated?" Treves replied that "an entire front has collapsed—the front of liberal democratic civilization" and that it was "an error of the intellect" to believe that the bourgeois state would defend the freedom of the proletariat.[75]

Treves could agree that an important source of the Left's inability to act after the First World War was derived from the split between an abstract revolutionary rhetoric and the pragmatic goals of reformism. Rosselli, adapting Salvemini's critique of both the maximalists and the reformists, saw the crisis of Marxism as crippling the power of the Left in Italy after the war. Rosselli answered Treves by claiming that the rebuke was expected, even welcomed, because it afforded an opportunity to clarify some points made in the first essay. It was necessary to acknowledge the (hopefully temporary) defeat of the Left and its causes without resorting to historical interpretations, using words like "inevitable," "determined," or "inescapable." Instead, the socialist leadership, according to Rosselli, was engaged in an intricate verbal ballet, "an elegant dialectical game" that arrived at the comfortable conclusion that in reality, there had been no defeat at all. Defending one of his more inflammatory statements (that "fascism may have been necessary"), Rosselli restated his line of thinking:

> When I affirmed that perhaps this tragedy was necessary so that Italian socialism would place moral values again in a position of honor; it would return to reality and finally gain some notion of the big political questions, I wanted to recognize the undeniable didactic value of fascism which has revealed to the Italians the real substratum of Italian life, which has again raised . . . fundamental problems that we cannot ignore . . . it is nothing if not the logical continuation of the "ancien régime."[76]

Here the influence of Gobetti and Salvemini is clear; fascism was not a "parenthesis" in Italian history but rather the manifestation of deep-rooted institutional deficiencies in Italian society. Although fascism was a "continuation of the old regime," Rosselli insisted that it was something new, a political hybrid that demanded a new type of opposition. And given the particular configuration of circumstances in Italy—the historical context, the evolution of economic development, the ethical, political, and cultural deficiencies—some of which was the responsibility of the socialist movement but much of which was beyond its control, the workers' movement had to adapt its ideology to these conditions. Socialist ideology, as it had developed in the early twentieth century, followed the pattern of German

Social Democracy and therefore appealed only to the "workers' aristoc-racy" of northern Italy. The crisis of Italian socialism could be traced back to the decade before the First World War, especially to 1908 when the debate between Arturo Labriola, Turati, Salvemini, and Modigliani came to a head. Parliamentary action could be seen in hindsight as not only the "greatest claim to glory of the movement but also its Achilles' heel." Rosselli denied the pessimism attributed to him by Treves. History, Rosselli wrote, teaches that there has never been a people that did not pass through some defining crisis such as the one that the Italians were now confronting. "Our conscience warns us that the road toward spiritual, political and economic autonomy cannot not be (I would say it must be) seeded with obstacles, defeats and suffering."[77]

The polemic between Rosselli and Treves drew others into the fray as well. Max Ascoli, Giuseppe Saragat, and Pietro Nenni continued the debate into the summer of 1926.[78] In truth, the project of an "autocritica" would be continued by Rosselli in exile through his book *Liberal Socialism* and through the publications of Justice and Liberty. The fierce debate, though, did not sever Rosselli's close ties with the leadership of the reformists.[79]

Yet the Pandora's box could not be closed. During the summer and autumn of 1926, *Il Quarto Stato* returned to the crisis of the Socialist Party, and Rosselli was forced to address the question several more times. In "Volontarismo," he posed what he called the "imperious dilemma": either the victory of fascism was due, at least partially, to the failures of socialism, or it must be admitted that the actions of the socialists had no bearing on Italian society. If the first were true, then it was necessary to examine the errors and act accordingly; if the second were true, the best course of action was to wait passively for the collapse of fascism.[80] Rosselli claimed that he had no desire to enter the lofty realm of philosophy ("fortunately, it is not a question of positivism nor idealism"), but that he would rather enter the realm of action. His conception of voluntarism was essentially a form of humanism. Arguing against the pessimism that was endemic on the Left after 1922, he would insist that pessimism had to be combated with volun-tarism, that is, with action. Here is another echo of his communist counter-part: in a letter to Pietro Sraffa, Gramsci had spoken of the "pessimism of the intellect, optimism of the will." For Rosselli the Aventine Secession was the nadir of antifascist pessimism. It was based on moral outrage but was incapable of action and symptomatic of the disease of pessimism. Perhaps the Aventine could have been supported in its early stages, but not after

3 January 1925 when the true nature and character of fascism was fully revealed. What was required after 3 January was action, the force of will, the audacious gesture that gave the lie to fascism's claim of universal obedience and consent.[81]

Since Rosselli and Nenni felt that their position was not fully understood, they devoted the eighteenth issue to a long editorial, "Chiarificazione" (Clarification). To begin with, the two wanted to put to rest any idea that the group around *Il Quarto Stato* was the nucleus of a future political party; their aim was more modest: to assist the socialist movement in freeing itself from the crisis in which it had been foundering since the failure of the Aventine Secession. The program of *Il Quarto Stato* could be reduced to four essential points: their position concerning fascism; their ideas on the political struggle; the institutional problem; and the question of socialist unity.

Contrary to the view of those who saw it as a transitory phenomenon or of those who in their pessimism saw it as identical with the Italian character, fascism was a much more complex problem. It could not be condemned simply as the last phase of capitalism and the mechanical reaction of the bourgeoisie. Italy's recent unification, *trasformismo,* the political inexperience of the masses, overpopulation, and the lack of a true democratic tradition, had to be addressed as factors in the rise of fascism. The socialists committed a fundamental mistake by ignoring these larger political questions in attempting to achieve what they saw as their essential function: that of lifting the working class from poverty with better salaries.

The method of the political struggle for *Il Quarto Stato* was the democratic method, both as a tool and as a goal. Democratic principles, such as popular sovereignty, a representative government, the respect for the rights of minorities, and freedom of the press and organization, are the basis of the political struggle in the more socially and politically advanced countries of Europe, such as Britain, France, Belgium, and Germany. Democracy, as both a method and a principle, was the fruit of the revolutions of the seventeenth and eighteenth centuries. "When we speak of socialist democracy, we mean by the word "democracy" something very different from the meaning used by the bourgeois parties. For us, political democracy is not real democracy, only the instrument to attain it. Real democracy means not only political autonomy, but also and above all economic freedom. A true democracy does not exist where there exists profound economic disparity."[82] Even the rule of the majority and popular sovereignty, in itself "sacrosanct," acquires a purely formal value when a minority holds the instruments of power for itself. Universal suffrage, when it is accompanied by poverty, is not substantial, but only formal democracy.

On the "institutional question," there could be no doubt that a socialist democracy could be only a republic. The problem arose when the socialists postponed the institutional question, which was in reality the overthrow of the monarchy, in favor of focusing attention on gaining better economic conditions for the working class. Those socialists who proposed that the institutional question be postponed until after the fall of fascism were mistaken; by 1926, Victor Emmanuel III had inextricably linked the House of Savoy with the fate of fascism. To believe that fascism came to power against the will of the King was "a fable of deluded monarchists."

The socialist schism was a historical error and a betrayal of the obligations toward the working classes. The socialists had forgotten that their task was to unite the workers, especially in moments of crisis. Strengthened by this essential principle, the socialist movement grew over decades. Tragically, the socialist schism did not end ideological disputes; if anything, philosophical hairsplitting continued in both the reformist PSU and the maximalist PSI. What Rosselli and Nenni proposed was that the dissension between the two socialist camps was less grave than appeared at first sight, that the disagreements were over situations that by now had ceased to exist, and that they had more in common than that which separated them. "What is important is to escape from the present state of paralysis . . . The time is pressing and we cannot avoid indefinitely our grave duties."[83]

During the final month of publication, Rosselli and *Il Quarto Stato* returned to the question of socialist unity. Matteotti's PSU, founded in October 1922, had been dissolved by fascist decree. It was reborn in Paris as the Partito Socialista dei Lavoratori Italiani (PSLI—the Socialist Party of Italian Workers), which continued the program of the earlier reformist PSU; that is, the program was gradualist and democratic as opposed to the revolutionary tactics of the PSI. Turati, Treves, and Saragat favored unification with the PSI on the condition that a reunified PSI adhere to the Socialist rather than the Communist International.[84] For his part, Rosselli remained cool to the debate raging on reunification. What was more important than resolving obscure theoretical points was to initiate action and organize the workers against fascism. He supported the PSLI, describing it as the only party, except for the Italian Republican Party, that was characterized by initiative, showed some signs of attracting young members, and engaged in the task of reexamining its position in the light of recent history. Yet he was careful not to fall into the trap of sectarianism, the congenital weakness of the Italian Left: "We do not make a fetish of the party," he once wrote; "we are sensible enough to understand that labels will not triumph, but only works."[85]

After the PSLI Congress had met in October 1926, an editorial appeared in the last issue of *Il Quarto Stato* (30 October), signed "Noi" (We) and was probably a collaborative effort between Rosselli and Nenni. The motions approved by the Congress were greeted with favor by the journal, since they addressed the institutional question and called for a broad antifascist front of the "manual and intellectual proletariat."[86] The Congress also reiterated its position on the rise of fascism and the character of Mussolini's regime, rejecting the communist theory as too simplistic. It also took an important step in defining antifascism in a positive sense—what it was for—as well as in a negative sense—what it was against. This was an important step forward and one that Rosselli would insist on in the future.

Il Quarto Stato was destined for a short life of only seven months. The day after the thirtieth edition appeared, 30 October 1926, there was another attempt on the life of Mussolini by a fourteen-year-old boy from Bologna, Anteo Zamboni. Zamboni was lynched on the spot, but there is some suspicion as to whether there really was an attempt on the life of Il Duce or whether it was an elaborate mise-en-scène to justify the swift and severe fascist reprisals that followed. The street gangs that had been contained by Mussolini were unleashed in a reign of terror, and the houses of Treves, Nenni, and Modigliani, among others, were destroyed. The attempted assassination eventually led to the passing of the Exceptional Decrees of 11 November 1926 that effectively signaled full dictatorship in Italy. In early November, with the help of Rosselli and Ferruccio Parri, Nenni fled to France, and the phenomenon of *fuoruscitismo* (antifascist exile movement) began.[87]

What had *Il Quarto Stato* accomplished in its short lifespan? Most observers, then and now, agree that the journal formed part of the conscience of antifascism in Italy and represented one of the first sustained attempts to forge an antifascist consensus among intellectuals. It addressed problems, questions, and ideas that were to be formulated in greater depth and complexity in exile, and it served to plant the seeds of a positive antifascism by arguing for a republic. *Il Quarto Stato* also continued the legacy of Gobetti by insisting that fascism was not an ephemeral phenomenon, noting the ties between fascism and the recent past. As a "socialist review of political culture," the journal became a model for other publications by antifascists both in Italy and in exile. It stressed that the forces of the Left had more in common than they realized, and it placed united political action above ideological consistency. For Rosselli it was his most sincere, and his last, attempt to reconcile himself with traditional socialism. Simultaneously, in articles like "Autocritica," there is the *heretical* Rosselli of *Liberal Socialism.* Here is the first elaboration of the general ideas of antifascism that were later to develop in the Antifascist Concentration and in Justice and Liberty. The project represented a rebirth of socialism after defeat, the beginning of a return through a new mentality that rejected the Aventine Secession and legalitarian methods. By 1926 both Rosselli and Nenni believed in the necessity of forming revolutionary antifascist militias that would spearhead the clandestine struggle against the regime and that would use violence. The communists of the time criticized the journal for its "bourgeois prejudice," but Rosselli would continue to insist that an effective antifascist coalition would have to forge an alliance among the industrial workers, the artisans, the peasants, and the advanced segments of the bourgeoisie, especially the intellectuals.

Turati's Escape

Most scholars point to 1926 and the Exceptional Decrees as the creation of the fascist dictatorship; indeed, Mussolini referred to 1926 as his "Napoleonic Year." On 5 November all political parties except the PNF were dissolved. All antifascist organizations were outlawed, and antifascist newspapers confiscated and suppressed. Four days later, the fascist majority in the Chamber of Deputies declared the seats of the 120 antifascist deputies who had participated in the Aventine Secession to be annulled, and Mussolini presented the Chamber of Deputies with a bill creating the Special Tribunal for the Defense of the State. The Chamber passed the bill on the spot, and the Senate followed suit on 20 November. The Tribunal began operating in February 1927 and continued until 1943, holding a total of 720 sessions in which 5,319 persons were tried. Of these, 5,155 were found guilty and sentenced, of whom 29 were executed and 7 given life sentences. Antonio Gramsci, despite his parliamentary immunity, was arrested, tried, and sentenced to a long prison term. At his trial, the prosecutor declared, "We must prevent this mind from working for the next twenty years." Ironically,

Gramsci's prison sentence and forced withdrawal from the daily political struggle allowed him to create his enormously influential prison notebooks that are today regarded as the most original reworking of Western Marxism.

Besides these measures, passports were canceled, and the regime revived the tradition of *confino* for political "criminals." *Confino* was the practice of forcing political opponents into "domestic exile": most were sent to islands such as Ponza and Lipari or to tiny villages in the interior of the South. Carlo Levi, perhaps the most famous of these prisoners and a member of Justice and Liberty in Turin, used this experience for his most powerful book, *Christ Stopped at Eboli*.[88] Carlo Rosselli also used his time in *confino* to write his most important theoretical work.

In 1926 the violent Blackshirt squads, held in check by Mussolini during the Matteotti crisis and its aftermath, were unleashed in all their fury. Many cities and provinces were again in the grip of terror. Filippo Turati was a virtual prisoner in his apartment in the Piazza Duomo of Milan. The death of his companion, Anna Kuliscioff, in December 1925 had provoked a period of severe depression in the reformist leader. To make matters worse, his own health was deteriorating, and he seemed to have given up the struggle, seeing a lifetime of work destroyed in a few short years. Outside his window, in the piazza of the great Gothic cathedral of Milan, fascist Blackshirts paraded and chanted "*Con la barba di Turati facciamo per lustrare gli stivali di Mussolini*" (With the beard of Turati we will shine the boots of Mussolini). It was in this atmosphere of fear and intimidation that Rosselli insisted on Turati's escape from Italy.[89]

Encouraged by the successful escapes of Claudio Treves and Giuseppe Saragat in the days after the Zamboni assassination attempt, Rosselli tried to convince Turati to flee to France, but the old warrior was weary and reluctant to undertake the dangerous risk. In the end, Rosselli's eloquence and insistence finally convinced Turati that his life was in danger and that the battle could be continued abroad. On the morning of 21 November, the day Nenni arrived safely in Paris, Rosselli had a "drammatico colloquio" with Turati; "If Anna were here . . ." began Carlo, hoping to inspire Turati; but the old man interrupted Rosselli to reply sadly, "Oh, let's not permit the dead to speak."[90] In the afternoon, Alessandro Levi brought Turati a letter from Treves that told of the latter's escape to Paris. That night, with the help of several accomplices, Rosselli ushered Turati out of his apartment under the not-so-watchful eyes of the fascist police. An elegant couple with a dog on a leash managed to distract the police who were watching the apartment, while Turati, clean shaven and bundled up in a greatcoat and large hat, left by another door. From that moment, Rosselli had consciously taken an irreversible step and placed himself outside the laws of fascist Italy.

Turati and Rosselli were fortunate in that the police did not realize something was amiss until two days later. Meanwhile, they fled by automobile to the villa of Giuseppe Albini, the "ferocious and very intelligent" drama critic of *Avanti!,* as described by Rosselli. In a sense, they were the victims of past success; because Nenni, Treves, Salvemini, Saragat, and others had managed to escape to France over the Alps, those roads were now closed and the mountain passes guarded by the fascist police. Another route would have to be found. Once the police discovered Turati's escape, they began a massive search of the homes of all his friends, relatives, and associates. Some people, terrorized by the police, surrendered information. Turati's doctor went to Marion Cave Rosselli and told her that by now, the police "knew everything."[91] It was only a matter of time before Albini's villa would be paid an unwelcome visit.

Aldo Garosci recounts the story of how a marriage that had been put off for some time was agreed to if the groom (who owned an automobile) would agree to bring Turati and Rosselli to the coast. Although never confirmed by Rosselli or Turati, the anecdote illustrates the romantic and adventurous—though still deadly serious—nature of the enterprise. Turati and Rosselli finally left Albini's villa and the area of Milan by car on 2 December, only a few hours before the fascist police arrived. Albini willingly served a prison term of eight months for his role in Turati's escape.

As the police concentrated their efforts in the Milan area and the mountain passes into France, Turati and Rosselli made their way south to the Ligurian coast. They spent a night hiding in a local hotel, signing in as father and son. They were helped in their efforts by the young socialist lawyer and future president of the Italian Republic, Sandro Pertini. Their destination was Savona, a small port city just west of Genoa. From there the trio rented a motorboat to reach French shores, but this boat proved too small to make the crossing to Corsica. Another and larger boat—the *Oriens*—was found and paid for by Rosselli, along with a sailor willing to take the risk, Italo Oxilia. Finally, on 12 December at eight o'clock in the evening, preparations were complete, and the small craft set sail for Corsica. "The large fish has broken the net and runs toward the high sea.

Pertini intones the *Internazionale,* while we watch the lights of Italy disappear." [92]

After twelve hours on a "diabolical sea," [93] the group arrived at Calvi, on the northwest coast of Corsica. News soon spread through the small town, and representatives of the local republican club were on the shore to welcome the old socialist warrior fleeing from fascist Italy. Turati, who had become seasick through the voyage, did not fail his hosts and somehow managed to overcome his illness, improvising on the spot a short and dignified speech in French for those who had gathered to greet the new exile. Parri would later recall that "the escape of Turati was a masterpiece of audacity and simple astuteness of Rosselli." [94] The next day, as Turati and Pertini were about to begin their journey to Marseilles, and in spite of their exhortations, Rosselli and Parri decided to return to Italy. Rosselli firmly believed that the antifascist struggle had to take place within Italy, as far as was possible. If it was absolutely necessary, as in the cases of Salvemini, Turati, and others, the older leaders could continue the battle in exile, while the younger followers, not as well known to the police, would continue the struggle in Italy. Rosselli and Parri reached Marina di Carrara on 14 December and were immediately arrested. Alessandro Levi recounts a visit to Rosselli in prison:

> Carlo was cheerful, he seemed proud to carry the handcuffs, and with his head held high . . . had an air of challenge and irony. One day Anna Kuliscioff had said in his presence that modern youth were afraid to go to prison. Those words of Kuliscioff, which seemed to Carlo in those dark times like "a ray of sunlight" were not a reproach to him. But the words of that very noble woman, who because of her ideals had suffered prison many times and in different countries, sounded like a criticism and an admonishment in the ears of Carlo Rosselli. In that gloomy December of 1926 he began to demonstrate that he did not have that fear, but he knew how to confront the sufferings and the material privations with cheerful courage. [95]

Rosselli and Parri were celebrated for their courageous action, but some criticized them for their return and almost certain arrest. In strictly rational terms, perhaps these criticisms were valid; but the expatriation of Turati should not be seen under the strict calculus of rationality. It was a heroic attempt, a clamorous and defiant gesture to challenge the power of the fascist state, an endeavor to demonstrate that there were those in Italy who would not allow themselves to be denied liberty and freedom. Rosselli's account of the episode years later emphasized this tragic yet heroic aspect of the entire operation: "Turati, leaving Milan and Italy, intuited that the voyage would be of no return, he had a presentiment that Death would seize him in exile like so many great Italians who because of too great a love for Italy were forced to flee the usurped land."[96]

Upon their arrest, Rosselli and Parri were transported to the local prison at Massa. They used their time to prepare a defense, knowing that Turati's escape had become common knowledge throughout Italy. After a week in prison at Massa, Carlo was transferred to the San Vittore prison in Milan, and from there to Como. Marion Cave Rosselli was expecting their first child at this time and rode in the same train as Carlo, in a different car. The police escort was kind enough to allow, contrary to regulations, husband and wife a few moments together (in police presence and with Carlo still in chains).[97]

After three months of prison in Como, Carlo was sent to Savona, where Parri was already being held. Italian law at the time stipulated that those accused of "non-authorized expatriation" had the right to provisional freedom while awaiting trial. Although the judicial authorities granted this privilege, the fascist police nonetheless sent all those accused to confinement on the island of Ustica, off the coast of Sicily. The train ride from Como in the north to Palermo in the south, as well as the Dantesque inferno of the notorious Ucciardone prison in Palermo, was described by Rosselli, who was shackled hand and foot all the way in the middle of a ferociously hot summer:

> Confusion and filth reign everywhere . . . After a while this promiscuity becomes torturous. Sudden quarrels, noisy dreams, subdued conversations, noises of every sort and nature—much nature—become confused.
>
> The prison slowly goes to sleep.
>
> The last bells sound . . .
>
> The sounds of outside life, of the other life, that which we call "normal," reach us. I was in Palermo seven years ago as a tourist, exactly in this month of May. Who knows how many times I passed the doors of Ucciardone without thinking?[98]

Outside the prison walls, the socialists renewed their attempts at opposition. Turati, Treves, Giuseppe Emanuele Modigliani, and Giuseppe Saragat resurrected the PSU in Paris as the PSLI in November 1926. In response,

Pietro Nenni revived the PSI a month later. There was broad support for the unification of the two parties; the PSLI gave its blessing in December 1929, and the PSI four months later. Yet a major sticking point soon emerged. Would the new unified party join the Communist or the Socialist International? Nenni was prepared to compromise, but the maximalists, led by Angelica Balabanoff, refused. Unification was achieved by compromise in July 1930: the newly reborn PSI was Marxist in character in its emphasis on class struggle and the final goal of a socialist society; but it stressed a commitment to democracy and a restoration of political and civil liberties.[99]

Rosselli, from his rather unorthodox confinement, followed these events closely. When he finally reached Paris in the summer of 1929, he threw himself into the ideological fray. However, enforced distance from these disputes was a blessing in disguise.

• • • •

CHAPTER THREE

Liberal Socialism

Liberty is the possibility of doubting, the possibility of making a mistake, the possibility of searching and experimenting, the possibility of saying "No" to any authority—literary, artistic, philosophic, religious, social, and even political.

IGNAZIO SILONE, *THE GOD THAT FAILED* (1949)

Socialism is nothing more than the logical development, taken to its extreme consequences, of the principle of liberty.

CARLO ROSSELLI, *LIBERAL SOCIALISM* (1930)

"Well-to-do, learned, intelligent, studious" was how a police report described Rosselli after his arrest.[1] He and Parri were detained at Massa prison for about ten days. Parri was "tall, slight, pale, his thick hair framing an intelligent face"; a marked contrast to Rosselli, who was "powerfully-built, with an eager, merry face and ringing voice."[2] "Occasionally at night," recalled Parri, "Rosselli sat up in bed, wiped the sweat from his brow, looked fixedly before him, looked at me, and laid down without a word."[3] "Until I met Parri," Rosselli wrote in 1929, "the Mazzinian hero had been to me a rhetorical abstraction. Now I see him before me in flesh and blood, with all the sorrow and energy of the world stamped on his features."[4]

Notice of their arrest arrived in Florence just as the Rosselli family was preparing for the marriage of Nello to Maria Todesco on 22 December. Despite his appointment to the Royal Institute of Modern and Contemporary History, Nello was arrested on his return from the honeymoon. Carlo was sent to Ustica, which was considered at the time, and with good reason, to be the worst of the islands of *confino*. To travel from Como to Ustica, it was necessary to traverse the entire peninsula. On Carlo's journey, two curious incidents occurred that point to the paradoxical nature of Italy in the years of fascism. Passing through Florence, the *carabinieri* (military police) who were accompanying Rosselli allowed him to spend the night in his boyhood home on via Giusti. Carlo passed the night with his family as the two *carabinieri* waited discreetly in the courtyard below. Occasionally they would raise their voices to inquire whether the prisoner was still there, and Carlo would simply lean out the window and reassure his captors that all was well. The next morning, all three boarded another train for Rome, where Rosselli was met at the station by his uncle Gabriele Pincherle, brother of Amelia. Weeks earlier at the Milan train station, Rosselli had been met by a colonel of the *carabinieri* (known by a mutual friend), who suggested draping Turati's great overcoat over Rosselli's handcuffed wrists while in the station. The good colonel thought that surely Rosselli, of a respectable bourgeois family, would not want to be seen in the very public Milan train station shackled like a common criminal; yet Rosselli waved him away, anxious that the people would see how the regime treated its citizens. "I shall never forget as long as I live," Carlo's wife, Marion, wrote, "the appalling impression, on those crossings to the islands, of the ship with its long files of political prisoners, chained one to the other, and the sinister clank of those iron chains. The sight always made me think of Tsarist Russia."[5]

On arriving at Ustica, Carlo was struck by its "tragic and naked beauty." Life on the island represented a liberation of sorts from the long months in prison. "What is this strange inebriation that takes hold of me? I seem to be born again. After a long prison stay, the first day of *confino* is an orgy, an explosion of the physical self."[6] Although he was on Ustica for only a month, the island left an impression on him, not only for its character but also for the friendships he forged there.

Personal events continued to crisscross with Carlo's public life. On 8 June 1927 Marion Cave Rosselli gave birth to their first child, Giovanni Andrea Rosselli, whimsically nicknamed "Il Mirtillino" (Little Blueberry Bush).[7] As so often happened in their lives, Carlo and Nello's fates were intertwined, sometimes in a positive way, but more often in a tragic manner. Two days later, Nello, presumed by the fascist authorities to be involved with the clandestine expatriations, was arrested and held for a month at Murate, the prison of Florence. The next day, his first in prison, Nello wrote to Amelia of the "tranquility of his conscience" and his "extraordinary serenity"; "I felt myself full of energy and youth; indeed I am grateful for this unpleasant experience, which serves as a test of nerves and character."[8]

However, Nello's asking to be sent to Ustica to be reunited with his brother created a bitter irony: Nello was in transit to the island when Carlo was being sent back for trial at Savona. Soon after arriving on Ustica, Nello received a postcard from Carlo that was sent from Ustica two weeks before. The younger brother remained in prison from July 1927 until February 1928; this episode was not his last taste of prison life.

By a curious and fortunate anomaly of fascist legislation, "clandestine expatriation," even for political reasons, did not fall under the jurisdiction of the feared Special Tribunal, which was established in November 1926 and began work in February 1927. Instead, Carlo Rosselli, Ferruccio Parri, and Sandro Pertini had the relative good fortune to be presented before the *magistratura ordinaria*, which had not yet fallen completely under the domination of the regime.

Rosselli and Parri decided to use the occasion of the trial to garner as much negative publicity against the regime as possible. The trial would be turned into a showcase for the foreign press, illustrating how civil and political liberties had been destroyed in an Italy where "the trains ran on time." During the long months between the capture at Marina di Carrara, the imprisonment at Como, and the internment on Ustica, Rosselli had decided irrevocably on fighting fascism with all his resources. Parri recalled long nights in prison when Carlo seemed possessed of an almost frightening determination. Together they decided to transform the trial into a political drama against fascism. In preparation for this, Rosselli read *The Confessions* of Rousseau (a "great book" he thought), the essays of Taine, a biography of Karl Marx, the writings of Ernest Renan, and Benedetto Croce's *Filosofia della pratica*. Besides reading, he was engaged in writing a work on utilitarianism.[9] With his mother, he argued over the merits of Gioacchino Volpe's recently published history of Italy. Volpe, professor of history at the universities of Milan (1905 to 1924) and Rome (1924 to 1940) began his career as a medievalist but became the foremost historian to support fascism. His *Storia del movimento fascista* of 1939 crowned his career as the official historian of the regime. Volpe's *L'Italia in cammino*, which was published in early 1927, was challenged only six months later by its antithesis, Croce's *Storia d'Italia*. As a fervent nationalist, Amelia Rosselli defended Volpe's work, but Carlo was stinging in his reply. Volpe's book was marred by "tepid evasions and contortions" and was neither acute nor profound. But Rosselli's most serious charge, characteristically, was that the book was not sincere. Nor did he fail to avail himself the opportunity to criticize his mother: "Scratch, scratch and in *mutter* [mother] one always finds a bit of nationalism."[10]

The trial, finally, opened in Savona on 9 September 1927 and lasted four days.[11] Rosselli had already set the stage for the drama with a letter to the judge, insisting on the political significance of the trial. He declared that Turati's escape was a political act. With stirring oratory, he declared that fascism was "the first and only subject responsible" for the present catastrophe in Italy and was "incriminated by the consciences of free men." Every possibility of legal opposition in Italy had been suppressed with "blind violence" and "unjust laws." It was a desperate struggle, made sacred by the blood of men like Matteotti, Gobetti, and Amendola. Helping Turati escape was "an austere protest," meant to be seen as "a cry of alarm to the civilized world, to offer a living proof of the definitive break between two Italies, between two moral races, between two opposite conceptions of life." Shrewdly, Rosselli cast himself in the tradition of the Risorgimento and reminded the judge of his personal history:

> I came to socialism after the defeat, in the conviction that the redemption of the workers must rest on an unshakable moral base and take back, integrating, the tradition of a Risorgimento that has remained the patrimony of a few . . . It comforts me to think that this substantial continuity that I claim between the struggle of today and yesterday finds a characteristic echo in the history of my family. A Rosselli secretly sheltered in Pisa a dying Mazzini, an exile in his own country. It was only logical that another Rosselli, a half century later, tried to save from fascist fury one of the most noble and unselfish spirits of the country.[12]

Inside and outside the courtroom, a large public had gathered, and despite the ominous presence of the fascist police and militia, they made no attempt to hide their support of the defendants. In addition, a large press contingent had arrived to follow the trial and had devoted ample coverage during the first few days; as a result, the prefect of Savona issued orders that the proceedings not be featured prominently in the local newspapers. Some of the best extant documents of the trial and its attendant atmosphere are the reports from a correspondent of the *Manchester Guardian,* Barbara Carter, who managed to slip into the courtroom by pretending to be the cousin of Marion Cave.[13] A *carabiniere* posted at the entrance of the courtroom heard her English accent and allowed her to enter. In one of her dispatches from Savona, Carter confessed that "everyone shared the pessimism of the young reporter from the newspaper *Il Lavoro* of Genoa, who, sitting next to me during the entire unfolding of the trial and finding himself within reach of the white collar of one of the lawyers wrote on it with a pencil while no one was looking: *Hic jacet mortua justitia* [Here, dead, lies justice]."[14]

As Carter had intuited, the full significance of the trial was not lost on the public. As the regime was consolidating its power, the trial was one of the last acts of Liberal Italy—the last gasp of freedom before the full implementation of the Special Tribunal for the Defense of the State. Parri at the time referred to fascism as "a parenthesis" (anticipating Croce's interpretation) and called for a second Risorgimento that would be the basis for the resistance movement.[15] Carlo Levi recalled that the trial had "all the characteristics of the absurd . . . a political and moral battle."[16] A moment of high drama took place during Rosselli's interrogation by Ispettore Generale Consolo, when the accused became the accuser:

Rosselli: In Milan there were no victims [of the fascists]?
Consolo: I said no.
Rosselli: And outside Milan?
Consolo: It doesn't concern me.
Rosselli: The antifascists, therefore, are undisturbed, Mr. Inspector General. The public order is not disturbed by the fascists?
Consolo: Yes.
Rosselli: You do not remember the events in Florence?
Consolo: They are not in my jurisdiction.
Rosselli: Did you hear that in Florence they killed the Honorable Pilati [member of the Chamber of Deputies]?
Consolo (weaker): This has no bearing . . .
Rosselli: The lawyer Delaini?
Consolo: I do not need to respond.
Rosselli: The railroad worker Becciolini?
Consolo: I do not need . . .
Rosselli: You know nothing of the "night of blood"?[17]
Consolo: I cannot . . .
Rosselli: Someone was killed in his bed.
Consolo: I cannot. . . .
Rosselli: By shots from a revolver.

Consolo: No.

Rosselli: It was the correspondent of *Avanti!* You know his name. Say it! Who was it?

Consolo (wearily, whispering): My brother.[18]

On the evening of the thirteenth, the three judges returned from their deliberations and announced the sentences: Turati, Pertini, Parri, Rosselli, Da Bove, Oxilia, and Boyancé were found guilty of article 160 of the Law of Public Security (6 November 1926, n. 1848). Oxilia was sentenced to one year, one month, and twenty days; the rest were condemned to only ten months. In light of the time already served and in the political context of the trial, the ten-month sentence amounted to an acquittal, as all those present immediately realized. Nearly twenty years later, the chief magistrate, Pasquale Sarno, revealed that the regime had an inordinate interest in the trial. "It was written to me that the Head of Government [i.e., Mussolini] was personally interested in the matter and was watching Savona; that my career depended on the outcome of the trial. But we obeyed only the voice of our conscience."[19] Upon the pronouncement of the sentence, the courtroom burst into a spontaneous delirium, and Sarno recalled that he restored order only after several long minutes during which the news made its way out into the street. Cries of "Viva il tribunale di Savona!" and "Viva la giustizia!" were met with threats by the assembled fascists, who called the sentence "an iniquity" passed by "antifascist" judges. The following day, Savona's fascist newspaper *Il Brandale* deplored the outcome and raged against "robed antifascism."

Rosselli, Parri, Pertini, and the others except for Oxilia, had been sentenced to only ten months; yet Mussolini, following the trial from Rome, telegraphed the *procuratore generale* of Genoa to appeal the sentence. As a result, five years' *confino* were appended to the sentences of them all. Carlo remained at Savona until the last week of December, when he was transferred to the penal island of Lipari. Elated by the original verdict and sentence, he was not discouraged by the intervention of Mussolini and the five-year sentence. In a characteristic gesture of defiance, he wrote that he would not pass five years on Lipari. "I have fallen from the clouds without, naturally, any harm. On the contrary!" Yet only six weeks later, awaiting transport to Lipari, he wrote that "1927 will remain for us the black year . . . in which we have touched bottom." He prepared a strenuous course of reading and writing to utilize the forced stay at Lipari, asking for De

Ruggiero's *History of European Liberalism* and various works of Taine, Labriola, and others; it appears that his greatest concern, besides the welfare of Marion and their son, was his imminent separation from Parri, who was being sent to Ustica.[20]

The judges themselves had lent an air of surrealism to the proceedings with their creative interpretation in arriving at a decision and sentence. Both Rosselli and Parri had unequivocally stated that they had assisted in Turati's escape for political reasons. They pointed to the massacres of October 1925 and November 1926 and to the fascist gangs that sang beneath Turati's window as proof that a "state of necessity" existed for Turati's flight. In their decision, though, the judges explicitly denied this argument, for to grant it would be implicitly to condemn the regime. They held that the affair was not politically motivated, in which case they would have been constrained to impose a sentence of between three and six years. Instead the judges forged a "creative" interpretation: Turati was old and sick; his only concern was to find somewhere in which a cure would be forthcoming. The judges could use this line of reasoning because of the testimony of Turati's doctor (Ghilardoni); yet reading between the lines, one can interpret "fascism" as the illness. As for Pertini, the judges decided that he had simply taken advantage of Turati's journey to remain in France to "look for work that in Savona he could not find" and to leave his family home, where conditions made "cohabitation impossible because of a brother who was a member of the fascists." Rosselli and the others were guilty merely of *concorso* ("attendance" or "cooperation"] and consequently were given the lenient sentence of ten months. "Ten of these trials," complained a fascist lawyer, "and the regime is done for." As for Carlo, he still had a sentence of five years *confino*. "I make no plans for the future," he wrote to Turati in Paris after the trial; "I believe though, that I will not remain more than a year in *confino*. Read between the lines."[21]

Lipari

If Ustica, as Rosselli wrote, was a parenthesis between the two prisons of Como and Savona, Lipari was "an open parenthesis."[22] He and Emilio Lussu joined several hundred other prisoners on the penal island of Lipari off the northern coast of Sicily on 28 December 1927. Lipari was a marked improvement over Ustica. Francesco Fausto Nitti, who was the nephew of the former prime minister and was familiar with the other penal islands, called it a "terrestrial paradise."[23] Two weeks before Rosselli's arrival, the fascist police on the island had uncovered a "conspiracy" to overthrow the regime; consequently, 250 persons were accused and held in prison for nine months before being acquitted by the court in Siracusa. It was into this atmosphere of suspicion and false rumors that Carlo landed on Lipari. Soon after his arrival, Marion joined him with little Giovanni, and after renting a small house, the small family settled down to a tranquil (if unorthodox) existence. Marion recalled those early days on Lipari as "another honeymoon."[24] When Amelia arrived to visit her son, Emilio Lussu remarked that she reminded him (even then) of the mother of the Gracchus brothers.[25] The Rosselli family, in truth, led a privileged existence on Lipari, able to rent and furnish a house and to find some small luxuries. Carlo, though immensely happy that his small family was reunited on the island, was brutally honest in recognizing his shortcomings as a husband and father: "I seek to foster my scarce sense of paternity. He who concerns himself with humanity in general finds it difficult to be a good father."[26]

Rosselli came to be regarded as a model prisoner by the island administrator. When information arrived from Rome concerning rumors that the model prisoner was planning an escape, the director of the penal colony replied that he wished all prisoners were like Rosselli. But it was all an elaborate charade. From the moment the sentence was announced, Rosselli had been planning an escape from Lipari, something that no one had yet accomplished. He established a rigid daily schedule, and the citizens of Lipari and the police came to expect his daily appearance on the streets at certain times, in a manner reminiscent of Kant's daily walks in Königsberg. In fact, he and Gioacchino Dolci spent many hours in reading Kant. Rosselli discussed with the landlord a project to bring up water from a well on the property, concerned himself with establishing a library for the prisoners, planned a course of reading and study, and even managed to rent a piano brought over from the mainland (there were none on the island) so that he could pass the evenings playing the music of Beethoven and Chopin. (The piano was to serve another, but clandestine, function.) All of this was done to establish in the minds of the police that the prisoner had accepted his fate and was resigned to passing five years on the island.

In reality, Rosselli—through Marion—had already contacted Francesco Fausto Nitti and Emilio Lussu about a possible escape. Lussu was a war veteran and Sardinian radical who had been arrested when he shot and killed a fascist *squadristra*, who was part of a mob that assaulted his home.[27] Acquitted in the courtroom on the grounds of legitimate self-defense, Lussu was, like Rosselli, nonetheless sentenced to *confino*. Nitti was the nephew of a former prime minister and son of a Methodist pastor. Together, the "modernist Jew" Rosselli, the lapsed Catholic Lussu, and the Methodist Nitti made for a strange trio. They were fortunate in finding Gioacchino Dolci on Lipari; he was a young worker from Rome who was active in the Republican movement. Dolci was eventually released and aided in organizing the escape effort of July 1929, as well as later in the founding of Justice and Liberty in Paris.[28] Along with Dolci, was Paolo Fabbri, a peasant from Molinella. Whereas Dolci was the intellectual— "There is in him a constitutional detachment from all that forms the ambition of the normal man . . . He struggles against bourgeois philistinism," Fabbri was the opposite: "Son of the earth, he has its concreteness and fertility . . . Fabbri is the proof of the vitality of socialism."[29]

The Rosselli house on Lipari soon became a focal point for the social and intellectual life of the close-knit community of political prisoners. Carlo forged strong ties with the anarchists and even invited the entire (admittedly small) anarchist community to his house. On the feast of the Epiphany, the tradition of the Befana (good witch) bringing gifts to small children was continued: Nitti dressed as the Befana, and 120 children of the *confinati* were given modest treats. While Carlo studied German with one group, Marion gave English lessons to another. This second study group was created for the express purpose of allowing Nitti and Lussu to frequent the Rosselli house without arousing suspicion.

Throughout 1928 and the early months of 1929, Rosselli continued to play the part of the resigned *confinato*, with a strenuous program of reading, yet his inner torment allowed for no real tranquility. He wondered whether he and his colleagues were unrealistic, noting that within Italy, life continued much as it had before. Prolonged existence in this unnatural state of heresy and prison created a world where all values seemed "strangely deformed."[30]

Plans for an escape were constantly being formulated, reformulated, abandoned, and revised. After several schemes had been voted down, including the possibility of a hydroplane's landing offshore, a consensus was reached. Rosselli, Lussu, and Nitti decided that the best possibility of success rested in swimming offshore to be picked up by a passing motorboat; the boat was to by hired beforehand and a time to be arranged for the pickup. On 17 November 1928, the prisoners carried out the first attempt.

After spending the day hoeing a small garden to allay any suspicions, that evening they made their way to the beach and swam offshore, waiting for a rendezvous that failed to take place. (The first boat that was rented was too small to navigate the rough waters that night.) Slowly it dawned on them that the motorboat would not be coming. Now the problem was to return to their houses before eight o'clock and the nightly rounds of inspection by the fascist police. Carlo recounted the close call after leaving the sea:

> I take the path of the fields. But my eyeglasses are lost and my eyes full of salt. I can see nothing. I forge ahead, stumbling often. I run. I crash into a wall of barbed wire. Four points puncture my eyebrow and cheekbone, and, it seems to me, an eye. Agitation. Blood. I wipe myself to find out if I can see. I see. Then go. In the last stretch, I slip into a tiny path. An extremely frightened little girl watches this giant, bloody thing. I enter the house panting. I run to the mirror.
>
> My face is all red with blood. Now I understand the fear of the little girl. I work feverishly to hide the evidence of the crime . . . I dress. After fifteen minutes, the patrol arrives.[31]

By the next morning, all had seemingly returned to normal. The other prisoners and the guards, on seeing Rosselli the next morning and knowing that Marion had left the island, assumed that Rosselli's injuries were the result of some amorous adventure. Carlo smiled sweetly at these conjectures and responded truthfully, "No, no, I fell in the garden yesterday."[32]

Though the first attempt at escape had ended in failure, an unexpected piece of good fortune was to come their way. Marion and Mirtillino soon returned to Lipari. Dolci had been released from Lipari on 7 December 1928 and eventually made his way to France in March 1929. There he coordinated new efforts with Alberto Tarchiani to free Rosselli, Lussu and Nitti. It was Tarchiani who spent two years first weaving and then reweaving the unraveled fabric of an escape plan. A new motorboat was purchased from an Egyptian prince in Tunisia (with Rosselli's money) and was registered to Marion's father.[33] Italo Oxilia, the pilot of the boat that brought Turati to France, was hired for another attempt in July.

On 23 June 1929, Marion and "Mirtillino" left Lipari smuggling a precious item off the island. On 26 July, Rosselli and his companions were again in the waters offshore, but again the motorboat failed to appear. That night Rosselli dreamed of a lion that was following him on a *tapis roulant* (flying carpet) Lussu interpreted the dream in a flash: the *tapis roulant* symbolized flight; the lion symbolized Africa.[34]

The next evening another attempt was made. This time the three remained in the surf long after the eight o'clock curfew. Under the noses of the prison director and fascist police, who were enjoying a summer ice cream by the shore, the three managed to climb aboard the silently waiting motorboat. The engine was started, and the motorboat sped away toward the North African shore. Contemplating the phosphorescent wake, the vanishing lights of Lipari, and his comrades left behind, Rosselli felt a "great sadness after the initial tumultuous joy."[35]

The motorboat made its way to Cape Bon in Tunisia, then on to Corsica and Marseilles, where ironically they were stranded because the French communists had declared a strike. Eventually they made their way to Paris. News of their escape electrified the antifascist community and focused new attention on political conditions within Italy. For Rosselli, "one thought will guide us in this hospitable land: to turn this personal freedom conquered with much difficulty into an instrument for the freedom of a people. Only in this way does it seem right to exchange a prison *in patria* with freedom in exile."[36] To all observers then, and to most historians afterwards, the escape represented a typical instance of fascist incompetence; yet Nicola Tranfaglia has implied that the escape may have been aided by the director of the penal colony on Lipari (perhaps bribed by the family?). Lussu himself obliquely remarked over thirty years later that the naval commander at Naples—by artfully delaying the order to give chase—was "consciously our accomplice."[37]

Liberal Socialism

It was while on Lipari (December 1927–July 1929) that Rosselli drafted what was to be his major theoretical work, *Liberal Socialism*.[38] Written clandestinely, it survived the many police searches in its hiding place in the piano and later in a rabbit hutch in the garden.[39] This was the precious item smuggled off the island by Marion Rosselli in June 1929, one month before Rosselli's escape. The work stands as the interpretive key in an understanding of Rosselli's heretical critique of socialism and Marxism, and it delineates his vision of a liberal socialism that is a viable alternative to both free-market liberalism and the apocalyptic seduction of Marxism. It can be read, parallel with Gramsci's *Prison Notebooks*, as a study of the defeat of democracy and socialism in the face of fascism, and it posits a viable position "beyond" liberalism, Marxism, or fascism.[40] Michael Walzer has written that Rosselli was "a socialist who has sailed away from the Marxist seas and touched land on the shores of liberalism,"[41] but the metaphor is incomplete: the shores of Rosselli's liberalism are sometimes caressed and sometimes buffeted by the Marxist seas. At a time when Gramsci's work was almost completely unknown and Croce had lost his appeal because of his tepid opposition to fascism, Rosselli's book came as a gust of fresh air. Alberto Cavaglion's reaction typified that of many: "Only one book exerted an influence comparable to that of Croce's works. This book was *Liberal Socialism* by Carlo Rosselli . . . Rosselli's opening, so bright and clear, succeeded in stirring its readers in a way that no volume of Croce's managed to do."[42] *Liberal Socialism* was not conceived as another contribution to the already vast literature of revisionism; Rosselli felt that although the revisionists were correct in stressing free will, it was impossible to insert voluntarism into Marxism. Nor was the book in the tradition of European social democracy; that camp had steadfastly refused to accept the precepts of nineteenth-century liberalism. Instead, Rosselli's book can be read as part of the literature of the "crisis of Marxism" that began with Bernstein's *Evolutionary Socialism* of 1899; in Italy, Giovanni Gentile's *La filosofia di Marx* appeared the same year, Croce's fundamental work on Marx appeared a year later and Georges Sorel's critical essays on Marxism were published in 1903. If there had been a "crisis of Marxism" fermenting for three decades, the same could be said for social democracy; *Liberal Socialism* was as much a criticism of the latter as the former.

The idea of a socialism seeking a synthesis between collectivism and individualism was not entirely new. The Hungarian Theordor Hertzka's 1890 utopian novel, *Freiland,* was described by G. D. H. Cole as "the most complete development of a social doctrine that is a mix of economic liberalism and socialist ideas." Immediately after the First World War, Cole also discerned a forerunner of liberal socialism in the German sociologist Franz Oppenheimer. An Italian historian has recognized a liberal socialism in the work of the French thinker Charles Renouvier, especially his *La nouvelle monodologie* that appeared, along with Bernstein's work, in 1899.[43] One of the earliest uses of "liberal socialism" was in Alfred Naquet's *Socialisme collectiviste et socialisme liberale.* Naquet, a medical doctor, was a Radical-Socialist member of the French Parliament in the Third Republic and was the first to propose a law legalizing divorce. Rosselli's book bears a striking structural and intellectual similarity to Naquet's work, although there is no evidence that Carlo had read Naquet. Both books begin with a trenchant critique of orthodox Marxism and collectivist socialism; the former was criticized because of the labor theory of value and the iron law of wages, and the latter because collectivism is a "pure utopia" contrary to a deep-rooted sentiment of human beings to assert themselves as individuals. If collectivism were to triumph, it would signal "the most frightful misfortune that could befall humanity."[44] Another predecessor of a "liberal socialism" was the anarchist Francesco Saverio Merlino, who had written convincingly of collectivism as a utopia and on the crisis of scientific socialism. With the decline of the anarchist movement after World War I, Merlino shifted to a revision of Marxism, advocating a "libertarian socialism" that had its roots in his earlier anarchism.[45]

Elements of L. T. Hobhouse's *Liberalism* are also discernible in Rosselli's work. Hobhouse was honest enough to realize that a reconciliation between the two was difficult, and he struggled to convince English liberals that liberalism and socialism were not antithetical. For Hobhouse a liberal socialist state would expand individual liberty while insuring social justice. Croce called Hobhouse's work "a fine eulogy and apologia" for liberal socialism.[46]

Although he was deeply influenced by Croce (less so by Gentile), Rosselli rejected Croce's starting premise of German idealism, turning instead to the tradition of British empiricism. Pasquale Villari had introduced into Italy the thought of John Stuart Mill in a way that emphasized Mill's later shift toward a vague socialism. Benôit Malon had also tied Mill to a French tradition of Henri de Saint-Simon, Auguste Comte, and Pierre-Joseph Proudhon. Italian political philosophy was strongly marked by the antipositivism and idealism of Croce and Gentile, but Rosselli's critique of Marxism derived more from the empiricist tradition. Nevertheless, he agreed with Gramsci that Marxism—as it had developed in Italy—was "contaminated by positivist and naturalist incrustations."[47]

In his attack against Marxism's economic determinism and continuing reliance on positivism (at least in Italy), Rosselli also pointed out the problems in the revisionist project that had begun with Bernstein's *Evolutionary Socialism*.[48] Like Bernstein, Rosselli attempted a revision of socialism from within its ranks; and like Bernstein, he was subject to the wrath of the orthodox against the heretic. No doubt Rosselli would agree with Peter Gay's assessment that "if there had been no Bernstein, it would have been necessary to invent him."[49]

Rosselli distinguished between Marxism as a determinist philosophy of history and as a method of historiography based on historical materialism. The first was to be rejected, but the second was to be retained. Although Marx's *Economic and Philosophical Manuscripts of 1844* might have blunted some of Rosselli's criticism, they were not published until 1932, and there is no evidence that Rosselli read them once they were available. Thirty years after the publication of *Liberal Socialism,* Ferruccio Parri recalled, "Rosselli said that if the *Communist Manifesto* had been the revolutionary gospel of a century, after the bitter experience of fascism there was a need for new promise, more human and richer in its emphasis on liberation."[50] Rosselli insisted that Marx had gained entrance to the pantheon of modern thinkers that transformed our consciousness of the world: Kant, Darwin, Freud. No one could argue that Marxism was not a necessary tool for a proper understanding of the world; no one could escape Marx's influence. Rosselli agreed with Croce that the introduction of Marxism into Italy represented a moral and an intellectual rebirth. Antonio Gramsci had remarked—and Rosselli would have agreed—that "everyone is a bit of a Marxist, without being aware of it."[51] While recognizing that Marx was undoubtedly part of modern consciousness, that the ideas and precepts of Marxism had embedded themselves in the psyche of contemporary society, Rosselli felt that the evolution of Marxism during the last decades of the nineteenth century and the first decades of the twentieth century had made it an obstacle to the emancipation of the laboring classes.[52] For the faithful, this heresy was tantamount to declaring that Christianity was an obstacle to the salvation of the soul.

Another avenue to understanding *Liberal Socialism* is to examine Rosselli's notes during his reading of the Belgian thinker Henri De Man's *Zur Psychologie des Sozialismus* that appeared in a French translation as *Au de là du marxisme* in 1927.[53] Rosselli was enthusiastic in his praise, calling it "the book that I have so often dreamed of writing . . . the courageous, honest, and very acute confession of a disenchanted Marxist."[54] As a university professor and an activist, De Man had been attracted to revolutionary Marxism in his youth, but the Bolshevik Revolution had revealed to him a deep scorn for individual freedom and democratic methods. His work was regarded as an important contribution by thinkers as diverse as Thomas Mann and Antonio Gramsci.[55] De Man realized that the crisis of Marxism was twofold: intellectual and political. Rosselli agreed with De Man that Marxism reduced men and women to being mere subjects of the social environment and that it denied the possibility of free will with its insistence on its "scientific" character. In addition, the Marxists offered a caricature of the working class: they refused to consider that the proletariat recognized in the bourgeoisie a better standard of living and, for better or worse, aspired to that standard. Rosselli was struck by De Man's thesis that "utopia, the vision of the future, in the isolated thinker as well as the masses, is born from repressed desires." Hence Rosselli's conclusion that "it is not possible to justify socialism only with reason."[56] Later, in *Liberal Socialism,* Rosselli returned to the psychological insights of De Man when he quoted the Belgian in that "mankind can assuage its deepest nostalgia, the victory over time, only by transforming its future ends into drives in the present, and thus incorporating a fragment of the future in the present." [57] De Man's plannism was reinforced in Rosselli's mind by his reading of Werner Sombart's *Der moderne Kapitalismus* (1908), which had appeared in an Italian translation in 1925 and which foresaw a modern mixed economy combining public and private property, limited competition, and increased cooperation.

Equally important in a rigorous reading of *Liberal Socialism* are Rosselli's fragmentary notes on Karl Marx, focusing on the problem of determinism and free will. The theory of class struggle has always been cited by Marxists and revolutionary socialists to prove that Marxism is not a determinist philosophy. The workers, reaching an unprecedented state of self-consciousness, insert their will into the historical process, thereby forcing the passage from one phase of society to another. But for Rosselli, Marx erred in stating that the workers acquire this consciousness only as a by-product of the organization of the means of production. Marx had often written that the formal, political revolution in social relations would occur only *after* the necessary changes had taken place in technology and production. The psychological transfiguration can happen only after the economic transformation; or as Rosselli wrote, "as the shadow follows the light." Economic reality in Marx is not the fruit of free activity but is completely conditioned. Class struggle appears as a necessary result of the existing contrast in things themselves. There is only one possibility out of this determinism: doubt as to whether the proletariat will arrive at the "logical conclusion" of historical consciousness. It is this doubt, according to Rosselli, which is evident most clearly in the *Communist Manifesto,* that permits the only instance of voluntarism in the entire system, later denied by the older Marx. In any event, the fundamental stimulus of the revolutionary process is not in propaganda, nor in the revelation of consciousness in the proletariat, but rather in the "pessimistic, dramatic, inevitable vision" of the laws of capitalist development. "Catastrophism," defined as universal poverty, periodic crises, and the injustice arising from the differences between the wealthy few and the desperate masses, provokes the proletarian rebellion and leads to a "messianic certainty."[58]

Rosselli's book begins with an apology, explaining that "the evident lacunae and lack of notes and bibliography" were the result of "the peculiar state of tension in which it was composed." Yet clearly, Rosselli had no intention of writing an academic book or of adding to the growing volume of revisionist literature. *Liberal Socialism* was to be "an explicit confession of an intellectual crisis that I know to be very widespread among the new generation of socialists."[59] The crisis was more profound than thirty years earlier when Bernstein's book first appeared, for now the very principles of Marxism were in crisis, not just their practical application. The first part of the book is a critique of Marxism and the revisionist tradition; the second half contains Rosselli's program of a "liberal socialism." The author admits that from the historical point of view, this formula might seem to contain a contradiction, since socialism arose as a reaction to nineteenth-century liberalism and especially to its economic doctrines. Yet he was convinced that history was moving to reconcile the two positions: "Liberalism has gradually become cognizant of the social problem and no longer appears automatically bound to the principles of classical economics. Socialism is stripping itself, though not easily, of its utopianism and is acquiring a new awareness of the problems of liberty and autonomy."[60] Was it that liberalism was becoming more socialistic, or that socialism was being infused with a touch of liberalism? For Rosselli the transformations were occurring simultaneously. Both liberalism and socialism contained "an exalted but narrow vision of life." Both had an ancient lineage:

> Greek rationalism and the messianism of Israel.
>
> The first contains a love of liberty, a respect for autonomy, a harmonious and detached conception of life.
>
> In the second the sense of justice is entirely terrestrial; there is a myth of equality and a spiritual torment that forbids all indulgence.[61]

Marxism was a closed, unified system and therefore could not be amended. With the materialist conception of history and the discovery of surplus value, "scientific socialism" had vanquished its ideological enemies and conquered the field. Marx had claimed to discover the underlying laws governing the unfolding of history. Communism was, therefore, neither an idea nor a proposition but was to be the result of a process immanent in history. Economic necessity was fundamental in human societies, and the historical process was the result of a dialectical play of forces. The expansive forces of production were constrained by the conservative nature of existing social relations, thus leading to class struggle. The capitalist system was "lacerated" by an inherent contradiction: while the system of production, symbolized by the factory, tended toward greater and greater collectivism, the means of production and exchange tended to remain in the hands of individuals or monopolies. This situation inevitably led to the conflict between the bourgeoisie and the proletariat, with the eventual victory of the proletariat assured.

It could be argued that Rosselli was merely setting up a straw man to knock over, and no doubt some of this analysis might verge on oversimplification. Yet it cannot be denied that he had correctly discerned a continuing "crisis of Marxism" in Italy and sought the causes of that predicament. Part of that crisis involved a conception of the role played by human will and actions in history. Under the influence of Feuerbach's radical humanism and historicism,[62] Marx had defended the effect of human will in history. But that defense gradually dissipated as Marx became convinced that history was governed by immutable laws, similar to the laws of nature. The result was that "psychologically speaking, the Marxian man is no more than the *homo oeconomicus* of Bentham." The Marxian conception of the world was based on the historical inevitability of *things* changing, not of the transformation of human beings. Eventually, the proletariat will revolt, but only after the external mechanisms of capitalist production change. The immanent laws of capitalism dictate that the capitalist hoards wealth and pays the workers the lowest possible wage to keep body and soul together; the proletariat cannot protest. With perverse irony, wrote Rosselli, *Capital* can be read as the most intransigent apologia for capitalism![63] Antonio Gramsci had made a similar argument in the wake of the Bolshevik Revolution that "in Russia, Marx's *Capital* was more the book of the bourgeoisie than of the proletariat . . . Events have exploded the critical schema determining how the history of Russia would unfold according to the canons of historical materialism."[64] The real problem is that once "human will" is entered into the equation of the historical process, sociological prognosis becomes impossible. Historical "inevitability" is contrary to free will and, consequently, to humanism and politics.

There is one aspect of Marxism that attenuates this determinism and allows for the element of human will: the theory of class struggle. How does Marx reconcile the idea that history is following immutable laws and the conception of class struggle that presupposes conscious human activity? He does so by arguing that the class struggle is the *necessary* result of the conflict that exists in things themselves; it is the human face of the dialectic immanent in things. The dramatic collision of the contradictory elements of capitalism is the catalyst for revolution, not the consciousness of the proletariat.[65]

At this point in his analysis, Rosselli suggests a provocative thought: using Marxism to write a history of revisionism. Such a history had not yet been written, although as Rosselli correctly pointed out, we should not expect the orthodox priesthood to give us the history of heresy. The revisionists themselves, like other heretics wishing to deny their heretical nature, have also failed in providing that history. Such a study would be both "singularly ironic and suggestive," since it would force Marxism to examine its own presuppositions and, in the process to "devour itself." If we accept Marx's position that ideology reflects the stage of development reached by the forces of production and class relations, then the profound economic and social transformations that have taken place since Marx's day would force us to undertake a substantial revision of Marxism—unless Marxist relativism applies to everything—economics, law, art, politics, and morality—except to Marxist doctrine itself. Here Rosselli cunningly turned Marx's radical historicism in on itself. In his notes on Marx, Rosselli concluded that if Marx had the opportunity to examine contemporary Europe, the German revolutionary would have radically changed his vision of the socialist movement.[66]

The history of Marxism could be defined in three stages: the religious, the critical, and the present. The first stage, ending around the turn of the century, saw Marxism as a new religion, promising secular redemption, and equated Marxism with socialism. Marxism was to be applied, not interpreted. While the rest of humanity was clouded in spurious ideologies and worshiped false idols, only the Marxists saw the path to the promised land. Marxism's great attraction for the masses was not in its critical understanding of the capitalist system but in the certainty that it instilled in its followers that they were on the right road in the teleological drama of history. A reading of the *Communist Manifesto* proves that Marx, that "irate library rat," trapped the reader with "his seductive logic" and could make "pronouncements worthy of the god of vengeance."[67] How could anyone resist that romantic dream of reason and justice allied with science? What did fatalistic determinism matter when Marx, like Joshua before the walls of Jericho, was proclaiming that victory was imminent? Yet revolution and victory failed to materialize. What appeared instead was the workers' movement: less apocalyptic, yet still suffused with a romantic spirit. The workers' movement led to political liberties, social legislation, and mass parties, not the Last Judgment of the expropriating revolution. The rise of the trade unions and cooperative movements taught the proletariat that the democratic method worked; it was no longer true that they had nothing to lose but their chains.

The second and critical stage, beginning at the end of the nineteenth century, was dominated by the revisionists. They were a varied group, from Bernstein to Sorel to Jaurès to Croce; what they shared was a psychological bond, a common urge, a single effort to emphasize the role of human will in the Marxist system. But Marxism, insisted Rosselli, was a dogmatic construct; "it cannot tolerate the germ of doubt," and the revisionists ended (like all heretics) in total subversion by questioning the concept of historical materialism itself. Revisionism rejected determinism and sought to reinsert human beings into the center of the historical process. It was imperative that social democracy concern itself with immediate causes, not with ultimate ends, and that the movement was everything, the end nothing. Yet by the first years of the twentieth century, the advances made by the revisionists had all been lost, partially because of the hypocrisy and blindness of the revolutionaries and partially because of the weakness of the reformists.

Rosselli held that Marxism was an artificial, "imported" phenomenon that never really managed to penetrate the socialist movement in Italy. How could it do so when the very social and economic conditions that Marx held as prerequisites for socialism were lacking? Italy was an overwhelmingly agricultural country, with an enormous rural population, a substantial artisan class, and a small proletariat, which was mostly concentrated in the northern industrial triangle of Genoa-Turin-Milan. As Rosselli so tellingly reminds us, for Italy the problem was not so much to convert to socialism; rather, it was to launch the process of development toward capitalism and modern life. What could be further apart than rural Italy and a Marxism that embodied historical materialism, Germanic discipline, Bentham and Ricardo, Feuerbach and Hegel, the industrialization of

Victorian England, and classical economics and the utilitarian calculus? Small wonder, then, that in southern Italy, Bakunin was more popular than Marx in the second half of the nineteenth century. Italian socialism was consequently trapped between its own rhetoric and the realities of Italian life; there had always been a lack of correspondence between its theory and practice, between its programs and action. The result was a "feeble and analytical style of reformism vitiated by a paternalistic conception of the state."[68]

The socialist tradition in Italy was nothing if not eclectic. Mazzini and Garibaldi were both claimed by the socialists as ancestors; Cattaneo had developed a federalist republicanism, while the "tenuous, noble vein of Malonian socialism" failed to attract the masses. Much of the socialist propaganda was based on what Rosselli considered its "Achilles' heel": "catastrophism," or the vision of increasing concentration of wealth in fewer and fewer hands, and accompanied by increasing misery for the proletariat, culminating in an explosive revolution. Still, during the first years of the twentieth century, socialism made great strides: Turati, who had once been condemned to prison for fourteen years, found himself being urged to assume power; Andrea Costa, from being a habitué of holding cells, was promoted to vice president of the Chamber of Deputies.[69]

Croce, Bernstein, and Sorel were the three thinkers most responsible for the diffusion of Marxism in Italy. Croce's experience was typical for many of his generation: a brief but intense immersion in Marxism, then a gradual recognition of its limitations. For Rosselli all the Italian revisionists, from Bissolati and Bonomi to Salvemini and Leone, Loria and Ferri, were eclipsed by Rodolfo Mondolfo whose exegesis of Marx provides "the best, and in fact the only, vehicle of Marxist education for the rising generation in Italy."[70] Mondolfo, Rosselli wrote in a passage that echoes with the insights of the philosopher Giambattista Vico, had discerned that

> The relation between man and his historical-social environment . . . is not a relation between two things each external to the other, but a relation of action and reaction, a dialectic relation within a single reality. The subject knows the object inasmuch as he produces it; the subject is social man, who, driven by his needs, by his perpetual dissatisfaction with the reality in which he lives, strives to alter the previously existing forms and social relations. It is in this striving, and thanks alone to this striving, that he gains consciousness of reality and its inadequacy. In order to interpret

the world, as Marx said in one of his theses on Feuerbach, it is necessary to change it.[71]

The Neapolitan philosopher Antonio Labriola strongly influenced the diffusion of historical materialism in Italy, but he warned against considering that conception as some "handy talisman." In language similar to Gramsci's, Labriola had insisted that the economic substructure "was not a simple mechanism from which institutions, laws, customs, and ideologies emerged as immediate mechanical effects." Labriola showed that the process of mediation was "extremely complicated, often subtle and tortuous, and not always decipherable." In fact, by 1908 the critical spirit of Marxism and revisionism had been spent: "In less than twenty years, socialism went from the thunderous revelations of Marx to a chorus of monotonous and repetitive followers . . . The living word had been transformed into a dead letter, faith into a rite, the rebel into a priest." The "war generation" was idealistic, voluntaristic, and pragmatic; it did not and could not understand the materialistic, positivistic, pseudoscientific language of its elders.[72]

One of the few in the socialist camp who acknowledged this crisis was Benito Mussolini. Rosselli described him as an "adventurer in the world of culture as he was in that of politics," having "no honest intellectual concern," only his own ambition. Yet Mussolini had recognized that the old socialist position no longer fulfilled the longing of the younger generation, and he claimed to revitalize Italian political life with an infusion of idealism, pragmatism and Bergsonian voluntarism. Mussolini's victory was facilitated by the "constitutional incapacity" of the old party to renew itself. The few correct diagnoses, such as had appeared in Salvemini's *L'Unità*, were ignored or suppressed. Rosselli was not subtle in his criticism: "The truth is that in the years leading up to the war, Italian socialism was intellectually dead. If it felt any stimulus at all, it must have been the drive to self-destruction . . . The war swept over this fragile intellectual edifice like an avalanche." The older tradition of reformist socialism was lost in the febrile postwar period "with its spinning vortex of new experiments." What was needed was a "rude intellectual shock to dislodge Italian socialists from their ideological passivity." Rosselli praised "the hard personal travail of search, of doubt, of conflict," from which would crystallize new values that would supersede the belief in the "thaumaturgic virtues" of orthodox Marxism.[73] Clearly, he intended that *Liberal Socialism* would function as that "rude intellectual shock."

Italian socialists were either unable or unwilling to pursue the process of revision to its logical conclusion—the break between socialism and Marxism. For Rosselli there were two consequences of the revisionist critique of Marxism; the first was paradoxical, the second, pragmatic: that one could be a Marxist without being a socialist; and that socialists who still believe that they can find a guiding principle in Marxism or concrete guidance for the socialist movement were fooling themselves.[74] The revisionists had claimed an original, fundamental nucleus in Marxism—the theory of historical materialism. Its application to the study of capitalist society would reveal the objective prediction of the inevitability of a socialist future. If the premise—historical materialism—proved shaky, then the entire socialist edifice of Marxism would collapse; and collapse it did: "today . . . in light of all the transformations that have taken place, it can no longer withstand close scrutiny . . . the relation between historical materialism and socialism had been turned upside down. That which had previously constituted a necessary conclusion now became a contingent premise."[75] If one wished to tie the philosophical theory of historical materialism to a practical program, the revisionist interpretation led not to socialism but to liberalism. From Marxism the road led to revisionism, and from revisionism, to liberalism; this progression was "inevitable."[76] Rosselli was prepared to make the paradoxical claim that historical materialism is a philosophy much better suited to the capitalist class than to the proletariat because the capitalist "possesses an awareness of his active participation in the transformation of the process of production. He is able to concretely insert his will into history, and his relation to economic life is typically one of action-reaction." The worker, instead, "only feels the effects or is forced to assist passively in the process of production," and thereby feels powerless to act.

The fetishization of Marxist tenets like historical materialism and the theory of surplus value served only as hindrances for the workers' movement. When fascism took to the streets, the socialists were unable to respond. Rosselli charged them with a modern version of the medieval Scholastic argument over how many angels could dance on the head of a pin: "In Italy the common dwelling was on fire, the flames from the houses of the workers were turning the sky red, and the inhabitants—the socialists—were squabbling among themselves about whether it really was a fire, what had caused it, whether it fell into this or that category, whether it had been foretold in the sacred books, whether it was burning only in Italy, and so on."[77]

The fascist onslaught, combined with the erosion of two fundamental myths, spelled the defeat of Marxism. Those two myths, the basis of all Marxist propaganda and the reasons for its success were, first, that the advent of communism was an inevitable outcome of the development of industrial capitalism; and, second, that communism was the only social system that could guarantee, through the rational ordering of production and distribution, an immense increase in productivity and well-being, freeing mankind from enslavement to material need. Marx's error was to have mistaken the prologue for the entire course of development, to have given transitory phenomena long temporal duration. Capitalism had discovered ways to reform itself and to attenuate the worst features of the system. Britain, the birthplace of the industrial revolution and "the Mecca of individualistic libertarianism," was an illuminating example with a wide range of social services and a mixture of nationalized or state-controlled enterprises. Communism was not the only social and economic system that could lay claim to rational planning. "In America especially, the process of economic rationalization has assumed such a rapid pace in recent years that it has eliminated the worst effects of unrestrained competition and fragmentation, realizing an extremely high level of productivity . . . The social revolution exploded in the most backward country, Russia; while the most developed country, the United States, survived the crisis with the least turmoil." [78]

In an imaginary debate between Marx and a cotton spinner from Lancashire or a cauldron producer from Birmingham, Rosselli held that Marx, ahead of his time and sensing the direction of economic progress, would certainly have won. But in a debate between an orthodox Marxist and Henry Ford, the American industrialist would point to unprecedented productivity, while the Marxist would make moral denunciations, defending qualitative values and the autonomy of the worker against the "appalling uniformity and leveling discipline" of modern production techniques. In short, the Marxist would be forced into a "liberal" position, reviving the scorned formulas of "utopian socialism." Rosselli seemed to revel in the twist: "There really is no end to the irony of history!" [79]

If Marxism has been superseded by the intervening events, what then, is to be the role of Marxism in twentieth-century Europe? Rosselli attempted an answer in his chapter "Overcoming Marxism":

I really do not mean to imply that nothing living or profound remains in his thought; quite the contrary. No one dreams of proposing a total (and totally absurd) denial of Marx . . . The son emancipates himself, but he cannot deny his father . . . today it is impossible to conceive of a modern individual, one endowed, that is, with a strong awareness of the problems of his time, who is not, within certain limits, a Marxist—meaning someone who has not incorporated into his being a whole ensemble of truths that, though they might with good reason have appeared revolutionary in Marx's time, have been comprehended by modern systems of knowledge and modern consciousness to such an extent that they have become almost banal.[80]

Marx's real triumph lies precisely in the fact that his thought has permeated all of modern social science; even his fiercest enemies are students of his work. In the social sciences, he occupies a position similar to Kant's in philosophy. The task for modern socialists is not to deny Marx but to emancipate themselves from his thought.

In his critique of Marxism, Rosselli also revealed his skepticism concerning the masses. Marxism was "the proper doctrine and pedagogy for the proletariat in its infancy." The "virgin and rebellious" crowd has two faces: "indistinct religiosity and material appetite." Marx's doctrine satisfied both: on the one hand, a "mythic, apocalyptic vision," and on the other, a glimpse of "a happy and rich society."[81] Marxism ascribes "attributes of divinity" to the proletariat, making it the "bearer of all the purest virtues. Rousseau's man in the state of nature became, in the nineteenth century, Mazzini's *popolo* and Marx's proletariat. The proletariat has risen to the rank of a philosophical category; history has become "an epic poem in which the proletarian hero defeats the bourgeois monster."[82]

The socialist movement needed to return to its ethical roots, when political action was inspired by the flame of moral indignation and outrage. Positivism and the obsession with proving itself to be "scientific" had robbed socialism of this impetus. The socialists must not be afraid of a "free, noble and frank reaffirmation" of idealism; for, in the end, socialism was an ethical ideal:

> Socialism is not socialization; it is not the proletariat in power; it is not even material equality. Socialism, grasped in its essential aspect, is the progressive actualization of the idea of liberty and justice among men: an innate idea that lies more or less buried under the sediment of centuries in the marrow of every human being. It is the progressive effort to ensure an equal chance of living the only life worthy of the name to all humans,

setting them free from the enslavement to the material world and material needs that today still dominate the greater number, allowing them the possibility freely to develop their personalities in a continuous struggle for perfection against their primitive and bestial instincts and against the corruptions of a civilization too much prey of the demons of success and money.[83]

Although Rosselli often admitted that the phrase "liberal socialism" sounded paradoxical, he maintained that it was not an oxymoron. He had no intention of introducing a new political terminology but wished to bring socialism back to its "first principles, to its historical and psychological origins," and to demonstrate that "socialism, in the last analysis, is the philosophy of liberty."[84]

The modern economy, with its mechanized, rationalized, and technocratic character that sacrifices the personality of the worker, forces socialists to become liberals in the sense that they must now defend the autonomy of the individual. Specifically, Rosselli defined liberalism as the political theory that "takes the inner freedom of the human spirit as a given and adopts liberty as the ultimate goal, but also the ultimate means, the ultimate rule, of shared human life." Liberalism is not a natural law, nor a fact of nature; rather, it is a historical and social product—a continual "becoming." Individuals are not born free, they become free and remain so by retaining an active and vigilant sense of their autonomy, by constantly exercising their freedoms. Echoing a sentiment common since the eighteenth century, Rosselli held that liberalism was based on a faith in man, in his potential for perfectibility and capacity for self-determination. All men, he felt, had an innate sense of justice.

Liberalism was the creation of modern critical thought, arising from the Reformation and the futility of the wars of religion. It flowered during the seventeenth and eighteenth centuries through the influence of the scientific revolution and the cultural ascendancy of the bourgeoisie. With the publication of the *Encyclopédie* and the French Revolution, the bourgeoisie had cemented its intellectual and political domination. Since then, liberalism had been transformed from the interests of a minority into the patrimony of all. "Socialism is nothing more than the logical development, taken to its extreme consequences, of the principle of liberty. Socialism . . . as the concrete movement for the emancipation of the proletariat, is liberalism in action; it means that liberty comes into the life of poor people."[85] The formal granting of liberty may signify an important development in the evolution of political theory, but the great majority are unable, because of material want and economic necessity, to exercise those freedoms. Socialism insists that material want and economic necessity be overcome so that all may benefit from liberalism. Three decades later in America, a similar argument was made by C. Wright Mills. "What is most valuable in classical liberalism," wrote the sociologist, "is most cogently and most fruitfully incorporated in classical Marxism . . . Marx remains the thinker who has articulated most clearly—and most perilously—the basic ideals which liberalism shares."[86] In words that Marx would no doubt have approved, Rosselli insisted that "liberty without the accompaniment and support of a minimum of economic autonomy, without emancipation from the grip of pressing material necessity, does not exist for the individual; it is a mere phantasm. In these circumstances, the individual is enslaved by poverty, humiliated by his own subjection . . . Free in law, he is in fact a slave."[87] The bourgeoisie had once been the standard-bearer of the idea of liberty; however, it no longer carried that standard. The bourgeoisie now used liberalism, along with an array of economic, juridical, and social principles, to safeguard its privileges from the masses and to halt historical progress. But liberalism is by definition historicist, dialectical, and relativist; it sees history as a perpetual flux, an eternal becoming and overcoming. It is the socialist movement that now seeks to carry "the dynamic idea of Liberty forward through the vicissitudes of history toward its actualization." Hence, socialism is the true heir of liberalism. Still, there is a fundamental difference between the liberalism of the bourgeoisie and that of the proletariat. For the bourgeoisie, "the conquest of political liberty was the sublimation and fulfillment of its own power," whereas for the proletariat, the demand and achievement of political freedom are the commencement of the struggle for economic emancipation.[88]

Political and economic freedom are by no means assured by the historical process. The liberal socialist is therefore in a position of doubt, a "virile relativism" that insists on the role of human will and action in history. The liberal socialist is tormented by a "critical demon" that continually forces one to review one's position in the light of experience. Liberalism is to be adopted as a strategy of means and as an end. Following the Sorelian definition of myth, Rosselli admitted that "our entire program is founded on the myth of liberty" and recalled that Jean Jaurès had reminded socialists that "one arrives at the ideal only through the real."[89]

The new socialist movement must adopt a principle of broad, intellectual tolerance as a philosophical and cultural attitude. Although individuals might strive for a consistency between theory and action, the attempt to impose such a rigid consistency on a broad-based movement can only strangle thought and inhibit political action. Or, as Rosselli warned, "Grief will result from trying to fetter a movement with a development spanning centuries, a movement irrepressibly polyphonic, to a single philosophical creed."[90] Italian socialism, desperately in need of a dose of realism, was presently incapable of formulating a constructive program. Before all else, the socialists must realize that Italy was a paradoxical country. The home of the Vatican, it still sheltered remnants of its pagan past just below the surface of a baroque Catholicism. In truth, there were two Italies: one that was modern, urban, and industrialized; the other, ancient and rural, still estranged from Western civilization, its people still pristine and enslaved. These people were far removed from the necessary conditions—economic, political, intellectual—of a socialist movement. What little workers' democracy existed in Italy could be found only in the trade unions; hence, Rosselli was "explicitly in favor of a reorganization of the socialist movement along the lines similar to the Labour Party in Britain".[91]

The book ended with a personal and political testament not included in the English translation. It contains—in as succinct a form as possible—the ideas developed in *Liberal Socialism* and later in exile. "My Reckoning with Marxism" is a curious document that is part humble confession and part ringing manifesto. Having "studied, suffered and meditated," Rosselli felt that he had come to understand something about Italian history. Socialism was first and foremost a moral revolution; its material aspect was distinctly secondary. As Camus succinctly wrote in October 1944, "We think that political revolution cannot do without a moral revolution that parallels it and gives it its true dimension."[92] Those who were striving for such a revolution had to recognize it in the present, not in the shadowy future; the revolution existed already in the conscience of those who labored on behalf of the working classes. It was necessary to recognize that there existed no necessary philosophical relationship between socialism and Marxism; indeed, the latter actually worked to hinder the former. Socialism without democracy meant "inevitable dictatorship, and dictatorship means servile men, numbers, not consciences, products and not producers, and means therefore the negation of socialism." As the standard-bearer of the oppressed and miserable, socialism was the heir to liberalism. Freedom, necessary for the moral life of the individual and the collective, was the most effective means toward the ideal of socialism. Socialization, as important as it may be, was merely a means and not an end unto itself. Socialism could not be imposed from above but had to be forged from below, "in the consciences of people, in the unions, in culture." The new socialist movement could not be cobbled together from the remnants of the old parties but had to be something entirely new, eschewing a single intellectual framework. Finally, the first act of liberation had to be self-liberation, freeing the individual to think and act differently, heretically if need be.[93]

If Rosselli had disturbed the waters with his early articles and "Autocritica," the publication of *Liberal Socialism* in 1930 generated a veritable tidal wave of indignation and criticism. Claudio Treves's review, which appeared in early 1931, was typical. Writing under a pseudonym, Treves felt that Rosselli's criticism of Marxism and the orthodox socialism went too far. Far from being superseded, Marxism was more relevant than ever. Noting the recent economic crisis precipitated by the stock market crash on Wall Street, Treves insisted that socialists retain their stress on economics, implying that Rosselli's emphasis on moral factors was misplaced. Of more importantance, Treves defended Marxism from Rosselli's most trenchant criticism: that it was not a humanism. The image of the automaton worker, completely unconscious of his or her role in history, is contrary to Marxism. Treves recalls Camillo Prampolini and his followers, who went into the countryside to teach illiterate peasants how to read and write so that they could be conscious of their role in history, and also that German Marxists had taken for their motto *Wissen ist Mach* (Knowledge is power). For Treves, socialism was not a deterministic philosophy; historical materialism was an "interpretive canon of social phenomena, a key that opened many locks." Rosselli, according to Treves, was a "revisionist" not content with merely revising Marxism; he called for its "total repudiation, without pity." Treves proposed the Manichean choice: either Marxism or fascism. He ended with a charge that Rosselli's work was neither socialist nor liberal.[94] Giuseppe Saragat, future president of the Italian Republic, following a similar tack and influenced by the Austrians Otto Bauer and Friedrich Adler, argued that Rosselli had ignored the stress on self-emancipation demanded by socialism.[95] Even Pietro Nenni was unsparing in his criticism, pointing out that Marxism did not neglect the problem of freedom.[96]

Palmiro Togliatti, leader of the PCI, was stinging in his condemnation:

Liberal Socialism was nothing more than the work of a wealthy, hypocritical, pseudointellectual, which betrayed the mentality of the petite bourgeoisie. Rosselli's defense of liberalism and democratic institutions was nothing less than a more polite version of fascism itself. *Liberal Socialism* could be read as part of a "fascist" body of literature and was merely a pernicious libel against Marxism.[97] In another essay, Togliatti had written that Rosselli was an example of "dissident fascism"[98] and vehemently criticized Rosselli's idea that antifascists had to make a distinction between nationalism and patriotism, denying the former but embracing the latter.

Rosselli responded that liberal socialism rested on an immutable premise, one that was denied by Marxism and the other variants of socialism. Liberal socialism began with the premise that human beings possessed the faculty of self-creation or, in the language of contemporary philosophical discourse, moral agency. His defense of liberal socialism as a variant of humanism followed. No one would deny that human beings are constrained by social, political, and economic realities; yet their very consciousness of those restraints entails the beginning of "liberation" and an awareness of the possibility of action in history. At the same time, a liberal socialism would refuse to absorb all facets of human life into itself; a clear distinction had to be made between the public and the private, and the state could not violate the latter. The liberal socialist began by recognizing the inviolable autonomy of the individual and ended by creating a society in which that individual would recognize the benefits of social equality.

Significantly, one of the few positive reviews was written by the anarchist Luigi Fabbri.[99] Other anarchists were wary of a socialism that was liberal rather than libertarian, but they welcomed Rosselli's critique of the State and his call for voluntary associations.

Although Rosselli was expecting criticism he was surprised by its vehemence. It confirmed his belief that he had struck a raw nerve in the socialist camp. But the most sustained and detailed critique of a "liberal socialism" came from Croce, who called it a "paradox." Croce accused Rosselli of succumbing to the "seduction of facile conclusions." Juxtaposing liberalism with socialism to obtain an artificial synthesis was illogical. Croce failed to realize that Rosselli was not attempting a synthesis, but rather a reconceptualization of socialism as the historical and ideological heir to liberalism. Socialism was not to be confused, compounded, or conjoined with liberalism; each retained its ideological distinctiveness. Socialism was not to replace liberalism but was to fulfill its promise. Croce compared liberal socialism to the hircocervus, a mythological beast that was half goat and half stag, "an absurd and aesthetically unpleasant combination that purported to attach the rough, rude, and shaggy body of socialism to the long and agile legs of liberalism."[100] Croce felt that liberalism should never be "contaminated" with socialism or democracy. The Neapolitan philosopher touched on a larger philosophical problem that has dogged thinkers for millennia: is it possible to combine a defense of individual liberties with an attempt to forge a just and equal society? For Croce nothing could claim precedence over liberty, the inherent dynamic and moving force of history itself. Rosselli's illogical synthesis of liberalism and socialism was replicated in the name given to the movement, Justice and Liberty. In modern times, the binomial liberty and equality have been joined since the French Revolution, but many—including Marx—have pointed out the logical inconsistencies involved in trying to tie the two together. By stressing individual rights and freedom, society may have to concede any possibility at social equality; conversely, if a community decides to strive for equality, individual liberties may suffer. Karl Popper eloquently defined this dilemma as "the beautiful dream" of combining freedom and equality, but ultimately he concluded that "freedom is more important than equality" and that "the attempt to realize equality endangers freedom."[101] Croce would not have hesitated to sacrifice equality on the altar of liberty but would have done so with loftier motives than those of contemporary neoliberals. Caught between Scylla and Charybdis, are we then forever politically suspended? Not necessarily: if we retreat from crass definitions of liberty (the ability to choose freely) and equality (a brutal redistribution of material resources), then the paradox collapses, especially if we speak of liberty itself as the entity to be equalized.[102] In fact, it was Nello's well-received book, *Mazzini e Bakunin,* which clearly demonstrated that liberal socialism neither was an abstraction nor was without a historical tradition in Italy.[103]

In an essay written in May 1943 and published in September, just days after Italy's surrender to the Allies and at the beginning of the Armed Resistance, with the ideals of justice and liberty again surfacing, Croce returned to this argument. He bitterly criticized a concept of "justice" as "an extravagant utilitarian and material equality" and as an "absurd transferal of a mathematical fiction to reality." Croce refused to acknowledge that Rosselli had never conceived of justice in such a crass manner. Irony of ironies, Rosselli had conceived of justice in impeccably Crocean terms: "the recognition of the spiritual dignity of every human being, coinciding with their intangible freedom."[104]

If Croce criticized Rosselli's coupling of liberalism and socialism in 1930 and the binomial "justice and liberty" after the war by refusing to join the Action Party, Guido de Ruggiero was closer to Rosselli's position. When *Liberal Socialism* first appeared in an Italian edition in the days immediately after the Second World War, De Ruggiero wrote a sympathetic review in the pages of *La Nuova Europa*. De Ruggiero called attention to the book's directness, efficacy, and conciseness. Rosselli's critique of Marxism was both lucid and sharp, and the various historical positions were characterized by "incisive passages that emphasized the essential elements." De Ruggiero was mistaken in thinking that Rosselli began as a Marxist who, at a certain point in his intellectual development, felt the insufficiency of that doctrine and therefore turned to revisionist socialism. The historian was correct that even in revisionism, Rosselli failed to find the answer to his doubts and his need for clarity. Revisionism, according to De Ruggiero, had all the characteristics of a "literary theology." Orthodox and reformists alike laid claim to Marx as to a sacred text; the indissoluble link between socialism and Marxism was for them an indisputable premise.[105]

De Ruggiero picked up an analogy made by Rosselli: the socialist movement resembled early Christianity. As it became apparent that the Second Coming (social revolution) was not imminent, apocalyptic visions gave way to an established Church (reform socialism and the workers' movement). De Ruggiero also agreed with Rosselli that Marxism was racked by an internal contradiction: economic and historical determinism could not be squared with Marx's earlier stress on free will. The efforts of the revisionists, from Bernstein to Labriola to Mondolfo, were an attempt to "reconcile the irreconcilable." Rosselli alone was willing to propose the heretical: a divorce between Marxism and socialism, without denying the contemporary significance of the former. Rosselli proposed justice and liberty as a new creed for the workers' aristocracy that had just emerged from an infancy marked by Marxism.[106] If De Ruggiero was defending Rosselli in 1945, Croce returned to his criticism of liberal socialism in a review of Aldo Garosci's biography of Rosselli that appeared in the same year.

The attempt to reconcile, synthesize, or join socialist and liberal principles in the modern period has a long and distinguished legacy, as Ira Katznelson (himself part of this tradition) points out: that of John Stuart Mill, John Dewey, Karl Mannheim, Bertrand Russell, John Rawls, Michael Walzer, and Norberto Bobbio. Nor is it a coincidence that some of the most ambitious attempts to revive a liberal socialism have come from Eastern

Europe. Established in 1961, the Klub Krzywego Kola (Club of the Crooked Circle) in Warsaw tried to reconstruct a humane and liberal socialism. In Prague, Charter 77 continued Alexander Dubček's search for a "socialism with a human face." In the process, they seem to have convinced neither liberals nor socialists. The Marxist critic Perry Anderson, ironically echoing Croce, feels that a liberal socialism is "an unstable compound" that might seem to attract the best elements of both ideologies but that is ultimately separate, leaving a more conservative liberalism.[107] Even such a staunch defender of liberal socialism as Norberto Bobbio has defined it as "an abstract doctrinal idea, as tempting in theory as it is hard to translate into institutional practice."[108]

Rosselli tried to explicate his conception of a liberal socialism with the inventive use of an apocryphal dialogue between two ideal "types": a critical, skeptical humanist; and an unwavering, orthodox Marxist.[109] The humanist begins by praising his colleague; both agree that fascism "denies that which is most noble in man: reason, moral autonomy, and responsibility." But the humanist is confused by the proliferation of different "socialisms"; there is a democratic socialism, a dictatorial socialism, a Christian socialism, and even a liberal socialism. The humanist is even more confused because of the recent appearance of a book, *Socialisme fasciste*.[110] The orthodox Marxist confidently declares that "fascism is the dictatorship of the capitalist class" and that Marxism strives for "a classless society of free and equal subjects, where the means of production are in the hands of the collective." The humanist is attracted by this scenario but suggests that there may be some disturbing resemblances between Marxism and fascism. The Marxist, understandably taken aback by this provocation, demands that the humanist explain himself. Orthodox Marxism, counters the humanist, affords small value to the individual, it has a negative conception of freedom, it worships the state (even while professing to destroy it), and therefore it ends with dictatorship. Marxism replaces concrete individuals with abstractions such as "the proletariat" or "the masses." The individual exists only to the extend that he or she fits into the abstract scheme. The humanist continues to reprove the Marxist: social man in the abstract does not exist, only men exist as they live and work in the factory, in the city, in the family. With infallible logic, the Marxist responds with another abstraction: "that which is true for all men is true for each man." The Marxist argues that when differences of class and economic oppression are abolished, all men will be free.

Here the humanist takes another road: both fascism and Marxism are reductionist theories. Fascism decrees that the individual has freedom only from being a member of the state; in fact, fascism holds that the individual exists only insofar as he is an organic member of the state. Marxism performs a similar reductionist argument in holding that freedom derives from economic conditions. Again, the Marxist replies with impeccable logic that "a man who dies of hunger, who is exploited, cannot be free." Here the humanist agrees but points out that the Marxist is confusing the essence of freedom—the "irreducible autonomy of the individual"—with the conditions necessary for its development. "Freedom," retorts the Marxist, "does not exist. Only the concrete and historical freedoms of class exist. Today bourgeois liberty. Tomorrow socialist liberty." But making freedom something external to human beings and a consequence of a particular economic system means reducing it to a relative value. The inevitable result is that autonomy, dignity, and freedom decline. The humanist points out an obvious contradiction: the Marxists claim to be fighting for freedom while extolling the dictatorship of the proletariat, even if that dictatorship is to be temporary. "The means must be in harmony with the ends. One does not arrive at freedom with dictatorship. Whoever battles dictatorship with dictatorship consolidates fascism." In reply to the Marxist's claim that Marxism wishes to destroy the state, the humanist points out that although claiming to destroy the state, Marxism actually makes it stronger. The choice is between an abstract, despotic, dictatorial state and the human person. Rosselli (in the guise of the humanist) repeats his assertion that "fascism is the perfect mass regime," thereby leaving himself open to the charge of being "an aristocrat disdainful of the masses," which he denies. "What I disdain is every form of collective life in which the humanity of each person is annulled." Instead the humanist calls for a society where the masses are not prostituted by demagoguery and where collectivization is replaced by free associations acting as "forms of redemption and liberation." The humanist looks forward to an Italy "repelled by demagogic festivals and fireworks," where the individual can extract the maximum of their faculties, enjoying freedom as the active life.

Although exile and war would push Rosselli further to the Left in his politics and thinking, he never abandoned this humanistic strain. Events in Paris and Spain would confirm his belief that a only humanistic socialism would attract enough men and women to defeat fascism and refashion Italian—and European—society.

Revolutionary Liberalism

Rosselli infused European antifascism with an impassioned plea and rational argument that echoed Gobetti for the revolutionary potential of liberalism—a liberalism forged out of the constant exercise of consciousness and existing as a force of the spirit before it was a force of politics.[111] The liberal who is sure in the use of reason is neither skeptical nor passive. In the classic eighteenth-century Enlightenment tradition, the liberal is a firm believer in the human spirit, who proclaims man as the only end and who possesses a faith in the perfectibility of the human race. At the same time, the liberal is driven by an awareness that this blessed state has never been reached and might possibly never be reached. A liberal is made, not born: made through incessant struggle and the perpetual excercise of one's faculties. The faith of a liberal is "a virile faith founded on reason." Paradoxically, this is both the great strength and the weakness of the liberal: strength because once gained, this position gives one a fuller sense of life; weakness because it lacks "lightning revelations." The liberal is marked (cursed?) by a perennial dissatisfaction with all commonplace positions. In short, the liberal is *tout court* modern man.

Rosselli moved beyond the earliest formulations of liberalism in affirming that liberalism could not exist in reference to individuals alone. True, the liberal defends the inviolable autonomy of the individual conscience. Yet since man is a political and social animal, the concept of liberty is necessarily a social one. Liberalism permits—indeed insists on—the autonomous grouping of associations, groups, and classes, and repudiates every form of violence. Defending liberalism against the charge that it is elitist or "aristocratic," Rosselli claimed that all ideologies, including Christianity and Marxism, in their initial forms, are aristocratic. The factor that determines whether an ideology is democratic or aristocratic lies not in its comprehensibility but in its function of serving the masses, of generating action and changing consciousness. Marxism generates its élan not with its theory of surplus value but with the concept of class struggle and the impetus of the *Communist Manifesto;* liberalism, as Croce had written, creates a force through its call to freedom, "leaven of history." Like Marxism, liberalism had penetrated all aspects of modern thinking. The socialism that arose as its "direct adversary" in the nineteenth century was now its "solemn avenger." Rosselli even discerned a liberal wing of communism in Leon Trotsky.[112]

All the active, revolutionary forces of history are, by definition, liberal. The early Christians, the Protestants, the Encylopedists, were all at one time liberals; so too the bourgeoisie at one time fulfilled the role of a liberating class against the absolutism of the monarchy and the dogmatism of the Church. Yet now the bourgeoisie had lost its liberal spirit and force. It no longer had a thirst for progress nor was it animated by a universal ideal. It sought to arrest the historical process at the present state, conserving its privileges with a recourse to violence. A new force arises to contest this sclerotic, petrified bourgeois liberalism—a proletarian liberalism. The proletariat is the "only modern revolutionary class"; liberalism and socialism, instead of opposing each other, are by now tied in a theoretical and practical relationship: "liberalism is the inspiring ideal force, while socialism is the practical, realizing force."[113]

Rosselli was careful not to fall into theoretical absolutes concerning class and human nature, which he recognized as mutable, paradoxical, and sometimes even contradictory. Human beings cannot be completely explained by reference to social and economic class. An individual can be conservative and revolutionary, dogmatic and liberal. "The bourgeoisie, almost always conservative concerning economic relations, is now almost always more liberal than the proletariat in the domain of culture and customs."[114] Yet even this picture must be qualified since there are strata of the bourgeoisie that act as catalysts of social and economic liberalism; many intellectuals and most of the leaders of the socialist and communist movements in Europe were from the middle class. In contrast, fascism had shown that considerable segments of the proletariat, because of their material and spiritual servitude, were easy prey for reactionary regimes. This point was another of Rosselli's heretical positions. Yet it does not invalidate the larger thesis: the majority of the proletarian forces are liberal, whereas the majority of the bourgeoisie had accepted dictatorship and reaction. In an unpublished, untitled, and unsigned document, Gobetti was given major credit for crafting the liberal philosophy of Justice and Liberty. His journal *La Rivoluzione Liberale* was a veritable "workshop of ideas" for the war generation. It was Gobetti who wrote stinging critiques of the older liberal tradition, and it was his journal that declared legal resistance after Matteotti's death to be "illusory."[115]

Rosselli defended the historical function of freedom, in contrast to the communists, who he felt saw the struggle for freedom as a conservative distraction to the primary goal of the socialist revolution. The communists failed to recognize that the struggle for freedom was essential, not an "idealist abstraction in the service of the bourgeoisie"; they confused contemporary liberals like Rosselli with the older, conservative liberals. Communists insisted that human beings, by definition, were not free because they were tied to the forms of economic production and distribution and the social relations they engender. The Marxist catechism, which underestimates the importance of freedom, is "morphine for the proletariat in a bourgeois society . . . it is a class concept, and therefore historical, relative and provisional."[116] For Marxists, concrete liberties such as freedom of the individual, of the press, of association, and of emigration, are "bourgeois sorcery," while those who fight for the freedom of all individuals and classes are "reactionary" and "social fascists." This critique was both sterile and contradictory, because "if the bourgeoisie is fascist, we, in as much as we are antifascist, are also anti-bourgeoisie. Or the bourgeoisie is not necessarily fascist, and then the communist model collapses."[117] The communists were correct in pointing out that the bourgeoisie was increasingly abandoning the liberal method; but what does this historical transformation signify other than that function was now passing to the proletariat? The communists lacked a sense of history: the freedoms acquired and conquered by the bourgeoisie in the struggle against the aristocracy can today be the tools and patrimony of the proletariat. In the context of the Ethiopian War and Spanish Civil War, Rosselli would seek a rapprochement with the communists, but it was always a strained relationship. The creation of the largest and most influential non-Marxist movement, Justice and Liberty, was Rosselli's defiant challenge to the communists, and it was nothing less than a mortal threat to fascism.

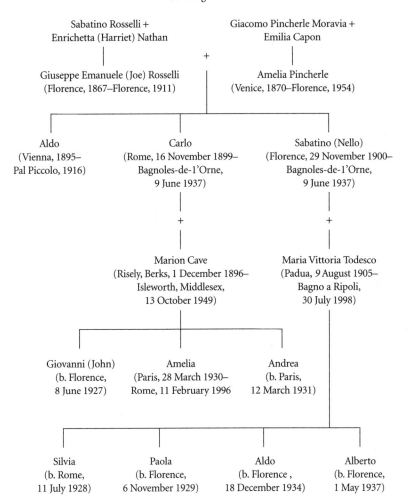

ROSSELLI-PINCHERLE
Genealogical Chart

Sabatino Rosselli +
Enrichetta (Harriet) Nathan

Giacomo Pincherle Moravia +
Emilia Capon

+

Giuseppe Emanuele (Joe) Rosselli
(Florence, 1867–Florence, 1911)

Amelia Pincherle
(Venice, 1870–Florence, 1954)

Aldo
(Vienna, 1895–
Pal Piccolo, 1916)

Carlo
(Rome, 16 November 1899–
Bagnoles-de-1'Orne,
9 June 1937)

Sabatino (Nello)
(Florence, 29 November 1900–
Bagnoles-de-1'Orne,
9 June 1937)

+

+

Marion Cave
(Risely, Berks, 1 December 1896–
Isleworth, Middlesex,
13 October 1949)

Maria Vittoria Todesco
(Padua, 9 August 1905–
Bagno a Ripoli,
30 July 1998)

Giovanni (John)
(b. Florence,
8 June 1927)

Amelia
(Paris, 28 March 1930–
Rome, 11 February 1996

Andrea
(b. Paris,
12 March 1931)

Silvia
(b. Rome,
11 July 1928)

Paola
(b. Florence,
6 November 1929)

Aldo
(b. Florence ,
18 December 1934)

Alberto
(b. Florence,
1 May 1937)

"The two families were part of an urbane, cosmopolitan, and polyglot cultural
aristocracy." Adapted from *Politica e affetti familiari: Lettere dei Rosselli ai Ferrero
(1917–1943)*, ed. Marina Calloni and Lorella Cedroni (Milan: Feltrinelli, 1997),
p. 277.

"Young men outraged by the corruption of the age and burning with zeal for justice." Carlo Rosselli, ca. 1917. (ISRT, AGL, Florence.)

"Truly worthy to be remembered among the great Italians of this century." Amelia Rosselli, ca. 1929. (Photograph by Mario Nunes Vais; Istituto Centrale per il Catalogo e la Documentazione, Gabinetto Fotografico Nazionale, Rome.)

The editors of *Non Mollare!* Left to right: Nello Traquandi, Tommaso Ramorino, Carlo Rosselli, Ernesto Rossi, Luigi Emery, Nello Rosselli. (ISRT, AGL, Florence.)

"I seek to foster my scarce sense of paternity. He who concerns himself with humanity in general finds it difficult to be a good father." Marion Cave, John Rosselli, Carlo Rosselli, ca. 1932. (ISRT, AGL, Florence.)

"The brothers were often inseparable, but they were a study in contrasts." Nello (left) and Carlo Rosselli, ca. 1937. (ISRT, AGL, Florence.)

24618 - Rosselli Carlo Alberto

"The greatest danger comes from Rosselli, and, in my view, it is absolutely necessary that he be suppressed." Fascist police photo. (ACS, CPC, busta 4421, fascicolo Rosselli Carlo.)

"Who am I? I am a socialist . . . a new and dangerous kind." (ISRT, AGL, Florence.)

Carlo Rosselli. Portrait by Carlo Levi, 1932, 61 cm × 50 cm, oil on canvas. (Fondazione Carlo Levi, Rome. © Estate of Carlo Levi/Licensed by VAGA, New York, N.Y.)

"What compels Justice and Liberty is . . . the development of
the Italian revolution, the self-liberation, the self-emancipation
of the Italian people; the raising—on the ruins of fascism—of a
new Europe." Flag of Justice and Liberty. (ISRT, AGL, Florence.)

"The prophets are no longer disarmed. And the descendants of the prophets,
with rifle in hand, have acquired a new consciousness." Rosselli (second from
left) at the front during the Spanish Civil War. (ISRT, AGL, Florence.)

18 June 1937 edition of *Giustizia e Libertà* announcing the assassinations of Carlo and Nello Rosselli. (ISRT, AGL, Florence.)

"The deaths of the Rosselli brothers signals the death of liberty in Europe." Funeral of the Rosselli brothers, Paris, June 1937. (ISRT, AGL, Florence.)

"The sad death in exile that appears almost inevitable for the finest sons of Italy." (ISRT, AGL, Florence.)

CHAPTER FOUR

· · · ·

Justice and Liberty

Heresy is the lifeblood of religions. It is faith that begets heretics.
There are no heresies in a dead religion.

ANDRÉ SUARÈS, *PÉGUY* (1915)

The only serious way to be antifascist is to be heretical.

CARLO ROSSELLI, "IL NEO-SOCIALISMO FRANCESE"
(1933)

The flight from Lipari took the refugees to Cap Bon in Tunisia, then
Corsica, Marseilles, and finally the large exile community in Paris. Rosselli
arrived in the French capital on 1 August and sent a telegram to Marion:
"Forgive the incorrigible; I am very well; send news; a hug to all; courage,
Carlo." [1] In his first letter from Paris to Amelia, Marion, and Nello, he wrote
that he felt with "absolute clarity" a "categorical sense of duty and mission." Only if he could transform his personal liberty into liberty for all
could he "find respite from my torment." [2] The escape, though, had un-
foreseen repercussions. Marion, pregnant with their second child, Amelia,
was arrested in retaliation. From Paris, Rosselli organized an international
campaign to secure her release. While Marion's father met with the Italian
ambassador in Britain, a rain of letters from England reached Marion in
prison, and former prime minister Nitti wrote directly to Lloyd George.
The international furor that ensued forced the regime to release Marion—a
British citizen—within a few days. Nello was not as fortunate and was sent
to *confino* on the prison island of Ustica. During the month of August,
Carlo Rosselli was literally besieged by newspaper correspondents from all
over the world. [3]

In an interview with a correspondent of *L'Italia del popolo,* a biweekly
republican journal published in Paris, Carlo concisely delineated the con-

ceptions and ideals developed first in *Il Quarto Stato* and further refined on Lipari. He stressed his belief in voluntarism and that the work of liberation could not wait for some deus ex machina but had to be the work of Italians themselves. Again he returned to his critique of the petrified orthodoxy of the socialists and Marxists: "The preoccupation to insert oneself in History with a capital H, to fix with perfect exactitude the civil state of one's time, to navigate along the course indicated by the Marxist compass, sometimes reduces even the most worthy to impotence . . . The man of action must, especially in certain moments, renounce being a historian of himself and his action." This was not to say that Rosselli glorified action for action's sake: "I hate blind action, brute action, action that is not supported by reason and not illuminated by moral light. I would not wish, in criticizing cerebralism and academicism, to fall into the contrary excess." For Rosselli the motto to keep in mind was Mazzini's *pensiero e azione* (thought and action). Antifascism was not a mechanical problem of simply overthrowing the fascist dictatorship. Action had to be accompanied by "a perfect ideological clarity." When the interviewer described Rosselli as "among those young socialists who perhaps more than any other defended the necessity of a profound revision of the theoretical and practical positions of the socialist movement," Rosselli responded that if anything, he was more convinced than ever of the necessity of undertaking a "courageous examination of conscience." The essential goal was a new conception of liberty: full, effective, positive, for all human beings and in all aspects of existence. Political and spiritual liberty was necessary as the premise for the struggle for economic autonomy in the future. "Our position is nothing less than the logical development, until its ultimate consequences, of the principle of freedom." [4]

Rosselli used his hard-won freedom by traveling extensively throughout Europe. He attended conferences in France, Belgium, and Germany; he wrote frequently to European newspapers and journals. He was particularly drawn to England and often wrote articles and letters to the editors at the London *Times* and the *Manchester Guardian*. In London he spoke at the National Liberal Club and the Royal Institute for Foreign Affairs. In France he often spoke for LIDU (The Italian League for the Rights of Man), an organization that unabashedly upheld the values of the French Revolution. But his most important and successful work was the foundation of a new movement.

Hammering together an unorthodox alliance of liberals, Mazzinian republicans, and democratic socialists, Rosselli was the driving force behind Giustizia e Libertà (Justice and Liberty). Present at its inception in the house of Alberto Tarchiani were the three escapees: Rosselli, Emilio Lussu, and Francesco Fausto Nitti; joining them were Nello Rosselli, Alberto Cianca, Gaetano Salvemini, Cipriano Facchinetti, and Raffaele Rossetti. Tarchiani had been born in Rome and spent time in New York City as a newspaper correspondent. Later he edited *Il Corriere della Sera* until it was taken over by the fascists in 1925. Although ideologically the most conservative of the founding members of Justice and Liberty, Tarchiani was paradoxically the most eager to engage in conspiratorial actions, including daring flights over Italian cities, bombings, and even plots to assassinate Mussolini. Mere months after the founding of Justice and Liberty, he was arrested by French authorities for possessing explosives and was accused of plotting an assassination attempt, but he was released after two months.[5]

Other activists that gravitated toward the new movement included the Roman journalist Alberto Cianca, who was instrumental in reviving the satirical journal *Il Becco Giallo* when he arrived in Paris in January 1927. Cianca had earned a law degree but was more influential as a journalist. He was director of Giovanni Amendola's *Il Mondo*, and his biting satire in *Il Becco Giallo* enraged the fascists. For his efforts, he was beaten several times until he fled to Paris. Vincenzino Nitti, eldest son of the former prime minister, lent his support, as did those who had been involved in the first attempt to rescue Rosselli from Lipari, Facchinetti and Rossetti. It was said to be the republican Raffaele Rossetti who suggested the name "Giustizia e Libertà," with its Risorgimento overtones, from poetry by Carducci. No doubt the example of the underground and conspiratorial Risorgimento movement, the *carbonari*, was in everyone's mind. Rosselli, however, tied the name of the movement to Bakunin's 1865 underground organization in Naples, "Libertà e Giustizia," noting that both movements posed the problem of replacing the "centralized, bureaucratic, military State" with an autonomous federation.[6] Symbol of the new movement was a flaming sword with the words Insorgere! Risorgere! (Revolt! Rise Again!), suggested by Lussu. The movement named a triumvirate as codirectors: Rosselli, Lussu, and Alberto Tarchiani. This selection revealed ideological divisions: if Rosselli advocated a revolutionary "liberal socialism," Lussu insisted that the movement transform itself into a new socialist party, and Tarchiani was to the right of both his colleagues, closer to a traditional liberalism. Radical

democracy, unorthodox socialism, classical liberalism, intransigent republicanism, and Gobetti's revolutionary liberalism were all present. Lussu
described the movement as comprising three currents: a radical socialist
(Rosselli), a Jacobin republican (himself), and a liberal democratic (Tarchiani). It was only Rosselli's charisma and enthusiasm that held these
disparate threads together. "Rosselli's impetuous youth was truly a force of
nature," Tarchiani wrote many years later. "He was certainly the most
powerful, complete, strenuous, indefatigable of the exiles in the cause of
Italian freedom."[7] A police spy in Paris reported to Rome that the members
of Justice and Liberty respected Rosselli in a way that bordered on "religious admiration."[8] When some protested that such a heterogeneous movement would be fatally flawed by these internal disputes, Rosselli defiantly
responded that "the hour of all heresies has sounded."[9]

Justice and Liberty attracted some of the most insightful intellectuals in
Italy and abroad. Umberto Calosso, who had worked with both Gramsci
on *L'Ordine Nuovo* and Gobetti for *La Rivoluzione Liberale* in Turin, was
forced into exile in 1931; he clearly traced Justice and Liberty back to
Mazzini's Giovane Italia movement just as the Risorgimento was the ante-
cedent for antifascism. Riccardo Bauer was another member that Rosselli
had met on Lipari. Bauer had collaborated with both Ferruccio Parri in
editing *Il Caffè* in Milan and Piero Gobetti on *La Rivoluzione Liberale* in
Turin. Like Rosselli, he too had received a degree in economics, was arrested for "clandestine expatriation," and was sentenced to Lipari.[10] Andrea
Caffi, born in St. Petersburg to Italian parents, had participated in the
Russian Revolution of 1905 in the ranks of the Mensheviks and had suffered three years in a Russian prison. Caffi had contributed a cosmopolitan
perspective to Prezzolini's review *La Voce* in Florence. Returning to Russia
in 1920, he was placed in prison again, this time by the Bolsheviks. Escaping to Paris, he sought out Rosselli and was a regular contributor to both
the newspaper and the journal of Justice and Liberty. Caffi was one of the
first to realize that although the March on Rome had been mere buffoon-
ery, Hitler's rise to power was a "great historic tragedy." Leone Ginzburg
had been born in Odessa and received his education in Italy, specializing in
literature at the University of Turin. Refusing to swear an oath of allegiance
to the fascist regime, he was dismissed from his teaching position but
remained in Turin to assist Justice and Liberty. He attacked the major
intellectuals of the regime, especially Giovanni Gentile and Alfredo Rocco,
as "corruptors." Arrested and brought before the feared Special Tribunal,

he was sentenced to prison but was amnestied in the wake of the Ethiopian victory in 1936. In Turin he collaborated with Luigi Einaudi and Cesare Pavese to make the Einaudi publishing house an oasis of culture and integrity during the fascist period. One of the most influential members of both Justice and Liberty and the Action Party, he edited the party's newspaper, *L'Italia Libera,* during the Armed Resistance. Captured in November 1943, he was imprisoned in the notorious Regina Coeli prison in Rome, where he died after torture under the Nazis in February 1944.

If Ginzburg charged Gentile and Rocco with moral corruption, Nicola Chiaromonte charged Giuseppe Prezzolini, Mario Missiroli, and Giovanni Ansaldo with petrified thinking. Chiaromonte had been born near Potenza and wrote for Giovanni Amendola's *Il Mondo* as well as other cultural reviews. In 1932 he met Rosselli for the first time and joined Justice and Liberty, only to leave the movement in 1935 when he felt Rosselli was moving rapidly to the left. During the Spanish Civil War, he participated in André Malraux's flying squadron. Lionello and Franco Venturi, father and son, along with Luigi Salvatorelli, valiantly exposed the abuses of history perpetrated by the regime. Lionello refused to swear the oath of allegiance to the regime and was dismissed from his chair at the University of Turin. Father and son were both forced into exile, first in France, later in the United States. Salvatorelli had been Professor of the history of Christianity at the University of Naples and had signed Croce's Manifesto of Anti-Fascist Intellectuals. His classic work, *Nazionalfascismo,* was published by Gobetti in 1923. Carlo Levi from Turin kept alive the memory and ideas of Piero Gobetti. Although trained as a medical doctor, Levi found greater satisfaction and solace in painting. Having joined Justice and Liberty at its founding, he wrote some of the most insightful works of the antifascist Resistance. With Ginzburg and Levi, Vittorio Foa, Augusto Monti, and Aldo Garosci lent their contributions to the Turin cell of Justice and Liberty, the most active and creative of those functioning in Italy. Emilio Lussu was a decorated war veteran and one of the founders of the Sardinian Party of Action which called for greater regional autonomy.

Silvio Trentin from the Veneto had renounced a teaching position in jurisprudence in 1926 and fled into exile. Beginning with Amendola's Unione Democratica Nazionale, Trentin moved to the PRI, but by the early 1930s, he had grown impatient with both the Republicans and reform socialism, which he called a "virus malefico."[11] One of the few not to settle in Paris, Trentin supported himself as a farmer, typographer and bookseller in Toulouse. His bookshop became the informal headquarters of Justice and Liberty in southern France. Trentin was on the radical left of the movement, and as Rosselli moved Justice and Liberty more to the left in the 1930s, Trentin became more influential; by 1934 he was a member of the Central Committee, since Lussu had dropped out because of political disagreements and ill health. Although disillusioned with the Stalinist betrayal of the Russian Revolution, Trentin was deeply influenced by Trotsky's theory of "permanent revolution," an idea that marked Rosselli's thinking in the context of the Spanish Civil War. Trentin's defense of the Russian Revolution caused some tension within the ranks of the movement. He is perhaps best known for his theory of combining political liberalism, a collectivist economy, and federalism. Trentin and Rosselli agreed that Justice and Liberty should be an elite, intellectual avant-garde that could then rally the masses.[12]

The concept of a political elite was to haunt Justice and Liberty long after its demise. The communists in particular never failed to portray the movement as a privileged group of bourgeois intellectuals, who were condescending in their relations with the proletariat. Rosselli, Trentin, Chiaromonte, Caffi, and the others agreed that the mass parties of the past had failed; it was time to experiment with new political forms. In fact, Chiaromonte wrote that "the essence of fascism is the negation of politics" creating the necessity to "think outside of politics." A revolutionary elite would have to be not only professional and passionate but also skeptical, tolerant, and humane, and would be drawn from the bourgeoisie, the artisanal class, the peasants, and the industrial workers.

"After three years of relative impotence," Carlo wrote, "I am full of energy . . . We will work—we will be victorious, even if the struggle takes another twenty years and demands the greatest sacrifices, life only has meaning if conceived this way."[13] By October 1929, Justice and Liberty was organizing centers in Italy, and Rosselli left his imprint on the movement from its birth.[14] That same month, the fascist police in Paris reported to Rome that Marion had "the intention of opening a political/intellectual salon accessible to all the emigrants and friends of Italian liberty," while her husband "dedicates himself to a vast project of propaganda and penetration, especially among the educated classes. The couple have large sums of money, acquaintances, sympathizers, and propose to create a vast movement of antifascism."[15] Justice and Liberty was to be a socialist-republican coalition that would attract and synthesize the most vital and activist currents among the antifascist exile intelligentsia. Its relationship with the older parties was ambiguous: some within the movement sought a possible renewal of the PSI and possibly an eventual integration of forces; on the other hand, Rosselli was to insist that Justice and Liberty was unlike the older, more established parties. "The socialism of Justice and Liberty," he wrote to Salvemini, "has nothing to do with traditional socialism."[16] Justice and Liberty was born in the crucible of fascism and therefore its essence was antifascism. Rosselli's critique of the older parties was the premise for insisting that GL remain a movement rather than a party. This eventually became the dominant ideological position, although not without internal disputes. An essential characteristic of the movement, this position allowed for an independence that was rare and could contribute to a free discussion of ideology and tactics. Sympathizers were active in France, Belgium, Britain, Brazil, and the United States, where Max Ascoli had fled in 1931; Salvemini, who had been in America on lecture tours, accepted the Lauro De Bosis chair in Italian civilization at Harvard University in 1934. The position had been established especially for him by Ruth Draper, fiancée of Lauro De Bosis, who had perished after a daring flight over Rome, dropping antifascist leaflets. From the United States, Salvemini, Ascoli, Giuseppe Borgese, Roberto Bolaffio, Michele Cantarella, Lionello Venturi, and Alberto Tarchiani supported Justice and Liberty, eventually forming the Mazzini Society in 1939. Salvemini was also instrumental, along with Aldo Garosci, the architect and architectural historian Bruno Zevi, the historian Enzo Tagliacozzo, and the aesthetic philosopher and art critic Renato Poggioli, in publishing the *Quaderni Italiani* from New York City.

What, then, were the tasks of a new revolutionary movement? Rosselli declared three areas that were of supreme importance: the formation of cadres, work among the masses and a certain type of action.[17] The Russian Revolution proved that a decisive, disciplined, and revolutionary minority could be successful. This nucleus need not be conceived of as a romantic, heroic elite, distanced from the masses, but rather as an avant-garde whose function would be to mediate between the minority and the masses. In fact, the first sign of class consciousness consists in the capacity for creating leaders. These leading cadres should not be tyrannical nor despotic nor centralizers of power; instead, they should use the Socratic, liberal method to inspire the masses. Rosselli recognized that the most delicate problem confronting the movement was that of creating and maintaining a constant psychological bond between the avant-garde and the masses.[18] Without this constant and reciprocal relationship, the avant-garde becomes a sect, impervious to everything else, and cuts itself off from the revolutionary process. Finally, actions were necessary that would capture the imagination and admiration of the people. The power of Justice and Liberty resided in the fact that "it was able to create a new type of movement, closely tied to the Italian spirit and the demands of the situation. It can combine virile revolutionary realism and romantic passion. Without this overwhelming passion, nothing serious and lasting can be accomplished in life, nothing. And even less in a revolution."[19]

Justice and Liberty began to implement its ideas immediately: before the end of 1929, the first issue of *Giustizia e Libertà*, a monthly underground publication, was ready to be smuggled into Italy.[20] Its masthead stated that GL was a "Revolutionary Antifascist Movement" and prominently featured quotes from the martyred Amendola ("In the darkest night, dawn is ever closer") and Matteotti ("You may kill me, but the idea that is in me is immortal"). Its first issue declared, "We will not win in a day, but we will win," and went on using the language of a manifesto:

> Justice and Liberty fights for the overthrow of the fascist dictatorship and for the victory of a free, democratic, republican regime.
>
> It acts on revolutionary terrain because the dictatorship has rendered any other form of struggle impossible.
>
> It summons to action all Italians who feel offended in their dignity by the present servitude and wish to actively participate in the insurrection.
>
> It affirms that the highest interests of the working classes are at stake in the present battle; because it can realize its ideal of economic and social justice only in a regime that guarantees judicial equality and political liberty.
>
> It affirms that the liberation of Italy must be the work of Italians.
>
> It declares that the battle is extremely difficult and imposes the greatest sacrifices. This is the price for the Second Italian Risorgimento.[21]

If Justice and Liberty managed to attract a heterogeneous group of young intellectuals, it was not without its critics. Palmiro Togliatti, to no one's surprise, followed the party line from Moscow in denouncing the new movement as an example of "socialfascism." For the PCI, GL was an "agency of Italian capitalism . . . an anticommunist organization . . . that seeks to trick the workers and separate them from the Communist Party."[22] More disturbing was the criticism from Pietro Nenni and Giuseppe Saragat. Both insisting that Italian socialism should remain faithful to Marxism, they were unwilling to follow Rosselli in a radical break. Saragat called the movement's program "utopian, petit bourgeois, antimarxist." Rosselli responded by recalling that Saragat himself had made some of the very same arguments now put forward by Justice and Liberty.[23]

A debate over the ideological reading of the Risorgimento was one of the permanent fissures of the movement. In the spring of 1935, the dispute became divisive. The Italian-Russian revolutionary, Andrea Caffi, deemed it a mistake for Justice and Liberty to base itself on the nineteenth-century Risorgimento. Mazzini, in particular, was a weak point who offered little for a modern, revolutionary movement. The "sacred memories" of the Risorgimento were the residues of "national vanity" and best abandoned.[24] Nicola Chiaromonte sided with Caffi in the dispute, while Franco Venturi and Umberto Calosso sided with Rosselli. They agreed that the "official" Risorgimento had been denuded of its true revolutionary potential, but they upheld its democratic, popular, and republican currents. It was this tradition that Justice and Liberty had to resurrect. Not surprisingly, the historian Franco Venturi suggested that moral and historiographical problems were conflated in the debate on the Risorgimento. Rescuing the more radical Risorgimento from the nationalistic and scholastic versions was both a political and an intellectual imperative.[25]

In a direct criticism of the passivity of the older parties, Justice and Liberty demanded that "We bury the past . . . we wish to break the spell . . . either fight or serve cowardly. There is no other way." GL was to be a revolutionary movement, not a party, and it demanded that Italians abandon the hope for divine intervention and have faith only in themselves. "Fascism holds in its fist weapons and says: 'I discuss only with arms.' It is necessary, therefore, to speak of war. This is the new language we intend to speak."

When it became clear that a more detailed program was necessary, Rosselli devoted considerable time to clarifying the position of the movement. He focused on the crisis of parliamentary institutions and the character of the fascist dictatorship.[26] Crucial in determining the nature of Justice and Liberty was Rosselli's highly critical judgment on the passivity of the older political parties. The raison d'être of the new movement, at least in the early years, was action. A month before his death, Rosselli recounted the founding principles of the movement:

> More than a common program, what tied us together was a state of mind:
> the revolt against the men, the mentality, the methods of the prefascist

political world, responsible for the miserable end of the Aventine Secession; an active will to struggle, which was to be also a redemption of the
humiliation of the battle not fought and the undeserved defeat; a convic-
tion that was not clear in its terms but very clear in its motives, of the
necessity of a renewal *ab imis* of the social and moral life of the country.[27]

It was not until January 1932, with the publication of the inaugural issue of
the *Quaderni di Giustizia e Libertà* as a theoretical journal, that the movement clarified its ideas into a coherent and formal program.[28] Since fascism
could be defeated only by a revolutionary movement, Justice and Liberty
could formulate itself only as the "concrete expression of the forces that
struggle on the revolutionary terrain against fascism." A wide-ranging and
detailed "Draft of a Program" took up where *Liberal Socialism* had left off:
an attempt to combine a reconquest of political and individual freedom
with a "principle of justice that renders democracy effective." The program
called for nothing less than a full-fledged revolution; a return to the past or
a superficial transformation was inadequate. Politically the revolution
would be driven by local councils, whose task would be to organize an
election based on universal suffrage for a Constituent Assembly. (Here
there were echoes of both the French and the Russian Revolution.) Italy
was to be a socialist republic, based on democracy. Fundamental freedoms
of association, the press, speech, and emigration would be reestablished.
The monarchy would be dispatched to the dustbin of history, while fascist
officials and their *fiancheggiatori* (supporters of the regime) would be tried
and their profits confiscated. The fascist corporations would be dissolved,
to be replaced by voluntary associations.

Agrarian reform was to be based on the old formula "Land to those who
work it." The program went on to detail the differences in large and small
holdings; noting that large holdings would require vast amounts of capital
and complicated technical direction, it suggested leaving the large agrarian
firms intact, simply transferring their ownership to the community. Share-
croppers, small tenants, leasers, and all others who cultivate the land would
acquire that land. In both cases, a small indemnity would be paid to the
present owners. This clause was to cause Rosselli and the movement much
grief and was dropped three years later in the face of strong opposition.
Consortia and cooperatives were to be established, assisting peasants with
loans, credit, mortgage debts, technical assistance, and educational programs concerning the use of technology, new crops, pesticides, and fertilizers. Landless peasants would be assigned to public or reclaimed land.

Industry and banking were to be fundamentally altered, in accordance with a transformation of relations within the heart of the industrial system, the factory itself. Workshop councils and shopfloor democracy would supplant the traditional hierarchy of relations. Workers would participate in the management of the factory, deciding on wages, production, schedules, hirings, and promotions. Simultaneously, and perhaps in blatant contradiction, the program called for a permanent organ to control and direct the nation's economy, tracing a plan for economic reconstruction (the influence of Russian and Belgian planning). Essential public services, such as those providing hydroelectricity, fertilizers, or private credit banking, would be nationalized, as would those industries that enjoyed monopolies (such as mining) and those that had survived and prospered by tariffs and subsidies (iron and steel, sugar, naval construction). Unlike fascist or postfascist Italy, management of the nationalized industries would not pass to the state but rather to autonomous agencies, avoiding bureaucratization and centralization. There would be a minimum wage and unemployment insurance (to be paid for the entire period of nonemployment). The properties of the fascist party and its organization would be confiscated and transferred to worker and peasant organizations. A progressive inheritance tax would be introduced, whereas the grain tax and other taxes on popular consumer goods would be abolished. Rents were to be reduced immediately; building construction would be in the hands of the local municipalities.

In the realm of foreign policy, the new republic would engage a program of peace and disarmament. Military spending would be reduced. There would be free trade in a united Europe. Although it did not renounce Italian colonies, the program called for a policy recognizing "the cultural and administrative autonomy of ethnic minorities" (presumably this would apply to Germanic peoples in the northeastern territory of the peninsula and to the African colonies).

After experiencing firsthand the arbitrariness of the fascist judicial system, the program called for a radical reform of justice and the penal system, based on the independence and tenure of judges. Education was to be free and available to all. "Teaching and culture will be considered essential to the life and progress of the Republic." There was to be a complete and radical separation of church and state; the immense properties and goods of the high clergy and religious congregations would be confiscated. There would be unconditional freedom of conscience and worship. The Lateran Treaty, Convention, and Concordat would be annulled.[29]

Several members, including Vincenzo Nitti, abandoned the movement, accusing it of a radical socialism; Tarchiani was unhappy but contained his misgivings for several more years until he too resigned. The response from the communists was furious, especially over the agrarian program; collectivization was the order of the day from Moscow. The socialists were mixed in their response: Nenni was more or less favorable; Saragat, however, was adamant in his criticism—only the proletariat could be entrusted with the task of the coming revolution.[30] The anarchists warmly welcomed the program.

Rosselli insisted that although the movement had been founded in Paris, the real work had to be carried out in Italy. Accordingly, cells were established in almost all the larger cities of northern Italy by the end of 1929. These cells were not to be considered as a heroic and romantic elite disconnected from the people. Rather, they were to be an ideal avant-garde. The key to the struggle was the connection between this avant-garde and the masses. Justice and Liberty would organically combine a "virile revolutionary realism" with a "romantic passion."[31] Ernesto Rossi and Riccardo Bauer were given the responsibility of forging these new groups. Bauer was especially successful in Turin, where he gathered the remnants of Gobetti's *La Rivoluzione Liberale* circle. Gathered around Augusto Monti were Cesare Pavese, Leone Ginzburg, Carlo Levi, Norberto Bobbio, and Vittorio Foa. The work south of Rome proved to be less fruitful. In the face of Croce's criticism concerning Rosselli's concept of a "liberal socialism" and "Giustizia e Libertà," only Tommaso Fiore, a friend of Salvemini, was able to attract some supporters and maintain contact with Rosselli and the others in Paris. The success of the GL cells is difficult to gauge. A major history of European socialism refers to the Italian socialists and communists as "pitiful émigré movements with only tenuous clandestine organizations inside Italy"[32] but fails to mention the partial success of GL. In the United States, antifascist exiles sympathetic to the ideology of Justice and Liberty later founded the Mazzini Society in New York in 1939 and published the *Quaderni Italiani.*[33]

An important task of the movement was the smuggling of antifascist writings back into Italy. Nello Traquandi, employed by the Italian postal system, was instrumental in this regard. He established an intricate web of contacts and postal workers across northern Italy to elude the censors. Every nucleus of the movement in each city had couriers who crossed the Italo-French border and returned with numerous documents and propaganda. Subterfuge was quickly refined and often subtle. The first issue of *Giustizia e Libertà* appeared carrying "Rome, November 1929" on its first page, although it was printed neither in Rome (but rather in Paris) nor in November. In this way, the movement sent the fascist police off on false leads, while protecting their couriers and distribution networks. Another tactic was to camouflage the publications of the movement within the covers of "respected" publications, such as the philosophical works of Croce or Gentile. Leone Ginzburg and Carlo Levi were given the task of reaching out to the youth in Italy; after more than a decade of fascism, many people had known no other political system.

Another facet of the movement's program was its criticism of the Catholic Church. Rosselli found Don Luigi Sturzo of the PPI (Italian Popular Party) a sympathetic figure. Sturzo had established the PPI in 1919 as a modern, mass Catholic party with a program of proportional representation, local autonomy, the "right to work," and the vote for women. He forcefully rejected any compromise with fascism, prompting the Vatican's 1923 order for him to resign and effectively dismantle the PPI; the Vatican had decided to side with fascism. Attacked by *squadristi,* Sturzo fled to London and in 1940 arrived in New York City after narrowly escaping a German air raid. From London he and Rosselli debated the position of the Church in Italian society.[34]

The most comprehensive expression of the movement's methods were published by Ernesto Rossi and Riccardo Bauer as "Advice on Tactics" in the eighteenth edition of *Giustizia e Libertà* in the summer of 1930.[35] The edition was so popular that a second edition was published a year later; it was perhaps the best and the most original, and certainly the most widely read of the various works of the early movement. Rossi and Bauer were explicit in the immediate objectives of the new organization. The first was what they called "passive resistance"—to create around the fascists an ambience of hostility in which they would feel isolated, scorned, hated, without being able to identify their enemies. This was to be a silent, diffused hostility that would discourage, demoralize, and disorient the fascists. Second was the "revolutionary organization," which would forge in every important city a nucleus of several dozen men and women, belonging to all the social classes and all political currents fighting against the dictatorship.[36]

Rossi and Bauer were eager to dispel the notion that the active resistance was privileged over the passive (as might be inferred from Rosselli's writings). Not all could be fighters on the front lines, but all could contribute to the antifascist cause. Possible modes of passive resistance included boycotting visits of the King or Mussolini (as was successful in Florence with the directives of *Non Mollare!*). Also, citizens should resist the temptations offered by the regime, particularly the Dopolavoro (After-work organization), which sponsored excursions in the countryside, pilgrimages, sporting events and the like. Justice and Liberty was highly conscious of the fact that the regime was attempting to forge a "consensus" and "hegemony" over the people, long before those words worked their way into the political lexicon. Those that were obligated to attend fascist functions were advised to arrive late and not to applaud; all were encouraged to stop smoking to decrease the regime's revenues from the tobacco tax, to boycott fascist stores, and to refuse to employ militant fascists. Others could help by distributing the clandestine publications or even lending the technology necessary to continue the clandestine writing; those that could were urged to assist the movement financially. Even the writing of graffiti such as "Viva Giustizia e Libertà!" if undertaken on a grand scale, could have an impact.

As could be expected, though, Rossi and Bauer were more explicit concerning the tactics of the "revolutionary organization." Although conceding that the various cells in different cities would be composed of varying political currents and would therefore have different characteristics, there were some tactics that all could agree on, as developed by the Central Committee of the movement that would give general directives and would coordinate the diverse initiatives. These included the establishment of a clandestine press; collection of dues based on one's ability to pay; infiltrating such unlikely places as the military, in addition to schools, universities, sporting clubs, and factories; establishing contacts in post, telegraph, telephone, and railroad offices; and acquisition of arms. The directives ended laconically with this advice: "Understand and accept that your life is at risk."

The second edition of "Advice on Tactics," which was published a year later in 1931, added fourteen more points, including the advice to be aware of, but not paralyzed by, the omnipresence of police spies. This advice was in response to the arrest of Rossi and Bauer, who were tried before the Special Tribunal and sentenced to twenty years in prison. It was the first of many severe blows to the movement.

Justice and Liberty was created in the midst of an exile community in Paris. As early as 1922, Italian socialists had fled to the French capital and had developed a tightly knit community, although not without internal disputes. This emigrant group expanded in 1925 to 1926, when the fascist regime unleased a concerted effort against its enemies.[37] Paris was home to Italian communists, revolutionary and reformist socialists, anarchists, Mazzinian republicans, radical democrats, and even dissident fascists. The early development of Justice and Liberty was characterized by an incessant desire for action and for concrete political gestures that would put the lie to Mussolini's claim to "consensus." But this is not to say that Rosselli neglected the theoretical framework for political action.

Also in Paris was LIDU, whose president, the photographer Giovanni Bassanesi, would figure in an important episode in the history of Justice and Liberty. In a way, Bassanesi was a typical member of the movement: it would be difficult to pin him down on the political spectrum. An observant Catholic and political liberal, he refused to adopt the informal *tu* (you)commonly used by the exile community and instead insisted on using *Lei,* the more formal word for *you,* as a form of address.[38] In early 1930, Bassanesi developed the idea of a daring midday flight over Italy to drop propaganda leaflets.[39] He first approached the communists in exile, who were understandably suspicious of him and his plan. Rosselli, though, was captivated by the idea, and Alberto Cianca accompanied Bassanesi in a few flying lessons. Unfortunately for Bassanesi, he suffered from unstable nerves, and every flight was a torture for him. Yet he persevered and acquired a grand total of thirty hours of practice before the actual flight. The many logistical problems (the purchase of a plane with Rosselli's money, finding an airfield, printing the manifestoes, and so on) were eventually ironed out, and Gioacchino Dolci was chosen to be the second pilot.[40] An airfield was found (or rather created) at Lodrino in the Swiss canton of Ticino, where a large Italian socialist community was eager to assist in the daring enterprise. Rosselli and Tarchiani personally brought the leaflets to the airfield in a small truck. To carry as many leaflets as possible (150,000), the two pilots relinquished their parachutes and took off.

A few minutes after noon on 11 July 1930, Bassanesi and Dolci were over Milan, dropping the manifestoes throughout the city, especially onto the Piazza Duomo, before the great Gothic cathedral and heart of the city. Some leaflets urged the people of Italy neither to smoke nor to pay taxes; another leaflet was an appeal to the workers; one simply stated, "Justice and Liberty salutes Milan, the City of the Five Glorious Days" [the uprising against the Austrians during the Risorgimento]; and in a direct challenge to the fascist regime, one *volantino* (leaflet) proclaimed with more bravado than truth that "Committees of Justice and Liberty have already been formed in thirty cities and are organized and armed for action."[41]

The episode struck Italy like thunder. In the middle of the day, in a great metropolis (the very birthplace of fascism), the antifascists had impudently dared to show themselves right under the noses (or more accurately, above the noses) of the fascist authorities. Mussolini had thundered that he could "darken the skies" with the new fascist air force and that Italy was impervious to attack; yet here were two inexperienced pilots who managed to circle over Milan undisturbed for nearly half an hour. It was, in a way, a repeat performance of the flight from Lipari. The rhetoric and bombast of the regime had been punctured by courageous action. This was no longer the academic, theoretical side of Italian antifascism; the use of modern technology, the audacity and the daring, captured the imagination of many young Italians. It was no surprise that new recruits began finding their way to the cells of the movement in Paris and in Italy.

Unfortunately, the flight was not an unmitigated success. On their return, Bassanesi and Dolci encountered mechanical difficulties, and the plane made a forced landing in the Gotthard Pass. Bassanesi was severely injured and was scarred for the rest of his life. He was arrested by the Swiss authorities, and in November he was placed on trial in Lugano, along with Rosselli, Tarchiani, and others charged with complicity. Dolci, for some unknown reason, managed to escape arrest; his role was not revealed until after the trial, which unfolded over three days in mid-November 1930. In the courtroom, Bassanesi's lawyer, speaking of the flight poetically defended his client, claiming that "freedom, banished from the earth, descends from the sky."[42] As in Savona, this was an opportunity for the antifascists to make their case before the public.[43] It soon became apparent that as in Savona, it was not Bassanesi and the others who were on trial, but rather Mussolini and the fascist regime. Filippo Turati and former Foreign Minister Carlo Sforza arrived to testify on Bassanesi's behalf. Newspaper correspondents from all over Europe attended the trial that took place only a few months after another, similar trial in Brussels of the Italian anarchist Fernando De Rosa for attempting to assassinate Prince Umberto, son of King Victor Emmanuel III.

Rosselli, Bassanesi, and the others took full advantage of the presence of the international press corps. Their ringing statements often elicited the spontaneous outbreak of cheers and applause. Their letter to the presiding judge was eventually leaked to the press.[44] And perhaps in one of his most poignant and powerful public statements, Rosselli recalled,

> I had a home: they destroyed it. I had a newspaper: they suppressed it. I had a professorship: I had to abandon it. I had, as I still have today, ideas, dignity, an ideal: to defend them I had to go to prison. I had teachers and friends—Amendola, Matteotti, Gobetti—they have killed them.[45]

Bassanesi had undoubtedly committed an infraction against Swiss law and so was sentenced to four months (because he had already been in prison since July, he was immediately released). There was no fine imposed, nor was he expelled; Rosselli, Tarchiani, and the others were acquitted.[46] An explosion of applause erupted in the courtroom and that evening a banquet was held in celebration. The return rail trip from Lugano to Paris was marked by enthusiastic demonstrations at every station, a sure sign that the trial had profoundly moved both the Swiss and the French people. There was, however, a tragic postscript to the successful story. In December 1931, Bassanesi attempted a repeat of his historic flight, only to encounter failure. The experience exacerbated his already fragile constitution, and he soon suffered a nervous breakdown. In 1932 he requested an amnesty from Mussolini's government and was expelled from Justice and Liberty.

Bassanesi's flight inspired other attempts; however, almost all ended in failure. The only other expedition that managed to carry out its intention of dropping leaflets was Lauro De Bosis's flight over Rome. Tragically, De Bosis went down somewhere in the Mediterranean Sea on his return. Sensing the outcome of the endeavor, he left behind a haunting essay, "The Story of My Death," written just before the flight.[47]

Until the flight over Milan, the fascist police had been slow in moving against the various branches of the movement. Several students at the University of Pavia who belonged to the movement had been arrested in the spring of 1930 but were released, and twenty-two persons were arrested in Bologna, but most were absolved; the few who were convicted received relatively light sentences. Publicity from the flight, combined with the movement's very public support of Fernando De Rosa and regicide, forced the fascist police to concern themselves with the new movement.[48] The police sought ways to infiltrate the organization and found a willing agent in Carlo Del Re, a Venetian with a shadowy past. On 4 October 1930, he had sought out former Foreign Minister Count Carlo Sforza, then in Brussels, awaiting the Lugano trial. Del Re insisted that the Italian antifascists had to engage in more violent opposition and tried to get Sforza to agree to some terrorist acts in order to compromise all the Italian exiles. Sforza, becoming suspicious, declined the offer.[49]

While in Rosselli's Paris apartment, Del Re first suggested that the antifascists send *panettoni* (traditional Christmas cakes) filled with dynamite to various fascist officials. Rosselli, Tarchiani, and the other members present looked at him in amazement, horrified at the thought of innocent women and children being killed on Christmas Day. They let Del Re know that they found the idea to be repugnant. Del Re then offered to help Ernesto Rossi and Riccardo Bauer in preparing an attack against tax collection centers in various cities. A chemical engineer, Umberto Ceva, was responsible for creating the phosphorous bombs that were to be used, and Del Re offered to help in their construction. The bombs were hidden in the countryside, driven there by Del Re himself; later he lead the police to the secret cache. Simultaneously information arrived at the Central Committee of Justice and Liberty in Paris that a spy had infiltrated their ranks. Del Re was present in Bauer's house in Milan when the letter arrived from the Central Committee, warning of an agent provocateur who was slightly disabled. Del Re, who had lost two fingers of his left hand, managed to maintain his composure. When confronted with the letter, he joked with perfect coldness that they could not possibly think him a traitor. Yet the damage had been done: at that very moment on 30 October 1930, twenty-four members of Justice and Liberty were arrested. Riccardo Bauer was apprehended in Milan, along with Umberto Ceva, Ferruccio Parri, and others; in Florence, Nello Traquandi was arrested; Ernesto Rossi was caught in Bergamo, where he had gone to teach.

Del Re made his way to Lugano, where on 2 November he telephoned Paris in an attempt to entice either Rosselli or Tarchiani into a trap. Belatedly suspicion had fallen on Del Re, and he was notified that no one would leave Paris; he would have to journey to Paris, where he arrived the next day and immediately made for Rosselli's house. There, in the course of incessant questioning by Rosselli and Tarchiani, he entangled himself in a web of contradictions. Foolishly, Rosselli and Tarchiani decided to continue their interrogation the next day and allowed him to leave. As could be expected, Del Re disappeared and was given a new name and identity by the fascist police. He had served his purpose and had been well compensated for his work. In 1930 when the average monthly salary in Italy was 1,000 lire, Del Re was paid 44,000 lire for his betrayal of the antifascists.[50]

Besides the misfortune of the arrests, his work left tragedy in its wake. On Christmas Day 1930, Umberto Ceva, held at the notorious Regina Coeli prison in Rome and afraid of betraying his "friend" Del Re under torture, committed suicide. In a note to his wife and two small children, he disclosed, "I have faith in three things: my country, my family, and liberty, but I cannot live in a country deprived of liberty."[51]

The stage was set for another trial. But there was to be one more adventure before the judicial proceedings began. Ernesto Rossi, arrested in Bergamo, was to be transported to Milan and then to Rome. Having made the trip several times, he knew that the train had to slow down near the resort town of Viareggio because of the nature of the terrain. Casually asking the two *carabinieri* guarding him if he could open the window for a breath of air, Rossi threw himself from the slow-moving train, handcuffed as he was. He evaded capture through the night and even managed to free himself from the handcuffs, but when he arrived at the home of someone he knew, the door was slammed in his face. In the morning, he was recaptured. In his account of the escape, Rossi commented on the common humanity he felt with his guards and repeated an idea that began with Gobetti and was to be a central pillar in the analysis of fascism as developed by Rosselli: "Fascism was not an accident attributable to the criminal initiative of Mussolini. It was the fruit of all our history. The regime would not fall because of internal disputes nor from economic crisis. To hope for a popular insurrection, to me, was folly. It was no longer the age of the barricades."[52]

Rossi and Bauer were to be tried before the Special Tribunal for the Defense of the State. The Tribunal was a military court with a president chosen from the generals of the various armed forces, five judges from the fascist Militia, and a prosecutor from the military judiciary. Crimes were made retroactive, and its sentences were not subject to appeal.[53] Since they were linked to the planned bombings, Rossi and Bauer faced a potential capital case. The prospect of two of the leading figures of Justice and Liberty being led before a firing squad pushed Rosselli and the others into feverish activity. Along with Salvemini, Rosselli mounted a campaign through letters to leading political figures and newspapers. The focus of this activity was Britain and, in particular, the *Manchester Guardian.* Liberal intellectuals from all over Europe, such as Arnold Toynbee, Bolton King, Ernst Cassirer, and Thomas Mann, lent their support to the campaign.[54] On 29 May 1931, the one-day trial began; all the accused carried themselves with an extraordinary grace that was noted by the journalists present. Bauer repeated the fundamental precepts of the movement:

> Our organization has a revolutionary character because the dictatorship has rendered any other form of political opposition impossible to all those who aspire to a free, democratic and republican regime in Italy. We call to action all those Italians who are offended in their national dignity and are ready to actively contribute to the rebirth. For us, the revolution is a necessity, a duty.[55]

Ernesto Rossi agreed, insisting that "ideas are worth little if one is not ready to sustain them with action."[56] Unfortunately, Rome was neither Savona nor Lugano, and the Special Tribunal was not ready to let another occasion slip by. Sentence was passed the next day in the so-called "trial of the intellectuals": Rossi and Bauer each received twenty years in prison; a month later, Nello Traquandi was sentenced to seven years. It was the most severe blow yet to the new movement.

Antifascism suffered still another blow when Filippo Turati died in Paris on 29 March 1932. Libertarian socialism had already lost one of its best with the death of Francesco Saverio Merlino two years earlier, and it would stagger under the death of the great anarchist Errico Malatesta soon after that of Turati. Together the deaths of Malatesta and Turati symbolized the end of an era.[57] The passing of the "grand old man" of Italian socialism presented Rosselli and the antifascist resistance with an opportunity to reflect on the history of Italian socialism and its present crisis in the context of fascism. Rosselli's desire to acknowledge Turati's pivotal place in Italian socialism led to one of his most important essays.[58] Tracing Turati's early life, Rosselli pointed out that as a student, Turati had been influenced by the legacy of the Risorgimento, the experience of the Paris Commune, the positivism of Ardigò, and the work of Loria. Ardigò, wrote Rosselli, like Feuerbach and Mill, never held the extreme positions of materialism and naturalism that reduced the subject to an object, and Ardigò passed on to Turati the recognition that consciousness—as an active and creative force—was the point of departure for a positivist philosophy. Therefore, Turati's was an "idealistic positivism or a positivist idealism."[59]

Characteristically, Rosselli, would not permit the traditional form and rhetorical tropes of the obituary (granted, at forty pages, this was no ordinary obituary) to keep him from a sharp critique of Turati's ideas and career. But as he explained, "While examining the work of Mazzini in 1860,

Alexander Herzen had written that 'Mazzini is so great that to refrain from a critique would be to offend him.'"[60] The best homage that could be paid by the younger generation was not "an indistinct panegyric," but instead an "affectionate effort of critical comprehension."

That Turati insisted on the dogma of a scientific socialism was the reason he found himself in a curious position: adored leader of the party, but rarely followed. Rosselli criticized the inconsistency between Turati's ideological position (supporting a republic) and his political position (temporary supporter of the monarchy). Nor could Rosselli share with Turati the rosy vision of socialist achievements during the fifteen years before World War I. Instead, it was precisely at that time when the symptoms of a profound moral crisis were manifest, not only in the party, but in the nation at large. Another criticism, which was developed not only by Rosselli but also by Salvemini and the *meridionalista* (southernist) Tommaso Fiore, was directed toward the unsophisticated conception of the working class as embedded in the official ideology of the PSI. Tied to an orthodox Marxism, the Italian socialists (both "revolutionary" and "reformist") concentrated on the industrialized proletariat. In Italy this group existed only in the North and only in a few large cities such as Milan, Turin, and Genoa. Most workers were agricultural and artisanal. Even universal suffrage, generally regarded as one of the great victories of the Left before the war, was tainted for Rosselli: the right to vote was won after a very small sacrifice; it was granted from above (by Giolitti in return for social peace), and the Italian people again came to benefit from a fundamental political institution without having sacrificed anything to achieve it. "No wonder that later, it did not know how to defend it." Rosselli donned the robes of the prophet in his critique:

In the not too distant future, Italian socialism must radically transform its constitutional structure. After the fall of fascism, with the revolution complete, the dominant problems will no longer be of opposition or propaganda, but of governing in the largest sense of the word. And the government must not then be consigned to the hands of only the party, always inclined to transform itself into a sect, but to the organic representatives of the working class, of the entire world of labor which through its network of worker, cooperative, and cultural institutions will constitute the new State. Only an organic, permanent, intimate contact between political and economic socialism, between party and unions, between elites and masses, will impede the possible oligarchical, bureaucratic, and sectarian degeneration of the party, favoring the rise of a substantial democracy.[61]

Croce had once written that Turati's Marxism performed an important liberal function in Italy. On one occasion, Turati wrote to Treves, in words that Rosselli approvingly quotes and that could just as well apply to the younger, heretical socialist: "Is this not our perennial destiny, the glorious labor that we have elected for ourselves, to march against the current, in hatred of all folly, to always be wrong today so that we will be right tomorrow?" For Rosselli, Turati embodied "the entire problem of the Risorgimento." He would remain as a symbol connecting the generation of 1848 and the generation of revolutionary antifascism, between the political Risorgimento of the nineteenth century and the social and moral Risorgimento embodied by antifascism.[62]

Nationalism and the Masses

The debate concerning exile was a natural extension of the debate over the character of the Risorgimento and the role of intellectuals such as Mazzini, Cattaneo, and Ferrari. It was absolutely vital that the antifascists address the issue of the Risorgimento, not simply for historiographical reasons, but to discern whether and what part of that tradition could be reconnected to the present struggle. If antifascists did not reclaim the Risorgimento legacy and instead abandoned the field, fascism would acquire, by default, a monopoly on the past and the Risorgimento. "Between the Italian State of 1860 and fascism," Rosselli wrote, "there is a connection—if not a filiation—of progressive degeneration that forces us (contrary to Croce) to place the end of Italian history not at 1914, but to follow it . . . to the march on Rome and beyond."

After the defeat of 1848–49, the character of the Risorgimento changed. It was captured by the moderates and the state of Piedmont, while its more radical demands were attenuated and the movement came to conceive of national unification solely in terms of expelling the foreigners. The consequence, according to Rosselli, was that there were in reality two *risorgimenti:* the official, moderate, Piedmontese and successful movement; and the popular movement, prepared between 1830 and 1848, with its crowning success of Garibaldi's Thousand cunningly defused by Cavour at Teano.

The leaders of the popular Risorgimento, such as Mazzini, Carlo Cattaneo, Luigi Ferrari, Carlo Pisacane, Giuseppe Garibaldi, Ausonio Franchi, and Giuseppe Montanelli, had always insisted that the problem of unification was intimately tied to the problem of freedom and social change. This transformation had to be the work of the Italians themselves, not to the overthrow of one political servitude for another. This was Rosselli's argument for the antifascist cause as well.

The antifascists had to return to the Risorgimento: not to the official movement as recounted in the schools and glorified through the work of conservative historians, but the forgotten movement and the defeated figures of Mazzini, Cattaneo, Pisacane, and Garibaldi. Even in fascist Italy, the embers of this popular Risorgimento had not died out, as demonstrated by the enormous success of works on Garibaldi and unification. All of which led Rosselli to examine the role of nationalism in unification and state-building and to note perceptively that nationalism was not an artificial construction, nor simply an "invention of the nineteenth century or the French Revolution." The sentiment of nationality may not be inherent in human nature, but to deny its influence because of its present "degeneration and deviations" was a fatal mistake for the antifascists. Nationalism cannot be wished away. By disregarding its power and influence and insisting on an abstract internationalism, the democrats and socialists were reducing themselves to impotence and hypocrisy. Rather, the sense of nationality should be turned to a Mazzinian ideal: a European force, a necessary rite of passage, education, construction, dissolving it from the statist, mystical, nationalistic, imperialistic tradition.[63]

Proof that nationalism was a potent force and had eclipsed international solidarity abounded in the 1930s. For Rosselli the event that crystallized this reality in his mind was the election that took place on 13 January 1935 in the Saar region, where the populace was given the opportunity to join France or Germany. The election results were a catastrophe for the united front and the socialists, who were expecting at least 30 to 40 percent of the vote, but a thunderous victory for German nationalism. By a nearly ten-to-one margin, the people of the Saar voted to join a Nazi Germany.[64] This in effect was a vote in support of the Hitler revolution two years after it had assumed power, and Rosselli drew the most drastic conclusion that traditional socialism, communism, the old ideologies, and the prefascist parties were all "liquidated"; it was proof of the "cadaveric impotence" of the older, traditional forces.[65] In addition, the vote led to the clearest attack on the passivity and malleability of the masses. The election results confirmed two concepts that Rosselli had insisted on in the face of criticism from orthodox socialists and Marxists: the first idea was the tremendous force of nationalism, especially in those countries that have only recently been united, like Italy and Germany, where it functions as a Sorelian myth for reactionary ideology; and the second idea was the absurdity of conducting the battle against fascism when allied solely with the proletariat. Rosselli, who never held out hope of a spontaneous mass uprising, came danger-ously close himself to denigrating the "masses," calling them "brutal, igno-rant, impotent, feminine, prey to he who makes the most noise, who has the most money, he who has success,"[66] and in a comment that infuriated his antifascist colleagues, held that "fascism is the most perfect mass regime in history."[67]

Fascist regimes could be defeated only by returning to the people a sense of autonomy, reason, and the value of freedom. This process would take place first among a minority of intellectuals and workers, and only then, perhaps, would spread to the masses. "We are not democrats, in the too–mechanical sense that the word has assumed; we do not attribute too much importance to majorities and minorities if the majorities conduct them-selves like sheep."[68] Several months earlier Rosselli had addressed the rela-tionship between GL and the masses, since the movement had often been criticized for ignoring the problem and accused of "individualism," "ro-mantic voluntarism," and the "cult of heroism." In fascist Italy, where the regime—through outright terror, legislation, and more subtle forms such as parades, sporting events, and the control of leisure—had effective con-trol of the masses, a policy of combating fascism on that level made no sense. The masses were inert and lacking political consciousness. Because of this situation in Italy—and in language that echoed Lenin—the only activity that could be carried out would be the responsibility of active and combative minorities that take up the essential task of educating the cadres for the revolutionary struggle.[69]

Indirectly related to the problem of nationalism was the fascist regime's economic policy of the corporate state. As developed by Alfredo Rocco between 1926 and 1929, corporativism attempted to synthesize syndicalism and nationalism. In theory, labor and capital were to be reconciled in an institutional arrangement that benefited both social categories. In reality, corporativism was a program to defuse the revolutionary potential of the proletariat, absorbing workers into obligatory and authoritarian corporations. By 1930 there were corporations controlling agriculture, industry, banking, commerce, transportation, the professions, and the arts. Supposedly a way to supersede the problems of free trade and class divisions emphasized by Marxists and socialists, corporativism contributed to the decline of living standards and wages for workers while increasing profits for industrialists and landowners. Rosselli, trained as a political economist, saw through the charade. The corporations were simply a new bureaucratic organ, without any autonomy, without any connection to real life, impotent to change the essential social structure of the country or relations between classes. "It could give neither bread, work, nor dignity to those that lacked bread, work, and dignity." The corporations were entities created for political, not economic, purposes. Fascism had arrived at a modus vivendi with the dominant social classes in Italy, fashioning a division of labor: the fascist oligarchy would control politics, whereas economics would be left to the bourgeoisie and workers would be left to their own devices. The corporate state was not a revolutionary solution to a millennial problem, but merely "a technical instrument of modern reaction."[70] Louis Rosenstock-Franck, a French economist and sociologist, agreed. In an article published in *Esprit*, he called corporativism "essentially the most ordinary, banal capitalism; obsequious to the demands of dictatorship and conserving its two fundamental attributes: liberal private property and profit." [71]

The insistence on nationalism's continuing power led Rosselli on to some dangerous ideological terrain. With events in Europe pointing toward a final crisis of democracy, he was willing to experiment in his search for allies, and became interested in the French neosocialists. In February 1934, a right-wing coup d'état was narrowly defeated even as Parisians took to the streets, chanting "Better Hitler than Blum!" The French socialists were divided because of the heresies propounded by neosocialists Déat, Marquet, and Montagnon. Marcel Déat was, like Blum, a graduate of the prestigious École Normale Supérieur; Adrien Marquet was mayor of Bordeaux, and Barthelemy Montagnon a former communist. Rosselli, ever ready to question established ideological truths, devoted several essays[72] to defending the "neos," a fact not forgotten later by his political enemies when their fascist sympathies became clear. The "neos" were serving a vital function in pointing out the persistence of nationalism as a potent, perhaps the most potent, ideology in the 1930s and the persistence of the capitalist system. Contrary to communist and orthodox socialist ideology, which saw fascism as the last gasp of a decadent capitalist order, the neosocialists insisted that the bourgeoisie was stronger than ever and that capitalism was transforming itself into an economic entity that could be flexible and could survive the present crisis. European socialists ignored this possibility at their peril and lacked the courage to admit this reality. For Rosselli there was in Europe a deadly and dangerous conservatism: the ideological conservatism of the antifascists. "Paris," he wrote bitterly in 1935, was a "museum of antifascism."[73] The resulting paralysis only played into the hands of the fascists, thus allowing fascism to reverse roles and present itself as an innovative force, while the antifascists were trapped in their orthodox ideologies. The "neos" were accused of being heretics and fascists. "We can be heretics," Rosselli countered, "without being fascists; indeed, the only serious way to be antifascist is to be heretical."[74] Even more fundamental for Rosselli, the true heart of the matter was not so much whether the "neos" were correct in their interpretations but rather was in the response of the other socialists and the conception of the revolutionary struggle. It was a historical error to transform the political party into a sect, a Church, a depository of eternal and immutable truths. The political party was an instrument for relative and contingent ends, prepared to work for an indefinite series of economic and social changes. Except for the Labour Party in Britain, all socialist parties had delineated a credo that could not be challenged without calling into question their entire ideological edifice.

The depression that was sweeping across Europe after the Wall Street crash of 1929 had economically destroyed the middle class in Germany. Yet the bourgeoisie refused to become "proletarianized"—to become the passive instrument of dialectical materialism—and had gone on the attack, "using the most bestial forms, armed with all the rancid prejudices of race and caste, with a primitive violence." Throughout Europe the middle class constituted the directive force, "the sinewy tissue of society," not only because of its economic position but also because of its social function. "Without its active participation, no great movement appears possible, no great movement has been created in the nineteenth and twentieth centuries."[75] For all the important movements of modern history, the bourgeoisie had been the decisive force. It was time to abandon the Marxist belief in the intransigent and historically bankrupt bourgeoisie. In order for socialism and antifascism to succeed, an alliance had to be forged between the proletariat and the enlightened elements of the bourgeoisie. The experience of Europe in the 1920s and 1930s gave ample proof that the proletariat was not in a position to gain power through either legal or illegal means.

Rosselli had allowed Déat to publish an article in the *Quaderni di Giustizia e Libertà* in which the French neosocialist had urged a "national socialism" for "blocking the path of fascism."[76] The reality of early-twentieth-century Europe, argued Déat, was the dominance of a neomercantilism, a permeating nationalism, and an entrenched bourgeoisie. This was the reality, not the prophecies of the *Communist Manifesto;* and if capitalism sought refuge in nationalism, socialism had to follow and attack it on a national level. The neosocialists suggested the impossibility of international socialist action in the present context, yet demanded some action, with all its risks and limitations. "I confess," Rosselli concluded, "that I agree with them."[77]

This obsession with renewing socialism, with trying to find some way out of the impotence of international socialism, explains Rosselli's attraction to the French neosocialist position. Impatient with the insipid socialism of Blum and willing to break the taboo of pacifism, Rosselli once again left himself vulnerable to ferocious criticism; indeed, he seemed to invite it, anxious to use the polemics to push the socialists and antifascists to reconsider their political assumptions. However, the "neos" were advocating a state socialism, something that Rosselli had always opposed and their slogan—*ordre, autorité, nation*—was appropriated, as Rosselli recognized, from the rhetoric of the Right.

As could be expected, Rosselli and the movement were criticized for being elitist, a "party of intellectuals" that denigrated the masses. "La lezione della Sarre" generated such a response that Rosselli devoted two more articles on the related topics of class and socialization.[78] Again he repeated that antifascism could not limit itself to fighting fascism only on the basis of class warfare. The simple, Manichean idea that the bourgeoisie was fascist and that the proletariat was antifascist actually hindered the struggle against the regime. With Italian fascism in power for over a decade and Hitler in Germany, the traditional "class" parties were forced to reconsider their positions. Previously, liberty, rights, and the law were considered "bourgeois"; now buffeted by "the fascist hurricane, they [the class parties] quickly and furiously reevaluate the old idols, they exalt them and recognize that the struggle for rights, freedom, and justice against the fascist 'barbarities' cannot be conducted on a strictly class terrain."[79] Rosselli was not denying the fact of class conflict but was only insisting that fascism was a phenomenon that went beyond mere class divisions to engulf all of civilization. In an argument that rejected Croce's "parenthesis" theory of fascism and anticipated Croce's later theory of fascism as "moral sickness," Rosselli pointed out that "fascism is the visible expression of the decadence and corruption of the world in which we live, in all its diverse aspects, in morale, culture, freedom, as in the economy and political life. It concerns all the people, *including a good part of the proletariat*. It is truly totalitarian."[80]

Influenced by his mother, by nationalist currents in Florence, and by the history of Italian Jews who saw their emancipation tied to the unification of the modern state, Rosselli had always insisted on the power of national-ism—but a cosmopolitan, enlightened, humane nationalism in the tradi-tion of a Herder or a Mazzini. The phenomenon of exile only fortified those ideas. As Said has perceptively pointed out:

> The interplay between nationalism and exile is like Hegel's dialectic of servant and master, opposites informing and constituting each other. All nationalisms in their early stages develop from a condition of estrange-ment . . . Triumphant, achieved nationalism then justifies, retrospectively as well as prospectively, a history selectively strung together in narrative form . . . Exiles feel . . . an urgent need to reconstitute their broken lives, usually by choosing to see themselves as part of a triumphant ideology or a restored people. The crucial thing is that a state of exile free from this triumphant ideology—designed to reassemble an exile's broken history into a new whole—is virtually unbearable, and virtually impossible in today's world.[81]

Rosselli's thinking and writing about exile and nationalism inevitably led to an examination of the role and function of the state in the modern age. In the twentieth century, and perhaps in all centuries, Rosselli believed, the state is "essentially an oppressive machine."[82] In a more biting critique, which was worthy of the best writings of the anarchists, he opened an essay with an echo of *The Communist Manifesto*, "There is a monster in the modern world—the State—that is devouring society."[83] The modern dicta-torial state has overthrown all human relations and substituted forced associations in the place of spontaneous, organic, creative ties. It is the logical conclusion of a process of statism in which there is no longer any place for human beings. *Homo sapiens* (thinking man) has been replaced by *homo servans* (servile man) serving the dictates of production, bureauc-racy, race, or empire. Completely subjecting human beings, the state com-pounds their degradation by demanding to be worshiped, by forcing its subjects to rejoice in their slavery. "The alternative by now is clear: either the State will crush us, Society; or we defeat the modern State, liberating Society."

In a direct criticism of Hegel—and even more so of his servile followers—Rosselli pointed out that the state has been transformed in the last century from being a part of society into an absolute, a universal, the divine idea manifest on earth. The only spiritual reality, the only true freedom could be achieved through the state, and the "total submission to its exalted ends . . . . In the beginning *the* State did not exist; only states existed." In contrast to the modern, despotic, centralizing state, there is the alternative of social federalism. The prototype of the "antistate" society were the medieval Italian communes with their free unions, representatives of the cities, the corporations, universities, confraternities, and societies. Even when the first lines of the absolutist state became obvious in the early modern period, there were associations and groups outside the sphere of the state, such as the Church or the aristocracy. The modern nation state was born with industrial capitalism and Jacobin democracy, both of which began as liberating forces; however, both degenerated into conservative and formal structures. In the space of little more than a century, because of modern war and economic crisis, citizens were transformed from voters into subjects. As modern war gave the state unlimited control over the blood of its subjects, the economic crisis gave it unprecedented control over society. "Masters of bread and blood, the State, in fascist countries, now commands the minds and consciousness of its subjects . . . The alienation of man in favor of the monster is thus complete. We are in full barbarism."

Explicitly relating his position to the anarchist tradition of Proudhon and Bakunin, Rosselli called for a strategy of a permanent, adversarial, and confrontational stance versus the state. His revolutionary, liberal socialism was the antithesis of the idea that equates socialism and statism as it had developed in Stalin's Russia. Rosselli approvingly quoted the Marx of the Gotha Program ("Freedom consists in transforming the State, the supreme organ of the society, into an organ that is entirely subordinate to society") and the Marx of *The Civil War in France* (the state is "the parasite that nourishes itself on the substance of society and paralyzes free will").

The only possible conclusion from this analysis was that the Italian revolution, built on the ruins of fascist capitalism, could not be anything but a federative association with the widest possible autonomy and freedom. Although there would still be a need for a central administration, it would be at the service of society. Or as Rosselli so succinctly concluded the essay, "Man is the end. Not the State."[84]

Antifascist Concentration

During the 1920s and 1930s, antifascism acted as a unifying force for those Italians who had emigrated to France for political or economic reasons. The most important antifascist group in exile was the Antifascist Concentration (AC), formed in May 1927 under the general direction of Pietro Nenni, which attempted to unite a wide range of ideological positions under a single umbrella organization.[85] Understandably and regrettably, there were several problems inherent in this enterprise. In Rosselli's mind, it simply re-created, in exile, the failed policies and mind-set of the Aventine Secession and was irrevocably trapped by its prefascist liberal mentality. Relations between the Antifascist Concentration and Justice and Liberty were therefore tense from the beginning. In September 1930, the two groups signed a Union and Action Pact, but the fundamental differences were not easily resolved. (As can be surmised, the anarchists and communists did not participate in the Antifascist Concentration, the former because they were suspicious of political hierarchies and the latter because the organization was *piccolo borghese*—petit bourgeoisie—and "social fascist"). The Antifascist Concentration still believed in a peaceful, or at least legal, stand against Mussolini's regime, whereas Rosselli was already insisting that the antifascist struggle had to adopt more active, revolutionary tactics. The various political parties that comprised the Antifascist Concentration were convinced that the regime was ready to fall at any moment and that Italy would return to the prefascist status quo ante. They were not alone: political thinkers, historians, and economists all over the world were predicting a short-lived regime. Then the old political parties would simply return to Italy and take up their positions again. This was to be a central point of contention between the various antifascist groups and Rosselli's movement; the former were mired in a "negative" antifascism— they stressed what they were against; Rosselli, on the other hand insisted that to attract adherents and to legitimate their quest for power, antifascists had to have a "positive" program as well. Only the communists would have a program as developed as Justice and Liberty.

Rosselli insisted also on attacking the *fiancheggiatori* such as the monarchy, the Papacy, and high capital, whereas the Antifascist Concentration, which was composed of Monarchists, Catholics, and Liberals, was much more muted in its criticism of these institutions. The Monarchy had been implicated with fascism since October 1922, and after 1929 the Vatican had irrevocably linked itself to the regime. In July 1930, *Giustizia e Libertà* carried as its lead essay "Contro Rinascenti Illusioni" (Against Renascent Illusions), in which it defended itself from charges that its republican and anticlerical position was harmful to the antifascist movement. The Antifascist Concentration was mistaken on at least three points: that the Monarchy could be an element of antifascism because the king was antifascist and the military supported the King, not fascism; that the Vatican was an important force because Catholic Action was loyal to the Pope and therefore antifascist; and that to fight without these forces would be a political error since fascism could not be defeated without their support. But, the article responded, didn't the Monarchy cede political power to the dictator, and hadn't the Pope declared that Mussolini was "the man sent to us by Providence?"[86] To ascribe antifascist sentiments to the King and the Pope was folly and self-defeating.

Rosselli had a delicate political balancing act to perform: he insisted that the antifascist struggle should encompass as many people and positions as possible, including Catholics and Liberals. At the same time, Rosselli and his colleagues were adamant in their conception of Italy as a republic. Consequently, they alienated the conservative and more moderate antifascist elements. The papal-monarchical antifascists, for their part, were caught in an inescapable contradiction. The Catholics insisted on a second Risorgimento; the essay pointed out that this was cynical hypocrisy since Pope Pius IX had vociferously opposed the first one, even to the point of inviting a foreign army into the country to prevent national unification and issuing *The Syllabus of Errors,* in which he condemned liberalism, materialism, and modernism in all its forms.

Rosselli's judgment of the Antifascist Concentration was not entirely negative. He recognized that it served an important function in the early antifascist emigration by maintaining an atmosphere of collaboration and cooperation among the exiles. It managed to preserve vital forces and present to the world another aspect of Italy and the Italians. Yet Rosselli agreed to join the AC only in 1932, almost three years after the founding of Justice and Liberty and only after lengthy negotiations concerning the autonomy of both groups and a clear division of labor: the AC would be responsible for all activity in exile, whereas Justice and Liberty was recognized as having responsibility for clandestine activity in Italy. On 12–13 November 1932, the General Council of the AC unanimously voted to accept the so-called "November Pact" with Justice and Liberty, which it recognized as "the unity of revolutionary forces consecrated in Italy" and agreed to fight for the following objectives:

1. A Democratic Republic, based on the working classes, organized on the widest foundation of autonomy, on the freedom of political and trade union associations, freedom of the press, a free, secular and unitary school, the separation of Church and State and the abolition of the Lateran Pacts;
2. A New Social Order that shatters the capitalist monopoly of the means of production and exchange . . . the socialization of essential industrial and financial institutions, factory control and democracy, land to the peasants, a home for everyone;
3. International Peace through a radical program of disarmament . . . the development of federalism and the absolute respect for cultural autonomy . . . free exchange of goods and labor, the collaboration of free people in the creation of a United States of Europe.[87]

Yet the accord could not hold. There was a fundamental difference in the character of the two organizations that Rosselli recognized as insuperable. The AC was legal, public, and pacific, whereas Justice and Liberty was illegal and revolutionary. Silvio Trentin had been appointed to represent Justice and Liberty in the Central Committee of the AC, characterizing the movement's leftward evolution. When in April 1934, the Central Committee of Justice and Liberty sent a proposal for a more formal unification with the AC, it was rejected, and the entire edifice of the Antifascist Concentration collapsed.[88] In its call for a unified revolutionary front, Justice and Liberty insisted on the trinity of "Liberty, Socialism, Republic" and suggested a congress be held on 10 June 1934—the tenth anniversary of Giacomo Matteotti's assassination—to consecrate the birth of a new Italian revolutionary, socialist, republican party that would synthesize the five components of the AC (PSI, PRI, PSLI, LIDU, and GL). The most controversial points in the "Proposta" were the suggestion of debating whether to join the Second International and the abolition of the various party journals and organs, to be replaced by one newspaper in exile and one in Italy. The "Proposta" specifically called for the dismantling of the Antifascist Concentration, which was to be replaced by a new revolutionary party. The

LIDU would direct a proletarian university in Paris with branches in all the principal centers of emigration. The CGL would become the liaison between the new party and the workers and peasants by adopting the structural form of the Belgian Workers' Party, in which the fusion of political and trade union forces would be complete.[89] Rosselli may have even assumed that these conditions would be rejected and thence precipitate the end of the Antifascist Concentration.

Sure enough, the PSI under the practical guidance of Nenni and the theoretical orientation of Saragat, had rejected the "Proposta" in early April, and on 5 May 1934 the General Council of the AC reviewed and approved the decision by the Central Committee to dissolve the organization. Meanwhile, Rosselli, undaunted and perhaps even spurred by the collapse of the Antifascist Concentration, continued his critique of traditional antifascism. In the last issue of *Quaderni di Giustizia e Libertà*, he made his strongest criticism yet of the old parties, declaring boldly that

> The old parties are dead. They survive in that museum of antifascism that is Paris, but in Italy they no longer have a hold. They died precisely because they were alive yesterday, because their function and essential motives are implanted in the old society that fascism decisively liquidated. To defeat fascism, one can no longer remain poised between two epochs; it is necessary, with open-mindedness, to impose oneself in the center of the fascist epoch, assuming fascism as the point of departure.[90]

The Antifascist Concentration was not the only group critical of Justice and Liberty; the PSI and the Italian Republican Party (PRI) also initiated polemics against the movement. In truth, the PSI had come through the fascist experience in worse shape than either GL or the PCI. The history of the PSI since the advent of fascism was a bewildering story of schisms, alliances, and ruptures. Founded in 1892, it had achieved important victories and had made great strides until January 1921, when at the Congress of Livorno, the PCI had been formed. What remained of the PSI was still divided between the maximalists and the reformists, a situation that led to another schism in Rome the next year, which saw the birth of the PSU. These divisions were carried over into exile. In March 1930, at a meeting of the PSI in exile, there was still another schism between "maximalists" under Angelica Balabanoff and *Avanti!*, published in Paris, and "fusionists" led by Pietro Nenni, with *Avanti! (L'Avvenire del Lavoratore)*, published in Zurich. A month later the "maximalists" withdrew from the Antifascist

Concentration. At the first Congress of the PSI in exile in July, the PSI and the PSULI [Partito Socialista Unitario dei Lavoratori Italiani] were unified. By July of the next year, a preliminary accord had been reached between the PSI and GL that paved the way for the entrance of the latter into the Antifascist Concentration in November.

The polemic with the PSI began with the publication of Emilio Lussu's essay "Orientamenti" in the *Quaderni*. In Lussu we hear an echo of Rosselli: "Today it is difficult to speak the language of socialism. Socialism is discredited . . . Bakunin used to say that for an uprising, one had to have the devil in the flesh. Continuing with the same figurative language, it can be said that democratic socialism . . . has had a sleeping angel in the flesh." [91] Italian socialists, Lussu argued, had to situate themselves historically between the French Jacobins and the Russian Bolsheviks; in other words, they had to reconcile the victory of individualism as conquered in the religious and political revolutions of the past centuries with the collective demands of production and exchange in modern civilization. The Sardinian radical insisted that "for the democratic revolution and even for the socialist revolution, living bourgeois are more necessary than dead socialists." The opportunity for an invigorating and historical renewal of Italian socialism had been lost because the PSI was extremely jealous and sensitive concerning its position as the only socialist entity in exile and refused to consider a fusion with the younger, heretical exiles in GL. The PSI felt it could not risk losing a possible alliance with the PCI by collaborating with GL; for its part, GL refused to abandon its conception of the political struggle and its desire to begin tabula rasa. [92]

Relations between GL and the PRI were also strained. In August 1930, the republicans Cipriano Facchinetti and Raffaele Rossetti resigned from the leadership of Justice and Liberty. A serious rift developed when the PRI created Giovane Italia as a clandestine group in Italy, modeled on Mazzini's subversive organization during the Risorgimento. When in June 1931, GL and the PSI signed an accord, the PRI saw this as an attempt to limit its influence in Italy. Rosselli continually had to insist on the republican credentials of GL. In a postscript to a letter sent to the Central Committee of the Antifascist Concentration on 1 December 1931, he decried the rumors that the split between the PRI and GL was occasioned by the "lack of confidence on the part of intransigent elements of the Republican Party toward the republicanism of Justice and Liberty." The schism, Rosselli maintained, was caused exclusively by personal motives, and no responsible person questioned the republican credentials of Justice and Liberty.[93]

Rosselli was criticized from all quarters and accused of killing the Antifascist Concentration; it was a charge, perhaps, that he willingly accepted. Perhaps the severest criticism came, ironically, from Angelo Tasca. Born into a working-class family, Tasca had been a colleague of Gramsci, Togliatti, and Terracini in the PCI and had developed into a fierce anti-Stalinist after spending 1928 in Moscow. For his heresies, he was expelled from the PCI in September 1929. Although he became a French citizen who collaborated with the Vichy regime during World War II, Tasca had earlier written an important and well-regarded study of the rise of fascism. In May 1934, Tasca accused Rosselli of provoking a crisis that could only benefit fascism; in fact, Tasca saw the dissolution of the Antifascist Concentration as fascism's greatest success since 1926. His criticism was acerbic: "From the ideological point of view, your group is heterogeneous and, it appears to me, lacking true originality. Nothing that goes beyond old-fashioned revisionism . . . A sequel of Gobetti and a pinch of activism are not enough to give your thought a critical and positive content sufficient that you can alone provide a doctrinal renewal of Italian socialism." Rosselli responded that very day, lamenting Tasca's misinformed criticism and insisting that even a "pinch of activism" was better than "a thousand Marxist exegeses."[94] But his impassioned defense of GL fell on deaf ears; Tasca remained unconvinced.

The PCI

Relations between Justice and Liberty and the PCI were often tense and not without acerbity. There was more here than a hint of sibling rivalry; the PCI, with good cause, perceived GL as its most serious competitor for the allegiance of young, active antifascists. This perception is borne out by the time, resources, and attention that the PCI devoted to attacking the ideological, theoretical, and organizational positions of the new movement. The two groups were the most vital, innovative, and well-organized of the exiled and underground antifascist organizations.[95] When GL was created in the autumn of 1929, the PCI was undergoing a particularly delicate moment in its history. Many of its leading lights were either in prison or in exile, the first implications of Stalinism were leaking out of Moscow, and bureaucrats were being criticized for their expulsion of both Angelo Tasca and Ignazio Silone. In early 1930, foreshadowing the doctrine of "social fascism," the PCI passed judgment on the general state of antifascism and on the Antifascist Concentration in particular: "All these movements today become fascistized quickly, in their ideology and the political orientation of their leading cadres and seek, or have already found, organic ties with fascism to fulfill a function of preserving the capitalist order threatened by the revolution."[96]

The first reference to Justice and Liberty in the communist press appeared in April 1930, in an anonymous review of Lussu's and Nitti's books chronicling their escape from Lipari. The reviewer was bitterly sarcastic and heaped scorn on the "romantic literature" that prized "exemplary action" and "the clamorous gesture."[97] A few months later, Ruggero Grieco unwittingly revealed his ignorance when he wrote that Justice and Liberty and the Antifascist Concentration were, for ideological purposes, identical.[98] In an attempt to paint the new movement as antiproletarian, Palmiro Togliatti wrote that "the men of Justice and Liberty are, amongst the social democrats, the furthest away from the working classes, the most decisively against every class agitation,"[99] whereas Giorgio Amendola, son of the murdered Giovanni Amendola, wrote, "That which social democracy conceals under a demagogic phraseology, [GL] declares openly . . . the men of Justice and Liberty do not hide their reactionary language."[100] This rhetoric underlay an inability or perhaps a refusal to acknowledge that Rosselli's movement went beyond the traditional thinking of European social democracy. Until 1936, Rosselli and Justice and Liberty were considered prime examples of what the Communist International had defined as "social fascism."

The theoreticians of the PCI were to examine and attack specific documents produced by the movement. In March 1931, *Giustizia e Libertà* published Rosselli's "Agli Operai," a direct appeal to the workers of Italy, aimed at socialists, republicans, communists, democrats and others in the antifascist cause. He went on to propose a program of "necessary freedoms" (association, organization, press, universal suffrage, and emigration); the establishment of a constituent assembly; the immediate release of all political prisoners; the immediate revision of all collective contracts of labor; the transferal to workers and peasant organizations of all the property of the fascist party and its organizations; the reestablishment of the internal factory workshop Commissions and the widening of their powers; an immediate reduction of the military budget; subsidies and public works;

the abolition of the grain duty and immediate reduction of the price of bread and foodstuffs; reduction of rents, construction of popular homes; the confiscation of the goods of those responsible for the dictatorship and a Revolutionary Tribunal for fascist leaders.[101]

The Italian communists could not allow such a program—so similar to their own—to go uncriticized. At the Fourth Party Congress of the PCI in Cologne (1931), Luigi Longo ("Gallo") was given the task of responding to Rosselli. In *Gli inganni e le menzogne di Giustizia e Libertà* (The deceptions and lies of Justice and Liberty), Longo accused the new movement of bringing together all the most heterogeneous and reactionary elements of bourgeois society, impeding the organization and action of the working class, and denying the possibility of a genuine communist revolution in Italy. The distinction that Rosselli and GL made between parliamentary democracy and fascism was a smokescreen to conceal class interests; the Soviet model for Longo was the only form of effective democracy.[102] Ironically, "Agli Operai" had pointed out the uncomfortable truth that fascist Italy had become the principal supplier of war material to Stalinist Russia. Indeed, on 25 September 1933, Potemkin, the Soviet ambassador to Italy, signed the "Friendship, Non-Aggression and Neutrality Pact" with Mussolini's regime.[103] Whereas Rosselli's criticism of Stalin's Russia was clear and unwavering, Silvio Trentin praised the Soviet Constitution of 1936, and Andre Caffi was more ambiguous in his judgment. All three—and the others in the movement as well—agreed, though, that Stalin was strangling the revolution with his bureaucracy and forced collectivization.

For Rosselli the first order of business was to defeat fascism; once the regime was defeated, each party would return to its own course of action. If the communists were to demonstrate in future elections that they had the consent of the majority, Justice and Liberty would be the first to recognize their right to govern.[104] But the communists, Rosselli insisted, in their scorn of "bourgeois values," failed to recognize that liberty was of paramount importance and that the essence of the antifascist resistance was the struggle for freedom:

Freedom is bread, it is dignity, it is the necessary condition for every transformation and every improvement, it is and will be justice . . . All men in all ages of history, among all the lands of the earth, have longed for freedom. The difference between men and animals is precisely in this aspiration of men for a life of freedom, for a life ordered by reason and justice . . . Freedom, in a word, is the people as master of *their own destiny.*[105]

Luigi Longo saw this language as appealing to the least politically conscious segment of Italian society, the petite bourgeoisie, and as characteristic of "the deceptions and lies" of the movement. Longo's diatribe was followed by a much more serious critique of Rosselli and GL, this time by Giorgio Amendola, whose essay "With or Against the Proletariat?" appeared in June 1931. Here for the first time was an analysis of Justice and Liberty rather than a polemical treatise commissioned by party leaders:

> These young intellectuals, nurtured under the Crocean influence of ideal-ist philosophy, lacking a knowledge of Marx because of the poverty of Italian Marxism, were marked by a pragmatism, a voluntarism (the influence of *La Voce* and Sorel) and had accepted the *moral* character of the antifascist struggle, seeing in the "moral question" not just a simple determination of the responsibility of single fascist leaders in this or that assassination, but the entire problem of the "liberation" of the Italian people, of its conscious participation in political life.[106]

Praising Gobetti and *La Rivoluzione Liberale* (and repeating the famous judgment passed on Gobetti by Gramsci), Amendola went on to criticize Rosselli and Nenni's *Il Quarto Stato* of 1925–26 as an example of how a generation educated in idealism tried with great effort to understand Marx, only to end with confused and disordered thinking. Justice and Liberty had managed to attract many of the forces of the Left and the ideological descendants of Gobetti and to forge them into a new movement. But, according to Amendola, the desire to maintain such a diverse group meant, in the end, total ideological confusion and equivocation—hence, the ironic and paradoxical intellectual poverty of GL, which had acquired a reputa-tion as a "movement of intellectuals."

Rosselli immediately recognized the force behind Amendola's critique and personally responded in the inaugural issue of the *Quaderni di Giu-stizia e Libertà*. Agreeing that Gobetti, the "master and sure guide for all," had been correct in understanding the social and historical function of the proletariat, Rosselli challenged the communists' "appropriation" of the martyred intellectual. Although they declared themselves followers of Gobetti, the young Turinese intellectual himself had once written, "In Marx, I am seduced by the historian and the apostle of the workers' move-ment. The economist is dead, with surplus-value, the dream of the aboli-

tion of classes, with the prophecy of collectivism . . . Historical materialism
. . . and the theory of class struggle are instruments forever embedded in
social science and are his glory as a theorist."[107] Rosselli went on to counter
the charge of "intellectual poverty." Yet the most urgent aspect of the
present situation was to defeat fascism by creating the largest possible
alliance for concerted action after a shameful period of inactivity and
impotence. As a countercharge, Rosselli accused Amendola and the communists of believing in the "grotesque phantom" of "social fascism."
Whereas Amendola and the communists saw the revaluation of the lira in
1927 as proof of the alliance between the bourgeoisie and the regime,
Rosselli pointed out that the revaluation, which was resisted by the banks,
was imposed on economics minister Volpi by Mussolini as a result of the
dictator's economic ignorance, in order to maintain the prestige of the
regime. "Where you see a proof of fascist-bourgeois identification, we see
one of the classic examples of the autonomy of the dictatorial mechanism
from the social forces that converged to create it." Fascism cannot be
identified with a single social and economic class; it springs from roots in
the Italian soil and expresses profound vices, latent weaknesses, and the
poverty of the entire nation. It was Gobetti, as Rosselli recalled, who
formed the "stupendous judgement" that "fascism is the autobiography of
a nation."

In concluding his essay, Rosselli addressed Amendola's question head-on:

> Your article opens with a question: With or against the proletariat? We
> close ours with the natural—the only possible—answer: with the prole-
> tariat. But we quickly add that there are diverse ways to serve the cause of
> the proletariat.
>
> Communism serves the proletariat by reducing it to a herd, imposing a
> jesuitical discipline, precluding autonomy, or freedom of criticism and
> judgment, deluding it with a perpetual exaltation of its virtues, the easier
> to render it the object of a bureaucratic dictatorship of the party.
>
> Justice and Liberty intends to serve the proletariat by developing in it
> the sense of dignity, of autonomy, of freedom; pushing it to struggle and
> sacrifice, without vain, flattering and humiliating adulation; to make of
> every worker a *man*, in the highest and most noble sense of the word, free
> in the workshop as well as life, before the *padrone* as well as before his
> conscience.[108]

Amendola's essay was part of a well-organized campaign to discredit
Rosselli and the new movement in the eyes of the antifascist resistance. At

least five major articles were published in the PCI party organ in exile, *Lo Stato Operaio,* between September 1931 and November 1932.[109] Togliatti began by recapitulating the standard line: Justice and Liberty shared many of the characteristics of the failed Aventine Secession (no mention was made of Rosselli's fierce condemnation of the Aventine); its exiled leaders were "reactionary ideologues"—indeed, the very fact that they were in exile was a "capitulation, a flight, a new betrayal" (no mention of Togliatti in Moscow). For Togliatti the new movement represented the attempt by the petite bourgeoisie to carve out an autonomous position in the antifascist crusade and to gain control of the entire resistance movement. But the petit bourgeois mentality inevitably becomes an instrument of counterrevolution and the carrier of the most reactionary solutions on the political and ideological field. Again the communists took up the cudgel of Gobetti with which to beat Rosselli. A rapprochement between Gobetti and Rosselli was not only impossible but also absurd.

> Gobetti was a poor intellectual, while Rosselli is a rich one, objectively and personally tied to the ruling capitalist classes . . . Gobetti was a scholar, passionately taken with ideas and had an original brilliance. Rosselli is a worthless dilettante, lacking any serious theoretical formulation . . . Rosselli's book [*Socialisme libéral*] is directly allied with fascist political literature . . . it is a thin, antisocialist libel and nothing else.[110]

Togliatti's appropriation of the martyred Gobetti was cynical maneuvering; when the young Turinese scholar was publishing his first journal in 1919, Togliatti had grouped him with "the parasites of culture."[111]

Two fundamental precepts of Rosselli's thought—the centrality of freedom and the need for a second Risorgimento—also come under attack. "The exaltation of 'freedom,'" according to Togliatti, "is a reactionary enterprise," whereas the antifascist revolution could be nothing less than a revolution "against the Risorgimento, against its ideology, against the solution that it had given to the problem of the unity of the State and all the problems of national life." This though, was precisely Rosselli's point: although the political outcome of unification was to be deplored, no one could deny the moral, spiritual, and ethical function that it had performed. Yet Togliatti concluded his first attack by declaring that Rosselli and the followers of GL were the "stupid and wicked servants of capitalism and fascism."[112]

After the hostile reception to the appearance of *Liberal Socialism,* this response was, in effect, Rosselli's second baptism of fire in the polemical world of antifascism. Yet the communist intrigue served only to make him work harder in diffusing the message of the movement. From Vienna where he was conducting research, Nello wrote to his older brother:

> I am proud of you and your work: little by little your name begins to be repeated by all as one who will one day be on the front line in Italy. Forward, therefore—but beware . . . choose your collaborators well . . . If at times you feel yourself alone or ignored, chase away the thought; there is a great deal of fire beneath the ashes in Italy . . . You will finish, we will finish with victory if you never give up, not even for a moment, not even an inch.[113]

In December 1931, Giorgio Amendola, using the false name "Fortunato," made his way back to Italy with the mission of establishing contact with GL groups in Milan and Turin, to try to enlist members into the PCI.[114] Justice and Liberty had begun a new publication, *Voci d'officina* (Voices from the workshop), with an inaugural article entitled "Prospettive della lotta rivoluzionaria in Italia" and signed "A group of students belonging to Justice and Liberty." The PCI now clearly saw a challenge to its hold over the proletariat. One brutally honest report was filed by a communist operative ("Marino") in Turin:

> One of the things most characteristic of this phenomenon [Justice and Liberty] and one of the most dangerous for the working class, is the indisputable intellectual honesty and sincere intentions of those that are building a revolutionary consciousness in Italy today outside the party. It is painful for a communist to say it, but I have had the impression that the aversion to fascism is clearer in certain sections of the intellectual petite bourgeoisie than in the proletariat of Turin.[115]

When GL published its revolutionary program[116] in January 1932, the PCI returned to the fray with this description: "a masterpiece of hypocrisy, lies and stupidity," that was not very different from the fascist program of 1919.[117] In truth, the new attack did not do much more than repeat the charges leveled by Togliatti several months before. A central tenet of this analysis was that there could be no revolutionary forces outside the proletariat; by definition, all other social and economic groups were reactionary.

One result of the Program of 1932 was to bring the problem of the peasantry and land-tenure into sharper focus. During the first decades of the twentieth century, socialists and communists had tended to focus on the industrialized proletariat in the North while the fundamental problems of the vast majority of the population went unheeded. Because of the work of Salvemini and Tommaso Fiore, Rosselli and GL had devoted more attention to the South. Now the PCI was faced with a specific proposal; it had to respond. The task was given to Ruggero Grieco, whose analysis of the *Mezzogiorno* was both sophisticated and subtle.[118] It had been a commonplace to argue that feudalism continued in the South: however, Grieco claimed that although there was a residue of feudalism, the essence of the problem was precisely in the tenacity of a usurious capitalism that determined social relations. Also, the plan to confiscate land and redistribute it to the peasants represented a golden opportunity for speculators.[119]

But the aspect of GL's agrarian program that aroused the most vehement criticism from socialists and communists alike was the concession to granting an indemnity for confiscated land. Here was proof, charged the communists, of the bourgeois mentality of Rosselli and his colleagues. In light of this vociferous criticism and Rosselli's shift to the Left, the proposal for an indemnity was dropped in the summer of 1935.

Rosselli defended Justice and Liberty from the charge that it had a fetish for private property; indeed, their position was even more intransigent than that of the communists. The defense of private property as developed by nineteenth- and twentieth-century liberals came under strong attack in Rosselli's writings. These liberals had written of private property as a necessary "social function" or self-interest as a "reward for abstinence" or individual initiative as "concrete morality." In truth, he felt that these were nothing more than "the fig leaves with which the bourgeoisie covers the economic reality of capitalistic puritanism."[120] Where Rosselli and the communists differed was that the socialization desired by GL came from below, through education and experience (ironically similar to Gramsci's position), not forced from above. The question of socialization went to the methodological and ideological heart of the matter. "There could be nothing more foolish," Rosselli argued, "more counter-revolutionary, more anti-Marxist, than the desire to pass from the theory to the practice of universal socialization in one blow; just as there is nothing more foolish than the wish to apply to Italy, where the revolution has not begun . . . discussions that refer to Russia, fifteen years after the revolution."[121]

Russia, of course, was another contentious point between GL and the PCI. Rosselli's first analysis of Russia had come immediately after the February-March Revolution, when he admitted the West's ignorance of the Russian people—"a people that spoke in a language of blood."[122] His own privileged position caused him to be acutely conscious of the vast gulf separating the rich and the poor in Russia. In the face of the deepening worldwide economic crisis after 1929, many people had become infatuated with the supposed rational management of the Soviet economy. By 1932 Rosselli could write that the Soviets were "in fashion" and that the mechanics of the Five Year Plan with their new productionist religion were seducing thinkers and politicians in Europe and America. This was a suspect philocommunism; "let us not forget," wrote Rosselli, "that the bourgeois admirers of Stalin and the Five Year Plan are the same people who for ten years have repeated that Mussolini saved Italy and that the trains run on time."[123]

Andrea Caffi and Silvio Trentin continued to defend certain aspects of the Russian Revolution. Both were morally offended by the Stalinist dictatorship, but they supported a planned economy directed by the state and marveled at the spirit of sacrifice among young Russians. Perhaps influenced by Sorel, Trentin often referred to the "mystical faith" in the cause; no revolution could survive without its own myth, above all the myth of justice and liberty.[124]

Rosselli's own position concerning the revolution was complex and insightful.[125] He did not blindly defend the revolution; nor did he dismiss it out of hand. The revolution should not be equated with the Stalin dictatorship. The historical fact remained that the Bolshevik Revolution destroyed the czarist regime and had given land to the peasants (only to take it back later). It was this revolution, Rosselli wrote, "that we loved and defended." If a choice had to be made between the capitalist society and the Bolshevik world, "we must resolve ourselves, not without anguish, for the second . . . But it is this alternative that we refute and repulses us; this coarse and brutal dualism—God or the Devil; communism or capitalism. Between God and the Devil, we stand, very simply, for Man. Our effort will be turned toward the overcoming of the disagreement in the name of a synthesis; in the name of a socialism informed by the idea of freedom in which Plans serve men, not where men serve Plans."[126]

The PCI, for its part, responded that "whoever has reservations, whoever protests, whoever is scandalized by some domestic or foreign policy of the USSR . . . is not a friend of the proletariat, supports reaction, and *is not a true antifascist.*"[127]

The relationship between GL and the PCI oscillated from outright hostility to attempts at reconciliation, often depending on international events. Hitler's rise to power and the Ethiopian War were two instances when the rivals sought avenues of cooperation. When the fascist regime announced a military mobilization in anticipation of hostilities in Ethiopia in February 1935, Rosselli sent a letter to the leaders of the PCI, asking to organize an allied, concerted response. A few months later, after little had been done, he again wrote to socialist and communist leaders, calling for a congress of Italian antifascists, not just to issue the usual "platonic" opposition statement that substituted words for action, but to initiate real work among the masses.[128] Yet when the PSI and PCI met in Brussels on the eve of the Ethiopian War, representatives from GL did not attend.[129] From Moscow, Togliatti voiced his disagreement, while Luigi Longo tried to persuade GL to join the crusade against the war. Rosselli sent off two letters in which he advocated the creation of a revolutionary alliance that would undertake extensive propaganda and parallel a "bread-peace-freedom" triad with "freedom-socialism-republic." He even suggested two names for the new organization: "Fronte Antifascista Rivoluzionario" or "Alleanza Rivoluzionaria Antifascista."[130] The essence of this new alliance would be (1) that the essential work had to take place in Italy; (2) that its end was a mass movement; (3) that a direct appeal must be made to the entire population; (4) that a major point of propaganda was that European fascism was planning a major war; and (5) that domestic and exile activities and propaganda be better coordinated and that theory and action be tied closer together.[131] Yet the response from the PCI was cool; it was not until May–June 1934 that the doctrine of "social fascism" was dropped in favor of united and popular fronts. Events in Spain were to overshadow even the Ethiopian conflict. The Ethiopian War and the Spanish Civil War combined to push Rosselli further to the left in an attempt to create a true, revolutionary alliance that would be capable of a mass uprising in Italy.

Meeting Trotsky

Another point of conflict between GL and the PCI was Rosselli's attempt to form an alliance with Leon Trotsky. As the wily Togliatti managed to evade the fascist police, he also succeeded in finding his way through the labyrinthine halls of power in Moscow. In the 1930s, with Gramsci in prison, Togliatti pushed the PCI closer to a Stalinist position. Rosselli's attempt to convince Trotsky to collaborate on the *Quaderni di Giustizia e Libertà* was a deliberate affront to the official hierarchy of the PCI. Hence the charge—throughout the 1930s and even after the Second World War—that Rosselli and his colleagues were "Trotskyists." Rosselli decided to approach Trotsky because the two shared a common antifascist strategy: only a social revolution could defeat European fascism.

"We believe it useful," Rosselli had written to Trotsky in late 1933, "that a man such as you, who fulfills such an important function in the present organization of revolutionary forces, would not distrust a living movement, the only original movement that antifascism has created in these last years. We would very much like to have your collaboration on our journal . . . because we believe that your thought could be singularly illuminative and provocative in Italy where there are numerous Trotskyist elements that only we are capable of reaching."[132] After Trotsky responded that he was interested in meeting Rosselli, the two revolutionaries had a revealing encounter in May 1934. Rosselli found Trotsky "youthful and vigorous" and—because of the danger of assassination—ironically dressed in impeccable bourgeois attire. The Russian revolutionary sported a blue silk necktie, which kept drawing Rosselli's eye throughout their hour-long meeting: "a romantic note" amid the dry and serious conversation. Rosselli's account of the visit was not only an acute psychological portrait of his guest but also perhaps inadvertently a veiled self-portrait: "Trotsky late? Impossible. The engineer and mathematician of the revolution could anticipate or precipitate; never tarry. A cold and very powerful reasoning rules all the acts of his life, as the mechanism of a clock. His genius—even in opposition—is as an organizer."[133]

Playing on the name of Justice and Liberty, Rosselli recalled that in 1897 a beardless Trotsky "scientifically" organized the workers, exhorting them with the words "The greatest joy is that of struggle for the great cause of justice and liberty." Twenty years later, the Russian was triumphant as a theoretician of the Revolution and as a leader of the Red Army. But his first victory, in Rosselli's mind, was a psychological one over his own passionate and explosive temperament. Trotsky managed to control the "formidable charge of internal dynamite" but in the process became less human. By age 54, the Russian had not only achieved immense victories but also suffered tremendous defeats. The dust of those defeats, though, was the "dust of Olympus, like the clouds that enraptured the warriors of Homer." All borders had been closed to him, most tragically, the borders of Russia where there was no longer a place for the heretical Trotsky. He was a genius to be admired, but from a distance; up close he was too dangerous. For Rosselli, Trotsky was infinitely greater than Stalin, who knew only how to "administer" the Revolution. Stalin's victory and his theory of "socialism in one country" meant the "diminution and the embalming" of the Revolution; Trotsky, on the other hand, would have turned the Revolution in a "Napoleonic" direction with his theory of permanent revolution.

In vain Rosselli sought to penetrate the shell that Trotsky had drawn around himself. The Russian had a role to play in the world that he could not relinquish; the man and the personality were by now one and the same.

Although Trotsky admitted he could write for "bourgeois" journals, using them strictly for utilitarian and pragmatic purposes, the *Quaderni di Giustizia e Libertà* were another matter entirely. Trotsky based his reservations on an intransigent and orthodox Bolshevism, and no argument was going to change his mind. Against Rosselli's liberalism and "bourgeois idealism," he posed class warfare and the dictatorship of the proletariat as eternal truths. Rosselli replied by pointing to Gobetti's *La Rivoluzione Liberale*, which had defended the Russian Revolution. Trotsky remained skeptical. "Today you are against Mussolini and fascism. It's natural. You are poor emigrants, but tomorrow? Tomorrow when you return to Italy and the abyss between classes gapes open, which side will you be on?"

Rosselli protested that GL had learned the lessons of the Russian Revolution: they would not accept a Constituent Assembly nor a Kerensky. Justice and Liberty could not be imprisoned in the old formulas and experiences of the past. In Rosselli's mind, Trotsky appeared conservative, and like many others who had experienced and accomplished much, he felt that the future could hold nothing new. With but little enthusiasm, the Russian admitted the possibility of future collaboration, and the talk ended on a cool note.

Afterwards Rosselli reflected that Trotsky possessed a crystalline and admirably organized mind as reflected in the elegant composition of his masterpiece, *History of the Russian Revolution*. His will was imperious, his personality, powerful. But the man had disappeared into the personality and had lost his humanity. Nature had furnished Trotsky with many gifts except that of a Socratic mind. He was too sure, perfect, and strong to be able to understand others. He was a prisoner of his past and the historic polemic with Stalin. He was the living personification of the Revolution: in the same way that the revolution devours its children without pity, Trotsky coldly used everyone and everything to reach his goal. He had no need of other individuals; he needed only the masses, the "people," a social drama, a revolution. "We doubt," Rosselli concluded, "that the people of the West would find him to be their man."[134]

A Socialist Humanism

In June 1935, European intellectuals gathered in Paris for an international conference in "defense of culture." Present there, in addition to Rosselli, Salvemini, and an anonymous fascist spy, were André Malraux, Julien Benda, Emmanuel Mounier, André Gide, E. M. Forster, and Bertold Brecht. Klaus Mann, son of Thomas Mann, came closest to Rosselli's position, castigating a general failure to distinguish that which was vital from that which was dead in European society. Part of the failure was the fashionable attack against liberalism and democratic institutions: "We have defamed the original, indestructible, and noble desire of European peoples for *freedom*," he charged, "because in many cases liberalism has been degraded to a worthless phrase and alibi for high profits." The solution was in safeguarding individual freedom without sacrificing collective goals. This, for Mann, was a "socialist humanism."[135]

Rosselli sought to infuse the movement with such a socialist humanism. Justice and Liberty launched two publications to publicize its ideology and tactics. *Giustizia e Libertà* was published monthly in Paris beginning in November 1929. In May 1934, with the collapse of the Antifascist Concentration, *La Libertà* ceased publication, and *Giustizia e Libertà* became a weekly.[136] Carlo had been thinking of such a project as early as March 1931. The idea was to engage in constructive work and the formation of a new elite. In a letter to Nello, he wrote that "I don't feel like pursuing a struggle only of action. It is necessary that we justify our ideals and that we prepare a work for the long term."[137] The newspaper was printed both in a large, tabloid format and in smaller versions that were easier to smuggle into Italy. As a weekly, it appeared every Friday and contained an editorial, usually written by Rosselli; several articles and essays dealing with the situation in Italy and Europe; press clippings from fascist Italy and the rest of Europe; and usually a book review or two. In its format, writing, and layout, it was meant to appeal to as wide an audience as possible—students, soldiers, intellectuals, workers, teachers, and the like. The title was in red, and the masthead carried an image of the Italian peninsula covered by a red torch, symbol of the movement. Subtitled "United Movement of Action, for Workers' Autonomy, the Socialist Republic, a New Humanism," the paper was quickly acknowledged as an authoritative voice of European antifascism.[138]

In January 1932, Rosselli published the first of twelve issues of *Quaderni di Giustizia e Libertà* (Notebooks of Justice and Liberty), which addressed more abstract and theoretical problems of the antifascist resistance.[139] The *Quaderni* appeared every three to four months, until January 1935. Rosselli was responsible for each issue, and it was not unusual for the lead editorial to be written by him, along with a shorter article and possibly a book review. Each issue was divided into sections, one that carried articles and essays, another that reproduced documents, another that was devoted to polemics with other antifascist groups, and one devoted to book reviews. In early 1933, Rosselli prepared a report to the Central Committee of GL concerning the first six issues of the *Quaderni:* by issue six (March 1933), the circulation had increased to 2,000 copies, with 600 copies for an Italian edition, 200 of a foreign edition camouflaged for smuggling into Italy, and 1,200 copies for France, Europe, and the Americas. Then 200 libraries began receiving the fifth issue. The total expenses for the first six issues amounted to 37,000 francs.[140] The *Quaderni* were created to clarify the "spiritual and ideological physiognomy" of the movement and proved to be highly effective in this regard. Much had changed in Italy and Europe since the imposition of the dictatorship in 1925–26. It was significant that much of the youth of Italy had come to political consciousness under the regime. The main task, therefore, was to increase and develop a plan of political education and propaganda directed at these youths. "It would be an error," Rosselli wrote, "to depend too much on men 35, 40 or 50 years old. Besides the ones that are in prison, on the islands, abroad, the others are all or almost all in a state of depression and painful skepticism." Whichever political party that managed to gain the allegiance of the young would "control the revolutionary situation tomorrow." That this was the proper course of action was proved, in Rosselli's eyes, by how the communists were criticizing the new movement. Carlo felt, mistakenly, that Justice and Liberty was hindered by "the lack of a myth, or if you wish, *un' idea forza* capable of influencing and attracting the youth, that permits us to speak a language completely geared toward the future."[141]

He sought that language in the tradition of European humanism. Several months after Hitler's ascension to power in Germany, Rosselli returned to the problem of European antifascism and its internal divisions:

In its essence, there is truly but one antifascism; it is the human problem, the struggle for values that are not tied to this or that country, but to humanity. It's a question of knowing why man is on this earth; if he is the purpose of life, or if his essence is to be humiliated as an instrument to another end; if he possesses his own sacred inviolable conscience, personality, freedom or if he must beg for his conscience, personality, freedom from the master that calls itself the State, that calls itself Capital; if, in short, man is to live humanly realizing himself according to his own original nature or if he is to be flesh for production and the cannon.[142]

It was no coincidence that antifascism began in Italy as an instinctive moral outcry, even before it was a sophisticated economic or political protest.

"Jewish" Antifascism

The late historian of Italian fascism and author of a six-volume biography of Mussolini, Renzo De Felice, insisted that although there were Italian Jews in the antifascist movements, it is "impossible to speak of a 'Jewish antifascism,'" even after 1938 and the imposition of the racial laws. Although the contribution of Italian Jews to antifascism was "numerically and qualitatively truly impressive," and though "Judaism has undoubtedly a certain democratic and liberal substratum," they participated as Italians rather than as Jews. Instead of speaking of "Jewish antifascism, one could only speak of antifascist Jews."[143]

Italian Jews were represented across the political spectrum from ardent fascists to fervent communists. Ettore Ovazza of Turin had participated, along with another 230 Jews, in Mussolini's "March on Rome" in October 1922. In 1934, Ovazza established a Jewish fascist newspaper, *La Nostra Bandiera* (Our Flag), and in a desperate attempt to "prove" the loyalty of Italy's Jews to fascism, he burned down the offices of a Zionist newspaper in Florence. He and his family suffered a gruesome death at the hands of the Nazis because his blind devotion to the regime prevented him from fleeing fascist Italy.[144]

At the helm of the PCI, along with Gramsci and Togliatti, were Umberto Terracini (a classmate from Turin) and Emilio Sereni. Terracini, one of the few Italian Jews who spoke fluent Hebrew, had suffered thirteen years in prison and *confino* during the fascist epoch. Paradoxically, his life was saved by a fascist official who warned him that the Nazis were rounding up Jews. Emilio Sereni abandoned his youthful Zionism (although his brother Enzo did not) and joined the communist underground. In and out of fascist prisons, Sereni escaped death several times and became a senator of the Italian Republic in 1948.

Two of Rosselli's colleagues in the socialist camp, Claudio Treves and Giuseppe Emanuele Modigliani, were Jewish. Treves had once fought a duel with Mussolini in which Treves had been slightly wounded. Both Treves and Modigliani were forced into exile in Paris, where Treves became editor of *La Libertà*, the newspaper of the Antifascist Concentration and where Modigliani (brother of the painter Amedeo) edited *Rinascita socialista*. Although he never abandoned the PSI, Modigliani was close to Justice and Liberty during his Parisian exile. He often referred to his Jewish origins, a trait that sometimes irritated Rosselli.[145]

Although there were Jews present in all political parties and all persuasions of antifascism, many seemed to gravitate to Justice and Liberty, which acquired a reputation as "the movement of Jewish intellectuals." When Sion Segre Amar, a young idealistic man from Turin, approached Carlo Levi about joining the movement, Levi could only moan, "Alas, another Jew." Levi made it clear to the young man that he didn't want Justice and Liberty to be known as a "Jewish" movement. Segre wittily asked whether he should first convert to Catholicism to join, or should he become a fascist just because he was a Jew?[146] Amar was clear on why Italian Jews were attracted to Justice and Liberty: "They felt fascism as an obstacle to their own ideologies and in Justice and Liberty they found a force (though very modest) for the struggle against that obstacle, but without mental constrictions or excessively rigid programs."[147] Without doubt, some were attracted by the charismatic personality of Carlo himself, who seemed to exert an enormous influence, especially over the younger members. Alberto Cavaglion insisted that for the youth of Italy, "only one book exerted an influence comparable to that of Croce's works. This book was *Liberal Socialism* by Carlo Rosselli."[148]

Although Carlo Levi had earned a medical degree in Turin, he never practiced professionally. In 1935 he was sent to *confino* in the Basilicata region of southern Italy. Out of that experience emerged his masterpiece of amateur anthropology and ethnography, *Christ Stopped at Eboli*. During the armed Resistance, he was active in the Action Party, the ideological heir to Justice and Liberty. His novel *The Watch* is a brilliant portrait of the waning days of the Parri government in late 1945. Levi spent more time at his painting than in practicing medicine. This pastime provided an excellent excuse for often having members of Justice and Liberty in his apartment in Turin, posing for paintings while discussing various antifascist projects.

Another member of the movement, Mario Levi, along with Sion Segre Amar, made it to the border town of Ponte Tresa on 11 March 1934 in an attempt to flee fascist Italy. Levi managed to swim to Swiss territory, but Amar was caught. According to the account in the fascist papers, Levi turned and shouted antifascist and anti-Italian insults from the safety of the other shore. Anti-Semitic fascists were quick to make the equation that antifascism was intimately tied to Zionism and "the Jew."[149]

Mario Levi's sister Natalia was also active in the movement and later achieved recognition as one of Italy's finest writers. She married Leone Ginzburg, a Russian professor of Slavic literature. Ginzburg had refused to sign the oath of loyalty that was demanded by the fascist regime of all university professors in 1931. In 1935 he was arrested with much of the Turin branch of Justice and Liberty. For his work in the Action Party, Leone Ginzburg died under nazi torture in Rome's notorious Regina Coeli prison in 1944.

Max Ascoli, although never formally a member of Justice and Liberty, worked closely with Rosselli on *Non Mollare!* and *Il Quarto Stato*. In 1933 he accepted a position as professor of political philosophy at the "University in Exile" in New York City. From New York, Ascoli helped to organize the Mazzini Society and the North American Federation of Justice and Liberty, with headquarters at 1133 Broadway in Manhattan, which published the *Quaderni Italiani*. He wrote tirelessly on behalf of antifascism in *The Nation* and even created a new journal, *The Reporter*.

As a young man of twenty-two, Vittorio Foa approached the movement in Turin in 1933 and was given responsibilities that belied his age. He too was arrested in the 1935 police sweep of Turin that virtually wiped out Justice and Liberty from that city for years.[150] Foa also went on to important positions in the Action Party during the armed Resistance; after the war, he was a highly regarded deputy of Parliament and one of the most respected voices in the country.[151]

Perhaps best known to American readers because of his memoir of the concentration camp, *Survival in Auschwitz*, was the writer and chemist Primo Levi. When captured by a fascist patrol in December 1943, Levi thought it wisest to acknowledge being "an Italian of the Jewish race," instead of admitting his role in the underground with the Action Party.

Levi, who had survived the horrors of the concentration camp, would take his own life in 1987, a victim of what he called "the survivor's disease."

As early as 1934, the regime was equating Judaism with antifascism.[152] The semiofficial newspaper of the regime, Telesio Interlandi's *Il Tevere* of Rome, commented that "the best of antifascism, past and present, is of the Jewish race: from Treves to Modigliani, from Rosselli to Morgari, the organizers of antifascist subversion were and are members of "the chosen people." [153] A spy who had managed to infiltrate the Turin branch of Justice and Liberty and who had noted the significant contributions of Carlo Levi, Leone Ginzburg, and others, concluded one report with the observation that "one senses easily existing among them a common link derived from race (they are all Jews)." Another report railed against the "vile Jew Rosselli." [154]

Rosselli himself, that "modernist Jew," would have been surprised at this characterization. In a letter to Harold Laski, he expressed his interest in and concern over the foundation in New York City of the "University in Exile," later the Graduate Faculty of Political and Social Science of the New School for Social Research:

> From the information I have received, it seems that the University, which has been constituted with Jewish funds, will recruit its teaching personnel solely from Jews. Although Jewish myself, it seems to me that this restriction is a great error and a great injustice. In Germany, it is not only Jews who are persecuted, but socialists, communists, pacifists, and free spirits. A University founded with Jewish money should consider its boast and obligation in not following a criterion of race or religion and should call to teaching elements of all currents of emigration and even various nationalities. Otherwise the reaction will be a reconfirmation of racial prejudice, and precisely on the field most delicate, that of culture.[155]

That most delicate field of culture was a constant concern of Rosselli's. As early as 1925, he had urged the Circolo di Cultura to publish works on history, economics, and politics that would be accessible to a wide audience. He took up that endeavor again in Paris. Justice and Liberty formed a small publishing cooperative and printed works by Lussu, Bolton King, Henri Béraud, Fernando De Rosa, and the last testament of the anarchist Michele Schirru, executed for an attempted assassination of Mussolini. Small editions examined fascism and the Special Tribunal, vilified the monarchy, and excoriated the Catholic Church; pamphlets were addressed to workers, students, and soldiers.[156]

The weekly *Giustizia e Libertà* always carried a section "Stampa amica e nemica" (Friendly and enemy press), which included short excerpts and reviews of recently published works. The *Quaderni* carried more extensive reviews that were often theoretically elaborate.

The Turin branch was most immersed in the cultural battle raging within Italy. Under the patronage of Giulio Einaudi and the Einaudi publishing house, Carlo Levi, Leone Ginzburg, Cesare Pavese, and Luigi Salvatorelli came together to form a new journal, *La Cultura*.

In short, antifascist Jews were attracted most to the PCI and to Justice and Liberty. In New York, Justice and Liberty's American counterpart, the Mazzini Society, assisted Jews seeking asylum from the nazi project of extermination.[157]

Women of Justice and Liberty

If the historiography of antifascism pales in comparison with that of fascism, the same is even more marked concerning treatments of women and antifascism. Although there is now a substantial body of work examining fascism and women,[158] there are but few studies in English on women activists and the special problems raised by their participation in what was a male-dominated movement.[159] As Victoria De Grazia makes clear, the problem of writing the history of women's participation in the Resistance "is tied up with the problem of writing the history of the antifascist Resistance as a whole." The work of new left social historians has challenged the traditional understanding of the Resistance; these scholars have turned their attention away from the traditional parties and political structures to the informal practices of everyday life.[160] According to the documents available, over 50,000 women participated in the armed Resistance, in addition to the 70,000 registered in the "Gruppi di difesa della donna." These Women's Defense Groups were established in Milan in late 1943 and worked with the Committee for National Liberation. More than 4,000 women were arrested; over 1,000 appeared before the Special Tribunal for the Defense of the State; nearly 4,000 were deported, and more than 700 were killed in action or executed.[161] This "silenced Resistance" deserves a study of its own; here we can only offer some superficial remarks and survey the activities of women associated with Justice and Liberty.

In two never-published letters to the editor of *The New York Times* during her American exile, Marion Cave Rosselli modestly wrote that she had been "secretary and general factotum" of *Non Mollare!* and that "as the wife (now the widow) of Carlo Rosselli, had some part in the Italian political situation." Gaetano Salvemini recalled that Marion had been part of the intellectual resistance from its inception, as an "instinctive reaction against [fascist] arrogance." Marion had personally typed all the issues of *Non Mollare!* and had hidden the paper in the Rosselli home in Florence. She had also distributed the paper throughout Florence by concealing it under her clothes as she made her rounds. In 1925 when Salvemini, Rosselli, Ernesto Rossi, and other Florentine antifascists wished to commemorate the murdered Matteotti, it was Marion who courageously took the wreath of flowers and led the men, ready to face down the fascists who had gathered threateningly to impede their small ceremony.[162]

It was Marion, pregnant with Amelia, who made numerous trips from Milan to Lipari in 1928 and 1929, preparing for the dramatic escape of her husband, along with Emilio Lussu and Francesco Fausto Nitti. Following their successful escape, she was immediately arrested, still pregnant with Amelia. She was, in the words of Salvemini, "the best part of our past."[163]

Marion Rosselli was assisted by several other remarkable women in Florence, Milan, and Turin. One of these was Renata Calabresi. Born in Ferrara, Calabresi received her doctorate in clinical psychology from the University of Florence in 1923. It was while in Florence that Calabresi entered the antifascist ranks, helping to distribute copies of *Non Mollare!* along with her brother, Dr. Massimo Calabresi. For her actions, she was briefly imprisoned by the regime and eventually fled into exile. Like many others, she arrived in the United States in 1940, fleeing the nazi invasion of Europe.[164]

Another formidable woman who worked with Justice and Liberty was Joyce Salvadori Lussu, from a noted liberal family. She was the faithful companion of Emilio Lussu and lived with him without the benefit of an official marriage until 1938, when Silvio Trentin and Giuseppe Emanuele Modigliani served as witnesses at their wedding in Paris.[165] In September 1943, they managed to find their way back to Florence to join in the clandestine reunion of the Action Party. Joyce Lussu recounted her participation in the Resistance in a volume published immediately after the German surrender.[166]

Bianca Ceva, sister of Umberto Ceva, who committed suicide in prison after the October 1930 arrest in Milan for fear of betraying his "friend" who was actually a fascist spy, wrote an account of her brother's activities and death in *1930: Retroscena di dramma*.[167] Thirty years after that tragic event, Bianca Ceva wrote how "for many days I felt myself immersed in a heavy atmosphere, where . . . the whole terrible face of life and the abyss of the heart appeared to me in their naked and pitiless truth." Bianca recalled that Umberto had left a note for his wife and children in which he wrote "you know that I have always adored Liberty." As Umberto's wife was leaving the prison after claiming her husband's body, an official asked her—without meeting her gaze—whether he could offer his condolences. When the trial of Rossi and Bauer finally took place in May 1931 for their conspiracy with Ceva, there was, in the courtroom, "the shadow of the Absentee." [168]

Bianca Ceva has also written about the antifascist resistance and postwar Italy.[169] Her colleague Barbara Allason participated in many projects of Justice and Liberty; her memoirs were published after the war.[170] Others who also participated were Natalia (Levi) Ginzburg, wife of Leone Ginzburg, and Vera Modigliani.

Perhaps the woman who was the most active in Justice and Liberty and later in the Action Party was the irrepressible and dynamic Ada Prospero Gobetti. Born on 23 July 1902, Ada had collaborated with the boy wonder of Turin, Piero Gobetti on his journals *Energie Nuove* and *La Rivoluzione Liberale*. In January 1923, as fascism was consolidating its power, they were married. A son, Paolo, was born in December 1925, just two months before Piero's early death in Paris after a vicious beating by fascist thugs.[171] Ada remained in Turin, translating, teaching, and publishing works on English literature (including studies on Samuel Johnson and on Alexander Pope, and an Italian edition of Boswell's *Life of Samuel Johnson*). During the war, the Gobetti house on via Fabro became a locus of the antifascist Resistance; a cage of canaries, moved from one window to another, alerted comrades in the street below whether fascist spies were watching the house. After the war, Ada was vice mayor of Turin, a member of the National Council, and a member of the executive committee of the Federazione Democratica Internazionale Femminile. In addition, she continued her passionate advocacy of education as editor of the pedagogical journal *Educazione Democratica*. Her biography of the communist militant Camilla Ravera appeared posthumously,[172] but her greatest work was undoubtedly the partisan diary she kept during 1943 to 1945. It is one of the great works of literature to come out of the Resistance.

> I dedicate these memories to my friends near and far, those of twenty years and those of a single hour. Because it is friendship—a bond of solidarity founded not on commonality of blood, nor of country, nor intellectual tradition, but on the simple human rapport of feeling yourself one among many—that appears to me the most significant aspect and sign of our struggle. And perhaps it really was. Only if we manage to save it, to perfect it or to recreate it despite the many errors and losses, if we manage to understand that this unity and friendship was not, and should not be, only a means to reach something else, but that it is an end in itself, because in it is perhaps the essence of man—only then can we rethink our past and see again the faces of our friends, living and dead, without melancholy or desperation.[173]

On the Nature of the Political Party

One of the most contested aspects of Justice and Liberty was whether the movement was a political party and, if not, whether it should transform itself into one. Rosselli had been very clear from the beginning: GL was to be a new, revolutionary movement, and its members were asked to put away party cards and to dedicate themselves to an inclusive, antifascist movement fighting for a democratic, socialist republic. Justice and Liberty was born outside the traditional political parties because of Rosselli's critique of their passivity and failed ideology, and because under the dictatorship it was impossible to conduct the fight against fascism in any other manner. The party is, by definition, the fruit of liberty, a delicate instrument. Where there exists no freedom of the press, of association, of organization, the party cannot exist. "To believe that the end of fascism will come from the metamorphosis and action of the political parties is absurd."[174] What remained in Italy were isolated groups of men and women who managed to conserve their dignity and a certain capacity for struggle; beside them were a minority of younger, more audacious Italians with an immense potential. It was to these groups that GL appealed.

Yet the older parties were not convinced. The PSI, the PCI, and the PRI all felt that GL either was already a new political party or was intending to transform itself into a rival on the political stage. Characteristically, Rosselli opened the pages of both *Giustizia e Libertà* and the *Quaderni* to those who disagreed with his position on this matter, both from within the movement and those from the older, traditional parties. Augusto Monti, who had collaborated with Gobetti on *La Rivoluzione Liberale*, argued that GL, with a program and a coherent ideology, was already a political party—a new Italian Socialist party. Lelio Basso took another tack: he held that GL was still too inconsistent and hazy in its ideology; it had to delineate its position and carve out space for itself on the political spectrum.[175] Following a respectful airing of their ideas, Rosselli responded. After acknowledging the criticism of both Monti and Basso, he delineated the essential characteristics of the modern political party:

> that which constitutes the definitive, peculiar character of the modern political party . . . is the fact that it cannot be conceived except in opposition to other political parties within a certain common political climate, which is the liberal climate of the nineteenth century . . . the concept of the "party" presupposes that of political struggle, of liberty and autonomy. A party does not exist where political parties do not exist; a party does not exist and cannot exist where political struggle does not exist; and political struggle does not exist where there is no freedom. All the political parties of our time . . . were born in a liberal climate with the assertion of fundamental liberties, such as the press and association.[176]

Rosselli insisted that all modern political parties were, in fact, miniature reproductions of the liberal state in which they were formed; they were, in microcosm, "working democracies" with elected officials, legislative and executive branches, freedom of discussion, and soon. The modern political party can be conceived only inside the state, even if its ultimate aim is the overthrow of that state. By rising to power, the party changes the nature of the state. "If, instead, the party is completely outside the State, it is in flagrant contradiction to the State, and in no way concurs with it; one no longer has a party, but a revolutionary movement, an anti-State." By this criterion, the Fascist Party in Italy, the Nazi Party in Germany, and the Communist Party in Russia were not political parties. Because they were single, totalitarian entities, they did not see themselves as "part of a whole, a moment in the dialectic of political forces, but as the whole, as the State. They are, therefore, States—antiliberal, antipolitical, that do not admit political parties, nor political struggle, and that logically designate their opponents as antistate."[177]

Rosselli never abandoned or modified this conception of Justice and Liberty as a revolutionary, transgressive, "anti-state." The fascist state was "an old acquaintance. It is the Leviathan of Hobbes, the absolute State of Louis XIV, the divine State of Hegel, Moloch." It is a "challenge against reason and humanity." Against this state, all free men, "without distinction of party or border are united in a common obligation to truth, justice and liberty."[178] Justice and Liberty was the seed of an entirely free and new state of the future that would arise from the revolution. It was to be the "explosive cell" of the future society. It was imperative that the members of Justice and Liberty live these values within the movement, without imposing a sectarian party discipline or a rigid body of doctrine. And in what may have been the first instance in history of a political movement conceiving itself as transitory, Rosselli wrote that in educating Italians of the "dignity of the political struggle," Justice and Liberty would be the nucleus of future political parties.[179] The other political parties—Liberal, Socialist, Communist, Catholic—all had roots in a prefascist past, hindering their conceptual grasp of fascism and the Resistance. As Norberto Bobbio has pointed out, "They passed through the Resistance; they did not see themselves as identical with it." All, that is, except Justice and Liberty, for Rosselli conceived of the movement as being identical to the essence of antifascism. Since fascism had been both antiliberal and antisocialist, antifascism could be neither purely liberal nor socialist, but had to be both.[180]

Fascist totalitarianism requires a diverse type of confrontation; after the defeat of fascism, a return to the older political order might be possible, and only then would it be time to discuss whether GL should become a political party. Until that time, the movement must remain as conceived by Rosselli—"the complete and revolutionary negation of fascism." Was the movement then condemned to be, in the words of Basso, "the democratic-republican-socialist cauldron of unhappy Aventine memory"? Rosselli refuted this outcome in no uncertain terms: Justice and Liberty was born as the absolute negation of the old mentality that led to the Aventine Secession.

A less optimistic view was propounded by Carlo Levi. After spending much of 1935 in *confino*, Levi returned to his colleagues in Turin. Rosselli and the movement had devoted much attention to the "Southern Question," based to a considerable degree on the work of the *meridionalisti* Guido Dorso, Gaetano Salvemini, and Giustino Fortunato. Levi's time in the *Mezzogiorno* had imbued him with the eternal fatalism of that condemned land to such a degree that even his most sincere antifascist collaborators could not understand; for Levi "they were all unconscious worshipers of the State." Whether the state they worshiped was the fascist state or "the incarnation of quite another dream," they thought of it as something that transcended both its citizens and their lives, hence the incomprehension between political leaders and the peasants. Levi's conception of the state was even closer to the anarchist vision than was Rosselli's; Levi shocked his friends when he told them that

> the State, as they conceived it, was the greatest obstacle to the accomplishment of anything. The State cannot solve the problem of the *Mezzogiorno*, because the problem that we call by that name is none other than the problem of the State itself . . . We must make ourselves capable of inventing a new form of government, neither fascist, nor communist, nor even liberal, for all these are forms of the religion of the State. We must rebuild the foundations of our conception of the State with the concept of the individual, which is its basis. For the juridical and abstract concept of the individual we must substitute a new concept, more expressive of reality, one that will do away with the now unbridgeable gulf between the individual and the State.[181]

Fascism

Rosselli and his colleagues in Justice and Liberty devoted themselves to an analysis of European fascism, or what Aldo Garosci called Hitler's "spiritual blitzkrieg."[182] An early work by Silvio Trentin, *L'aventure italienne: légendes et réalités,* which was published in Paris in 1928, and dedicated to Giovanni Amendola, proposed a theory of fascism as an "accident" of Italian history. If Trentin was closer to Croce's interpretation in 1928, his subsequent experience with Justice and Liberty pushed him further to the Left. Other scholarly works followed (*Antidémocratie,* 1930; *Aux sources du fascisme,* 1931; *La crise du droit et l'état,* 1935) in which he carefully laid bare the intellectual and political failure of fascism.[183]

Rosselli, Levi, and Parri developed a conception of fascism that would be echoed several decades later in the work of the German-born psychoanalyst and social philosopher, Erich Fromm.[184] "Freedom is a burden," Rosselli noted in an unpublished essay. "This duty to keep oneself free, to follow reason and the critical spirit is insupportable."[185] Italians were lacking neither political intelligence nor the capacity to create new systems of thought. What was absent, according to Rosselli, was "character, the will to fight, the obstinacy of sacrifice, the coherence between thought and action."[186] Carlo Levi agreed, seeing the deep roots of fascism in the "inherited incapacity to be free" and in the "fear of passion and responsibility." The "morally weak" Italians felt a need for "an exterior order" that would replace an "inexistent morality."[187] Levi's poetic and powerful indictment of the moral failure of the Italians, written in the waning days of World War II, *Paura della libertà,* was inaccurately translated as *Of Fear and Freedom,* rather than the more accurate, and telling, *Fear of Freedom.*[188] Emilio Lussu, for his part, agreed with Gobetti, Rosselli, and Levi that the Italians had inherited a moral conscience that had been brutalized by centuries of feudalism and Catholicism. "It is not intelligence that Italians lack; they have enough to export. It is character that is missing."[189] In truth, Rosselli and his colleagues were close to Croce's later formulation of fascism as "moral sickness" with roots in rabid nationalism, fanatical imperialism, romantic decadentism, and the First World War. By defining fascism first as a "parenthesis" in the unfolding history of liberty in Italy and then later as a "moral sickness," Croce was crafting a strategy that could deny that there was anything specifically "Italian" about fascism. Ferruccio Parri instead condemned the entire experience of Liberal Italy, from unification to the Great War, as responsible for the rise of fascism.[190] Parri's condemnation of Liberal Italy was similar to Rosselli's claim that "between the Italian State after 1860 and fascism there is a connection; if not of filiation, of progressive degeneration."[191]

Rosselli was undoubtedly influenced by Croce, as the following passage makes clear:

Fascism does not exhaust itself in a fact of simple class reaction. It is accompanied by such a complex of factors, especially moral, that it assumes the character of a real and true "national crisis." The causes of this crisis are many; but it is certain that they involve the entire life of the nation, proletariat included.

Fascism does not only offend the rights of one class for the benefit of another class. It offends modern civilization, the rights of the human personality, the most elementary sense of morality and humanity. The division between fascists and antifascists is not determined only on the basis of class relations; there is, between fascists and antifascists a differ-

ence of moral sensibility . . . which gives the struggle for freedom an
almost religious value.[192]

Rosselli's analysis of fascism was derived in part from Piero Gobetti. As
such, it was idiosyncratic, heterogeneous, "heretical," above all in his insistence that fascism could not be explained simply as class reaction. Gobetti
had understood that fascism was "a catastrophe; it is an indication of
decisive puerility because it signals the triumph of facility, of confidence, of
optimism, of enthusiasm."[193] Gobetti and Rosselli shared the idea that
fascism—paradoxically—represented something very old and yet radically
new in the history of politics. The supremely repugnant fact about fascism
was not its suppression of freedom—something common to all tyrannies
and part of Italian history—but was its creation of "a fabric of consensus,
in the active servility that it demands from its subjects." Mussolini had the
Italians under a "sadistic subjugation. I enslave you and you must tell me
that you freely accept being a slave; you must proclaim, after Gentile, of
being a free slave."[194] The Italian people had been passive subjects of their
history; the intervention of a deus ex machina—Pope, King, or Duce—answered a psychological need. "From this point of view the Mussolini government is anything but revolutionary. It is linked to tradition and pro-
ceeds along the line of least resistance. Fascism, all appearances to the
contrary, is the most passive development in Italian history." In words that
directly echoed the martyred Gobetti, Rosselli pointed out that "fascism
has in some sense been the autobiography of a nation that rejects the
political contest, that worships unanimity, and shrinks from heresy."[195] The
economic, moral, and political roots of Italian fascism were to be found in
a failed Risorgimento and in the corrupting influence of Giolitti's *trasformismo*.[196]

Moreover, there were other forces that contributed to the rise of fascism:
hundreds of thousands of people who supported the mechanism of the
"bureaucratic-dictatorial" state; the cult of violence, a taste for adventure,
and authoritarian tendencies generated by the war; a religion of nationalism; and weakness of character on the part of the Italians, centuries of
servility, the influence of the Church, and political apathy. In short, fascism
was both class reaction and moral crisis, and those who fought only the
former were fighting only half the battle.[197] By the manipulation of nationalism, the press, and even sports, the regime could "corrupt and distract"
the masses. Sports became a modern version of the Roman *panem et*

circences. Mussolini had shrewdly realized that it was not a question of smothering every passion, but of directing and channeling those passions in ways favorable to the regime.[198] As Carlo Levi discerned in a brilliant essay, "Sport," Italians under fascism had been reduced to enjoying only individual and private passions, such as self-interest and sex. (And even these, lamented Levi, "how limited and tired!"). Cinema was a "passive occupation" permitting "easy evasion." The only collective passion left was sport. Sport—which previously had signified personal initiative, a fair contest, moral autonomy, and honorable struggle—was antithetical to fascism; but the regime was careful in appropriating whatever it could. Cycling and soccer generated such fanaticism as to be "symptoms of an illness." As De Man had already noted, sports fanaticism was "the principal phenomenon deriving from the repression of instinct generated by the monotonous and brutalizing character of industrial work." For Levi this enthusiasm could represent something positive (individual fortitude and character in the case of cycling) or collective enterprise (in the case of soccer). But the regime could not permit the expression of such enthusiasm to go uncontrolled. Sport under fascism had become an industry and "cooperated in a most efficacious manner in keeping the country in the beatific state of infancy."[199]

Rosselli clearly saw that Hitler's ascension to power in January 1933 radically changed the nature of politics on the continent and posed a threat to all of Western civilization. Between 1922 and 1933, fascism could be conceived of as the "autobiography" of Italy; national socialism in Germany meant that fascism was a European, and not just an Italian, phenomenon. The nazi revolution took up where the fascist revolution had stopped. Italian fascism had "degenerated" into a reactionary regime, but national socialism was the universal aspect of fascism. Hitler was an "authentic barbarian, a sincere barbarian," whereas Mussolini was a "false barbarian, an actor" who never really believed in the fascist revolution. More than a tyrant, Mussolini was a corrupter, and like all corrupters, was corruptible himself. Hitler, instead, was the true "anti-Europe."

What was "infinitely painful" and "grotesque" was the seemingly unstoppable collapse of an entire world of German democracy, social democracy, and communism. There was something diabolical as well as paradoxical that the long-awaited "crisis of capitalism" in Germany gave way to the victory of national socialism. "The manner, the rapidity, the enormity of the submersion superseded the limits of the imagination." Hitler's victory was symbolic of a "tragic moral failure" in Germany and Europe.[200]

There was no question that fascism in Europe was victorious, but what did this victory signify? "Impotent to create, [fascism] presents itself as a tremendous gravedigger of worlds, myths, men." The historical function of a "dictatorship of iron and blood" was to reveal the precariousness of the foundations of European society. A disillusioned Alexander Herzen had written in 1848 that "we live in a sad age, where all that was virtuous in the past has disappeared; the decrepit world no longer has faith and defends itself with desperation, because it is afraid; it forgets its gods; it overturns the rights upon which it was built; it renounces intellectual development and honor, it becomes a ferocious beast, persecuting and killing."[201] If Rosselli could sympathize with the defeated Russian revolutionary, he did not despair. Hitler's victory in Germany meant that the ideals of Justice and Liberty, until now the ideals of a minority, would now become the ideals of the majority; if not, European civilization would end.[202] There were even elements of grotesque comedy in the tragedy of Italian fascism. After a decade in power, fascism was a "pseudo-revolution" still desperately seeking its "*raison d'être* before history."[203]

A similar analysis appeared in the *Quaderni* by Nicola Chiaromonte, who explicitly conjoined European fascism with death. There had been a progressive moral, social, and political degeneration since 1914; Europe was now reaping what it had sown. Political assassination and the systematic use of terror meant that fascism was an outlaw state, the first of its kind in history. Fascism had not substituted a liberal state, but one that was already "totalitarian" in spite of itself and that had developed a conception of the nation as a "myth of salvation."[204]

Perhaps Rosselli's most penetrating and prophetic analysis of fascism and the one that generated the most commentary among European antifascists was his essay "La guerra che torna"[205] (War Returns). He challenged the pacifists and their refusal to recognize that their faith in peace had to be questioned. He was especially harsh toward the French socialists and their policy, even after Germany's withdrawal from the League of Nations in October. The paradox was that those who had worked so hard against fascism and those who had already made the equation that fascism equals war were now reluctant to draw the logical conclusions from this development in Germany. With Hitler in power, "the illusion of peace is ended . . . Peace returns to that which it has always been in history: a negative and precarious state, a parenthesis between two wars."[206]

Hitler's Germany in 1933 may have still been militarily weak, but it abounded in audacity, desperation, and folly. Not only was its "socialism" a "war socialism," its ideology was pan-Germanism rather than socialist internationalism. Rosselli saw immediately that Hitler would drag Germany "into the very depths of the abyss."

> Without a complete reversal, war is coming, war will come. It will come because it is inevitable that the same causes produce the same effects; because millions of youths have been raised in the delirium of war, because fascism, master of half a continent, will be dragged into it as the ultimate test, because poverty and hunger have always been, as Proudhon taught us, the most powerful motives for war, because the struggle between fascism and antifascism appeals to the judgment of God, because the old Europe that we believed dead and buried with the ten million who died on the battlefields, rises again.[207]

It might be two, five, or ten years, but eventually Germany would become powerful enough to challenge all of Europe. Rosselli theorized that war might break out among the signers of the Treaty of Versailles, as a "large international police action." A preventive war, as some were advocating, had little chance of becoming reality. Although he insisted that a preventive war could prevent a longer, more bloody catastrophe, the reality of domestic and international politics in democratic countries like Britain and France made such a scenario unlikely. Public opinion in those countries would be against any war, and there was no possibility of fighting a war in the name of the Treaty of Versailles that, in the words of Rosselli, was "condemned in the consciences of the people" and that would isolate France rather than Germany.

Until now, antifascism had been completely defensive, caught in a siege mentality, clear only about what it was against. The only possibility of preventing a European bloodbath in the future was a revolutionary intervention in Germany, which would be tied to revolution in other parts of Europe. These possibilities were dreams, admitted Rosselli; the Western democracies were not made of such stuff. Revolutionary democratic socialists were lacking in France and Britain; instead, they clung to the formula of nonintervention. "Non-intervention? Since when have revolutionaries raised the banner of non-intervention? Since when have they affirmed that tyrannies, even if based on centuries of tradition and a passive consensus, were the domestic affairs of a people? The authentic revolutions, those that aspire to a universal principle, were always interventionist."[208] A true democracy, according to Rosselli, must show itself capable of a continual transformation, a "permanent revolution." This is what the English called "the price of liberty."[209]

The antifascists were accused of instigating war, believing that only by war could fascism be defeated. Rosselli had anticipated this criticism and responded that it was fascism and not antifascism that was responsible for the coming war. "We would prefer to be bad prophets, but we feel that already today, part of the German people fanaticized by Hitler will go to war with frenzy, with joy." The rhetoric, the symbolism, and the mind-set fostered in fascist Italy would also send a part of Italian youth off to war in exaltation. In 1932, on the tenth anniversary of the "March on Rome," machine-guns were solemnly presented to the avant-garde fascist youth, not as a commemoration of the past but as an augury of the future. "War is coming, war will come. There is only one way to think about it: it must be prevented. Prevent it with a resolute action, with a revolutionary intervention in those countries where fascism dominates and overthrow it with a civil war."[210] And yet Rosselli had no illusions that such a policy would be enacted. The tragedy was that when the catastrophe arrived, it was too late to do anything about it. For the small band of antifascist revolutionaries, the path was clear: "We will not retire in pilgrimage to the wall of lamentations; nor will we resign ourselves to the fascist war. We will serve the war against fascism. We will transform the fascist war into a social revolution."[211] Rosselli was suggesting nothing less than a preemptive, revolutionary strike against Hitler and Mussolini. In the midst of the Ethiopian War, he returned to this theme, arguing that fascism's entire raison d'être (origin, mentality, philosophy, politics, economics, tactics, organization, and vocabulary) was war. Since 1925 fascism had done nothing else than prepare for war. Instead of the "permanent revolution" boasted of by Mussolini, it was more proper to speak of a "permanent war." "Fascism is a class war that begins domestically and transfers itself, not capriciously, but for the supreme reason of self-conservation, abroad."[212]

Again Rosselli had touched a raw nerve among his antifascist collaborators. The socialists responded critically and almost in unison.[213] Nenni answered that he felt that "Hannibal was not at the gates," that perhaps Justice and Liberty was exaggerating the danger, that the edifice of peace was not collapsing, and that the intervention advocated by Rosselli would inevitably degenerate into an "imperialist intervention." War for Nenni could never be revolutionary, nor democratic; it was by its very nature reactionary. The duty of socialists was to oppose war wherever and whenever it might break out. Modigliani concurred; only Giuseppe Saragat among the socialists was willing to suspend judgment and admit the possibility that Rosselli might be right. Rosselli's obstinate advocacy of a preventive, revolutionary European war proved to be another obstacle in his relationship with the Antifascist Concentration and the exile community.

Rosselli responded in a letter to Nenni that until January 1933, he had agreed with Nelli's position; but Nazism in Germany had radically changed the equation. The antifascists were caught in a Catch-22: to prevent war meant first and above all to defeat fascism on the continent; to defeat fascism meant war. "It seems to me that you remain strangely indifferent to the catastrophe that threatens, to the fascist wave that submerges all peoples one after the other, to the collapse of a willful, active politics of the Left, of revolutionary socialism. According to you, there is nothing to be done." [214] If any doubt remained concerning the brutal nature of Hitler's regime, it was dissipated on 30 June 1934, in the "Night of Long Knives" massacre of Ernst Roehm, chief of staff of the *Sturmabteilung* (Brownshirts), and his associates. The bloody nazi purge had an admonishing historical value: it demonstrated the real substance of the fascist dictatorships—they rested on a political and moral foundation of "blood and depravity." [215]

Fascism had been victorious in Europe because of the weakness of the opposition and its lack of new, innovative ideas. Fascism had an immense technical and psychological superiority, while the rest of Europe witnessed the collapse of the old world and its ruling class in a twilight of ideas. "Fascism is the child of a corrupt and weak democracy. And like a good child, it buries the father."[216] Although not denying the seriousness of Hitler's rise to power, Rosselli ridiculed the Western democracies' cringing attitude before the new Germany. This sense of inferiority rested on the fact that the Western states no longer believed in their fundamental principles and myths. Germany's power rested not so much in her military, but rather in the nazi mystique.[217]

Justice and Liberty continued to insist that "fascism is above all an instrument of war." Fascism had been born from the domestic, fratricidal war and claimed war as a legitimate foreign policy to acquire a justly deserved "Empire." With fascism confined to Italy, the threat was remote, but with Nazism in Germany, the last remaining democracies in Europe were in danger. Those democratic countries could not escape partial responsibility for the wave of fascism in Europe, but they were the only countries in which the working class could make its voice heard. In this atmosphere that was suffocating Europe, "Justice and Liberty cannot and should not limit itself to an inert political or historical critique . . . Democratic antifascism . . . must prepare itself, spiritually and materially, for the eventuality of a war." Fascism had usurped the rhetoric of patriotism, contaminating it with that of nationalism. It was necessary that Italians recognize that "the *patria* was not the army, the Empire, or colonies. Rather the *patria* is in the homes, the fields, the factories, the workshops, free labor, in the thought and work of Italians . . . The enemy is within, and not beyond, our borders."[218]

Rosselli had realized early that fascism was not just the Leviathan of Hobbes nor the absolute state of Louis XIV. Fascism could not be compared with classic reactionary regimes; its leader was an ex-revolutionary, "an adventurer without scruples," a "demagogue serving his own ambition, yet knowing his adversaries perfectly well." Fascism was not simply class reaction but moral crisis, a human crisis, a crisis of civilization.[219] "Conscious, therefore, of the responsibility that we assume before the country and the world, we are ready, more than ever, to throw ourselves against the fascist barbarities; and we will consider our lives well spent if our sacrifice will contribute in giving Italy political freedom and social justice, and if it becomes the avant-garde of the democratic, socialist, and republican reconstruction of Europe."[220]

Justice and Liberty continued to explore ways to fight the regime, including the possibility of political assassination. If one accepted the premise that fascism equals Mussolini, a premise that the Duce himself was eager to sustain, then assassination was a legitimate political tactic. Rosselli and GL may have been influenced by the romantic example of the anarchists who had killed several heads of state before the Great War, including King Umberto of Italy at the racetrack of Monza.

Rosselli had become Mussolini's bête noire. Besides guiding a dynamic antifascist movement, Rosselli was also reputed to be involved in several assassination attempts against the Duce as early as March 1931, including a rumored plot to bomb Mussolini's office in Palazzo Venezia by air.[221] With Rosselli's money, an airplane was even purchased in France, but nothing more developed. In public Mussolini often shrugged off assassination attempts, but he was understandably concerned for his physical safety. The socialist deputy Tito Zaniboni, the Anglo-Irish Violet Gibson, the anarchists Gino Lucetti and Michele Schirru, and the young Anteo Zamboni (son of an anarchist) had all tried to assassinate Mussolini. Zaniboni and Lucetti were imprisoned. By one of those strange ironies of history, Zaniboni was joined by Mussolini himself in *confino* on the island of La Maddalena (a further irony—Garibaldi's final resting place) after the Duce had been deposed. Gibson was declared insane, and Mussolini humanely permitted her to return to Britain; sixteen-year-old Zamboni was literally torn to pieces on the spot by fascists, and his body paraded around the city of Bologna. Aldo Garosci, Max Salvadori, and Gioacchino Dolci all implied years later that Justice and Liberty had indeed planned to assassinate Mussolini.[222] Rosselli had made some ambiguous comments concerning assassination, but it was the mild-mannered liberal Tarchiani who seems to have been most active in fomenting assassination plots. He may have had a hand in arming the anarchist Angelo Sbardellotto, who, like the republican Domenico Bovone, had planned to kill Mussolini. By the 1930s, Mussolini's complacency had turned to ferocity; both Sbardellotto and Bovone were executed. OVRA uncovered another plot by Angelo Adam, also a member of Justice and Liberty; in addition, a spy reported that Rosselli and Lussu discussed with him an attempted assassination of Mussolini, including the possible use of explosives or a pistol in the Chamber of Deputies, the Senate, or somewhere more feasible in Rome. The spy even reported an expedition with Rosselli to the outskirts of Paris to test a bomb. Thus began a "brutal chess match" between the movement and the regime[223] that would ultimately end with Rosselli's death.

· · · ·

CHAPTER FIVE

The Tragic Hero

Thou Paradise of exiles, Italy!
PERCY BYSSHE SHELLEY, *JULIAN AND MADDALO* (1819)

. . . the sad death in exile that appears almost inevitable for the
finest sons of Italy.
CARLO ROSSELLI, "FILIPPO TURATI E IL SOCIALISMO
ITALIANO" (1932)

The particular problems created by exile were often uppermost in Rosselli's
mind. He had insisted from the earliest days of his active participation in
the antifascist cause that the struggle was to be carried out within Italy and
not from abroad. Exile did not change his position; if anything, he continued to argue that the important work was to be done in Italy, among the
youth, workers, and middle class. Rosselli was highly conscious of the exile
tradition of the Risorgimento and often related his life and thought to men
like Mazzini, Cattaneo, and others in the nineteenth century. Many *fuorusciti* (exiles from fascism) saw themselves as the inheritors of an exile tradition that could be extended even further. Although few consciously evoked
it, there was a legacy of the exiled intellectual in Italy that stretched back to
Dante, through Machiavelli, and into the nineteenth and twentieth centuries. The role of the public intellectual has always been of critical importance in Italy, where a proximity to political power has often led to their
special influence and their critical position vis-à-vis established institutions. Besides Russia there is perhaps no other country that has such a
tradition of exiling its most important thinkers. Perhaps Rosselli even unconsciously thought of himself in the tradition of the exiled Hebrews and
of the moral and social catalyst of the Biblical prophets when he wrote

that "the messianism of Israel" was one of the foundations of modern socialism.[1]

Because of unprecedented upheavals and conflicts, the twentieth century's sign has been exile. As the cultural critic Edward Said reminds us, modern Western culture has been shaped to a large degree by exiles, émigrés, and refugees; in the process, exile has been transformed into a powerful and enriching motif of art and literature. The literary critic George Steiner has developed the thesis of a genre of twentieth-century writing as "extraterritorial," literature created by and for exiles: "It seems proper that those who create art in a civilization of quasi-barbarism, which has made so many homeless, should themselves be poets unhoused and wanderers across language."[2]

Rosselli devoted much thought to the "exile question" and the problems that exile produced. From Lipari, he once wrote to his mother: "In truth I regret nothing. Neither studies nor career abandoned, nor the forced separation from all of you and my normal life. If there has been anyone who freely chose his own destiny, that would be me. I have never hesitated, I have never doubted . . . Pity him who resists his nature . . . I confess, despite everything, that I love this life as it unwinds under the mind's eye."[3] Rosselli constantly sought to overcome and transform the exile experience into a catalyst for the antifascist struggle and a renewal of European culture. "My mind and my heart," he wrote soon after the flight from Lipari, "are in Italy. There lie our hopes, there is our field of action. [Lussu and I] do not consider ourselves *fuorusciti*, but *estromessi*, prisoners who have reconquered their freedom with the sacred duty of reconquering it one day for all."[4] Recalling a page from Macaulay's *History of England,* Rosselli quoted the English historian that exiles were "people of strong character and noble soul, but scarce intelligence." The exile continues to conceive of the country as it was when he left, trapped in time. This misconception leads to only one of what Rosselli called "the dangers of exile."[5] By 1934, after more than a decade of fascist rule, most exiled antifascists could not understand that for the youth of Italy, fascism was the norm. Many in Italy had no experience of prefascist Italy, and for some, Italy without fascism was almost inconceivable. As much as they detested this mental state, the exiles were forced to recognize its truth if they wished to compete for the allegiance of the youth in Italy. Other mistakes, such as the habit of always depicting fascism on the verge of collapse, were the consequence of exile and more wishful thinking than rational analysis. If Mussolini could weather the Aventine Secession and the Matteotti crisis, how much stronger was the regime after the abolition of all legal opposition and the free press and the creation of the Exceptional Decrees and the Special Tribunal? Fascism, according to Rosselli, had proved that it was capable of surviving, and its overthrow did not seem imminent in the 1930s; the antifascists had to be prepared to work another decade or more, if necessary.

The errors of exile were damning and included exaggerating the importance of the traditional parties; failing to attack fascism at its roots, harboring "sentimental motives" and cultivating an "aristocratic antifascism." Furthermore, there were those who were defending the "so-called prefascist democracy" or existing "pseudo-democracies" and not insisting enough on the positive elements of antifascism. The antifascist resistance in exile was still symbiotically tied to the prefascist parties; this connection was their single greatest weakness, because it prevented them from acknowledging that fascism represented something completely new in European politics and because it prevented them from considering new, revolutionary and possibly "illegal" tactics. History confirmed that intellectuals in exile were instrumental, both from an ideological and a practical point of view, in developing a revolution.

Ironically, on publication of this essay in late 1934, Mussolini himself used it to "prove" the "fatal errors" of the antifascist emigration. Rosselli answered the charges within a week.[6] A few months later, Libero Battistelli, a republican and Mason who had fled to Brazil and who had been active in the antifascist resistance and a member of GL, wrote that the situation in Italy, after more than a decade of fascism, made free intellectual life impossible.[7] Agreeing that the political and cultural life of most Italians had precipitously declined, Rosselli argued that there still existed a minority of young people (and some older intellectuals) who count for a lot more than the *fuorusciti*, who because of the intrigues of exile life, were losing vigor and spontaneity. "In every Italian city, in every university, and even in various working centers, there exist groups of young people that, if for now manage to accomplish little in politics, nevertheless manage to read, study and debate with an open-mindedness and intelligence that are rarely found in exile." Rosselli made reference here to the large number of translations of foreign works carried out in Italy, and he remarked that "someone must read them." It was only after the war, in the late 1940s and the 1950s, that he was proven right in his assessment of intellectual life among the youth of Italy. Writers, artists, and filmmakers commented that for all the claims of "totalitarianism," many could experiment and prepare the ground for that explosively fertile cultural life after the war. In and of itself, exile "is not a force," wrote Rosselli. "It is a fact that leaves open every alternative. *Fuoruscitismo* counts only insomuch as it is the expression, the combative and living part of a movement *in patria*."[8]

One who shared Rosselli's experience and perception of exile was Ignazio Silone. Born appropriately enough on 1 May 1900 as Secondo Tranquilli in the rugged Abruzzi region, Silone joined the PSI, moved to the PCI when it was created in January 1921, and changed his name while in a Spanish prison in 1924 (*secondino* is Italian for "guard"). When the Special Tribunal for the Defense of the State ordered his arrest, he fled to Switzerland. Disenchanted with communism after visiting Moscow, he was expelled from the Swiss Communist Party in 1930, with the blessing of both the PCI and the Communist International. A year later his younger brother Romolo died after being tortured in a fascist prison. Silone spent the next fifteen years in exile, turning away from active politics to literature. His most famous and powerful work, *Fontamara* (Bitter Spring) set in a poor Abruzzi village, recounted a horrific tale of fascist brutality. First published in German, the book was translated into several languages and immediately became a best-seller, changing the opinions of hundreds of thousands of people concerning fascism. In a review, Rosselli called it "a beautiful and painful book," noting that it had received a favorable review from no less than Leon Trotsky. It was the work of "an authentic writer," recommended to all antifascists and anyone who sought "a reflection of humanity in a work of art." Rosselli had insightfully gathered that the protagonist of Silone's novel was not an individual but a social category—the peasantry. It was a scathing revelation of the all-too-common social state of poverty. A scene where the peasants are physically forced to renounce a day's work—and wages—to attend a fascist demonstration definitively reveals the artificial "fabric of consensus" boasted by fascism. No revolutionary program, wrote Rosselli, could ever be as effective and convincing as Silone's book. It was, in short, probably "the best Italian social novel."[9]

Although expelled from communism, Silone still saw class struggle as the key to Italian history since unification. Like Rosselli he was fierce in his condemnation of the prefascist past and the passivity of the political parties, especially reform socialism. "Fascism did fall from the sky," Silone argued after Gobetti, nor was it inevitable. "History is always self-critique." ("La storia è sempre autocritica.") Because Silone fervently believed in the "consciousness, the will, and the force of man," he concluded that "the future belongs to socialism. The future belongs to liberty."[10]

Rosselli recognized in Silone a kindred spirit (Silone had once described himself as "a socialist without a party, a Christian without a church"), and so in shared exile, a correspondence began. Rosselli wrote urging Silone to participate in Justice and Liberty. Silone responded with affirmations of solidarity but pointing out that he had withdrawn from active politics and propaganda. Silone refused to write about tactics or political programs; his experience with the communists was still too fresh in his mind. The expulsion from the party was a liberation, "una vera fortuna," and "not even Christ could make me speak" on things better said by others. Instead Silone was willing to write on cultural issues such as the historical problems of the Italian revolution or the general crisis of socialism, even if, as he himself admitted, the "schoolmarmish presumption and arrogance of a Leninist functionary" marred his previous writings on these subjects. Rosselli recognized Silone's fate as "tragic" yet insisted on his collaboration since *Fontamara* had served the cause of freedom better than all abstract theories.[11] Although Silone contributed several short pieces to the *Quaderni,* he retained his distance from active antifascism.

As the American critic Irving Howe wrote in an introduction to Silone's *Bread and Wine,* but which applies equally well to Rosselli, there are "two encompassing visions" always in "severe tension" in Silone's imagination: "the secular promise of socialist liberation and the Christian promise of spiritual transcendence."[12] Silone was much closer to Rosselli's position than has been acknowledged; when he returned to active politics during the Second World War, he wrote that "today [1942] the usual term, in Italy and abroad, to define our thinking and to distinguish it from traditional socialdemocracy is *liberal socialism.*"[13]

Silone was not an isolated case; characteristically, Rosselli offered the pages of both the newspaper and the journal to a wide range of thinkers and writers. The liberal historian Guido De Ruggiero contributed, as did the radical socialist Lelio Basso, the anarchist Camillo Berneri, and the communist Angelo Tasca. European writers included the Austrian socialist Otto Bauer, the French neosocialist Marcel Dèat, the Hungarian socialist Bela Menczer, the Russian-French sociologist Georges Gurvitch, the Austrian journalist Hans Kaminski, and the French economist Louis Rosen-stock-Franck. *Giustizia e Libertà* and the *Quaderni* thus represented the wide range of European antifascism.

Ethiopian War

On 15 May 1935, the Turinese group of Justice and Liberty was decimated by mass arrests. A month before, to quell domestic criticism in preparation for the Ethiopian War, Mussolini had instructed the police to prepare a roundup of dissidents. The members in Turin were betrayed by a pornographer and police spy, Dino Segre, who was known as "Pitigrilli."[14] Among the more than two hundred persons arrested were Michele Giua, professor at the Military Academy of Turin (sentenced to fifteen years); Vittorio Foa, lawyer (fifteen years); Massimo Mila, writer and music critic (eight years); Augusto Monti, teacher of a generation of young writers, including Cesare Pavese (five years); and Carlo Levi.

On hearing the news in Paris, Carlo Rosselli immediately recognized the significance of the arrests. The Turin branch of GL was the largest, most active and most creative of the cells in Italy. For Rosselli, who had always insisted that the real antifascist struggle had to take place in Italy, the destruction of the Turin organization was a tremendous blow. The problem of police spies infiltrating the movement was crippling, and Rosselli was often criticized for not doing enough to prevent such lapses. Furthermore, the arrests could not have come at a worse time. Emilio Lussu had withdrawn temporarily from active work because of illness; soon he resigned from the Central Committee of GL in a dispute with Rosselli. He eventually moved to Switzerland and returned to active antifascism only in 1937.[15] Nenni and Tasca were continuing their criticisms of Rosselli. A new group of extreme republicans, the ARS (Azione Repubblicana Socialista) presented itself as a rival to Rosselli's movement. Justice and Liberty was preparing a concerted campaign against the Ethiopian War but had become isolated from the other antifascist parties because of its polemic with the Antifascist Concentration, Rosselli's criticism of the socialists and communists, and his interest in the French neosocialists.

The Ethiopian War marked another turning point in Rosselli's analysis of Italian fascism.[16] Although he had written in 1933 that fascism and national socialism inevitably led to war, he had perhaps underestimated Mussolini's regime, believing that it would not risk a confrontation with

Britain or France over Ethiopia. When in February and March 1935 preparations were being made for an armed expedition to Ethiopia, Rosselli was
forced to recognize that Mussolini's regime would be going to war, despite
what France, Britain, or the League of Nations might say. War with Ethiopia would represent a radical break with the past. Along with Liberia,
Ethiopia was the only African country independent from European rulers.
A war would be long and bloody; revenge for the Italian defeat at Adowa in
1896 could be achieved in a few months against a people without modern
military technology, but "it will take years, decades, to subdue, or rather
exterminate, a free people of ten million."[17] Not without reason, Rosselli
saw the Italian war in Africa as an opportunity for nazi Germany to "colo-
nize" Austria, which was recognized to be within the Italian sphere of
influence since the end of the Great War. As the Italian-Turkish War of
1911–12 forecast the European conflagration of 1914–18, the Italian-Ethio-
pian War would signal a new European war. A month later, Rosselli listed
the reasons why Justice and Liberty was against the Ethiopian "adventure":

> We are against the African war:
>   (a) because it is a fascist war;
>   (b) because it is a capitalist-statist war;
>   (c) because it is a colonial war;
>   (d) because it is a war.[18]

Yet Rosselli was mistaken in believing that the regime's decision to go to
war in Africa could only lead to civil war in Italy. Between April and May
1935, he devoted three articles to the propaganda campaign against the
war.[19] A realistic analysis of the forthcoming war would reveal that the
fascists had every possibility of victory. Fascist propaganda was promising
all things to all people: unemployed workers and land-hungry peasants
were presented a picture of a wealthy colony to be exploited; middle-class
citizens were promised easy positions in a colonial bureaucracy; the adventurous youth were assured of a new challenge and an evasion of the bore-
dom of normal life, with the possibility of glory. Rosselli had noted what
the historian Victoria De Grazia was to point out sixty years later: that the
war was the "perfect war for mass consumption."[20] Or in Rosselli's words,
"Abyssinia will function as a diversion on a grand scale." How were the
antifascists to combat this line of propaganda? Rosselli insisted that *the
African war is absolutely unpopular.*"[21] Here Rosselli may have been himself
a victim of exile; although hotly contested, the Ethiopian War was a great

success for Mussolini's regime. Rosselli was closer to the truth in seeing the Ethiopian War as an example of the "new imperialism." The older empires had been built on a conception of economics and politics that was by now superseded by events like the Industrial Revolution and modern warfare. Germany had developed into a world power in the thirty years after its unification although it had no colonies or empire to speak of. "Yankee capitalism," wrote Rosselli, colonizes the world without "taking" countries; as in the Philippines, it "liberates" countries, the better to subject them to American markets. The new economic crisis could not be solved by acquiring colonies but had to be solved at home, "revolutionizing a social system that makes modern technology a force for impoverishment and by renouncing idiotic dreams of autarky." Ordinary logic dictates that colonial wars are fought for territorial expansion. But Mussolini and fascism, for Rosselli, were not logical. What, then, were the reasons for this war? In the third essay of the series, Rosselli attempted a psychological profile of Mussolini to discern the reasons. Mussolini was 53 in 1935, "on the threshold of old-age . . . what will he leave behind?" With the Monarchy and the Papacy still intact, Mussolini could claim neither a social nor a political revolution. The dictatorship might claim roads, buildings, land reclamation schemes, but nothing that could not have been accomplished, and better, by another political regime. In foreign policy, the picture was not much brighter: no expansion of frontiers, no conquest of Dalmatia, no wars won. Mussolini's only claim would be to have "saved Italy from Bolshevism," inaugurating a series of mass, reactionary regimes in Europe—an ironic boast for a former revolutionary socialist. A restlessness had been creeping into Italian society, and a great, diversionary spectacle was necessary for the people. Once again the myth of Imperial Rome was brought out for public consumption, and generals began to emulate the ancient Roman general Scipio. The Ethiopian campaign was not just a capitalist war, caused by the Italian bourgeoisie in their incessant search for profits; of more importance and more to the point, it was a war that revealed the desperation of the fascist regime.[22]

The antifascist opposition to the war, according to Rosselli, had been extremely weak for several reasons. For one thing, the old mentality of the prefascist past was still alive in parties, programs, and individuals. Secondly, because of the mechanics of totalitarianism, the antifascist opposition had been reduced for years to a position of negation—a permanent *no*, which can be proof of character but was not sufficient to generate enthusiasm and sympathy. It was necessary that antifascism pass from *no* to *yes,* affirming itself no longer, or not just, as *anti*-fascism, but as a positive, renovating force of Italian society. How ironic, wrote Rosselli, that Italian youths were asked to bring "civilization" to African "savages" when they themselves were "convinced that the present civilization is false and corrupt and cannot renovate itself without revolution and internal war." The antifascists should instead prepare for war against the dictatorship to return dignity to man; war against capitalism and the bourgeois mentality; war against the Papacy, "the great center of corruption of our history"; and war against the "monarchy, rhetoric, venal patriotism, corporative red-tape, reactionary and reformist socialists." This would not be a traditional war for "old diplomacies, the old States, the old Europe" but rather a war in the name of "a socialist and liberating humanism."[23]

Although Rosselli, in truth, did not offer much in the way of tactics to oppose the war beyond a renewed propaganda campaign, his analysis of the war was insightful. In July (well before military operations began in October) he wrote that the war was unlike any other colonial venture; in its logistical and economic demands, it had to be compared with a war on the European continent. Victory would be worse than defeat because it would confirm Mussolini and the fascists in their belief in the imperial myth and because the war itself would lead to political and economic ruin.[24] As for the fascist argument that land in Ethiopia would relieve overpopulation and land scarcity in the *Mezzogiorno* (an argument especially attractive to Italian immigrants in other countries), Rosselli asked how it would be possible for Italy to find the necessary capital to develop Abyssinia when the capital could not be found to develop the *Mezzogiorno*. Emigration cannot be easily directed, just as population cannot be easily manipulated. This undertaking was a "great illusion."[25] Although Rosselli was too optimistic in believing that "Abyssinia will be for Mussolini's Italy what Spain was for Napoleon's France,"[26] he correctly foresaw that France and Britain would not risk a major conflict with Italy over Abyssinia while Hitler reigned in Germany[27] and that Mussolini was engaging in a foreign war for reasons of domestic politics.[28]

In the context of an impending war in Africa, Rosselli proposed an alliance with the communists to consecrate all available forces against the regime. The communists refused to join any alliance in which it had to share power or modify its principles. A trip to England confirmed Rosselli's suspicions that the British were unwilling to risk a confrontation with Mussolini. Conditions had changed in Britain; perhaps nothing symbolized this change as much as the fact that the editor of the *Times,* a newspaper that had done so much to secure Marion's release from prison after Carlo's escape from Lipari, was now a fervent supporter of the fascist regime in Italy.

In October 1935, communists, socialists, republicans, democrats, anarchists, and members of the LIDU met in Brussels for a Congress of Italians Abroad to deal with the Ethiopian War and to debate the question of sanctions. The Congress concluded its work by sending a telegram to the president of the League of Nations, Edvard Beneš, demanding that a firm policy of sanctions be applied against fascist Italy. Rosselli had declined to attend the Congress, believing that the event would be more words than action and would not achieve anything concrete. Instead Justice and Liberty held its own congress a month earlier in Paris. The result was a "Manifesto agli Italiani" written by Rosselli and Umberto Calosso.[29]

When in early 1936 it became obvious that Mussolini was close to victory in Ethiopia, Rosselli was honest enough to recognize his error in thinking that the African campaign would take years.[30] Instead it represented the symbolic closing of one era and the opening of another, more dangerous period. Yet victory in Africa, in the end, would be a "ball of lead" for the regime. In possession of an "empire," Italy would have to devote scarce and precious resources to "pacify" the Ethiopians. One day it would become clear just what a folly it was to launch Italy on a path of imperial competition with Britain or France when it lacked the necessary economic and industrial potential. For Rosselli, the Ethiopian War was to foreign policy what Mussolini's speech of 3 January 1925 was to domestic policy— a conscious move to overcome a crisis of regime.[31] After Mussolini declared the formation of the "Empire" from the balcony of Palazzo Venezia in Rome on 9 May 1936, Rosselli wrote that "it is better to recognize with a virile frankness that fascism, at least domestically, emerges reinforced, consolidated by this crisis."[32]

The Prophet Armed

The Spanish Civil War was the last act in the Rosselli drama. Paraphrasing Machiavelli's critical judgment of the fervent reformer of Renaissance Florence, Savonarola, Rosselli instead boasted that "the prophets are no longer disarmed. And the descendants of the prophets, with rifle in hand, have acquired a new consciousness."[33] As he had foreseen, victory in Ethiopia pushed fascism, with a renewed yet false sense of confidence, into new adventures. Even before victory was proclaimed in Africa, the regime was setting its sights on other parts of Europe. In Spain on 16 February 1936, the republicans were elected after the so-called *bienio negro*, or two black years, of conservative rule. In 1934 the Republic had been threatened but had been saved by an uprising of peasants and workers in the Asturias. Meanwhile, a coalition of French socialists and radicals were victorious in the spring elections of 1936, in what seemed like an effective response to the attempted coup d'état of February 1934.

Although it might have appeared that the forces of the Left were finally responding to the fascist threat in Europe, Rosselli saw continued signs of weakness. He criticized the Italian version of the Popular Front as defensive and insufficient in answering fascism by re-creating the old party coalitions of the past. In the very month (June 1936) that the Popular Front published a ringing manifesto calling for the governments of Europe to resist fascism in Europe, the conservative British government announced in the House of Commons that the effort to impose sanctions against Italy for the Ethiopian War would be abandoned. For Rosselli it was a fundamental mistake to appeal to the League of Nations or the national governments when they had so clearly and obviously "betrayed their mission." The Popular Front was making the fatal error of repeating the strategy of the Aventine Secession. The call for an uprising in Italy was premature, and totalitarian Italy was not democratic France. The fascist victory in Ethiopia forced the antifascists to rethink their basic ideas, regroup, and reorganize.

On 4 July 1936, the League of Nations officially ended the sanctions against Italy. Rosselli's response was summed up in one word: nausea.[34] Stephen Lux, a Viennese Jew, Czech citizen, and journalist for *Prague Presse,* committed suicide during the 4 July session in order to call attention to the plight of the Jews in Hitler's Germany. For Rosselli the suicide of Lux was an individual and symbolic gesture of the collective suicide of democratic Europe. Mussolini and Hitler had reduced the League of Nations to insignificance and could now proceed with their plan for the fascistization of Europe. Their only conclusion would be that a Britain that did not go to war over the Mediterranean would not go to war for central or eastern Europe; and that a France that did not go to war over the Ruhr valley would not go to war over Austria or Czechoslovakia.

Several days after the attempted coup d'état of 18 July 1936 in Spain, various members of Justice and Liberty met in the offices of the journal on

Rue Val-de-Grâce. Rosselli proposed a quick and decisive intervention of a united volunteer force of antifascists in Spain; here was the opportunity to transform antifascism from a negative, passive idea into a positive, active force. "In view of the fact that fascism won by force and rules by force, in view of the fact that the most basic freedoms have been snuffed out; in view of the fact that in certain hours a deed is worth more than a thousand speeches, we Italian exiles, volunteers of freedom, will begin to combat fascism with force in Spain."[35]

Unfortunately, the reform socialists were hesitant, and the communists were awaiting word from Moscow on how to proceed. Only the maximalist socialists and the anarchists agreed with Rosselli's demand for a volunteer force to leave immediately for Spain.[36] For the next ten months, Rosselli fought the fascists while trying to convince the supporters of the Spanish Republic that this was not just a civil war to defend the Republic but was the first scene of the last act of the drama of European fascism. Rosselli conceived of the Spanish Civil War as the first real opportunity to combat fascism on equal terms, on the field of battle, with the only element understood by fascism—force. In a letter from the front after his first battle, he recalled Ernesto Rossi's motto that "Ideas are worthless if one is not ready to serve them with action."[37] The Marxists and anarchists instead saw the war as the opportunity to create a Marxist or an anarchist society. This differing vision of the Spanish Civil War was to cripple the effort to defend the Republic.

Spain had occupied Rosselli only sporadically in the 1930s. He had visited the country twice in the spring of 1931 in an attempt to organize another propaganda flight over Italy. The first issue of the *Quaderni di Giustizia e Libertà* had published the complete text of the Constitution of the Spanish Republic. It was not until three years later that he returned to the subject.[38] After the uprisings in Vienna and Spain, Rosselli concluded that fascism could not come to power except through civil war. Also, the power and the importance of Spanish anarchism had to be recognized, even if it contained certain inherent problems. The really fatal error of the Spanish revolution of 1932 was the failure to implement land reform. Without casting doubt on the good faith and high moral standard of the revolutionary leader Manuel Azaña, Rosselli criticized his conception of the Republic as "platonic and quixotic." The position of both the Marxists in the POUM (Partito Obrero de Unificación Marxista) and the anarcho-syndicalists in rejecting the "bourgeois republic" was another mistake in

Spain. Yet for all his criticism of the leading players and forces in Spain, Rosselli sought out both Spanish Marxists and Spanish anarchists.

One week after the attempted coup, Rosselli's first editorial on the Spanish crisis appeared in *Giustizia e Libertà*. The traditional reactionary forces—Church, Army, Monarchists, large landowners—had launched the "supreme attack" against the Republic, and the people of Spain were well aware that their destiny was at stake. The uprising in Spain represented more than just a "clerical-feudal" reaction against the Republic; the future of Spain was at stake. The civil war contained a lesson for antifascists: "a revolution, if it does not wish to be ephemeral, cannot stop halfway, and that the respect for democratic legality . . . is the tomb of revolutionaries."[39] The situation was, in the literal sense of the word, a crisis in that after the uprising, Spain would be either socialist or fascist; all intermediary positions had been swept away. The outcome would determine the social struggle in Europe for years to come. If Francisco Franco and his forces were successful, it would signify "the death toll for the last European democracies."[40] In a letter to Marion in early August,[41] Rosselli mistakenly thought that the conflict would take weeks "or perhaps months" to be resolved. The policy of "nonintervention" was a pathetic spectacle. It was a "scandal" that the French government refused to send airplanes when Mussolini had already sent twenty-one.[42] Hitler had sent twenty-four Junker transport planes to Morocco by late July. Léon Blum was caught in his knowledge of the gravity of the situation and his usual doubts. The Catholic Church, for its part, issued the papal encyclical *Divini Redemptoris* in March 1937, blessing the crusade against "atheistic communism."[43]

With his arrival in Barcelona during the first week in August 1936 being noted by the police,[44] Rosselli was received by a contingent of FAI (Federación Anarquista Ibérica) and introduced to members of the CNT (Confederación Nacional del Trabajo) and POUM. He wrote back to Marion that "for now, it is a not a real war, a modern war, but rather a slow siege"[45] and managed to hammer together an accord with the regional government of Catalonia to create an Italian antifascist column of volunteers. Members of Justice and Liberty joined with Italian anarchists to create the Ascaso Column.[46] Together, Rosselli and the Republican Mario Angeloni shared command of this first group of 130 Italian volunteers: 90 infantry under the command of Rosselli and 40 machine gunners under Angeloni. Of this group, approximately seventy to eighty were anarchists, twenty were members of Justice and Liberty, and the remainder were either socialists, communists, or republicans.[47] After a week, Rosselli returned to Paris, where he tried to convince the other antifascists to volunteer in Spain. At the end of the month, he was back in Spain, on the Aragon front. By October 1936, the first elements of the International Brigades had come together in Spain.

The Loyalists lacked everything except valor and enthusiasm. Arms were desperately needed, and Rosselli placed what remained of his family patrimony at the service of the Republic. The attempts to purchase arms sometimes led to confusion, as when two representatives (one from Justice and Liberty, the other a socialist) went to Belgium: presenting themselves as fascist arms merchants, they arranged for an arms shipment to be sent to Spain. However, the workers who were to transport the arms, on hearing of the "fascist" buyers, went on strike. The two representatives had to approach the leaders of the workers and reveal their true identity, after which the material was allowed to pass.[48]

Rosselli was also instrumental in helping to form André Malraux's air squadron, the only air defense of the Republic before the arrival of planes from the USSR. The pilot Giordano Viezzoli, a member of GL, volunteered for service in Malraux's squadron, but on 30 September 1936, he was killed during a dogfight over the skies of Madrid.[49] The fascist police, efficient as usual, were aware of an important meeting that took place in Malraux's house in the summer of 1936. Malraux had invited his friend Leo Lagrange, Minister of Sport in the French government, to discuss the possibility of French support for the Spanish Republic. Rosselli and Viezzoli were also present, along with the Russian writer Ilya Ehrenburg.[50] Malraux personally intervened that night to effect a reconciliation between Rosselli and Nicola Chiaromonte. Chiaromonte had left Justice and Liberty in 1935 when Rosselli moved further to the Left, and he had gravitated to the anarchist groups in exile and had edited a volume of Andrea Caffi's writings called *A Critique of Violence*. During the Spanish Civil War, though, Chiaromonte abandoned his pacifism and fought with Malraux's air squadron. In his book *Man's Hope*, Malraux based the character of Scali, the art historian who reads Plato at the front, on Chiaromonte.

Although constantly moving from the front to Barcelona to Paris, Rosselli managed to set down his personal thoughts in a diary.[51] After meeting the anarcho-syndicalist leader Santillán ("one of the rare anarcho-syndicalist intellectuals"), Rosselli inquired as to when they would be leaving for the front. "*Mañana,*" came the reply. In panic Rosselli tried to explain that the column was not ready, that the men were exhausted, and that it would be a few days before they were even familiar with their weapons and the most rudimentary tactics of warfare. It was only later that he began to realize that in Spain, *mañana* really meant some ambiguous and vague moment in the future. "*Mañana*—that fatal word—the key to the psychology and the technique of this adorable, but slow and disorganized, people. With the ample music of its three *a*s, *mañana* seems to open up the entire future."[52]

After several weeks, *mañana* finally arrived, and the volunteers set off for the front: "The Ascaso Column leaves in three rows. The *compañeros* make sure not to march in step, they make a concerted effort to not march in step. They do not wish to be confused with soldiers. They sing, they raise their fists. The joy of those departing is as visible as the vexation of those that remain behind."[53] And in a passage reminiscent of George Orwell's description of the "multiform" rather than the uniform, Rosselli wrote in his diary for 19 August 1936, in Barcelona:

> Only the anonymous genius of the revolution could have invented this extraordinary, but at the same time natural, uniform: overalls. The war of the workers will be made with the uniform of labor. On 19 July, there was no time to undress. The workers left the factories in overalls to launch themselves against the soldiers. Five hundred died. But the revolution was victorious in the cities and now the workshop extends its sovereignty over the barracks.
>
> The anarchist worker would have refused the uniform. He wears instead, without coercion, the overalls, his everyday dress. You fascists that minutely study the composition and colors of uniforms; Hitler, who recounts in *Mein Kampf* of having spent entire days in consultation with his tailor, and you, dogmatic revolutionaries, here is how the new uniform emerges. Carlyle could add a note to his *Sartor Resartus*. Yes, the clothes make the revolution.
>
> The intellectual who dons the overalls for the first time feels an ineffable sentiment of joy. Here, I slough off my past, my bourgeois habits and wants, to consecrate myself to the cause of the workers. I enter the revolution with only body and soul. We will be brothers, comrades in overalls. Every distinction and rank disappears.[54]

During that first eventful month of August in Spain, Rosselli reflected on his life in exile and the turn that it was now taking. After ten years of prison, deportations, escapes, and exile, it was now the moment to take up arms. After having preached the necessity of intervention, it was only right that the intellectuals now participate personally. "Besides, this human experience and this effort of consistency is worth more than any political mission."[55] That "human experience" characterized Rosselli's time in Spain, from the moment he crossed the border by train. Here is his description of a stop at the town of Tarrasa on the night journey by rail to the front. It deserves to be quoted at length:

The night swallows me up.

It is one o'clock. We are stopped in a station. A tremendous crowd—thousands and thousands—has invaded the sidewalks and tracks. Shouts, applause, they climb onto the car. Quick, grab. From the small window, where there is already a horde of comrades, every gift of God enters. Melons, watermelons, bread, prosciutto, salami, wine, cheese.

"Long live the revolution!"

"Long live Spain!"

"Long live Italy!"

It is the offering of Tarrasa to those departing for the front. The women are the most enthusiastic. During ten minutes, there is a frenetic discussion between train and station, between volunteers and the people. The entire city of Tarrasa is in the station to greet the Italian volunteers. Everyone. The large industrial town has not slept for fifteen days. Every night it goes to greet the trains, to fête the volunteers.

Tarrasa, Tarrasa! The heart breaks. The conversations become more private. The *compagno* has found his *compagna*.

Now the train is ready to depart.

A speaker of the committee salutes us. "Answer," my comrades yell. I yell our thanks and our best wishes, in a Spanish-Italian. The train moves, the crowd is gripped as if by a trembling, my comrades sing at the top of their voice to cover their emotion. I too have tears; here is the revolution in the moment of its immense fraternity; oh Spain, how worthy it is to fight for you, oh how one can be ready to give one's life, after Tarrasa, for Tarrasa, for all the infinite, grey, monotonous, working-class Tarrasas.

The secret anguish of the departure has disappeared from everyone's face. During the night, the train hosts an explosion of life. We pound each other on the shoulders, yell, and look deeply into each others' moist eyes, and between a slice of watermelon and a sandwich, we shamelessly confess our faith.

Yes, it is worthwhile. Our Dulcinea is now called Tarassa.[56]

The Italian Ascaso Column received its baptism of fire at Monte Pelato on 28 August 1936, where, though outnumbered and lacking proper weapons, they held their own against Franco's forces. Tragically, Angeloni was killed in this first action, and thus command of the Ascaso Column passed exclusively to Rosselli, who was slightly wounded by "an intelligent bullet." The battle raged for four hours in the early morning hours, ending abruptly at half past nine.[57] As Rosselli wrote in his diary: "The terrain and the sun direct the war. I have learned from conversations with the Spanish soldiers that war is conducted until nine in the morning. Afterwards, the heat and the dryness impede any combat. And then the hours for the *comida,* meals, are sacred on both sides."[58] Although Rosselli often made light of the dangers at the front, especially in his letters to Marion, the dangers were real enough: at Monte Pelato, the Italian Column lost Angeloni, and six others were killed, including Giuseppe Zuddas, a colleague of Emilio Lussu's in the Sardinian Action Party and a member of the Central Committee of GL. Aldo Garosci and three others were wounded. "Angeloni died like a classic hero: 'Farewell comrades'—he cried from the embankment where he was overexposed. He sang the *Internazionale,* spoke of his family and was conscious until the end . . . He told the Spaniards that is was beautiful and easy to die for freedom."[59] Rosselli himself was lost to the volunteers as he retreated to a Swiss ambulance to tend to his wound.[60]

After the battle of Monte Pelato, the Italians were regarded with new respect, and Rosselli was asked to participate in several "war councils" at the front. Although this recognition granted him greater influence in the planning of the war, it diminished his efficiency as commander of the Ascaso Column. Two larger problems were to hinder the Loyalists: the first problem was a dispute between Rosselli and the Italian and Spanish anarchists; the second, indirectly related to the first, was the vehement debate surrounding the "militarization" of the volunteers.[61]

Central to this dispute was the relationship between Rosselli and the Italian anarchist Camillo Berneri.[62] Writing for both Salvemini's *L'Unità* in Florence and Piero Gobetti's *La Rivoluzione Liberale* in Turin, Berneri had joined the anarchist circles after a brief membership in the Socialist Party. He had been among the early supporters of the *Non Mollare!* group in Florence in 1925 and had fled to France but was expelled in 1934. He eventually found his way to Spain, where he joined the members of Justice and Liberty in the Ascaso Column and fought at the battle of Monte Pelato. Even before Spain, Rosselli and Berneri had worked together; in the pages of *Giustizia e Libertà,* Berneri had written a long defense of anarchism and the compatibility of that doctrine with Rosselli's thinking.[63] For Berneri, Rosselli's critique of Marx was in a long line of Italian anarchist thinkers such as Errico Malatesta, Stefano Merlino, and Luigi Fabbri; yet there were also points of diversion between the two camps. Rosselli was clear in pointing out that anarchism was still tied to the nineteenth century, whereas Justice and Liberty represented a "new phenomenon . . . that responded to the demands of a diverse society."[64] For all the infighting between the anarchists and Justice and Liberty, Rosselli remained a strong admirer of the anarchists and their "revolt against history." They were one of the "heroic avant-gardes of the western revolution . . . creating a new world."[65] "Catalonian anarchism," Rosselli declared in a speech over Radio Barcelona, "is a constructive socialism, sensitive to the problems of freedom and culture. Every day it furnishes proof of its realistic qualities."[66] When the Italian anarchist Antonio Cieri was killed at the front of Huesca, Rosselli wrote a sincere and moving obituary in the pages of *Giustizia e Libertà*.[67]

Catalonia, the stronghold of Spanish anarchism was, for Rosselli, the "bulwark of the revolution." Anarcho-syndicalism, which had been defamed and misunderstood, was showing itself to be capable of constructive work. Catalonian anarchism was in the great tradition of Bakunin and Proudhon; from Sorel, it had recognized the danger and paralysis of bureaucratic and reformist socialism. Its greatest figure was the educator and martyr Francisco Ferrer. Catalonia was now witnessing the birth of a new form of social democracy, the synthesis of the theory and praxis of the Russian experience with the legacy of the West. Catalonian anarchism was a "libertarian humanism."[68]

In a way, the debate taking place in Spain resembled the conflict with the Antifascist Concentration in Paris. Were the volunteer columns representatives of the old parties, or should they be, as Rosselli maintained, the nuclei of new political formations? The problem of military discipline was compounded by the fact that many volunteers had never been professional soldiers. The large contingent of anarchists naturally viewed with suspicion any attempt to impose a hierarchy. In a clear indication of the prevailing sentiment, posters appeared in the streets of Barcelona: *Soldato? Nunca! Miliciano del pueblo.*[69] Rosselli's close ties with the military and political leaders in defense of the Republic made him a favorite target of those who thought that no military organization or discipline was necessary. Fernando De Rosa's death on 16 September, because of inadequate preparation and organization, lent force to Rosselli's argument.

During the first days of September 1936, the representatives of the various antifascist organizations fighting in Spain gathered, at the behest of the socialists and communists, to examine the possibility of a united antifascist front against Franco. The meeting ended with a proposal to form a Popular Front at the service of the Republican government still in Madrid. Representing Justice and Liberty were Alberto Cianca and Franco Venturi. Ironically, the very position that Rosselli was insisting on—the formation of a united antifascist front—was the development that would diminish his influence in Spain. Finally culminating in the formation of the Garibaldi Battalion, this strategy left Rosselli with less power than in the first days of the insurrection. Yet he maintained an almost naive optimism during 1936.[70]

Rosselli left Paris, where he had gone to recuperate from his wound, and returned to Barcelona on 7 November. Toledo, forty miles south of Madrid, had fallen to Franco's rebel forces just a few weeks earlier. Relations with the anarchists were increasingly strained, requiring "the patience of Job," as he wrote to his wife; "I feel within me an enormous energy, but also an inadequacy and pain for such a wait. It's a problem with all revolutions, with all creations."[71] Recognizing that the question of an efficient control and use of men and arms was the central problem of the revolution, Rosselli proposed the transformation of the volunteer brigades into formal, fully mechanized divisions capable of offensive strikes.[72] It was absolutely necessary that the volunteers be reorganized on a more technical basis without in any way abandoning or losing their revolutionary fervor. It was not possible to continue with the present system, geared to a "war of position," and incapable of an offensive or a "war of movement." The "state of siege" mentality of the Loyalists was suicidal and prohibited fighting the war as a social revolution.[73]

The same day that Rosselli sent the proposal, he gave over Radio Barcelona what was to be his most important speech. It was an act that probably sealed his fate. The Loyalists had effectively used the radio for propaganda, and so Rosselli was asked to do a broadcast that would be transmitted into Italy. In stirring and ringing phrases, he urged Italians in Italy to support the Spanish Republic as the first step in overthrowing fascism in Europe:

Comrades, Italian brothers, listen.

An Italian volunteer speaks to you by radio from Barcelona to bring you the greetings of thousands of exiled Italian antifascist volunteers who are fighting in the ranks of the revolutionary army.[74]

Rosselli tied the volunteer and exile tradition to the most famous and glorious names in recent Italian history: Santarosa in Greece; Garibaldi in the Americas; Mazzini in England; and Pisacane in France—all fighting for justice and freedom. What were the volunteers fighting for? A new order based on freedom and social justice:

> In revolutionary Spain, and above all in libertarian Catalonia, the most audacious social advances are being made respecting the personality of man and the autonomy of human groups. Communism, yes, but libertarian communism. Socialization of the large industries and large-scale trade, but not statolotry; the socialization of the means of production and exchange is conceived as a means to free man from all forms of slavery.[75]

In a direct appeal to Italians, Rosselli told them that

> Every day airplanes furnished by Italian fascism and piloted by mercenary aviators who dishonor our country launch bombs against defenseless cities, killing women and children. Every day Italian bombs constructed with Italian hands, transported by Italian ships, launched by Italian cannons, fall in the trenches of the workers. Franco would have already lost some time ago, if it were not for the powerful fascist aid. It must be shameful for Italians to know that their government, the government of a people that was at one time in the avant-garde of the struggle for freedom, attempts to assassinate the freedom of the Spanish people![76]

Carlo had somehow managed to inform Nello in Florence of both the hour and the frequency of his broadcast. Nello, according to his son Aldo, sensed that Carlo had taken an irrevocable step that might lead to tragedy.[77] Four days after this radio broadcast, a report was submitted by the fascist police: "Rosselli is the most outstanding personality of Italian antifascism in the Spanish Civil War . . . and participates in the most important executive committees. He enjoys great popularity among the antifascist soldiers who recently joined to designate him the only possible successor to Mussolini."[78]

Two weeks later, Rosselli was sent a telegram by Garcia Oliver, who requested his assistance in Valencia. Since his ties with the Italian Ascaso Column had continued to degenerate because of disputes with the anarchists, Rosselli submitted his resignation on 6 December 1936. Unfortunately, a relapse of phlebitis was to prevent him from taking up his new duties in Valencia. In letters to Alberto Cianca, who had remained in Paris to assume editorial responsibilities for *Giustizia e Libertà*, Rosselli wrote that by December a definitive rupture had occurred in the Italian section. The conflict was not between Spaniards and Italians, but between *giellisti* and anarchists. "In Catalonia, there is a period of rather acute crisis. A minority faction of anarchists opposes semi-militarization which is now indispensable."[79] And he concluded, "The old Italian section no longer exists. There exists a new Giacomo Matteotti Battalion, open to all."[80]

By the end of 1936, Rosselli's characteristic optimism was giving way in the face of mounting difficulties. His close relationship with Salvemini had become strained; Rosselli was moving further to the Left, and Salvemini was becoming more pessimistic. "You hope for a popular revolution in Italy," Salvemini wrote to Rosselli from Harvard University; "I have lost all faith in the revolutionary proletariat."[81] The continued "nonintervention" of France and Britain, along with the war matériel flowing to Franco's forces from fascist Italy and nazi Germany, made the international picture bleak. In France, Leon Blum defended the policy of "nonintervention." Winston Churchill was particularly pleased and noted with characteristic bluntness that by attacking the Spanish Republic, Mussolini had performed a historic role. "Liberty was lost," Churchill observed, "but Italy was saved."[82] Within Spain there were continuing disputes among the defenders of the Republic, with ideological demands hindering the prosecution of the war. A note of exasperation began to creep into Rosselli's letters.[83] Slow, disordered, and sometimes chaotic, Spain (not unlike Italy, it should be admitted) was also hindered by a certain mentality that Rosselli thought he detected in the people—"the tragic *mañana*"—that was incompatible with fighting a revolution.[84]

Back in Paris to recuperate from his wound and phlebitis, Rosselli continued to organize men and arms for the Spanish republicans, although he was often suffering from the twin scourges of "nostalgia and temptation."[85] He returned to the offices of *Giustizia e Libertà*, where he wrote several penetrating essays on the course of the war in Spain and the unfolding of developments in Europe.[86] In February, speaking to volunteers in Argenteuil about to depart for the front, Rosselli reiterated the reasons for fighting in Spain. The volunteers were headed for "the ideal *patria*," the one that the exiles had been fighting for in Italy. As for many others, fighting for the Spanish Republic was a defining experience; for Rosselli, it even could be considered a metamorphosis: "I must confess that after the long years of exile, it was only when I passed the borders of Spain, when I enrolled in the peoples' militia and donned the overalls, the symbolic uniform of armed labor and embraced the rifle that I felt a free man again, in the fullness of my dignity."[87]

After more than a decade of persecution, arrests, trials, imprisonment and exile, the antifascists could finally feel themselves to be part of a larger community. The stigma of exile, though worn with fierce pride, could be set aside in a larger cause. After years of having to ask, beg, and receive, the antifascists were finally able to give, to contribute, to establish themselves as a positive force, fighting *for* something. The Spanish experience had opened new horizons and possibilities. Rosselli recounted the episode at the train station of Tarrasa to the departing volunteers as an example of the tremendous cauldron of humanity that they were about to enter. Spain was a decisive turning point in the history of Italian antifascism: "The myth of an antifascist that does not fight is ended. The defamation of an Italian proletariat incapable of reacting to fascism is ended. The academy of exile in which an ungrateful destiny seemed to condemn us is ended."[88] The intervention in Spain would be the bridge that would bind the antifascists to Italy and act as a catalyst for a humanistic, socialist revolution in Italy. The antifascists would lead the Italian people from their servitude and passivity into a new period of history when they would be active, conscious agents of their own fate. For Spain, for Italy, for the new socialist revolution, "it is worth it—if necessary—to die."[89]

That necessity was borne by Antonio Gramsci, who died on 27 April 1937 after eleven years in fascist prisons. *Giustizia e Libertà* devoted a six-column headline and the entire first page to his death, calling it a "slow assassination."[90] Rosselli's commentary placed Gramsci along with Gobetti as a heroic martyr: "Ils seront reconnus un jour comme les prophètes de l'Italie libre qui se construit aujourd'hui par l'esprit et par une lutte très dure." For Rosselli, Gramsci was the very incarnation of the revolutionary ascetic. With his death, "humanity has lost a genius and the Italian revolution lost its leader."[91] On 22 May, at the Gymnase Huygens in Paris, a commemoration was held in Gramsci's memory. Among the speakers (besides a fascist spy) were Marcel Cachin, editor of the French communist paper *L'Humanité*, Egidio Gennari of the PCI, Bruno Buozzi of the PSI, and Carlo Rosselli. In his speech, just two weeks before his own death, Rosselli contrasted Gramsci and Mussolini as embodying two different types of politics and two different types of humanity. Whereas Mussolini was "bruyant, irrationnel, improvisateur, démagogue, aventurier, traître à l'idéal de sa jeunesse," Gramsci was "intime, réservé, rationnel, sévère, ennemi de la réthorique et de toute sorte de facilité, fidèle à la classe ouvrière dans la bonne comme dans la mauvaise fortune."[92]

Last Project

Rosselli's last theoretical project was a series of five essays devoted to the goal of the political unification of the Italian proletariat.[93] The essays clearly reveal that the experience of the Spanish Civil War and the evolution of developments in Europe had pushed Rosselli further to the Left in his thinking. Whereas previously he had insisted that an enlightened, minority fraction of the bourgeoisie would lead the socialist revolution, that vital role now passed to the proletariat in light of the irreparable crisis of capitalism and the moral-political failure of the European middle class to prevent the rise and spread of fascism. Still, he never accepted a rigidly class-based definition of fascism, even in his last and most radical phase.[94]

The aim of unifying all the political currents of the proletariat to forge a truly effective revolutionary force was of the utmost importance. In effect, the essays were the culmination of Rosselli's political thinking and activity since 1925 and of the work of *Non Mollare!* in Florence. Throughout all the developments of the fascist period, from the declaration of the totalitarian state in January 1925 to the formation of Justice and Liberty to the Ethiopian and Spanish Civil Wars, Rosselli had insisted on the creation of a united, revolutionary front against Mussolini's regime. This undertaking could come about only after the unification of the proletariat; after nearly a decade and a half of fascism, the present situation of nearly half a dozen political parties' vying for the allegiance of the working class was self-destructive.[95] In the face of totalitarian oppression, there was no valid reason why ideological differences—bordering on theological disputations—should perpetuate these divisions. The advantages in combining forces would outweigh any inconsistencies or sacrifices in ideological purity. The theoretical mutations that had taken place within the PSI and the PCI over the last few years had rendered obsolete the rationale for the schism of 1921 at Livorno. The two parties had already forged a "pact of unity and action," which was then of limited scope. Would it not be possible to strengthen and expand that pact? Justice and Liberty was open to such efforts and willing to make "reasonable concessions."[96] In a sign of his continued insistence on the complex nature of fascism and yet of his desire to mend fences with the communists, Rosselli ended the first essay with a revealing appeal to Marx:

> Fascism is not only ferocious class reaction. It is the social destruction of all classes and all values. The central, directing force of the working class must use all its forces and all its effective reasons of revolt against fascism, inspired by the vision of Marx who saw in the emancipation of the working class the emancipation of the entire human race.[97]

The communists' dynamic potential and rapprochement with the socialists in the face of the Hitler threat made the communists more attractive to Rosselli after 1936. Simultaneously, dissension was growing between Rosselli and the socialists, since the latter felt themselves to be the only party that could claim to be both democratic and socialist, a claim also made by GL. In 1936 and 1937, Rosselli was prepared to work more with the dynamic PCI than with the PSI, which he felt to be moribund. He moved beyond polite generalities to address the problem of how to reach the masses who had been manipulated by more than a decade of fascist propaganda and socialization.[98] Another problem was to dissociate the antifascist present and future from the prefascist past. This purpose, as we have already seen, had been part of Rosselli's thinking from the days of the Aventine Secession in 1924. Looking to the past and its political formulations would cripple the antifascist cause and effectively prevent transforming antifascism into a revolutionary program for a republican, democratic, and socialist Italy in the future. Rosselli subjected the idea of reconciliation between the PSI and the PCI to more critical scrutiny. After 1921 both parties had developed their own structures, organizations, and cadres that they were unwilling to abandon. The reconciliation, therefore, was ineffective, an outcome brought about because each side perceived its own weakness and thus continued to conceive of the problem of the political party as the problem of formulating ideology at the center and diffusing it out to the members and the masses. In reality, according to Rosselli, the real problem was to perceive the political party as the vehicle for effecting the antifascist revolution. As an oblique criticism of the communists, he insisted that the proletarian revolution was not simply a matter of economic emancipation, but rather the formation and implementation of an "integral humanism." "Today," he confessed, "we are all infinitely more sensitive than twenty years ago to the problems of freedom, democracy and even morality and culture."[99]

Rosselli's assessment of the PCI was balanced, and on the whole, rather positive. He acknowledged that it was "the most conspicuous force" among the Italian proletariat. The communists had displayed admirable courage and determination after the advent of fascism, especially after the imposition of the dictatorship in 1925 and the Exceptional Decrees of 1926. They carried on the struggle with "admirable energy," and even if their autonomy could be questioned, there was no denying their "moral and combative valor." Also, there was no doubt that "if fascism fell today, it would be the strongest proletarian party."[100] One of the criticisms that could be brought against the PCI before 1936 was its theoretical formulation of the doctrine of "social fascism." With the aim of destroying any potential rival for the allegiance of the working class, the communists deemed all the various currents of democratic socialism as "deviant," "petit-bourgeois," and "servants of the fascists." Accordingly, the communists violently opposed any accord with the forces of democratic socialism. Rosselli seemed to excuse this mistaken policy by conceding that the schism in 1921 had naturally made the party wary of those on its immediate right and that nearly all the bourgeois parties of the center failed to vigorously oppose fascism in 1922. With an increased dependency on Moscow and the Third International, the PCI increasingly turned to attacking social democracy, the Antifascist Concentration, and GL in particular. If this policy could be defended in the 1920s, it could not be defended after the rise of Hitler in Germany. The *svolta*, or "turn," came in 1934, not because of some internal evolution within the PCI, but because it was dictated from Moscow. Accordingly, the entire vocabulary and rhetoric of the party changed: "dictatorship of the proletariat," discussion of the soviets, and class warfare passed out of fashion, to be replaced by an emphasis on "bread," "peace," "freedom," and "democratic rebirth." The party also rediscovered national traditions. Rosselli responded that "the new communist policy is correct in its intentions, correct in its premises, yet erroneous in its application." Its intention to pull antifascism out of "the closed hothouse in which it had been vegetating" was praiseworthy; its premise that it must reestablish contact with the masses and emerge from a sectarian isolation was to be welcomed. What was suspect in Rosselli's eyes was the party's ability to launch the revolution. To speak constantly about revolution without being able to create even the most elementary conditions to bring it about was sterile and counterrevolutionary. The political struggle could not be reduced merely to a tactical or theoretical instrument; instead was the essence of antifascism. Rosselli traced the problems of the PCI back to an excessive centralism, an almost military hierarchy that was both its great strength and its weakness. Once a policy was decided, the party followed it to its extreme consequences with a tenacity that was truly admirable. The PCI probably could not alter its internal structure and character; yet it could be a great service in bringing its organization, its discipline, its enthusiasm to a new, united, revolutionary proletarian party in which it would find the intellectual freedom and critical ferment that it lacked. Only in such activity, Rosselli believed, would the PCI fulfill its mandate.[101]

If Rosselli was cautious in his criticism of the PCI, he did not hesitate in pointing out the many deficiencies of the PSI.[102] Although it had been the "propulsive and organizing center of the entire proletarian struggle for thirty years" (1892–1921), it was now clear that the PCI claimed that title. The PSI had left an indelible stamp on Italian society, especially in the northern and central parts of the country, where the masses had transformed themselves and the conditions of their labor, acquiring civil dignity and class consciousness.[103] Recounting his earlier criticism, which he had made in his essay on the death of Turati, Rosselli now pointed out that in its early years, the PSI had attracted the youth of Italy with the party's intransigent idealism but that the possibility of fruitful reformism degenerated into opportunism. Whereas earlier the party's simple preaching had awoken the masses and persecution had stimulated the militants of the party, recently the PSI had been paralyzed between a revolutionary rhetoric and reformist actions. Its revitalization during the Libyan War of 1911–12 had been only temporary and based on a "verbal Blanquism, demagogic rather than seriously revolutionary."[104] In 1914 the PSI confirmed itself as indecisive and inconsequential with its neutralism and policy of "neither support nor sabotage" for the approaching war. In 1918–19 it failed to assess accurately the postwar conditions, tied as it was to prewar politics. In January 1921 came the schism in Livorno with the communists, and in October of the following year, the split between maximalists and reformists. In truth, the Italian Socialist Party was defeated. Fascism had found it ridiculously easy to destroy the little that schism had left standing.

What was left of the PSI after nearly a decade and a half of fascism? Here a distinction had to be made between socialism as an ideal that informed antifascism and socialism as a political party "no longer able to insure the political unity of the proletariat." Although there were still hundreds of thousands of people in Italy that considered themselves socialist, they were from the prefascist era; the few new recruits to the party were usually intellectuals rather than workers. Accordingly, their socialism was of a critical, humanistic Marxist variety, and they were often not closely tied to the party. The socialists in exile continued in two separate parties, the PSLI—which followed the Second International and continued the reformist tradition—and the PSI—which held to its maximalist position. The latter had become petrified in its thinking and was merely a "cult of memory"; only the PSLI could be said to have remained an active, vital party, especially with the infusion of new members like Pietro Nenni (who had left the PSI), Angelo Tasca (who had come from the PCI), Giuseppe Saragat, and others. The PSI had been the instrument of political action and the vehicle for the political education of the working class in the prewar era; that era had been superseded by fascism, which completely changed the rules of the game, forcing a rethinking of old ideas and a new plan of action. Or, as Rosselli so accurately observed, "Every epoch and every struggle creates its own instruments of action."[105]

The "instrument of action" for the present epoch—that of fascist totalitarianism—was, as Rosselli made explicit, Justice and Liberty. To begin with, it was a *new* political movement without precedent in "the traditional political landscape." The fact that Justice and Liberty managed to survive proved that it possessed something that was lacking in the other political parties—a clear understanding of what fascism really was, what it meant to Italian and European society, and what were the means needed to combat and defeat it. Because GL was the only political movement to arise in the fascist era, Rosselli in effect thought of it as the inverse image of fascism:

> Justice and Liberty can be defined as the first integrally antifascist European movement, because it sees in fascism the central fact, the tremendous *innovation* [*novità*] of our time, and because its opposition derives not from a defense of positions acquired previously or from a simple extension of the schemes of the anticapitalist struggle, but from a will to liberation that springs from the prison of that fascist world and the practical experience of struggle. What compels Justice and Liberty is . . . the development of the Italian revolution, the self-liberation, the self-emancipation of the Italian people; the raising—on the ruins of fascism—of a new Europe.[106]

This "compulsion" and "will to liberation" were the source of its open-minded and almost "experimental" character and action, its "intellectual restlessness." It was what lent the members of Justice and Liberty the reputation of being les enfants terribles of the antifascist camp—a reputation that Rosselli seemed to court and relish. The members did not come from any single party but from all over the political spectrum: socialists, communists, democrats, and republicans; students of Gobetti, Gramsci, and Salvemini; intellectuals without a party; the very young who came to political rebellion by their own paths in the solitude of tyranny; revolutionary workers formed during the struggle in the factories and the streets of Italy; and old militants tired of waiting for the promised revolution. This disparate group was held together by the charisma of Rosselli and a state of mind that condemned the prefascist political world. The first three years of the movement (1929 to 1932) had been characterized by incessant activity such as the escape from Lipari, the flight over Milan, and even plans for the attempted assassination of Mussolini. Politically it was a period of a united democratic-socialist-republican action. Within Italy, GL had attracted young, intelligent, and committed antifascists to such an extent that it became a major force in the antifascist struggle. These younger antifascists were drawn to Justice and Liberty because of the conception of antifascism as the self-emancipation and the second Risorgimento of the Italians. The youth were also attracted because GL refused to make the political and moral compromises that had marked the prefascist parties. The movement was unique not only for conceiving of antifascism as the second Risorgimento, for its intransigence, but also for its insistence that in order to defeat the totalitarian state—a creation of the twentieth century—new methods must be used. In this way, the movement captured the fantasy and imagination of the masses and utilized all the technological means at its disposal to agitate the energies of the people.

By 1932, because of mass arrests, the first phase of Justice and Liberty had ended. A decade of fascism, glorified in bombastic spectacle, had made substantial impact on Italian society. The youth of Italy now saw fascism not as a temporary parenthesis but as a point of reference that could not be ignored. For the movement, it was a delicate moment of transformation when it moved away from audacious acts and gestures to forge a coherent political program voiced through the *Quaderni di Giustizia e Libertà* (January 1932–January 1935). The new ideology claimed Piero Gobetti's *La Rivoluzione Liberale* and Antonio Gramsci's *L'Ordine*

Nuovo as inspiration. Although there was a multiplicity of voices and of ideological positions, the principal themes of the *Quaderni* were liberation of the worker, agrarian reform, the role of the proletariat and the structure of the state.

Whereas the first phase of the movement had concentrated on action, this second phase risked falling into a sterile intellectualism. Events in Europe, such as the uprising in Vienna, the insurrection in Asturias, and the attempted coup d'état in France in 1934, forced GL to reexamine the possibility of concerted political action. The spread of fascism in Europe required that Rosselli and the others expand their vision of the movement to include the self-emancipation of all the peoples living under tyranny and the creation of a new Europe. This self-emancipation could come about only through the proletariat, since the bourgeoisie had amply proved its complete incapacity as a ruling class.

Contemporary political categories did not apply to Justice and Liberty:

> Using this terminology, we would have to define ourselves as socialists, communists and libertarians simultaneously (revolutionary socialists/liberal communists) . . . In socialism we see the animating idea-force of the entire workers' movement, the substance of every real democracy, the religion of the century. In communism [we see] the first historic application of socialism, the myth but above all the most energetic revolutionary force. In libertarianism [we see] the element of utopia, the dream, the powerful (even if coarse and primitive) religion of the individual.[107]

GL was the synthesis of these powerful currents, something that could not be attributed to any of the other political parties. In creating that synthesis, it could direct the battle against fascism on two levels: the first, and more elementary, was the reawakening of the people, the stirring of the masses, and the creation of a vital consciousness among the working classes; the second, and more theoretical, was the formation of a new ruling class that would comprise the elite of a social and humanist revolution opposing the barbarity of fascism.

Until now, the proposals formulated for the defeat of fascism were inadequate: the Popular Front strategy could only fail, since among its conditions for success were a democratic political life and parties that were strong—neither of which existed in Italy. Moreover, the "Unity of Action Pacts" signed by the socialists and communists were also destined to failure, since they only increased the rigidity of ideological positions and hindered rather than fostered cooperation. What, then, was the alternative?

The best way to defeat fascism, according to Rosselli, was the creation of a new, original movement that would be based on the proletariat, capable of conducting a "practical, political, and cultural struggle against the totalitarian colossus." This new movement should not be considered in terms of traditional political parties, but instead as a larger social force, the "anticipation of the future society, a social microcosm." GL could bring to this project a renewal of the proletarian struggle; its experience of action and initiative; and a lucid interpretation of fascism and an intimate understanding of the culture and history of the country. GL addressed some of the most important problems of modernity in Italy, such as the formation of ruling classes, the development of the *Mezzogiorno,* federalism, and the alliance among urban workers, peasants, and intellectuals. Above all, it was concerned with liberty, not in the abstract, formal sense, but based on concrete action, as a positive, emancipating force.[108]

Death in Exile

This type of antifascist—the prose hero—was destined to be killed.[109]

Still afflicted with painful phlebitis, Carlo left Paris and arrived at the mud-bath resort of Bagnoles-de-l'Orne in Normandy on 27 May 1937. He took a room at the Hôtel Cordier just outside the town of Tessé-la-Madeleine. Coincidentally (or perhaps not), the Duke of Ajmone, of the Royal House of Savoy, was also in the resort town.[110] Marion soon joined him, and Nello arrived on 6 June, leaving Maria and a newborn son, Alberto, in Florence. "We reverentially kneel before your demographic superiority," Carlo had humorously written to his younger brother on hearing the news of his nephew's birth, "but now that you have achieved a balance between boys and girls, I hope you will stop yourselves."[111] Nello's request for a passport had been granted with such efficiency and so quickly (three days) that friends, especially Piero Calamandrei in Florence, were suspicious. Calamandrei warned Nello not to go to France, fearing that agents of the regime were following him and preparing some kind of action against the brothers. Nello could not imagine anything so dramatic; had not Gioacchino Volpe, official historian of the regime and director of the Istituto Storico in Rome, pulled some strings to get Nello permission to use the

Library of the British Museum for his research? Nello was more concerned with the care of his newborn Alberto and the need to leave his other children, Silvia, Paola, and Aldo. Carlo was in France, and Nello felt that both their lives had reached a crisis point; he had to speak with his older brother.[112]

Carlo had established a daily routine at the spa, taking the cure in the morning, working in his room until the late afternoon, and then going for a drive in the countryside with his Ford car that had survived the front in Spain. This routine was duly noted by several spies who had also arrived in the resort town soon after him.[113]

On the afternoon of the ninth, Carlo and Nello drove Marion to the train station and watched her depart for Paris, where she would help celebrate Mirtillino's tenth birthday. On his return trips to the hotel, Carlo usually avoided the heavy traffic of the main road and turned instead onto a side road that led past the forest at Couterne. Knowing of this habit, the assassins had pulled their car over to the side of the road, giving the impression of mechanical failure. As the brothers arrived where the "disabled" vehicle was parked, they stopped their car and approached to assist the driver. It was at this point that they were attacked and murdered. Carlo was killed by four dagger thrusts, two of which severed the carotid artery. Nello was attacked by less efficient murderers; he suffered many dagger wounds and apparently tried to resist in some desperate attempt at defense. An autopsy later revealed bullet wounds as well. The bodies were dragged a short distance and left in the underbrush by the side of the road, with a dagger nearby. The assassins drove off, taking Carlo's Ford and abandoning it several miles later. It was found the next day, and in the back seat, there was a bomb, whose fuse had failed. The bodies were not found until two days later. There was an eyewitness: Hélène Besneux, a hairdresser, was bicycling on the road by the forest when she came upon the scene of the assassinations. Three days later, on 12 June, she reported to the authorities that she had seen a pool of blood and that one of the men had seen her, given her a murderous look, and then driven off.[114]

Back at the Hôtel Cordier, lying on Carlo's desk was a postcard from Mirtillino in Paris, anxiously awaiting his mother's return for his tenth birthday.[115]

News of the double assassination shocked and stunned the antifascist community. A crowd estimated at between 100,000 to 200,000 people attended the funeral services in Paris, and the cortege made its way to the Père Lachaise cemetery accompanied by the music of Beethoven's Seventh

Symphony.[116] There the brothers were laid to rest, with the following inscription on their monument:

> Carlo and Nello Rosselli
> Murdered Together
> 9 June 1937
> Expect Together
> That the Sacrifice of Their Youth
> Will Hasten
>
> . . .
>
> The Victory of Their Ideals
> Justice and Liberty

On orders from the French government, which feared offending Mussolini, an ellipsis had been inserted where originally "In Italy" was to appear. The two words were carved into the monument only after the liberation of France. Almost thirteen years later to the day, the antifascist cause was struck by "a second Matteotti case."[117] In a perhaps related event, two days after the funeral, Leon Blum submitted his resignation as Premier of France.

The fascist press tried to link the assassinations to conflicts within the antifascist community, explicitly accusing the communists, anarchists, and allies of GL. The recent murder of the anarchists Camillo Berneri and Francesco Barbieri at the hands of Stalin's agents in Spain gave this story "credibility." It was no coincidence that the most aggressive support of this theory was taken up by *Il Telegrafo,* the daily newspaper of Livorno, under the editorship of Giovanni Ansaldo and controlled by Count Galeazzo Ciano, Minister of Foreign Affairs and Mussolini's son-in-law.[118] But the antifascists were not fooled. For Salvemini, "all roads lead to Rome."[119]

Although most observers immediately assumed that Mussolini was the author of this crime, there is no smoking gun to implicate him directly. There is, instead, this cryptic comment to his secretary Yvon de Begnac in July 1937: "History will decide the reason of their fate. Power is not always able to control the apparatus that it represents."[120] Mussolini's foremost Italian biographer, Renzo De Felice, devotes a few revealing paragraphs to the Rosselli assassinations in his massive biography of the dictator. For De Felice, the Rosselli murders are merely a "parenthesis" (a word used twice) in Mussolini's biography.[121] Instead, the Rosselli assassinations must be read as a signifying moment in the history of the regime, comparable to the assassination of Matteottti and to Mussolini's order to execute Italian anti-fascists captured in Spain. "The dead," Mussolini mistakenly remarked to Ciano, "tell no history."[122] Could the Rosselli assassinations be the work of the security apparatus without Mussolini's knowledge or approval? In his dispatches from Italy during World War II, Herbert Matthews of *The New York Times* wrote of Galeazzo Ciano's complicity in the assassinations. At the time of Ciano's own execution by Mussolini's Italian Social Republic in 1944 (even after Mussolini's daughter, Edda, pleaded with her father to spare her husband's life), Marion Cave Rosselli wrote to *The New York Times* and pointed out that along with Ciano, General Emilio De Bono and Giovanni Marinelli were also executed; both had been implicated in the Matteotti assassination twenty years earlier. In his refusal to show mercy to his own son-in-law and colleagues, Mussolini effectively silenced those who might have revealed his role in three assassinations thirteen years apart.[123] Despite attempts by the regime to accuse the Left, proof of fascist (if not Mussolini's) authorship of the assassinations is provided by the regime itself. In the Archivio Centrale dello Stato in Rome, a document prepared by the Director of the Political Police Division on 1 February 1939 lists more than fifty antifascist volunteers killed in the Spanish Civil War. Listed as #12850 is "Carlo Rosselli, founder of Giustizia e Libertà, wounded at Monte Pelato, assassinated near Paris, *by fascists*, the 11th [sic] June 1937, with his brother Nello."[124]

In public Amelia Pincherle Rosselli bore the deaths of her two sons with dignity and stoic resignation, yet letters to Nello's widow reveal a deep, private despair. Years later Sandro Pertini wrote that she seemed to emerge from the terrible events of June 1937 "like the heroine of a Corneille tragedy." [125] Marion lived for another twelve years, but as Salvemini wrote at her passing in 1949, after the death of Carlo, her life was "a painful descent toward death."[126]

It soon became clear that the assassins were members of the French *Cagoule,* a secret extreme right-wing sect known for the hooded cape of its followers; the sect had ties to the French secret services and the secret society CSAR (Comité secret d'action révolutionnaire).[127] Evidently the assassins had been closely following Rosselli for at least several months, if not longer. On 15 February 1938, Marion Rosselli recognized one of those arrested in the case, Fernand Ladislav Jakubiez, who had posed as a traveling carpet salesman and who had appeared one morning at the Rosselli house in Paris during the autumn of 1936, asking suspicious questions about Carlo. In the spring of 1936, a certain Carlo Zanatta presented himself to members of GL in Paris, claiming to be an army deserter with information against a Communist Party member. Under questioning, it became apparent that Zanatta's entire story was false; bursting into tears, he revealed that he had concealed a loaded pistol in the belt of his trousers. He had been approached by an agent provocateur at the Italian Consulate in Paris with instructions to assassinate Rosselli.[128]

The assassination of the Rosselli brothers forced the French authorities to investigate the *cagoulards*. Their work turned up more than one hundred individuals. On 12 January 1938, The French Minister of the Interior, Max Dormoy, announced plans to arrest seven individuals related to the Rosselli murders: Jean Filliol, Fernand Jakubiez, Robert G. E. Purieux, Jean Marie Bouvyer, L. C. Huguet, André Tenaille, and J. Foran. Five were already under arrest; Huguet and Filliol were still being sought. One of the automobiles used in the assassination belonged to Eugene Deloncle, one of the leaders of the CSAR. A serious shortcoming of the investigation was that it failed to admit that there was any Italian connection to the assassinations. In January 1938, the French daily *Matin* reported that Dormoy had noted that the weapons of the *cagoulards* came from beyond France's borders; another official in the French police force cited "the number of arms, rifles, machine-guns of Italian manufacture" found in the investigation.[129] The new French Premier, Daladier, sought to appease Mussolini at all costs in the futile hope of distancing Italy from nazi Germany. Consequently, for reasons of international politics, all future work on the assassinations and the *cagoulards* was confined within France's borders. With the fall of France and the creation of the Vichy regime, all those implicated in the assassinations were freed under Marshal Pétain. Dormoy was arrested by the Vichy regime and later killed during the night of 25–26 July 1941 by a bomb placed under his bed.

With the fall of the Pétain regime and the end of the war, a new inquiry was initiated against the *cagoulards*. André Tenaille had died fighting for the Nazis on the Russian front; for his services, he was posthumously awarded the Legion of Honor by the Pétain government.[130] Eugene Deloncle, after entering the service of the Nazis, was killed by the Gestapo; François Mètenier became head of Pétain's bodyguard.[131] Mètenier, Jakubiez, and Puireux were arrested and imprisoned; Filliol, Bouvyer, Foran and Huguet could not be found. On 6 June 1945, Jakubiez revealed that "Carlo was killed in an instant. His brother, gravely wounded, had fallen into the ravine. I stabbed him two or three times with a dagger; Filliol finished him off with the pistol . . . Filliol searched the bodies and took some papers, that were sent to Italy, as I discovered later."[132] The fate and content of the papers taken from the Rosselli brothers have never been revealed.

Although Jakubiez had confessed in June 1945, the trial of the *cagoulards* did not take place until 11–28 November 1948. Jakubiez was sentenced to life at hard labor; François Méténier was sentenced to twenty years hard labor; Puireux, four years of hard labor; those charged in absentia were sentenced to death. (Curiously and conveniently, both in France and in Italy, death sentences were usually handed down to those in absentia). No mention was made of any Italians involved in the assassination. Yet the evidence proves that the Italian fascist police were watching Carlo Rosselli at the Hôtel Cordier.[133]

In Italy the prosecution of those responsible for the Rosselli assassinations degenerated into absurdity. Attempts to place high fascist officials on trial were often haphazard, with some minor officials being convicted while major party functionaries were either ignored or forgotten. As early as July 1944, a High Commission for Sanctions against Fascism had been established under the general direction of former Foreign Minister Carlo Sforza. The Decreto that brought the High Commission into existence called for the creation of four commissions: one to deal with property seized from the Fascist Party; another to sequester fascist profits; a third, under the direction of Mario Berlinguer, to be concerned with prosecuting fascists; and a fourth, under Mauro Scoccimarro, to purge fascists from the government.[134] Those responsible were eventually brought to trial. The first document entered into evidence at the trial of Italian officials involved with the murders was prepared by the SIM (Servizio Informazioni Militari—Military Intelligence). After specifying various acts of sabotage (including germ warfare), the document states simply,

5. Suppression of bothersome persons in various localities.
Means: various, preferably poison.[135]

Judge Italo Robino of the High Commission questioned General Cesare Amé, of SIM—the agency responsible for espionage and counterespionage under Mussolini. At one point in the interrogation, when the secretary who was recording the question was absent, Amé said to Robino: "Why don't you seek those responsible for the real and true bloody crimes committed by fascism? The Rosselli murders, for instance." Robino asked what Amé knew about the Rosselli assassinations, and the general replied, "I know nothing, but there is a certain Emanuele, I believe an official, who must know many things." "Are you trying to say," Robino asked, "that he participated?" Amé responded with a sphinxlike "Perhaps." Later, he was to deny ever saying anything of the kind, and he even denied being questioned.[136]

Sante Emanuele was a retired colonel of the *carabinieri* who testified before the High Court of Justice that Colonel Paolo Angioi gave him the order to eliminate Carlo Rosselli. Emanuele passed the order to the head of the counterespionage center in Turin, Major Roberto Navale. It was Navale who contacted the French *cagoulards*. "The initiative came from Ciano."[137] Emanuele stated that he had met Ciano and Anfuso after the assassination of the Rosselli brothers and "I can say specifically that the attitude of Ciano was such as to clearly show that the decision was his. The attitude of Anfuso was that of one who cooperated."[138] Filippo Anfuso was cabinet chief at the Foreign Ministry and as such, close to Ciano. Loyal to Mussolini after the coup d'état of 24–25 July 1943, he served in the Republic of Salò and was appointed ambassador to Berlin. Another high-ranking member of the fascist hierarchy to be implicated was General Mario Roatta, commander of the losing fascist side at the battle of Guadalajara and twice Chief of Staff of the Italian Army. Since 1934 he had been the head of SIM and was rumored to be involved in the assassination of King Alexander of Yugoslavia. He was the highest-ranking Italian military officer who was helping Franco in Spain, along with his German counterpart Admiral Wilhelm Canaris.

The climax of Italian efforts to attain justice in the Rosselli affair was the trial held in Rome before the High Court of Justice for the Punishment of Fascist Crimes, from 29 January to 12 March 1945, better known as the "Roatta Trial." The accused were charged with "espionage, denunciations and reprisals against antifascists, of shipwrecks, train wrecks, the arson of buildings, ships, and transports, of the diffusion of germs to provoke epidemics, of facilitating assassinations and homicides among those that of Bonomini and the Rosselli brothers, Carlo and Nello, the last assassinated at Bagnoles-de-l'Orne (France) the 9th June 1937."[139] When questioned by Judge Lorenzo Maroni on 31 January 1945, Emanuele replied:

> The elimination of Rosselli was certainly not an isolated fact, but must be inserted into the matrix of actions relative to the war in Spain. The

Rosselli "affair" must be considered as an act of sabotage to eliminate the activity of Carlo Rosselli who was recruiting "red" troops. I transmitted this mission to the Turin center, directed by commandant Navale . . . It was this center that took care of all the details. Major Navale organized everything, independent from me.[140]

Emanuele's testimony implied that Ciano and Anfuso decided on Rosselli's assassination without conferring with Mussolini. Although there exists no hard evidence, it is highly unlikely that either Ciano or Anfuso would have undertaken such an action on their own. On 22 March 1937, Navale had met with members of the *Cagoule* in Monte Carlo. The French asked for one hundred Beretta semiautomatic weapons in exchange for "the suppression of troublesome persons." Anfuso admitted to participating in this meeting with Navale and Emanuele.[141] The dagger left behind by Jakubiez was used by the fascist papers to "prove" that it was an antifascist crime: fascists would not be so foolish to leave behind such evidence. Yet Vittorio Cerruti, former ambassador to Berlin and Paris, testified that when he met Ciano after the assassination, the Foreign Minister said to him: "'You must admit that the idea of the dagger was really a brilliant idea.' I deduced that the dagger was placed there, by orders of Ciano, with the intention of accusing the antifascists of the assassination."[142]

Before the sentences were handed down, Emilio Lussu, Aldo Garosci, Randolfo Pacciardi, and Piero Calamandrei were permitted to address the court.[143] On 12 March, sentence was passed on all the accused: Anfuso (in absentia) was found guilty and sentenced to death by firing squad; Roatta, Emanuele, and Navale were all found guilty and sentenced to life in prison; their sentences were to be published in all the daily papers of Rome. Angioi was sentenced to twenty years and six months; Alberto Pariani, to fifteen years; Manlio Petragnani, to twelve years.[144] Only Roatta, Emanuele, and Petragnani were under arrest at the time, and the court was to "lose" Roatta in the middle of the trial. Roatta, who had been complaining of ill health, was in the military hospital on Via Giulia in Rome. On the night of 4 March, he simply walked out of the hospital and disappeared. Although a halfhearted attempt was made to find the General, he easily made his way to Franco's Spain, where he found a warm welcome. Several days later, on 7 March, the Leftist parties organized a mass demonstration of 15,000 at the Coliseum; after marching up the Via dei Fori Imperiali, the crowd was fired upon by *carabinieri* who were "protecting" Prince Umberto at the Quirinale Palace.[145] The travesty of justice continued when the Supreme Court of Cassation annulled the sentences of Navale, Angioi, and Pariani. The Navale case was sent to the Court of Assizes of Rome, which recognized his guilt, yet reduced the sentence to seven years. The Supreme Court of Cassation also annulled the sentences of those guilty in the death of Giuseppe Amendola. Another trial in Perugia in 1949 absolved Anfuso, Emanuele, and Navale. In 1953 Anfuso was elected to Parliament as a deputy from the MSI (Movimento Sociale Italiano—the neofascist party that arose after the Second World War) and served as the editor of the party's newspaper, *Il Secolo d'Italia*. Roatta returned to Italy and died a free man in Rome in 1968.

Questions concerning the Rosselli assassinations surfaced again in 1951 with the publication of Alberto Moravia's *Il conformista*. Moravia, whose real last name was Pincherle, was a first cousin to the Rosselli brothers; his father Carlo was Amelia Rosselli's brother. Interviewed by the noted critic Enzo Siciliano in 1972, one year after Bernardo Bertolucci had directed his cinematic version of *The Conformist,* Moravia revealed that his novel was indeed based on the Rosselli assassinations.[146]

The Rosselli brothers, representing two different types of resistance, were thus inducted with Piero Gobetti, Giovanni Amendola, Giacomo Matteotti, Antonio Gramsci, and others who had refused to consider any moral compromise with the regime, into the pantheon of martyrs to fascism.

Conclusion

Men reject their prophets and slay them, but they love their martyrs and honor those whom they have slain.

FYODOR DOSTOYEVSKY, *THE BROTHERS KARAMAZOV*
(1880)

You'll try to reveal what should remain hidden, you'll try to incite people to learn from the past and rebel, but they will refuse to listen to you.

ELIE WIESEL, *A BEGGAR IN JERUSALEM* (1970)

Today the historical legacy of antifascism in Europe is under attack on several fronts. Politicians openly question the most basic tenets of democracy and seek to redeem past regimes; moreover, some intellectuals consciously foster a "culture of nostalgia" that later manifests itself in various guises within the realm of popular culture. Although the nature of the antifascist resistance has been closely examined and criticized from within, we are now witnessing a concerted effort to rewrite history and to denigrate the struggle against totalitarian and authoritarian regimes. "Revisionists" grasp for academic legitimacy, while their political counterparts mask strategies of domination with the rhetoric of national pride. A favored technique among neofascists (or as they prefer to call themselves, "postfascists") is to place themselves on the same moral plane as their victims and as antifascists. In the view of postfascists, fascists were "victims" as much as Jews, antifascists, and partisans. The 25 April holiday in Italy, celebrated after the war as a national holiday of liberation from fascism and nazism, should now—according to the leader of the postfascist National Alliance, Gianfranco Fini—be conceived of as a "day of national reconciliation." For Fini's colleague Maurizio Gasparri, "Togliatti and Pinochet are the same."

In the winter of 1933, Rosselli had presented a talk on fascist foreign policy at the Royal Institute of Foreign Affairs in London. He warned that fascist nationalism led inevitably to imperialism, racism, and war. Sixty-two years later, Fini was invited to the Royal Institute, where he declared that fascism and antifascism have passed into history and should be treated accordingly.[1] Historians find themselves central to this debate concerning writing, memory, and the preservation of a particular vision of the past. The fiftieth anniversary of the end of the Second World War generated a debate in Italy similar to the German *Historikerstreit*, in this case over the nature of fascism and the antifascist Resistance.[2] In addition, the fiftieth anniversary of the end of the war was an occasion for historians to convene and reassess the Resistance legacy.[3]

The assassination of the Rosselli brothers was a devastating blow to Justice and Liberty and to European antifascism. Nello had been widely respected for his courageous insistence on remaining in Italy to continue his scholarly work, and Carlo was universally recognized for his boundless energy and selfless dedication to the struggle. Even Carlo's bitterest ideological critics were quick to acknowledge that European antifascism had lost one of its best. Palmiro Togliatti, so acid in his condemnation of Justice and Liberty, wrote that Rosselli represented a figure of "civic courage and devotion to the cause of freedom" that was seldom to be found in the bourgeoisie. Togliatti recognized the profound conflict between Justice and Liberty and the PCI, refusing to "throw a hypocritical veil over our differences," yet insisting that "our dissent was admissible within the framework of democratic socialism."[4] As Tarchiani recalled,

> Twelve hours on end at the steering wheel, exhausting journeys, nights at the desk, hair-raising risks, moral sufferings, bitter disappointments, desertions, painful surprises, betrayals, nothing was spared him and he faced it all . . . He was the most persevering, the most humble, the most disciplined of us all . . . He gave peace neither to himself nor to his comrades in the struggle nor to his enemies.[5]

Nenni recorded in his diary from the Spanish Civil War that "we all feel that antifascism suffers an irreparable loss."[6] Lussu wrote that he would always picture Rosselli "so strong that he seemed immortal, even physically; like a Greek god."[7] A day before the funerals of the Rosselli brothers took place in Paris, Romain Rolland wrote a scathing indictment of European democracies, charging that they could defend neither themselves nor their own defenders like Rosselli. André Breton, Paul Langevin, Fernand

Leger, Emmanuel Mounier, Pablo Picasso, and others signed a public statement declaring "The assassination of Matteotti signaled the death of liberty in Italy; the assassination of the Rosselli brothers signals the death of liberty in Europe."[8]

Rosselli's assassination had brought Lussu back to Justice and Liberty. In July 1943, he was a leader of the antifascist underground in Rome, organizing a GL cell for the armed Resistance, and he served in the government of Ferruccio Parri. The movement continued to work against fascism and to publish *Giustizia e Libertà* until the fall of France in June 1940. Leadership of the movement passed to Lussu, Alberto Cianca, and Aldo Garosci. Yet the various ideological tensions that had given the movement a dynamism while Rosselli was alive now worked to hinder its effectiveness. Alberto Tarchiani, who represented the liberal wing, had resigned from his position on the Central Committee when Rosselli clearly was moving further to the left in the context of the Ethiopian War. After Rosselli's death, he left the movement. In 1940, in the face of the nazi invasion, Tarchiani fled Europe and arrived in New York, where he joined Gaetano Salvemini, Max Ascoli, and others in the Mazzini Society. As secretary of the society, he edited its newspaper and actively participated in the Resistance. On the basis of his extensive contacts with the U.S. State Department, he served as Ambassador of Italy to the United States after the war (1945–1955). Ascoli was named president of the Mazzini Society in 1940; after the war, he was editor of *The Reporter* for twenty years and a member of the Council on Foreign Relations.

Emilio Lussu had also distanced himself from Justice and Liberty in 1935, arguing—against Tarchiani—that the movement was not radical enough and should reformulate itself as a new revolutionary socialist party. Contrary to Tarchiani, though, Lussu returned to Justice and Liberty after Rosselli's death and attempted to forge an alliance of republicans, socialists, and communists to infuse the movement with a democratic, revolutionary idealism. He served as minister in the government of Ferruccio Parri and, until his death in 1975, continued to insist—contrary to Giuseppe Saragat—that the PSI should not cooperate with the Christian Democrats. Lussu was joined by Silvio Trentin, and together they were perhaps the two most radical members of Justice and Liberty in attempting to keep the movement alive. Trentin became active in the French Resistance and founded the partisan movement *Libérer et fédérer* that combined liberalism and federalism in a revolutionary program. In September 1943, he returned to Venice, only to suffer a heart attack in a fascist prison and then to die at home six months later. Lionello and Franco Venturi, father and son, fled fascist Italy to France and the United States. Lionello joined the Mazzini Society and along with Salvemini, voiced criticism of American policy toward Italy. Lionello was already a noted art historian; his son Franco became an eminent historian.

Giuseppe Emanuele Modigliani, who had never turned in his PSI party card but who had collaborated with Justice and Liberty in Paris, was hunted by fascists and Nazis alike. He and his wife Vera were saved by another member of the movement, Joyce Lussu. The couple fled Paris in 1940, just before the SS raided their house. Rudolf Hilferding, leader of Austrian social democracy, who had been staying in the Modigliani house, was not so fortunate and was arrested. Aldo Garosci also fled from the nazi invasion of France and arrived in the United States, where he worked with Gaetano Salvemini in editing the *Quaderni Italiani,* which was published in New York, and in continuing the work of the *Quaderni di Giustizia e Libertà.* After the war, he was appointed to the chair of modern history at the University of Turin and became one of the most prolific and persistent defenders of the exiled resistance.[9] Joining Garosci in Turin was Augusto Monti, teacher and moral inspiration to the *giellisti* in that city, including Carlo Levi, Leone Ginzburg, Vittorio Foa, Cesare Pavese, and Norberto Bobbio. Monti, too, had joined the Action Party, and his *Realtà del Partito d'Azione* succinctly recapitulated Rosselli's thinking. Marxism and liberalism were the necessary factors in a "necessary product." Both were "inevitable," and "in the dual adaption of this dual inevitability—of the liberals to communism and the communists to liberty—lies the secret of tomorrow's rebirth."[10]

The Rosselli families spent the next decade in exile, first in Switzerland and then in England. In 1940—the same year that Marshal Pétain pardoned those who were responsible for the assassinations—Amelia, Maria, and Nello's four children made their way to the United States and settled in Larchmont, New York, with Marion (who was active in the Mazzini Society), Mirtillino, Amelia, and a third child, Andrea. They were all shepherded by the indomitable elder Amelia, who was then in her midseventies and still fiercely proud of her sons. Gaetano Salvemini, then teaching at Harvard University, visited Amelia at the house in Larchmont, where they both lamented their dead: Amelia her beloved Aldo in 1916, and then Carlo and Nello; and Salvemini recalling the deaths of his wife and five children in the 1908 earthquake.[11] Salvemini died in 1957. In a posthumous essay, he candidly revealed that he had wandered for many years in the labyrinth and reached the conclusion that he had understood nothing. Yet he left an admonishing note: "Whoever is convinced of possessing the infallible secret for making men happy is always ready to slaughter them."[12]

In 1946, Amelia, Marion, Maria, and the children returned to Italy. Marion moved to England in 1947, where she died in 1949. Amelia died in 1954.[13] John Rosselli returned to the United States and was trained as a historian. He eventually settled in England and became professor of history at the University of Sussex.[14] Andrea also returned to America, where he became an engineer. Amelia (Melina) moved to Rome and gained recognition as a major avant-garde poet. In an interview (1987) she reminisced:

> I remember my father as a serene, affectionate person and my mother a bit remote, preoccupied. Our relationship with our parents—I speak of myself and Andrea who was my younger brother—was a bit evanescent. One must not disturb the children speaking of impending dangers. But at the table, when they spoke between themselves, one intuited something. Of my father, besides affection, there rests a sense of incorporeality. When he left for Spain in 1936, I was six years old, and therefore don't remember much.

She recalled that terrible day in June 1937 when her mother had to tell the children of the assassinations:

> My mother called Andrea and me. I don't know if she had already spoken with John, our older brother, I suppose she did. About two years older than me, he was already very mature. She called us into her room. She was in bed, with a sense of defeat, a woman who had been tested. But essentially she was calm. She asked us: "Do you know what the word 'assassination' means?" We answered yes; then all I remember is that we returned to our room.[15]

Later Amelia spent time in libraries, trying to reconstruct the figure of her father, "almost totally forgotten by me." The death of Marion in 1949 caused a nervous breakdown in her sensitive daughter. When asked whether her poetry served to keep alive the memory of her parents, she replied ambiguously, "Perhaps."[16] But the tragic fortunes of the Rosselli family continued: on 11 February 1996, she telephoned a friend that she was again considering suicide. A few hours later, she jumped to her death from her apartment window. Her cousin Aldo told authorities that Amelia had a persecution complex and had never recovered from the assassination of her father and the death of her mother.[17]

Justice and Liberty managed to weather the loss of Carlo Rosselli, although it never was the same. In May 1940, with the fall of France imminent, it drafted a manifesto against fascism, reiterating many proposals first brought forth by Carlo Rosselli. During that summer of 1940, a new political voice emerged from the University of Pisa. Guido Calogero, a philosopher, drafted a Manifesto calling for a liberalsocialism. A second manifesto a year later echoed Rosselli:

> Liberalism and socialism, considered in their best substance, are not contrasting ideals nor disparate concepts, but parallel specifications of a single ethical principle, which is the universal canon of all history and every civilization. This is the principle by which we recognize the personhood of others in contrast to our own person and assign to each of them a right equal to our own.[18]

Rosselli's federalism survived in the Manifesto of Ventotene (another island of *confino*). From there, in 1941, Altiero Spinelli, formerly of the PCI, and Eugenio Corloni, of the PSI, were joined by former *giellisti* Ernesto Rossi and Riccardo Bauer. Spinelli and the others harked back—as Rosselli had done—to Carlo Cattaneo's concept of a United States of Europe. Two years later, from his refuge in Lugano, Rossi wrote *Gli Stati Uniti d'Europa,* a fervent appeal and the only hope to save the continent from war. In January 1945, while the war still raged in northern Italy, Piero Calamandrei spoke at the first official congress of the European Federalist Association in his capacity as Rector of the University of Florence, arguing that "federalism is not a utopia."[19] He was a member of the Constituent Assembly that gave Italy its Constitution, and in 1944 he founded the journal *Il Ponte* that keeps alive a tradition of liberal socialism to this day.

As the fascist regime began to crumble under the onslaught of war, many members of Justice and Liberty made their way back into Italy, where they reorganized themselves in January 1943 as the Action Party, combining the liberal socialism of Rosselli with the liberalsocialism of Calogero. From Milan they published a newspaper, *L'Italia Libera*. Also the party published a new journal that laid claim to the earlier movement, *Nuovi Quaderni di Giustizia e Libertà,* in which it outlined a formal political program based on regional autonomy, agrarian and industrial reform, progressive taxation, mass education, and development of the *Mezzogiorno*. Italy was to be a secular, republican state within a European federation.[20] Of the five parties that made up the CLN (Committee of National Liberation), it was arguably the most intransigent, refusing to collaborate (unlike Togliatti and the PCI) with either the Badoglio government or the Catholic Church.

Though it was a formal political party, the Action Party remained true to Rosselli's vision of the movement. In many ways, it was the most radical of the parties involved in the Committee of National Liberation—the political arm of the Italian Resistance.[21] When Togliatti returned from Moscow in 1944, he announced the *svolta* (reversal) of the PCI—its willingness to collaborate with the Badoglio government and to postpone questions on the Monarchy and the Vatican Accords. The Action Party, instead, was adamant in demanding the abdication of Victor Emmanuel III, the declaration of the Republic, and the complete separation of Church and State. Parallel to the political activity of the Action Party was its military contribution to the Resistance. Brigades were formed—the "Rosselli," the "GL," and the "Italia Libera"—which were second only to the communists in their strength and importance. Participation in the armed Resistance was central to the ideology of the Action Party. Italians would now be active protagonists in a "Second Risorgimento," one that was truly popular, social, and just. Armed struggle against fascism, nazism, and the prefascist state was a redemptive act, forging a consciousness that had previously been lacking among the masses. Leone Ginzburg, before he was tortured to death by the Nazis in a Roman prison in 1944, wrote that "the Italians have now taken their place among the peoples who struggle for liberty."[22]

The Action Party was to play a significant role in the immediate postwar landscape. It advocated a solution that was neither Marxist nor anti-Marxist. Known as "the party of the intellectuals," its fatal flaw—like that of Justice and Liberty—was an inability to capture a mass base.[23] Both Emilio Lussu and Ernesto Rossi served in the short-lived (June–November 1945) government of Ferruccio Parri.

Even before the fighting was over, a struggle took place over how to define the postwar order and the nature of the antifascist resistance. The Actionist Ugo La Malfa, later leader of the small but highly respected and influential PRI, echoed Rosselli when he argued in May 1944 that a broad coalition of antifascist parties would be necessary to effect the necessary break with the prefascist past. La Malfa charged that "Italy has never been a real democracy" and called for a "progressive democracy" that avoided the injustices of both the liberal and the Marxist state.[24] This indictment of the status quo ante could not go unchallenged. In a radio broadcast on 1 September 1944, Pope Pius XII offered a religious justification of private property, while Alcide De Gasperi would write that "antifascism is a contingent political phenomenon, which will at a certain moment be overturned by other political ideals more in keeping with the . . . feelings of Italian public life, for the good and the progress of the nation."[25] Ada Gobetti spoke for many in this later recollection: "In a confusing way I sensed, however, that another struggle was beginning: Longer, more difficult, more tiring, even if less bloody. It was no longer the question of fighting against arrogance, cruelty, and violence . . . but . . . of not allowing that little flame of solidarity and fraternal humanism, which we had seen born, to die in the calm atmosphere of an apparent return to normal life."[26]

Both the potential and the problems of the Action Party were embodied in Ferruccio Parri, who became the first prime minister of postwar Italy. Parri, who had been imprisoned with Rosselli, symbolized the spirit and idealism of the antifascist Resistance. He also revealed that idealism was no match for the political cunning of the Christian Democrats under De Gasperi. Appointed prime minister by the CLN on 19 June 1945, Parri's program of institutional reform was sabotaged by the Christian Democrats in alliance with the British[27] and, to a lesser extent, with the Americans. In a famous speech on 26 September 1945, Prime Minister Parri shocked his audience by echoing Gobetti and Rosselli: "I do not believe that the governments we had before fascism can be called democratic." For the new prime minister, the legacy of the antifascist Resistance was that it was the only democratic movement in the history of Italy that the masses had supported. With the Resistance, both fascism and the nineteenth-century liberal state based on formal law had been superseded. "We can say that in the history of antifascism all the best traditions of the Italian spirit . . . are summed up and gathered together and guide it to successive liberating stages, beginning with the first enlightenment revolution of the eighteenth century."[28] It may be argued that Parri represented the most noble strain of the Resistance, even more radical and true to form than the PCI after Togliatti's *svolta di Salerno*.[29] But by the end of 1945, Parri's attempt to institute a purge of former fascists was undermined by both the Liberal and the Christian Democratic parties. When the Liberal Party, with the support of the Christian Democratic Party, withdrew from the governing coalition on 24 November, the Parri government collapsed, and he was forced to resign. Parri did not mince words in calling the collusion between the PLI and the DC a coup d'état that would ensure the "resurgence and reorganization of fascist and reactionary forces, sabotaging the future of democratic Italy."[30]

The best analysis of this short-lived period of high expectations that were based on the ideals of the Resistance is to be found in Carlo Levi's work, *The Watch*. Continuing an argument he began in *Paura della libertà*, Levi showed how Italy and the Italians were afraid and unable to take that final leap of faith and to radically break with the past.[31] Profiting from the "coup d'état," Alcide De Gasperi became prime minister in December 1945 and initiated a reign of Christian Democratic rule that would remain unbroken for four decades. After the 2 June 1946 elections—in which the Action Party won only 1.5 percent of the vote and seven seats—that party was officially disbanded. The members made their way to the various parties of the Left, some finding their way to the PCI, some to the PSI, and many to the small but highly respected and influential PRI.

In September 1944, members of the Circolo di Cultura, devastated by the fascists on New Years' Eve 1924, gathered in Florence. They formed the Circolo di Cultura Politica "Fratelli Rosselli," which still exists today in the Piazza della Libertà.[32] Many members of Italia Libera, *Non Mollare!*, Justice and Liberty, and the Action Party contributed to a new cultural review, *Il Ponte* (The Bridge), which successfully kept alive a vital current of liberal socialism in the postwar period. Calamandrei had founded *Il Ponte* in 1944 in Florence, when the Nazis were still in the city and Carlo Levi was in hiding, writing his mythical-poetic masterpiece, *Paura della libertà*. Calamandrei went on to become a member of the Constituent Assembly, and as a specialist in legal philosophy, he helped draft the 1948 Constitution of the Italian Republic. Carlo Levi drifted to the PCI and was named a senator in 1943. In 1947 the socialist leader and journalist Lelio Basso, Gobetti's former colleague on *La Rivoluzione Liberale*, became secretary general of the PSI and founded a new journal, *Quarto Stato*, that explicitly recalled the efforts of Nenni and Rosselli twenty years earlier. Ignazio Silone returned to a brief stint in active politics, joining the PSIUP (Partito Socialista Italiano di Unità Proletaria) in 1942, but then turning to Giuseppe Saragat's more moderate PSLI (Partito Socialista dei Lavoratori Italiani) in 1947. Nicola Chiaromonte turned his attention to literature and history after the war; with Silone, he founded the journal *Tempo presente*, which continued the discussion concerning socialism, liberalism, and communism. Joining *Il Ponte* and *Tempo presente* was a resurrected *Il Mondo,* first published by the assassinated Giovanni Amendola. Many members of Justice and Liberty and of the Action Party found a warm reception in its pages; Aldo Garosci, Ernesto Rossi, Gaetano Salvemini, Ugo La Malfa, and Leo Valiani were joined by Benedetto Croce, Luigi Einaudi, and Lelio Basso.

Although Justice and Liberty and the Action Party did not survive into the postwar era, their ideals were kept alive by many independent intellectuals of the Left. Even the PCI began to echo many ideas first broached by Rosselli in the 1930s. If Togliatti continued to criticize the bourgeois socialism of Justice and Liberty, his successors sounded a different note. Commenting on the 1973 coup d'état that brought down Salvatore Allende in Chile, Enrico Berlinguer wrote that "the essential task" was "to rally the vast majority of people around a program of struggle for the democratic renewal of our society and the state." The task of the PCI was to "build a coalition of political forces that corresponds to this majority and this program and is capable of realizing it. Only this line, and no other, can isolate and defeat the conservative and reactionary groups; only this line can give democracy solidarity and invincible strength; only this line can advance the transformation of society."[33] The challenge to the establishment of a liberal socialism today comes not from communists on the Left but from neoliberals on the Right.

If Italian communists were finally coming around to Rosselli's position, former members of Justice and Liberty and the Action Party continued to uphold those ideals. Parri and Pertini continued to play an important role in the political life of Italy. Pertini became president of the Republic in 1978: it was, as many would agree, "an extraordinarily felicitous choice":

> The tiny and frail old man invigorated the office of the President. His outspoken advocacy of democratic values, his constant re-evocation of his anti-Fascist youth, his invitation every year to thousands of schoolchildren to come and meet him in the Quirinale, left an indelible impression on Italian public opinion. Pertini became the most popular President that the Republic ever had. Thirty-five years after the Parri government, the Resistance returned memorably to the highest echelons of the State. As a consequence, Italian democracy was much strengthened.[34]

It was no coincidence that Pertini called on the republican Giovanni Spadolini to become prime minister in 1981, the first time after Parri in the history of postwar Italy that the prime minister was not a Christian Democrat. Spadolini was one of the Italian political leaders who clearly associated themselves with the legacy of Justice and Liberty and the Action Party.[35]

In December 1993, in the wake of the massive corruption scandals that rocked the country, surviving members of Justice and Liberty and the Action Party gathered in Rome and resurrected the old movement. Appropriately enough, Aldo Garosci was named president, while Leo Valiani, Bruno Zevi, and Alessandro Galante Garrone were named to the Executive Committee. The new organization was named the "Movimento d'Azione Giustizia e Libertà," which has put forth members for local elections, organized conferences, published books, and even created a Web site.[36] The symbol of the new movement is a red, flaming sword superimposed over the Italian peninsula in green, with the letters G and L on either side in white. The background is blue, with stars in gold around the peninsula, a reminder of the movement's European and federalist tradition.

The last half century has witnessed a sustained effort by the Italian Left to reexamine its own legacy. Krushchev's revelations of Stalin's atrocities at the Twentieth Party Congress in February 1956 was a political and ethical earthquake, as was the invasion of Hungary several months later. In 1968 the suppression by Russian tanks of the "Prague Spring" in which Alexander Dubček attempted to create a "socialism with a human face" precipitated a final and definitive break with Soviet socialism, acting as a catalyst for Eurocommunism. In 1975 the debate concerning the nature of the intellectual and armed Resistance again flared anew. The opening salvo was fired by Giorgio Amendola, a leading figure of the PCI and an important protagonist in the antifascist struggle. From the pages of the PCI newspaper L'Unità, Amendola called for a new and comparative history of Italian antifascism that went beyond the traditional hagiographical and mythical treatments that were so common after the war.[37] In asking for a more rigorous historiography of antifascism, Amendola cited the work of the PCI as a model, while lamenting the fact that any criticism of the PSI or GL raised "a chorus of indignant reactions."[38]

Amendola's contention that only the communists had engaged in a critical historiography of their past was immediately challenged by an equally respected member of the antifascist struggle, Leo Valiani. In an interview that appeared two weeks after Amendola's critique, Valiani admitted that

Justice and Liberty had been mistaken on some points but asserted that the movement had neither ignored nor hidden its past errors; the history of Justice and Liberty had been written many times, and with critical detachment.[39]

In response to Valiani, Amendola elaborated on his earlier statements with the assertion that Italian antifascism was ill prepared for the tasks set before it in 1943 to 1945 and that the causes of its failure were to be found in the early development of antifascism that led to political, organizational, and cultural deficiencies. For Amendola, the socialists and members of Justice and Liberty were most responsible for this state of affairs. The debate grew in intensity when Valiani defended Justice and Liberty from accusations of ideological and political confusion: in a barely veiled reference to the PCI's past ties to Moscow, Valiani wrote that Rosselli was working for a "democratic, libertarian, even socialist revolution, but not for a new dictatorship."[40]

Amendola neglected to mention that as early as 1931, he and Rosselli had already considered these issues in two important essays.[41] Still the debate raged on as the future president of the Italian Republic, Sandro Pertini, entered the fray, as did the republican leader Ugo La Malfa.[42] In truth, the Amendola-Valiani exchange in 1975 resurrected a debate that was almost a half-century old concerning the theoretical and ideological differences between the PCI and the heterogeneous amalgam of independent Leftist thinkers that eventually gravitated toward Carlo Rosselli and his movement. It is revealing that in an interview published a year later, Amendola conceded that "a true analysis of fascism in the noncommunist antifascist emigration began in 1929 with the arrival of Rosselli [in Paris] and the formation of Justice and Liberty."[43]

Carlo Rosselli's place in the history of Italian antifascism is a curious one. Although he is acknowledged as a central figure in the struggle of the 1920s and 1930s against European fascism, his thought suffered a period of benign neglect after the war, only to be revived in the 1970s. One Italian scholar has commented on the paradox that Carlo Rosselli is "very famous but not well known"[44] in the sense that even though there is a street or a monument named after the Rosselli brothers in every large Italian city, Carlo's thought remained lost to thinkers during the Cold War period. Nicola Tranfaglia has called attention to what he calls the historiographical *sfortuna* (misfortune) that characterized Rosselli in the thirty years after the war.[45] With the dissolution of the Action Party, which had inherited the political and intellectual legacy of Justice and Liberty, Rosselli was relegated to the pantheon of antifascist martyrs, and thus his thought was conveniently neglected, except by a few independent intellectuals of the Left, such as Giovanni Spadolini and Norberto Bobbio.[46]

Meanwhile, historical and political developments within Italy had created the context for a new look at Rosselli. During the 1970s, the PCI loosened its ties with Moscow and set course for Eurocommunism. Both the PCI and the PSI began to reformulate their positions regarding the complex relationship between liberty and socialism along lines that Rosselli had already developed in the 1930s. By the mid-1970s the PCI had adopted Rosselli's ideas so thoroughly that a popular quip in Europe proposed, "Scratch a French communist and you find a Stalinist; scratch an Italian communist and you find a liberal." Or in an earlier version told to Claire Booth Luce, who was horrified by the power of the PCI, "In Italy the Communists are really not communists, the Socialists are not really socialists, and the Christian Democrats are not really democrats."[47]

Why was it that Rosselli and Justice and Liberty would not be studied seriously until the 1970s? It may be that the highly politicized realm of Italian culture and publishing resisted Rosselli in favor of more fashionable intellectual currents. In addition, postwar Italian society was divided as the Christian Democrats acquired and maintained a monopoly over national politics while the Communists could dominate the cultural arena. Italian historiography, intimately tied to the great mass political parties of the postwar period, was not ready to engage the heretical Rosselli.

The remains of Carlo and Nello Rosselli were brought back to Florence from Père Lachaise cemetery in 1951. Their bodies lay in state in the magnificent Sala dei Duecento of the Palazzo Vecchio. On 29 April, solemn ceremonies took place in the Piazza della Signoria. Salvemini, who had returned from his American exile to his old teaching post at the University of Florence, spoke of the brothers' heroic sacrifice before they were interred at the cemetery of Trespiano, overlooking their beloved city—the "Athens of Italy."[48] The single stone that marks both graves bears a flaming torch, the symbol of Justice and Liberty, and states simply, "Carlo e Nello Rosselli / Giustizia e Libertà / Per Questo Morirono / Per Questo Vivono" (Carlo and Nello Rosselli / Justice and Liberty / For this They Died / For this They Live).

What does Rosselli represent in the aftermath of the Cold War and the collapse of the First Italian Republic in the wake of the corruption scandals? Rosselli was a prophet crying out in the wilderness: heard but not heeded. Justice and Liberty and the Action Party represent "roads not taken." Historians, who are trained as social scientists, are admonished not to grapple with the question, What if? But the historian as humanist might recognize the tragedy of a historical alternative not pursued. With the collapse of state socialism between 1989 and 1991, and notwithstanding the triumphal cries of neoliberalism, Rosselli's liberal socialism may be one of the few viable alternatives. Perhaps the collapse of 1989 to 1991 will allow a reexamination of certain ideas that had previously been dismissed out of hand. Recent trends (wildly fluctuating business crises, the concentration of wealth in fewer hands, increasing poverty) may even bring us back to some insights of the *Communist Manifesto* after 150 years, an irony Rosselli would have approved of, for he was a romantic ironist who managed to escape the "ironist's cage."[49]

Along with the "dissidents" of the Risorgimento, such as Mazzini, Cattaneo, Garibaldi, Pisacane, and Ferrari, and their modern counterparts such as Gobetti, Amendola, Matteotti, and Gramsci, Rosselli had set sail for an infinitely receding shore: a society combining a concern for social justice and equality with an insistence on personal liberty. Or as one political scientist has written, "Perhaps liberal socialism will prove an impossible subject, but I remain persuaded, as our hero George Orwell was, that it is an inescapable one."[50] With his intransigent resistance against fascism; with his refusal to bow before an unprecedented barbarism; with his heresy, exile, and tragic death, Rosselli personified the intellectual and armed prophet of our age.

. . . .

ABBREVIATIONS

NOTES

SELECTED BIBLIOGRAPHY

INDEX

. . . .

Abbreviations

AC	Antifascist Concentration.
ACS	Archivio Centrale dello State, Rome.
AGL	Archivio di "Giustizia e Libertà."
BNF	Biblioteca Nazionale Firenze.
CGL	Confederazione Generale di Lavoro.
CLN	Comitato di Liberazione Nazionale.
CPC	Casellario Politico Centrale (Rome).
DC	Democrazia Cristiana (Christian Democracy).
DS	Democratici di Sinistra (Democrats of the Left).
FR	Fondo Rosselli in the Biblioteca Nazionale Firenze.
GL	The movement Giustizia e Libertà (Justice and Liberty) founded in Paris in 1929.
GL	The newspaper *Giustizia e Libertà*.
INSMLI	Istituto Nazionale per la Storia del Movimento di Liberazione in Italia (Milan).
ISRT	Istituto Storico della Resistenza in Toscana (Florence).
LIDU	Italian League for the Rights of Man.
OVRA	Three interpretations have been suggested: Organizzazzione di Vigilanza e Repressione dell'Antifascismo (Organization for Vigilance and Repression of Antifascism); Organo di Vigilanza dei Reati Antistatali (Organ of Vigilance for Antistate Crimes); and Opera Volontaria di Repressione Antifacista (Voluntary Agency for Antifascist Repression).
PCI	Partito Comunista Italiano (Italian Communist Party; officially PCd'I [Communist Party of Italy] from 1921 until 1943).

PDS	Partito Democratico della Sinistra (Democratic Party of the Left).
PNF	Partito Nazionale Fascista (National Fascist Party).
PPI	Partito Popolare Italiano (Italian Popular Party).
PRI	Partito Repubblicano Italiano (Italian Republican Party).
PSI	Partito Socialista Italiano (Italian Socialist Party).
PSLI	Partito Socialista dei Lavoratori Italiani (Socialist Party of Italian Workers).
PSU	Partito Socialista Unitario (Socialist Unitary Party).
QGL	*Quaderni di Giustizia e Libertà.*
SIM	Servizio Informazioni Militari (Military Intelligence Service).

· · · ·

Notes

Introduction

1. The first remark is by the late Costanzo Casucci, former Director of the Central State Archives in Rome and editor of several volumes of Rosselli's writings, in an interview with the author in Rome, 23 June 1993; the second is from Claudio Pavone, interviewed in *La Stampa,* 29 May 1993, p. 17.

2. See the note by the editors (Mitchell Cohen and Michael Walzer) that precedes Nadia Urbinati, "The Liberal Socialism of Carlo Rosselli," *Dissent* (Winter 1994): 113.

3. Massimo Mangilli-Climpson, *Men of Heart of Red, White, and Green: Italian Anti-Fascist Volunteers and the Spanish Civil War* (New York: Vantage Press, 1985), p. 131.

4. Walzer's "Camus" comment was made at ceremonies marking the publication of the English translation of Carlo Rosselli's *Liberal Socialism* at the Italian Cultural Institute in New York City, 31 May 1994.

5. H. Stuart Hughes, *Prisoners of Hope: The Silver Age of the Italian Jews, 1924–1974* (Cambridge, Mass.: Harvard University Press, 1979), p. 56. Joel Blatt, "Carlo Rosselli's Socialism," in *Italian Socialism: Between Politics and History,* ed. Spencer Di Scala (Amherst: University of Massachusetts Press, 1996), p. 91.

6. *Uomini e volti del fascismo,* ed. Ferdinando Cordova (Rome: Bulzoni, 1980), pp. 87–88.

7. Celestin Bouglé, *Depêche de Toulouse,* 28 June 1937; quoted in Gaetano Salvemini, *Carlo and Nello Rosselli: A Memoir* (London: For Intellectual Liberty, 1937), p. 69.

8. Gerd-Rainer Horn, *European Socialists Respond to Fascism: Ideology, Activism and Contingency in the 1930s* (New York; Oxford: Oxford University Press, 1996), p. 156.

9. Nadia Urbinati, Introduction to Carlo Rosselli, *Liberal Socialism,* trans. William McCuaig (Princeton, N.J.: Princeton University Press, 1994), p. lii.

10. In February 1999, the DS organized a conference in Rome, "Socialism and Liberty: Remembering Carlo Rosselli," recognizing Rosselli as an ideological ally and forerunner of contemporary Italian democratic socialism.

11. Christopher Pierson, *Socialism after Communism: The New Market Socialism* (University Park: Pennsylvania State University Press, 1995), pp. 84–85.

12. "Socialism is dead," proclaimed Ralf Dahrendorf in *Reflections on the Revolutions in Europe* (New York: Times Books, 1990), p. 38; wheres the "end of history" was proclaimed a decade ago in Francis Fukuyama's essay of the same title in *The National Interest* (Summer 1989): 3–18; see also his *The End of History and the Last Man* (New York: The Free Press, 1992).

13. Police report dated 11 June 1934, in the ACS, Ministero Interno, Direzione Polizia Politica, busta 141, fascicolo K/110; quoted in Joel Blatt, "The Battle of Turin, 1933–1936: Carlo Rosselli, Giustizia e Libertà, OVRA and the origins of Mussolini's anti-Semitic campaign," *Journal of Modern Italian Studies* 1, n. 1 (Fall 1995): 42 (hereafter cited as Blatt, "The Battle of Turin, 1933–1936").

14. Although the literature on fascism in English is vast, the works on antifascism are not as plentiful. The classic study and point of departure for all students of the subject is by Charles F. Delzell, *Mussolini's Enemies: The Italian Anti-Fascist Resistance* (Princeton, N.J.: Princeton University Press, 1961 [reprint, New York: Howard Fertig, 1974]); see also the important study by Frank Rosengarten, *The Italian Anti-Fascist Press, 1919–1945* (Cleveland: Case Western Reserve University Press, 1968). Excellent general studies include Larry Ceplair, *Under the Shadow of War: Fascism, Anti-Fascism, and Marxists, 1918–1939* (New York: Columbia University Press, 1987); Alexander De Grand, *The Italian Left in the Twentieth Century* (Bloomington: Indiana University Press, 1989). More recent works are David Ward, *Antifascisms: Cultural Politics in Italy, 1943–1946* (Madison, N.J.: Fairleigh Dickinson University Press, 1996); Gerd-Rainer Horn, *European Socialists Respond to Fascism* (New York: Oxford University Press, 1996); *"Never Give In": The Italian Resistance and Politics,* ed. Alastair Davidson and Steve Wright (New York: Peter Lang, 1998).

15. Urbinati, *Liberal Socialism,* xxxi; on the influence of Rosselli and his movement in the United States, see Max Salvadori, "Giellisti e loro amici negli Stati Uniti durante la seconda guerra mondiale," in *Giustizia e Libertà nella lotta antifascista e nella storia d'Italia. Attualità dei fratelli Rosselli a quaranta anni dal loro sacrificio,* ed. Carlo Francovich (Florence: La Nuova Italia, 1978), pp. 273–302 (hereafter cited as *Giustizia e Libertà nella lotta antifascista*).

16. "Historicism" has been a notoriously slippery concept for the past two centuries, often defined in contrasting ways. Fundamental to the development of historicism is its distinction between *Geisteswissenschaften* (the human, cultural, or "social" sciences) and *Naturwissenschaften* (the natural or "hard" sciences). It was the Neapolitan philosopher Giambattista Vico (1668–1744)

who first elaborated a critique of the Enlightenment and Cartesian epistemology in his *Scienza nuova* (1744). For Vico, *verum factum,* or "the true and the made are convertible." In a famous passage he spoke of a "truth beyond all question: that the world of civil society has certainly been made by men, and that its principles are therefore to be found within the modifications of the human mind." *The New Science of Giambattista Vico,* ed. Thomas G. Bergin and Max H. Fisch (Ithaca, N.Y.: Cornell University Press, 1948), pp. 52–53. For Benedetto Croce, nothing existed outside of history. Hayden White, in the introduction to his translation of Carlo Antoni's *Dallo storicismo alla sociologia* (Detroit: Wayne State University Press, 1959), argues that a confluence of romanticism, post-Kantian idealism, and Darwinism resulted in the modern form of historicism. As understood here, historicism is an antinaturalist and antipositivist epistemology recognizing that the subject and object of study are not as ontologically different as in the natural sciences and that a consciousness of the historical context is critical for understanding any human enterprise. As Rosselli made clear in his critique of Marxist determinism, there were no "laws of history," and he followed Vico in believing that human beings—having made history through their free will and actions—could understand history.

17. Ira Katznelson, *Liberalism's Crooked Circle* (Princeton, N.J.: Princeton University Press, 1996), pp. 34–36; on the intellectual as "double agent," see Morris Dickstein, *Double Agent: The Critic and Society* (New York: Oxford University Press, 1992).

18. Piero Gobetti, "Il nostro protestantismo," *La Rivoluzione Liberale* 4, n. 20 (17 May 1925): 83; Michael Walzer, *The Revolution of the Saints: A Study of the Origins of Radical Politics* (Cambridge, Mass.: Harvard University Press, 1965).

19. In the vast literature on Rosselli, I have found only one reference tying Rosselli to the Frankfurt School, but this topic may be a possible avenue for further scholarship and insights. See Jan Petersen, "Giustizia e Libertà e la Germania," in *Giustizia e Libertà nella lotta antifascista,* p. 236.

20. Alberto Moravia, *The Conformist,* trans. Angus Davidson (New York: Farrar, Straus and Young, 1951), pp. 217–218. For the gift of *Crime and Punishment* and Moravia's criticism of the Rosselli family, see Enzo Siciliano, *Moravia* (Milan: Longanesi, 1971) pp. 30, 91.

21. Quoted in Blatt, "Carlo Rosselli's Socialism," in *Italian Socialism: Between Politics and Politics,* p. 88n62.

22. Marcel Cachin, *L'Humanité,* 15 June 1937; quoted in Pierre Guillen, "La risonanza in Francia dell'azione di GL e dell'assassinazione dei fratelli Rosselli," in *Giustizia e Libertà nella lotta antifascista,* p. 249.

23. AGL, sezione I, fascicolo I, sottofascicolo 103.

24. Marherita Repetto Alaia, "Women and Mass Politics in the Republic," in Di Scala, *Italian Socialism: Between Politics and History,* p. 126. An exception is Giuseppe Fiori, author of biographies of Antonio Gramsci, Enrico Berlinguer, the anarchist Michele Schirru, Emilio Lussu, Silvio Berlusconi, and most recently, *Una storia italiana: vita di Ernesto Rossi* (Turin: Einaudi, 1997).

25. "I will tell you what I will do and what I will not do. I will not serve that in which I no longer believe whether it call itself my home, my fatherland or my church: and I will try to express myself in some mode of life or art as freely as I can and as wholly as I can, using for my defence the only arms I allow myself to use—silence, exile, and cunning." James Joyce, *Portrait of the Artist as a Young Man* (New York: Penguin, 1987), p. 247.

26. Edward Said, "Reflections on Exile," in *Altogether Elsewhere: Writers on Exile,* ed. Marc Robinson (Boston: Faber and Faber, 1994), p. 137.

27. Carlo Rosselli, *Dall'esilio: Lettere alla moglie, 1929–1937,* ed. Costanzo Casucci (Florence: Passigli, 1997).

28. Quoted in Urbinati, *Liberal Socialism,* p. x.

29. Salvemini, *Carlo and Nello Rosselli,* p. 38.

30. Carlo Rosselli, *Dall'esilio,* p. 32.

31. Carlo Rosselli to Amelia Rosselli, 16 March 1934; letter confiscated by fascist police; now in ACS, CPC, Busta 4421, fascicolo 4.

32. "Filippo Turati e il socialismo italiano," *QGL,* no. 3 (June 1932): 42.

1. Younger Brothers

1. Amelia Rosselli, unpublished *Memoriale,* AGL; quoted in Nicola Tranfaglia, *Carlo Rosselli: dall'interventismo alla Giustizia e Libertà* (Bari: Laterza, 1968), p. 13; (hereafter cited as Tranfaglia, *Carlo Rosselli.*) English translation in Susan Zuccotti, *The Italians and the Holocaust: Persecution, Rescue, Survival* (New York: Basic Books, 1987; reprint, Omaha: University of Nebraska Press, 1996), p. 242.

2. One of the most decorated officers in the Italian Army was General Emanuele Pugliese. There is an extensive bibliography on the Jews of Italy. See especially Renzo De Felice, *Storia degli ebrei italiani sotto il fascismo,* 4th ed. (Turin: Einaudi, 1993); Attilio Milano, *Storia degli ebrei in Italia* (Turin: Einaudi, 1963); Sergio Della Pergola, *Anatomia dell'ebraismo italiano* (Rome: Carucci, 1976); Gina Formiggini, *Stella d'Italia, stella di Davide: gli ebrei dal Risorgimento alla Resistenza* (Milan: Mursia, 1970). In English, Meir Michaelis, *Mussolini and the Jews: German-Italian Relations and the Jewish Question in Italy, 1922–1945* (New York: Oxford University Press, 1978); H. Stuart Hughes, *Prisoners of Hope: The Silver Age of the Italian Jews, 1924–1974* (Cambridge, Mass.: Harvard University Press, 1983); Susan Zuccotti, *The Italians and the*

Holocaust: Persecution, Rescue and Survival (New York: Basic Books, 1987); Alexander Stille, *Benevolence and Betrayal: Five Italian Jewish Families Under Fascism* (New York: Summit Books, 1991).

3. Pellegrino Rosselli even piously recorded the hour of Mazzini's death: 1:35 P.M. See Aldo Garosci, *La vita di Carlo Rosselli*, 2 vols. (Rome: Edizione U, 1945; reprinted as *Vita di Carlo Rosselli*, 2 vols. [Florence: Vallecchi, 1973]), I, p. 12; (hereafter cited as Garosci, *Vita*).

4. Their courtship is examined through an extensive epistolary exchange in Aldo Rosselli, *La famiglia Rosselli: una tragedia italiana* (Milan: Bompiani, 1983), pp. 9–66.

5. Alberto Moravia, Preface to Aldo Rosselli, *La famiglia Rosselli*, p. 2.

6. Foreward to Aldo Rosselli, *La famiglia Rosselli*, p. vi.

7. Letter of 25 March 1928; reprinted in *Epistolario familiare: Carlo, Nello Rosselli e la madre (1919–1937)*, ed. Zeffiro Ciuffoletti (Milan: SugarCo, 1979; reprinted as *I Rosselli: Epistolario familiare 1914–1937* [Milan: Mondadori, 1997]), pp. 412–414; hereafter cited as *Epistolario familiare*.

8. Besides the letters collected in *Epistolario familiare*, others are in the Archivio Giustizia e Libertà (AGL) in the Istituto Storico della Resistenza in Toscana (ISRT), Florence. See also Riccardo Bauer, "I Rosselli e l'epistolario familiare," *Risorgimento* 32, no. 1 (February 1980): 1–11.

9. Tranfaglia, *Carlo Rosselli*, p. 17.

10. Ibid., pp. 16–17.

11. On the cultural life of Florence just before World War I, see Walter L. Adamson, *Avant-garde Florence: From Modernism to Fascism* (Cambridge, Mass.: Harvard University Press, 1993).

12. Tranfaglia, *Carlo Rosselli*, p. 17.

13. Nello Rosselli, *Mazzini e Bakunin: Dodici anni di movimento operaio in Italia, 1860–1872* (Turin: Einaudi, 1927); *Carlo Pisacane nel Risorgimento italiano* (Genoa: Orfini, 1936); *Saggi sul Risorgimento e altri scritti*, preface by Gaetano Salvemini with an introduction by Alessandro Galante Garrone (Turin: Einaudi, 1946); *Nello Rosselli, uno storico sotto il fascismo: Lettere e scritti vari (1927–1937)*, ed. Zeffiro Ciuffoletti (Florence: La Nuova Italia, 1979).

14. Alessandro Levi, *Ricordi dei fratelli Rosselli* (Florence: La Nuova Italia, 1947), p. 59.

15. The remark is by Giorgio Spini, one of Italy's most respected historians and a Methodist lay preacher, in "Florentine Antifascism: The Jewish Milieu," in *Italian Socialism: Between Politics and History*, ed. Spencer Di Scala (Amherst: University of Massachusetts Press, 1996), p. 102.

16. Garosci, *Vita*, I, p. 20n1.

17. Carlo Rosselli, *Liberal Socialism*, ed. Nadia Urbinati, trans. William McCuaig (Princeton, N.J.: Princeton University Press, 1994), p. 6.

18. De Felice, *Storia degli ebrei italiani,* p. 91.

19. AGL; quoted in Tranfaglia, *Carlo Rosselli,* p. 13. Emphasis in the original.

20. Amelia to Carlo, 31 January 1919; *Epistolario familiare,* pp. 91–92.

21. *Epistolario familiare,* p. 235.

22. The best study of Nello's religious beliefs is Bruno Di Porto's essay "Il problema ebraico in Nello Rosselli," in *Giustizia e Libertà nella lotta antifascista,* ed. Carlo Francovich (Florence: La Nuova Italia, 1978), pp. 491–499. Nello's speech is quoted in De Felice, *Storia degli ebrei italiani,* pp. 89–90; English translation quoted in Susan Zuccotti, *The Italians and the Holocaust* (New York: Basic Books, 1987), p. 246. Nello published his thoughts on the Livorno conference in the Zionist journal *Israel* on 20 November 1924; reprinted in *Il Ponte* 12, no. 6 (June 1957); reprinted as "Ebraismo e italianità," in "Carlo e Nello Rosselli: Socialismo liberale e cultura europea (1937–1997)," in *Quaderni del Circolo Rosselli,* ed. Ariane Landuyt, no. 11 (1998): 115–118.

23. Carlo Rosselli, *Liberal Socialism,* p. 76.

24. Hughes, *Prisoners of Hope,* p. 56. The three scholars who have pointed out the influence of Rosselli's Judaism are Giorgio Spini, "Florentine Antifascism: The Jewish Milieu," in *Italian Socialism: Between Politics and History,* pp. 100–104; Joel Blatt, "The Battle of Turin, 1933–1936," *Journal of Modern Italian Studies* 1, no. 1 (Fall 1995): 22–57; and Alberto Cavaglion, "L'ebraismo in Carlo e Nello Rosselli," in "Carlo e Nello Rosselli. Socialismo Liberale e cultura europea 1937–1997." *Quaderni del Circolo Rosselli,* no. 11 (March 1998): 69–75.

25. Margherita Sarfatti, *The Life of Mussolini* (London: Butterworth, 1925), p. 176; Angelica Balabanoff, *My Life as a Rebel* (reprint Bloomington: Indiana University Press, 1973, 1st ed., London, 1938), p. 244. Both quoted in Jasper Ridley, *Mussolini: A Biography* (New York: St. Martin's Press, 1998), pp. 49, 97.

26. "Corradini, Enrico" in Philip V. Cannistraro, ed., *Historical Dictionary of Fascist Italy* (Westport, Conn.: Greenwood Press, 1982), pp. 140–141; Ronald S. Cunsolo, "Enrico Corradini e la teoria del nazionalismo proletariato," *Rassegna Storica del Risorgimento* 65 (July–September 1978): 341–355.

27. Amelia Rosselli, *Fratelli minori* (Florence: Bemporad, 1921); quoted in Corrado Tumiati, "Amelia Rosselli scrittrice," *Il Ponte* 12, no. 4 (April 1956): 585–586.

28. Recommended by his commanding officer for the Gold Medal of Honor, he was posthumously granted the Silver Medal. Garosci, *Vita,* I, p. 22n1; Tranfaglia, *Carlo Rosselli,* p. 14.

29. For an excellent treatment of the "war generation," see Dan S. White, *Lost Comrades: Socialists of the Front Generation, 1918–1945* (Cambridge, Mass.: Harvard University Press, 1992).

30. "Inchiesta sui giovani (Guerra e fascismo)" in *Libertà!*, 10 May 1924; quoted in Tranfaglia, *Carlo Rosselli*, p. 23.

31. Letter of 16 November 1928; *Epistolario familiare*, p. 427.

32. "Inchiesta sui giovani (Guerra e fascismo)" in *Libertà!*, 10 May 1924; quoted in Tranfaglia, *Carlo Rosselli*, p. 23.

33. Carlo Rosselli, "Il sindacalismo rivoluzionario," in *Socialismo liberale: Opere scelte di Carlo Rosselli*, ed. John Rosselli (Turin: Einaudi, 1973), I, pp. 16–17; hereafter cited as *Opere scelte*.

34. "Compito nuovo," in *Vita* 7 (20 May 1919); now in *Opere scelte*, I, pp. 5–8.

35. Alexander De Grand, *The Italian Left in the Twentieth Century: A History of the Socialist and Communist Parties* (Bloomington: Indiana University Press, 1989), p. 37.

36. Quoted in Ridley, *Mussolini*, p. 102.

37. Garosci, *Vita*, I, pp. 27–28.

38. "L'esame di Ginevra," *GL*, 9 August 1935. Balbo's American biographer wrote that this is "probably an apocryphal story" and "credits" Rosselli for its origin; see Claudio Segrè, *Italo Balbo: A Fascist Life* (Berkeley: University of California Press, 1987), pp. 29, 411n24.

39. "Il sindacalismo rivoluzionario," thesis of June 1921 at the Istituto di Scienze Sociali "Cesare Alfieri"; deposited in the AGL; now in *Opere scelte*, I, p. 10.

40. "Il sindacalismo rivoluzionario," *Opere scelte*, I, p. 12; see also Maurizio Degli Innocenti, "Carlo Rosselli e il movimento sindacale: Dalla tesi di laurea a *Socialismo liberale*," in Francovich, *Giustizia e Libertà nella lotta antifascista*, p. 56.

41. "Il sindacalismo rivoluzionario," in Carlo Rosselli, *Opere scelte*, I, p. 18.

42. Tranfaglia, *Carlo Rosselli*, pp. 58–59; see also Paolo Bagnoli, "L'esperienza liberale di Carlo Rosselli, 1919–1924," *Italia Contemporanea* 28 (October–December 1976): 29–42.

43. "Libera Russia," *Noi Giovani* no. 4 (March 1917); quoted in Tranfaglia, *Carlo Rosselli*, p. 19.

44. "Il sindacalismo rivoluzionario," p. 19.

45. Ibid., p. 21.

46. Roberto Vivarelli, "Carlo Rosselli e Gaetano Salvemini," in Francovich, *Giustizia e Libertà nella lotta antifascista*, pp. 69–98.

47. Norberto Bobbio, *Ideological Profile of Twentieth-Century Italy*, trans. Lydia G. Cochrane (Princeton, N.J.: Princeton University Press, 1995), p. 82.

48. Cited in Garosci, *Vita*, I, p. 39.

49. Ibid.

50. *Epistolario familiare*, p. 131.

51. The literature on Croce is vast. In English see Edmund Jacobitti, *Revolution-*

ary Humanism and Historicism in Italy (New Haven: Yale University Press, 1981); David D. Roberts, *Benedetto Croce and the Uses of Historicism* (Berkeley: University of California Press, 1987); M. E. Moss, *Benedetto Croce Reconsidered* (Hanover, N.H.: University Press of New England, 1987); A. Robert Caponigri, *History and Liberty: The Historical Writings of Benedetto Croce* (London: Routledge & Kegan Paul, 1955).

52. Letters of 23, 28 February 1923 and 5 March 1923; *Epistolario familiare,* pp. 165–170.

53. Quoted in Tranfaglia, *Carlo Rosselli,* p. 120.

54. Piero Calamandrei, *Uomini e città della Resistenza* (Bari: Laterza, 1965), p. 58. There were nearly one hundred newspapers, reviews, and journals in the Circolo, from the leading Italian dailies to foreign papers such as *Les Temps, The Times, Deutsche Allgemeinezeitung,* and *The Chicago Tribune;* in addition, there were important journals such as *The Nation, The Atlantic Monthly,* and the *Manchester Guardian.* See "Nel nome dei Rosselli," in *Quaderni del Circolo Rosselli* 11, 1 (January 1991): 30.

55. Piero Calamandrei, "Il manganello, la cultura e la giustizia," in *Non Mollare 1925* (Florence: La Nuova Italia, 1955), p. 71; Carlo Francovich, "Il Circolo di Cultura: l'ultima espressione di vita democratica a Firenze," *Quaderni del Circolo Rosselli* 11, 1 (January 1991): 80–84.

56. Calamandrei "Il manganello, la cultura e la giustizia," pp. 72–76.

57. Quoted in Aldo Rosselli, *La famiglia Rosselli,* p. 150.

58. Iris Origo, *A Need to Testify: Portraits of Lauro De Bosis, Ruth Draper, Gaetano Salvemini, Ignazio Silone* (San Diego: Harcourt, Brace, Jovanovich, 1984), p. 128.

59. Garosci, *Vita,* I, p. 43. On Salvemini, "The man who would not conform," see Origo, *A Need to Testify,* pp. 128–190; and Giovanni Minervini, *Salvemini e la democrazia* (Manduria: Lacaita, 1994).

60. Ernesto Rossi's obituary of Salvemini, *Il Mondo,* 17 September 1957.

61. Gaetano Salvemini, "Empirici e teologi," *Il Ponte* 24 (May 1968): 40–50; cited in Bobbio, *Ideological Profile,* p. 89.

62. Quoted in Origo, *A Need to Testify,* p. 162.

63. Gaetano Salvemini, "Marion Rosselli," *Il Ponte* 5, no. 11 (November 1949): 143.

64. Garosci, *Vita,* I, p. 37; quoted by Urbinati in Carlo Rosselli, *Liberal Socialism,* p. xxi.

65. Garosci, *Vita,* I, p. 44.

66. Calamandrei, "Il manganello, la cultura e la giustizia," p. 79.

67. *Non Mollare 1925,* p. 80.

68. Tranfaglia, *Carlo Rosselli,* p. 135.

69. *Epistolario familiare,* pp. 210–213.

70. De Grand, *Italian Left in the Twentieth Century,* p. 54.

71. Quoted in Aldo Rosselli, *La famiglia Rosselli,* p. 116.

72. Nello Rosselli, *Carlo Pisacane nel Risorgimento italiano* (Turin: Bocca, 1932).

73. Letter of 21 December 1932; now in Carlo Rosselli, *Scritti dell'esilio,* I, *"Giustizia e Libertà" e la Concentrazione Antifascista (1929–1934),* ed. Costanzo Casucci (Turin: Einaudi, 1988), p. 170; hereafter cited as *Scritti dell'esilio,* I.

74. "Filippo Turati e il socialismo italiano," *QGL,* no. 3 (June 1932): 42; reprinted in *Scritti dell'esilio,* I, p. 133.

75. Piero Gobetti, *Risorgimento senza eroi* (Turin: Einaudi, 1956).

76. Clara M. Lovett, *The Democratic Movement in Italy, 1830–1876* (Cambridge, Mass.: Harvard University Press, 1982), pp. 4–5, 28.

77. The phrase is from Louis J. Rosenberg, *Mazzini* (Chicago: C. H. Kerr & Co., 1903).

78. Lovett, *Democratic Movement in Italy,* pp. 13, 18.

79. "Eroismo assoluto," *GL,* 3 April 1936; now in *Scritti dell'esilio,* II, p. 338.

80. Giuseppe Ferrari, *Scritti politici,* ed. Silvia Rota Ghibaudi (Turin: Einaudi, 1973), p. 391.

81. For Garibaldi as "knight of liberty," see Jean Burton, *Garibaldi* (New York: Knopf, 1945); on Garibaldi as "myth," see Romano Ugolini, *Garibaldi* (Rome: Edizioni dell'Ateneo, 1982).

82. For more on the concept of these thinkers as "dissidents," see Ugo Dotti, *I dissidenti del Risorgimento: Cattaneo, Ferrari, Pisacane* (Rome: Laterza, 1975).

83. De Grand, *Italian Left in the Twentieth Century,* p. 51.

84. Giacomo Matteotti, *Discorsi parliamentari,* 3 vols. (Rome: Stabilimenti tipografici C. Colombo, 1970), II, pp. 873–888. Matteotti's accusations are reprinted in *The Fascisti Exposed,* trans. E. W. Dickes (New York: Howard Fertig, 1969; first English publication, 1924).

85. Guido Gerosa and Gian Franco Venè, eds.,, *Il delitto Matteotti* (Milan: Mondadori, 1972), p. 24. Note the historical parallel with Henry II and Thomas Beckett; see also Gaetano Arfè, *Il delitto Matteotti* (Bologna: Cappelli, 1973).

86. For the story of this underground newspaper, see Piero Calamandrei, Ernesto Rossi and Gaetano Salvemini, *Non Mollare 1925* (Florence: La Nuova Italia, 1955); also Frank Rosengarten, *The Italian Anti-Fascist Press 1919–1945* (Cleveland, Ohio: Case Western Reserve University Press, 1968), pp. 64–67; Charles F. Delzell, *Mussolini's Enemies: The Italian Anti-Fascist Resistance* (Princeton, N.J.: Princeton University Press, 1961), pp. 30–32.

87. Churchill made his remark at a 1926 press conference in Rome. Martin Gilbert, *Churchill: A Life* (London: Heinemann, 1991), p. 480.

88. "Eroe tutto prosa," in *Scritti dell'esilio,* I, p. 265.

89. Ibid., pp. 267–268.

90. The letter is partially reprinted in Lelio Basso and Luigi Anderlini, eds., *Le*

riviste di Piero Gobetti (Milan: Feltrinelli, 1961), p. lxxxiv; the original is held at the Archivio Centro Gobetti in Turin.

91. Tranfaglia, *Carlo Rosselli,* p. 179.

92. Luciano Zani, *Italia Libera: Il primo movimento antifascista clandestino (1923– 1925)* (Rome, Bari: Laterza, 1975), p. 3.

93. Zani, *Italia Libera,* p. 173; Ernesto Rossi, "L'Italia Libera," in *No al fascismo,* ed. Ernesto Rossi (Turin: Einaudi, 1957), p. 48.

94. Rossi, "L'Italia Libera," pp. 42, 48.

2. Autocritica

1. Guido De Ruggiero, *The History of European Liberalism,* trans. R. G. Collingwood (London; New York: Oxford University Press, 1927), p. 435; originally published as *Storia del liberalismo europeo* (Bari: Laterza, 1925; reprints, 1984, 1995).

2. Quoted in David Ward, *Antifascisms: Cultural Politics in Italy, 1943–46. Benedetto Croce and the Liberals, Carlo Levi and the "Actionists"* (Madison, N.J.: Fairleigh Dickinson University Press, 1996), p. 43.

3. Giuseppe A. Borgese, *Goliath: The March of Fascism* (New York: Viking, 1937), pp. 25, 473.

4. Ibid., pp. 288–289, 299–300.

5. On Prezzolini see entry in Philip V. Cannistraro, ed., *Historical Dictionary of Fascist Italy* (Westport, Conn.: Greenwood Press, 1982), pp. 441–442; and Walter L. Adamson, *Avant-Garde Florence: From Modernism to Fascism* (Cambridge, Mass.: Harvard University Press, 1993), pp. 234–235, 240–244, 256– 257.

6. Norberto Bobbio, *Ideological Profile of Twentieth-Century Italy,* trans. Lydia G. Cochrane (Princeton, N.J.: Princeton University Press, 1995), p. 127.

7. Carlo Rosselli, "La lotta di classe nel movimento operaio," *Critica Sociale* 33 (1–15 February 1923): 444–446; "Per la storia della logica," *La Rivoluzione Liberale* 2 (15 March 1923): 27–28; "Contradizzioni liberiste," *La Rivoluzione Liberale* 2 (24 April 1923): 48; and "Luigi Einaudi e il movimento operaio," *Critica Sociale* 34 (15–31 May 1924): 158–159. The last three have been reprinted in *Opere scelte,* I, pp. 29–51.

8. "Contradizzioni liberiste," *Opere scelte,* I, p. 42.

9. "Per la storia della logica," *Opere scelte,* I, p. 30.

10. "La lotta di classe nel movimento operaio," *Opere scelte,* I, p. 45.

11. "Liberalismo socialista," *Critica Sociale* 33 (1–15 July 1923): 203–204; reprinted in Piero Gobetti's *La Rivoluzione Liberale* (15 July 1924): 114–116; reprinted in *Opere scelte,* I, pp.107–128.

12. The letter is in the ACS, Ministero Interno, Direzione Generale, Pubblica

Sicurezza, gen. ris. (1903–1940), busta 501, and partially reprinted in Giuseppe Rossini, ed., *Il delitto Matteotti tra il Viminale e l'Aventino* (Bologna: Il Mulino, 1966), pp. 129–130, and in Tranfaglia, *Carlo Rosselli,* pp. 121–122.

13. Letter of 21 July 1923; *Epistolario familiare,* p. 172.

14. *La Rivoluzione Liberale,* 15 July 1924; Rosselli's essay and Gobetti's commentary are reprinted in *Opere scelte,* I, pp. 107–128.

15. Tranfaglia, *Carlo Rosselli,* p. 172n53; *Epistolario familiare,* pp. 228–229.

16. "Liberalismo socialista," *Opere scelte,* I, p. 111.

17. "1935," *QGL,* n. 12 (January 1935): 6.

18. "Liberalismo socialista," *Opere scelte,* I, p.109.

19. Harold Laski, *The Decline of Liberalism* (London: Oxford University Press, 1940), p. 21.

20. De Ruggiero, *History of European Liberalism,* p. 434.

21. For a recent discussion of "liberalism as method," see Ernesto Paolozzi, *Il liberalismo come metodo: Antoni, Croce, De Ruggiero, Popper* (Rome: Fondazione Luigi Einaudi, 1995).

22. "Liberalismo socialista," *Opere scelte,* I, pp. 116–117.

23. Ibid., p. 119.

24. Ibid., p. 120.

25. Ibid., p. 124.

26. For Rosselli's critique of these Marxist ideas, see his unpublished, handwritten notes in AGL, sezione I, fascicolo 7, sottofascicolo 1, documento #5.

27. "Liberalismo socialista," *Opere scelte,* I, p. 127. Emphasis in the original.

28. "La crisi intellettuale del Partito Socialista," *Critica Sociale* 33 (1–15 November 1923): 325–328; "Aggiunte e chiose al 'bilancio marxista,'" *Critica Sociale* 33 (1–15 December 1923): 359–362; both are reprinted in *Opere scelte,* I, pp. 83–106.

29. "La crisis intellettuale del Partito Socialista," *Opere scelte,* I, 83.

30. Ibid., pp. 83–84.

31. Croce's assessment is from a fundamental essay, "Concerning the Form of Scientific Materialism," which first appeared in 1896. Benedetto Croce, *Historical Materialism and the Economics of Karl Marx,* ed. Michael Curtis (New Brunswick, N.J.: New Transaction Books, 1981), p. 3. Quoted by Nadia Urbinati, ed. Carlo Rosselli, *Liberal Socialism* (Princeton, N.J.: Princeton University Press, 1994), pp. xlii–xliii. "Non si può non essere marxisti," and Norberto Bobbio, Introduzione, Carlo Rosselli, *Socialismo liberale* (Turin: Einaudi, 1973), pp. xi–xii.

32. "La crisi intellettuale del Partito Socialista," in *Opere scelte,* I, p. 86.

33. Ibid., p. 87.

34. Ibid., p. 88 Emphasis in the original.

35. Ibid., p. 94.

36. Alexander De Grand, *The Italian Left in the Twentieth Century: A History of the Socialist and Communist Parties* (Bloomington, Ind.: Indiana University Press, 1989), p. 34.
37. "Aggiunte e chiose al 'bilancio marxista,'" *Critica Sociale* 33 (1–15 December 1923): 359–362; now in *Opere scelte*, I, 96–106.
38. Ibid., p. 101.
39. Ibid., p. 103.
40. "Contributo a un chiaramento di idee," *Critica Sociale* 34 (1–15 January 1924): 14–16.
41. Rodolfo Mondolfo, *Umanesimo di Marx: Studi filosofici 1908–1966* (Turin: Einaudi, 1968).
42. John Stuart Mill, *La libertà* (Turin: Einaudi, 1925); Tranfaglia, *Carlo Rosselli*, p. 173n61.
43. Tranfaglia, *Carlo Rosselli*, p. 159. On the history of Marxist revisionism in Italy, see Enzo Santarelli, *La revisione del marxismo in Italia* (Milan: Feltrinelli, 1977).
44. *Epistolario familiare*, pp. 247–249.
45. Frank Rosengarten, *The Italian Anti-Fascist Press, 1919–1945* (Cleveland, Ohio: Case Western Reserve University Press, 1968), pp. 10, 11–14.
46. Ibid., p. 17.
47. Gaetano Salvemini, "Il Non Mollare," in *Non Mollare 1925* (Florence: La Nuova Italia, 1955) p. 3.
48. Ernesto Rossi, "Il Non Mollare," *Il Ponte* 1, no. 8 (August 1945): 235.
49. Garosci, *Vita*, I, p. 55, and Salvemini, "Il Non Mollare," p. 5.
50. The document is reproduced in full in *Non Mollare 1925*, table 9; emphasis in the original.
51. Ibid., table 13.
52. Ibid., table 17.
53. Salvemini, "Il Non Mollare," p. 11.
54. Gaetano Salvemini, *Memorie di un fuoruscito* (Milan: Feltrinelli, 1960), pp. 14–15.
55. Alessandro Levi, *Ricordi dei fratelli Rosselli* (Florence: La Nuova Italia, 1947), pp. 79–80.
56. *Non Mollare*, April 1925; reproduced in *Non Mollare 1925*, table 24.
57. *Non Mollare 1925*, table 30.
58. *Non Mollare 1925*, table 35.
59. *Non Mollare*, 5 October 1925; reprinted in *Non Mollare 1925*, table 43. Emphasis in the original.
60. Alessandro Levi, *Ricordi dei fratelli Rosselli*, p. 72.
61. Letter of 2 April 1926; *Epistolario familiare*, p. 298. For the fascist police

version of the event, see the document from the Prefecture of Genoa in ACS, Pubblica Sicurezza 1926, Busta 15, inserto A1. An open—and threatening—letter to Rosselli appeared in the fascist newspaper *Il Littorio*, "Schiaffeggio per la seconda volta al Professore Rosselli" on 4 May 1926.

62. Frank Rosengarten, *Silvio Trentin dall'interventismo alla Resistenza* (Milan: Feltrinelli, 1977), p. 87.

63. Paolo Bagnoli, "La battaglia socialista de 'Il Quarto Stato,'" in *Giustizia e Libertà nella lotta antifascista*, ed. Carlo Francovich (Florence: La Nuova Italia, 1978), pp. 113–146.

64. Quoted in Giuseppe Tamburrano, "Survival in Defeat: Pietro Nenni," in *Italian Socialism: Between Politics and History*, ed. Spencer Di Scala (Amherst, Mass.: University of Massachusetts Press, 1996), p. 62.

65. Pietro Nenni, "Lo scampolista," *Almanacco socialista 1938* (Paris: PSI, 1938), p. 147; quoted in Tranfaglia, p. 330n3.

66. The letter is reprinted in Domenico Zucàro, ed., *Il Quarto Stato di Nenni e Rosselli* (Milan: SugarCo, 1977), pp. 309–310.

67. Ibid., p. 10.

68. AGL, sezione I, fascicolo I, sottofascicolo 80, inserto #9.

69. Giorgio Amendola, *Intervista sull'antifascismo* (Bari: Laterza, 1976), p. 60.

70. *Il Quarto Stato di Nenni e Rosselli*, pp. 309–313.

71. "Autocritica," *Il Quarto Stato*, 3 April 1926; *Opere scelte*, I, pp. 129–132.

72. "Autocritica," *Opere scelte*, I, pp. 130–131.

73. Ibid., p. 132. *"Transformismo"* was Giolitti's tactic of co-opting—or transforming—political adversaries into allies.

74. Garosci, *Vita*, I, p. 74.

75. "Rabano Mauro" (Claudio Treves), "Autocritica o demolizione," *Critica Sociale* 36 (7–15 April 1926): 93–96.

76. "Autocritica non demolizione," *Il Quarto Stato*, 1 May 1926; *Opere scelte*, I, p. 133.

77. Ibid.

78. Alcuino, "Autocritica per ricostruire," *Critica Sociale* 36 (16–31 May 1926); Observer, Max Ascoli, and Franz Weiss, "Polemica sull'autocritica socialista," *Il Quarto Stato*, 15 May 1926; Roberto Rigola, Giuseppe Saragat, and Observer, "Ancora polemica sull'autocritica socialista," *Il Quarto Stato*, 22 May 1926; Pietro Nenni, "La nuova fase," *Il Quarto Stato*, 12 June 1926.

79. Letter of 16 May 1926; *Epistolario familiare*, pp. 303–304.

80. "Volontarismo," *Il Quarto Stato*, 12 June 1926; *Opere scelte*, I, p. 145.

81. "Contro il pessimismo," *Il Quarto Stato*, 26 June 1926; *Opere scelte*, I, pp. 155–160.

82. "Chiarificazione," *Il Quarto Stato*, 24 July 1926.

83. Ibid.

84. De Grand, *Italian Left in the Twentieth Century,* p. 63.

85. "Un congresso e i suoi problemi," *Il Quarto Stato,* 9 October 1926; *Opere scelte,* I, pp. 167–171.

86. "Il Congresso del PSLI," *Il Quarto Stato,* 30 October 1926; *Opere scelte,* I, pp. 172–178.

87. On the phenomenon of *fuoruscitismo,* see Aldo Garosci, *Storia dei fuorusciti* (Bari: Laterza, 1953); Paolo Alatri, *L'antifascismo italiano,* 2 vols. (Rome: Riuniti, 1973); Gaetano Arfè et al., *L'emigrazione socialista nella lotta contro il fascismo, 1926–1939* (Florence, Sansoni, 1982); Charles F. Delzell, "Il fuoruscitismo italiano dal 1922 al 1943," in *Movimento di Liberazione in Italia* 5, n. 23 (March 1953): 3–37; Antonio Bechelloni et al., eds., *Italia in esilio: L'emigrazione italiana in Francia tra le due guerre* (Rome: Presidenza del Consiglio dei Ministri, 1993); Marina Tesoro and Elisa Signori, *Antifascismo in esilio: fra repubblicanismo e socialismo* (Florence: Le Monnier, 1987).

88. Carlo Levi, *Cristo si è fermato a Eboli* (Turin: Einaudi, 1945); printed in English as *Christ Stopped at Eboli,* trans. Frances Frenaye (New York: Farrar, Straus and Giroux, 1947).

89. For Rosselli's account of the way he convinced Turati to flee and their subsequent flight, see his "Come Turati lasciò Italia," originally published in *La Libertà,* 14 April 1932; now in Carlo Rosselli, *Scritti politici e autobiografici* (Naples: Polis Editrice, 1944), pp. 17–27. The original manuscript is in the AGL, sezione I, fascicolo 2, sottofascicolo 2, inserto 17.

90. Carlo Rosselli, *Scritti politici e autobiografici,* pp. 19–20; see also his "Turati e il socialismo italiano," *QGL,* no. 3 (June 1932): 1–42.

91. Garosci, *Vita,* I, p. 100.

92. "Come Turati lasciò Italia," Carlo Rosseli, *Scritti politici e autobiografici,* pp. 23–24.

93. Filippo Turati, *Avanti!,* 15 August 1927.

94. Ferruccio Parri, *L'Umanità,* 9 October 1948.

95. Alessandro Levi, *Ricordi dei fratelli Rosselli,* p. 99.

96. "Come Turati lasciò Italia," Carlo Rosselli, *Scritti politici e autobiografici,* p. 18; see also Enzo Tagliacozzo, "L'evasione di Turati," in *No al fascismo,* ed. Ernesto Rossi (Turin: Einaudi, 1957), pp. 49–70; and Alessandro Schiavi, *Esilio e morte di Filippo Turati, 1926–1932* (Rome: Opere Nuove, 1956), pp. 294–297.

97. Gaetano Salvemini, *Carlo and Nello Rosselli: A Memoir* (London: For Intellectual Liberty, 1937), p. 13.

98. "Fuga in quattro tempi," Carlo Rosselli, *Scritti politici e autobiografici,* pp. 33–34.

99. De Grand, *Italian Left in the Twentieth Century,* p. 64.

3. Liberal Socialism

1. From the Prefettura of Milan, ACS, CPC, Busta 4421, fascicolo 2.
2. Gaetano Salvemini, *Carlo and Nello Rosselli: A Memoir* (London: For Intellectual Liberty, 1937), p. 27.
3. For Parri's account, see "Con Carlo Rosselli dalla fuga di Turati al processo di Savona," in *Non Mollare*, 8 June 1947.
4. "Fuga in quattro tempi," *Opere scelte*, I, p. 510.
5. Quoted in Salvemini, *Carlo and Nello Rosselli*, p. 24.
6. "Fuga in quattro tempi," *Opere scelte*, I, p. 514.
7. Aldo Garosci mistakenly has written that John [Giovanni] Rosselli was born on 10 June (the anniversary of Matteotti's death) and that his middle name was Giacomo (after Matteotti); the correct information was supplied to me by John Rosselli himself, who also noted that the source of the nickname came from the blueberry bushes that surrounded his parents while they were vacationing in the Alps when Marion was pregnant with John; Carlo turned to her and said, "You'll see what a beautiful little blueberry bush we'll make."
8. *Epistolario familiare*, p. 323.
9. The letters are from 21 and 28 March, 4 and 10 April, 17 June 1927; all in AGL with 4 April and 17 June reproduced in *Epistolario familiare*, pp. 335–336 and 346. The 148 pages of notes for the work on utilitarianism are collected in the AGL, sezione I, fascicolo 3, sottofascicolo 1, inserto 10.
10. Letter of 27 September 1927; *Epistolario familiare*, pp. 355–356. The German *mutter* is in the original.
11. On the trial, see Tranfaglia, *Carlo Rosselli*, pp. 343–360, and Alessandro Levi, *Ricordi dei fratelli Rosselli* (Florence: La Nuova Italia, 1947), pp.109–116. The complete transcript of the trial is preserved in the Archivio di Stato (Savona). For a reconstruction of the trial, see Vico Faggi, ed., *Il processo di Savona* (Genoa: Teatro Stabile, 1965).
12. BNF, FR, cassetta 1, inserto II, n. 4.
13. AGL, fascicolo III, sottofascicolo 5.
14. Barbara Carter, *Il Mese*, 30 July 1945.
15. Ferruccio Parri, *Scritti: 1915–1975* (Milan: Feltrinelli, 1976), p. 45.
16. Carlo Levi, "Ricordi del processo," *Il processo di Savona*, pp. 95–97.
17. The *notte di sangue* was a massacre carried out by fascists in Florence in October 1925.
18. This dialogue, found in Faggi, *Il processo di Savona* (pp. 53–54), is based on the transcript of the trial in the Archivio di Stato at Savona.
19. *Il Mondo*, 17 January 1956, p. 3.
20. *Epistolario familiare*, pp. 363–375.

21. The remark was overheard by Rosselli at the end of the trial and conveyed to Turati in a letter of 18 September 1927; AGL, sezione I, fascicolo 1, sottofascicolo 120.

22. "Fuga in quattro tempi," *Opere scelte*, I, p. 514. Documents pertaining to Lipari are in the AGL, sezione I, fascicolo 7, sottofascicolo 1.

23. Francesco Fausto Nitti, *Nous prisons et nous évasions* (Paris: Edizioni di Giustizia e Libertà, 1930). After the war, an Italian edition appeared as *Le nostre prigioni e la nostra evasione* (Naples: Edizioni Scientifiche Italiane, 1946); see also Nitti's *Escape: The Personal Narrative of a Political Prisoner Who Was Rescued from Lipari, the Fascist "Devil's Island"* (New York: Putman, 1930). Emilio Lussu recounts his version in *Road to Exile: The Story of a Sardinian Patriot*, trans. Mrs. Graham Rawson, with a preface by Wickham Steed (New York: Covici & Friede, 1936), pp. 226–238; first published as *Marcia su Roma* (Paris: Casa Editrice Critica, 1933); a more recent English translation of Lussu's account appeared as *An Autobiographical Account by a Leading Sardinian Republican Politician of Resistance to Fascism in Sardinia from 1919–1930*, trans. Roy W. Davis (New York: Edward Mellen Press, 1992).

24. Garosci, *Vita*, I, p. 126.

25. Emilio Lussu, "Carlo Rosselli," *GL* 25 June 1937.

26. "Fuga in quattro tempi," in *Opere scelte*, I, p. 514.

27. Lussu's correspondence with Rosselli is found in *Lettere a Carlo Rosselli e altri scritti di Giustizia e Libertà*, ed. Manlio Brigaglia (Sassari: Libreria Dessi, 1979). For his account of Lipari, see *La catena: dalle leggi eccezionali alle isole* (Paris: Edizioni di Giustizia e Libertà, 1929).

28. BNF, FR, cassetta 1, inserto III, no. 1.

29. "Fuga in quattro tempi," p. 516.

30. Letter of 16 February 1928; *Epistolario familiare*, p. 403.

31. "Fuga in quattro tempi," p. 519.

32. Ibid.

33. Alberto Tarchiani, "L'impresa di Lipari," in Ernesto Rossi, ed., *No al fascismo* (Turin: Einaudi, 1957), p. 107.

34. "Fuga in quattro tempi," p. 523.

35. Ibid., p. 524.

36. Ibid., p. 525.

37. Nicola Tranfaglia, *Il labirinto italiano: Il fascismo, antifascismo, gli storici* (Florence: La Nuova Italia, 1989), p. 182.

38. According to a fascist police report, the book was to be titled *Marxisme, socialisme et liberté*. Although they may have been mistaken on the title, the police did know in advance that the book was to be published by Librairie Valois at 7 Place du Panthéon, just next door to the Rosselli home in Paris. ACS, CPC, Busta 4421, fascicolo 2. The first edition appeared in a French

translation as *Socialisme libéral,* trans. Stefan Priacel (Paris: Librairie Valois, 1930). The first Italian edition appeared in 1945, with a letter by Marion and Treves's critical review. There were printed 3,100 copies of this first Italian edition: 10 copies for the family, 90 for libraries, 100 for the press, and the remaining 2,900 for the public. Since the original manuscript was still in the hands of the family, which had fled France before the oncoming German Army in 1940, this first Italian edition was based on the French edition of 1930 and was published under the supervision of Aldo Garosci and Leone Bortone. After the war, the original manuscript, written on tiny pieces of paper to facilitate its being hidden (from the police) in the piano, was deposited in the Biblioteca Nazionale di Firenze, and forms the heart of the Fondo Rosselli. It was not until 1973 that a new edition was published in Italy under the direction of Carlo's son John. On the vicissitudes of the manuscript and its complicated publication history, see John Rosselli, "Nota editoriale a *Socialismo liberale,*" in Carlo Rosselli, *Socialismo liberale* (Turin: Einaudi, 1973). The first English translation was *Liberal Socialism,* edited by Nadia Urbinati and translated by William McCuaig (Princeton, N.J.: Princeton University Press, 1994). A Spanish edition appeared as *Socialismo liberal,* translated by Diego Abad de Santillán (Madrid: Pablo Iglesias, 1991). A recent study is Salvo Mastellone, *Carlo Rosselli e "La Rivoluzione del Socialismo"* (Florence: Leo S. Olschki, 1999).

39. "As an expression of a noble character, devoted to a single ideal—the betterment of the Italian working classes—the book has a place in the history of political thought in Italy." Marion Cave Rosselli, "Lettera della moglie," in Carlo Rosselli, *Socialismo liberale* (Rome: Edizioni U, 1945). This letter, which serves as a foreword to the first Italian edition, was written while the Rosselli family was in exile in Larchmont, New York, during the Second World War (November 1944).

40. Urbinati, Introduction to Carlo Rosselli, *Liberal Socialism,* p. xxxiv.

41. Michael Walzer, "Introduction to *Liberal Socialism,*" *Dissent* 41 (Winter 1994): 123.

42. Quoted in *The Italian Refuge: Rescue of Jews During the Holocaust,* ed. Ivo Herzen (Washington, D.C.: Catholic University Press, 1989), p. 89.

43. Theodor Hertzka, *Freiland: Ein sociales Zukunftsbild* (Leipzig: Duncker & Humblot, 1890); translated as *Freeland: A Social Anticipation,* trans. Arthur Ransom (New York: Appleton, 1891); Reinhard Opitz, *Der deutsche Soziallib-eralismus, 1917–1933* (Cologne: Pahl-Rugenstein, 1973); Franz Oppenheimer, *Die soziale Frage und der Sozialismus: eine kritische Auseinandersetzung mit der Marxistischen* (Jena, Germany: G. Fischer, 1912); Charles Renouvier, *La nuovelle monodologie* (Paris: Colin, 1899), cited in Giovanna Cavallari, *Charles Renouvier filosofo della liberaldemocrazia* (Naples: Jovene, 1979).

44. Alfred Naquet, *Socialisme collectivisme et socialisme liberal* (Paris: Dentu,

1890); see Gian Biagio Furiozzi, "Alle origini del Socialismo Liberale: Alfred Naquet," in "Carlo e Nello Rosselli: Socialismo liberale e cultura europea (1937–1997)," ed. Ariane Landuyt, no. 11 (1998) of the *Quaderni del Circolo Rosselli* (Florence: Giunti, 1998): 160–161.

45. Francesco Saverio Merlino, *L'utopia collectivista e la crisi del "socialismo scientifico"* (Milan: Fratelli Treves, 1898); *Formes et essence du socialisme* (Paris: Giard & Briere, 1898); *Revisione del marxismo* (Bologna: Minerva, 1945); *Concezione critica del socialismo libertario,* ed. Aldo Venturini and Pier Carlo Masini (Florence: La Nuova Italia, 1957).

46. L. T. Hobhouse, *Liberalism* (Oxford: Oxford University Press, 1911); Croce's comment was from his essay "La concezione liberale come concezione della vita" of 1927, now in *Liberismo e liberalismo,* P. Solari, ed. (Naples: Ricciardi, 1957), p. 14.

47. Antonio Gramsci, "The Revolution against *Capital,*" in *Selections from Political Writings, 1910–1920,* ed. Quentin Hoare, trans. John Mathews (New York: International Publishers, 1977), p. 34.

48. Eduard Bernstein, *Die Voraussetzungen des Sozialismus und die Aufgaben der Sozialdemocratie* (Stuttgart: J. H. W. Dietz, 1899); *Evolutionary Socialism,* trans. Edith C. Harvey, introduction by Sidney Hook (New York: Schocken Books, 1961).

49. Peter Gay, *The Dilemma of Democratic Socialism: Eduard Bernstein's Challenge to Marx* (New York: Collier Books, 1962), p. 99.

50. Ferruccio Parri, "Nascita del Giustizia e Libertà," *Il Ponte* 13 (June 1957): 860.

51. Antonio Gramsci, "Our Marx," *Il Grido del Popolo,* 4 May 1918; reprinted in David Forgacs, ed., *An Antonio Gramsci Reader: Selected Writings, 1916–1935* (New York: Schocken Books, 1988), p. 36.

52. AGL, sezione I, fascicolo 7, sottofascicolo 1, document no. 7.

53. An English translation appeared as *The Psychology of Socialism,* trans. Eden and Cedar Paul (London: Allen & Unwin, 1928).

54. BNF, FR, cassetta 2, inserto VIII, n. 1.

55. Albert S. Lindemann, *A History of European Socialism* (New Haven: Yale University Press, 1983), p. 245; Gerd-Rainer Horn, *European Socialists Respond to Fascism* (New York, Oxford: Oxford University Press, 1996), p. 76.

56. BNF, FR, cassetta 2, inserto VIII, n. 1.

57. Carlo Rosselli, *Liberal Socialism,* ed. Nadia Urbinati, trans. William McCuaig (Princeton, N.J.: Princeton University Press, 1994), p. 82.

58. AGL, sezione I, fascicolo 7, sottofascicolo 1, document no. 5.

59. Carlo Rosselli, *Liberal Socialism,* p. 5. All references will be from the English translation. I have slightly changed the translation in places.

60. Ibid., p. 6.

61. Ibid.

62. For an example of Feuerbach's historicism and humanism, see his *The Essence of Christianity*, ed. E. Graham Waring and F. W. Strothman (New York: Frederick Ungar, 1957); on Feuerbach's influence on Marx and Engels, see Frederick Engels, *Ludwig Feuerbach and the Outcome of Classical German Philosophy* (New York: International Publishers, 1941).

63. Carlo Rosselli, *Liberal Socialism*, p. 14.

64. Antonio Gramsci, "The Revolution Against *Capital*," signed "a.g.," in *Avanti!* 24 December 1917; reprinted in *An Antonio Gramsci Reader: Selected Writings, 1916–1935*, pp. 32–36.

65. Carlo Rosselli, *Liberal Socialism*, pp. 14–15.

66. AGL, sezione I, fascicolo 7, sottofascicolo 1, documento no. 5.

67. Carlo Rosselli, *Liberal Socialism*, p. 18.

68. Ibid., p. 33.

69. Andrea Costa was the most prominent of anarchists to convert to the socialist cause and maintained a faith in radical democracy and collectivism. Although he joined the PSI in 1882, he never considered himself a Marxist.

70. Carlo Rosselli, *Liberal Socialism*, p. 44. For Mondolfo see his *Mazzini e Marx* (Milan: Critica Sociale, 1972); *Umanesimo di Marx* (Turin: Einaudi, 1968); and *Sulle orme di Marx* (Bologna: Il Mulino, 1948).

71. Carlo Rosselli, *Liberal Socialism*, p. 45.

72. Ibid., pp. 40–41, 48–50.

73. Ibid., p. 53.

74. Ibid., p. 56.

75. Ibid., p. 57.

76. Ibid., p. 59.

77. Ibid., p. 62.

78. Ibid., pp. 66–67. Rosselli was not blind to the negative aspects of the American economy. See, for example, his review of Henry Ford's memoirs in "Le memorie di Henry Ford," *La Riforma sociale* 32 (September–October 1925): 451–469.

79. Carlo Rosselli, *Liberal Socialism*, p. 68.

80. Ibid., p. 71.

81. Ibid., p. 74.

82. Ibid., p. 77.

83. Ibid., p. 78.

84. Ibid., p. 84.

85. Ibid., p. 86.

86. C. Wright Mills, *The Marxists* (New York: Dell Publishing, 1962) p. 14; quoted in Ira Katznelson, *Liberalism's Crooked Circle* (Princeton, N.J.: Princeton University Press, 1996), p. 61.

87. Carlo Rosselli, *Liberal Socialism*, p. 86.

88. Ibid., pp. 87–88.

89. Ibid., pp. 109–110.

90. Ibid., p. 119.

91. Ibid., p. 127.

92. James D. Wilkinson, *The Intellectual Resistance in Europe* (Cambridge, Mass.: Harvard University Press, 1981), p. 62.

93. Carlo Rosselli, *Socialismo liberale* (1979), pp. 143–144.

94. "Rabano Mauro" (Claudio Treves), *La Libertà*, 15 January 1931, reprinted in Carlo Rosselli, *Scritti dell'esilio*, I, pp. 294–299.

95. Giuseppe Saragat, "Fuori strada," *Avanti! L'avvenire del Lavoratore*, 30 January 1930; now in Carlo Rosselli, *Scritti dell'esilio*, I, pp. 307–311; see also Saragat's "Rosselli e *Socialisme libéral*," *Avanti! L'avennire del Lavoratore*, 10 January 1931; now in Giuseppe Saragat, *Quarant'anni di lotta per la democrazia* (Milan: Mursia, 1965), pp. 179–182.

96. Pietro Nenni, "Il socialismo e la lotta per la libertà," in *Avanti! L'avennire del Lavoratore*, 10 January 1931, now in *La battaglia socialista conto il fascismo, 1922–1944*, ed. Domenico Zucàro (Milan: Mursia, 1977), pp. 264–268.

97. "Ercoli" (Palmiro Togliatti), "Sul movimento di Giustizia e Libertà," *Lo Stato Operaio* 5, no. 9 (September 1931): 463–473; now in Palmiro Togliatti, *Opere*, ed. Ernesto Ragionieri (Rome: Riuniti, 1967–1979), vol. III, pp. 411–422.

98. Palmiro Togliatti, "Caldara e gli altri," *Opere* II, p. 392.

99. Fabbri's review appeared in a journal he edited in exile, *Studi sociale: Rivista di libero esame*, 16 August 1931. See Rosselli's letter to Fabbri in *Scritti dell'esilio*, I, pp. 170–172. On the relationship between the two, see Clara Aldrighi, *Antifascismo italiano en Montevideo: el diálogo político entre Luigi Fabbri y Carlo Rosselli* (Montevideo, Uruguay: Universidad de la República, Facultad de Humanidades y Ciencias de la Educación, 1996).

100. Quoted by Nadia Urbinati, Introduction to Carlo Rosselli, *Liberal Socialism*, p. l. For Croce's criticism of Rosselli, see his *L'idea liberale: Contro le confusioni e gli ibridismi* (Bari: Laterza, 1944), pp.16–20; and *Nuove pagine sparse* (Naples: Ricciardi, 1929), pp. 194–197.

101. Karl Popper, *Unended Quest: An Intellectual Autobiography* (La Salle, Ill: Open Court, 1976), pp. 33, 36; quoted by Urbinati, Liberal Socialism, lii–liii. More recent works on the subject include Frank Cunningham, *Democratic Theory and Socialism* (Cambridge: Cambridge University Press, 1987), and Richard Bellamy, *Liberalism and Modern Society* (University Park: Pennsylvannia State University Press, 1992).

102. Steven Lukes, "Equality and Liberty: Must They Conflict?" in Lukes, *Moral Conflict and Politics* (Oxford: Clarendon Press, 1991); see also Ira Katznelson, *Liberalism's Crooked Circle*, pp. 51–53.

103. Giorgio Spini, "Florentine Antifascism: The Jewish Milieu," in *Italian Socialism: Between Politics and History,* ed. Spencer Di Scala (Amherst: University of Massachusetts Press, 1996), p. 101.

104. Benedetto Croce, "Libertà e Giustizia," *La Critica,* 20 September 1943; reprinted as *Libertà e Giustizia: revisione di due concetti filosofici* (Bari: Laterza, 1944), pp. 12–14.

105. Guido De Ruggiero, "Il socialismo di Rosselli," *La Nuova Europa* (16 September 1945): 9.

106. Ibid.

107. Katznelson, *Liberalism's Crooked Circle,* pp. 57–59.

108. Norberto Bobbio, *Liberalism and Democracy,* trans. Martin Ryle and Kate Soper (London: Verso, 1990), p. 80.

109. "Socialismo e fascismo," *GL* (1 February 1935): 1. In the original dialogue, "socialism" refers to orthodox, Marxian socialism; consequently, the "socialist" of the dialogue is rendered here as a Marxist.

110. Pierre Drieu La Rochelle, *Socialisme fasciste* (Paris: Gallimard, 1934).

111. Carlo Rosselli, "Liberalismo rivoluzionario," *QGL,* no. 1 (January 1932): pp. 25–29; see also his "Il programma rivoluzionario di Giustizia e Libertà" and "Chiaramenti al programma" in the same issue.

112. See the anonymous review of Trotsky's autiobiography in *QGL,* no. 1. (January 1932): 48–51.

113. Carlo Rosselli, "Liberalismo rivoluzionario," *QGL,* no. 1, (January 1932): 26.

114. Ibid., p. 27.

115. Untitled document, typewritten in French, AGL, sezione III, fascicolo 1, no. 13.

116. "Liberalismo rivoluzionario," *QGL,* no. 1 (January 1932): 28.

117. Ibid., pp. 28–29.

4. Justice and Liberty

1. The telegram was intercepted by the fascist police and is now in the ACS, CPC, Busta 4221, fascicolo 2.

2. *Epistolario familiare,* pp. 455–459.

3. In one day, he granted eight interviews; AGL, sezione II, fascicolo 1, sottofascicolo 51, no. 1. Among the newspapers that carried the story of the escape from Lipari were *The New York Times, The New York Herald,* and *The Chicago Times* in America; *The Daily Chronicle, The Daily Express,* and *The Daily News* of England; the *Volkische Zeitung* of Berlin; *La Prensa* of Buenos Aires; and numerous others.

4. "Pensiero e azione per la conquista della libertà," in *Scritti dell'esilio,* I, pp. 3–9.

5. For Tarchiani's account, see his "Introduzione" to the reprint publication of *Quaderni di Giustizia e Libertà* (Turin: Bottega d'Erasmo, 1975), pp. 1–18.

6. "'Libertà e Giustizia' e 'Giustizia e Libertà,'" *QGL*, no. 2 (March 1932): 53–54.

7. Tarchiani, "Introduzione" to *Quaderni di Giustizia e Libertà*, p. 4.

8. ACS, DPP, Busta 114; quoted in Joel Blatt, "The Battle of Turin, 1933–1936," *Journal of Modern Italian Studies*, 1, no. 1 (Fall 1995): 28.

9. "Fra Manzanarre e Sprea . . . ," *QGL*, no. 4 (September 1932): 5.

10. Riccardo Bauer, "Carlo Rosselli e la nascita di GL in Italia," in *Giustizia e Libertà nella lotta antifascista*, ed. Carlo Francovich (Florence: La Nuova Italia, 1978), pp. 205–216.

11. Silvio Trentin, "Bisogna decidersi," *QGL*, no. 11 (June 1934): 103.

12. Silvio Trentin, *Riflessione sulla crisi e sulla rivoluzione* (Marseilles: ESIL, 1933); idem, *La crise du droit et de l'Etat* (Paris: L'Eglantine, 1935); on Rosselli and Trentin as "theorists of the Italian revolution," see Frank Rosengarten, "Carlo Rosselli e Silvio Trentin, teorici della rivoluzione italiana," in Francovich, *Giustizia e Libertà nella lotta antifascista*, pp. 261–272.

13. Letter to Bertha Pritchard, 23 August 1929; AGL, sezione I, fascicolo 1, sottofascicolo 94, inserto 1.

14. Riccardo Bauer, "Carlo Rosselli e la nascita di Giustizia e Libertà," in Francovich, *Giustizia e Libertà nella lotta antifascista*, pp. 205–215.

15. ACS, CPC, Busta 4221, fascicolo 2.

16. Letter of 13 April 1934, in the Archivio Salvemini, ISRT; quoted in Roberto Vivarelli, "Carlo Rosselli e Gaetano Salvemini," in Francovich, *Giustizia e Libertà nella lotta antifascista*, p. 88.

17. "La situazione italiana e i compiti del nostro movimento," *QGL*, no. 5 (December 1932): 1–13.

18. Ibid., p. 10.

19. Ibid., p. 13.

20. The collection of *Giustizia e Libertà* as a monthly is conserved in the AGL, sezione IV, fascicolo 2, sottofascicolo I, inserto 2.

21. *Giustizia e Libertà*, no. 1, November 1929; AGL, sezione IV, fascicolo 2, sottofascicolo 1, inserto 2, no. 1.

22. "Giustizia e Libertà," *Bollettino Stampa del Partito Comunista* (20 February 1932): 3; Rosselli's response is in *QGL*, no. 2 (March 1932): 47–51.

23. "Il critico di sè stesso," *QGL*, no. 2 (March 1932): 16–17.

24. "Andrea" [Andrea Caffi], "Appunti su Mazzini," *GL*, 29 March 1935.

25. "Gianfranchi" [Franco Venturi], "Sul Risorgimento italiano," *GL*, 5 April 1935.

26. "Linee essenziali di un programma costruttivo," AGL, sezione III, fascicolo 1, no. 6.

27. "Per l'unificazione del proletariato italiano: V. Giustizia e Libertà," *GL*, 14 May 1937; now in *Scritti dell'esilio*, II, p. 531.

28. *QGL,* no. 1 (January 1932); especially the three pieces by Rosselli, "Il programma rivoluzionario di Giustizia e Libertà," pp. 1–8; "Chiarimenti al programma," pp. 9–20; and "Liberalismo rivoluzionario," pp. 25–29.

29. "Schema di Programma," *QGL,* no. 1 (January 1932): 4–8.

30. Nenni's reponse was in *Avanti! L'Avvenire del Lavoratore,* signed "Noi," 30 January 1932; Saragat's essay "Fuori strada" (Wrong Road) appeared in the same issue.

31. "La situazione italiana e i compiti del nostro movimento," *QGL,* no. 5 (December 1932): 8, 10, 13.

32. Albert S. Lindemann, *A History of European Socialism* (New Haven: Yale University Press, 1983), p. 289.

33. Documents of the Mazzini Society are preserved in the AGL, Fondo "Mazzini Society," and include letters of Max Ascoli, Lionello Venturi, Gaetano Salvemini, Michele Cantarella, Alberto Tarchiani, and others. On the resistance to fascism in America, see John Patrick Diggins, *Mussolini and Fascism: The View From America* (Princeton, N.J.: Princeton University Press, 1972), pp. 344–345, 406–418; and his essay "The Italo-American Anti-Fascist Opposition," *Journal of American History* 54 (December 1967): 579–598.

34. AGL, sezione I, fascicolo I, sottofascicolo 114. For the position of Justice and Liberty on ecclesiastical matters, see Pier Giorgio Zunino, "Giustizia e Libertà e i cattolici," in Francovich, *Giustizia e Libertà nella lotta antifascista,* pp. 323–330; and idem., *Giustizia e Libertà: Attegiamenti nei confronti della politica ecclesiastica fascista* (Bologna: Il Mulino, 1972).

35. "Consigli sulla tattica," *Giustizia e Libertà* no. 18, n.d. (but Summer 1930). AGL, sezione IV, fascicolo 2, sottofascicolo 1, inserto 2, no. 2.

36. Ibid.

37. For an excellent examination of the historical and historiographical problems of this emigration, see Simona Colarizi, "Problemi storiografici sul fuoruscitismo e sull'antifascismo all'estero," in *L'emigrazione socialista nella lotta contro il fascismo (1926–1939),* ed. Francesca Taddei (Florence: G. C. Sansoni Editore, 1982), pp.1–12.

38. Garosci, *Vita,* I, p. 212. The fascist regime replaced the "feminine" *Lei* with the more "virile" and "Roman" *Voi.*

39. The best study of Bassanesi and the antifascist tactic of propaganda flights is Franco Fucci's *Ali contro Mussolini: i raid aerei antifascisti degli anni trenta* (Milan: Mursia, 1978). On the flight and the trial, see Egidio Reale, "Il volo su Milano," in *No al fascismo,* ed. Ernesto Rossi (Turin: Einaudi, 1957), pp. 159–175.

40. For Dolci's account see "Il racconto dell'Osservatore," in *Almanacco Socialista 1931* (Paris: PSI, 1931), pp. 56–62.

41. Garosci, *Vita,* I, p. 214n1.

42. Fucci, *Ali contro Mussolini,* p. 35.

43. *Giustizia e Libertà,* no. 22 (January 1931); AGL, sezione IV, fascicolo 2, sotto-fascicolo 1, inserto 2, no. 14.

44. BNF, FR, cassetta 1, inserto II, n. 3.

45. Rosselli's testimony at the Bassanesi trial was published in the monthly *GL* in January 1931 and is now reprinted in *Scritti dell'esilio,* I, pp. 20–22.

46. Fucci, *Ali contro Mussolini,* pp. 50–51.

47. Massimo Salvadori, "Il sacrificio di De Bosis," in Rossi, *No al fascismo,* pp. 215–230; Iris Origo, *A Need to Testify* (San Diego: Harcourt, Brace, Jovanovich, 1984), pp. 33–78. For Origo, De Bosis was "a modern Icarus." The French text of "The Story of My Death" was released, according to instructions left by De Bosis, to the French press by his friend Francesco Luigi Ferrari on 6 October 1931. It appeared on 14 October in *The New York Times,* the London *Sunday Times, Le Soir* in Brussels, and in most of the other important European papers. The first Italian translation was by Gaetano Salvemini, *La storia della mia morte* (Turin: de Silva, 1948).

48. On the fascist police, see Franco Fucci, *Le polizie di Mussolini: La repressione dell'antifascismo nel "ventennio"* (Milan: Mursia, 1985).

49. Garosci, *Vita,* I, p. 217.

50. Fucci, *Le polizie di Mussolini,* pp. 144–145.

51. Bianca Ceva, *1930: Retroscena di un dramma* (Milan: Ceschina, 1955).

52. Ernesto Rossi, "Fuga dal treno," in Rossi, *No al fascismo,* p. 183.

53. Cesare Rossi, *Tribunale speciale* (Milan: Ceschina, 1952); and *Aula IV: Tutti i processi del Tribunale speciale* (Milan: La Pietra, 1976).

54. Garosci, *Vita,* I, p. 222n1.

55. Riccardo Bauer quoted in Manlio Magini, "Il processo degli intellettuali," in Rossi, *No al fascismo,* p. 213.

56. Ibid.

57. On Turati's exile and death in Paris, see Alessandro Schiavi, *Esilio e morte di Filippo Turati, 1926–1932* (Rome: Opere Nuove, 1956); for Malatesta, see *Errico Malatesta: His Life & Ideas,* ed. Vernon Richards (London: Freedom Press, 1984).

58. "Filippo Turati e il socialismo italiano," *QGL,* no. 3 (June 1932): 1–42; now in *Scritti dell'esilio,* I, pp. 85–133. The original manuscript is in the BNF, FR, cassetta 1, inserto II, n. 2.

59. "Filippo Turati e il socialismo italiano," *QGL,* no. 3 (June 1932): 6.

60. Ibid., p. 42.

61. Ibid., p. 33.

62. Ibid., pp. 37, 42.

63. Carlo Rosselli, "Discussione sul Risorgimento," *GL,* 26 April 1934; now in *Scritti dell'esilio,* II, pp. 152–157.

64. 447,000 voted for reunion with Germany; 46,000 were opposed.

65. "La lezione della Sarre," *GL*, 18 January 1935; now in *Scritti dell'esilio*, II, pp. 95–97.

66. Rosselli apologized in the lead editorial a week later for using the "feminine" adjective in this maner.

67. "La lezione della Sarre," *Scritti dell'esilio*, II, pp. 96–97.

68. Ibid., p. 97.

69. "Giustizia e Libertà e le masses," *GL*, 20 July 1934; now in *Scritti dell'esilio*, II, pp. 25–28.

70. "Corporazione e rivoluzione," *QGL*, no. 10 (February 1934): 3–12.

71. Louis Rosenstock-Franck, "Le corporativisme fasciste," *Esprit*, 1 January 1934; reprinted in *QGL*, no. 10 (February 1934): 13–15; Rosenstock-Franck published a book on the subject, *L'économie corporative fasciste en doctrine et en fait: ses origines historiques et son évolution* (Paris: La Librairie sociale et économique, 1934).

72. "Il neo-socialismo francese," *La Libertà*, 17 August 1933; "Lo spirito e i fini del neo-socialismo francese," ibid., 24 August 1933; "Il neo-socialismo francese nel quadro internazionale," ibid., 31 August 1933; all are now in *Scritti dell'esilio*, I, pp. 226–243; and "Ancora sul neo-socialismo francese," ibid., 14 December 1933, in AGL, sezione II, fascicolo 22, no. 2; also "Due Congressi: SFIO-Neos," in *GL*, 1 June 1934; now in *Scritti dell'esilio*, II, pp. 7–10.

73. "1935," *QGL*, no. 12 (January 1935): 3.

74. "Il neo-socialismo francese," *Scritti dell'esilio*, I, pp. 226–227.

75. "Lo spirito e i fini del neo-socialismo francese," *Scritti dell'esilio*, I, p. 235.

76. Marcel Déat, "Come sbarremo la strada al fascismo," *QGL*, no. 8 (August 1933): 21–30.

77. "Il neo-socialismo francese nel quadro internazionale," *Scritti dell'esilio*, I, p. 243.

78. "Classismo e antifascismo," *GL*, 25 January 1935; and "Socialismo e socializazzione," ibid., 8 February 1935; both are reprinted in *Scritti dell'esilio*, II, pp. 98–102, 110–114.

79. "Classismo e antifascismo," *Scritti dell'esilio*, II, p. 99.

80. Ibid., p. 100. Emphasis in the original.

81. Edward Said, "Reflections on Exile," in *Altogether Elsewhere: Writers on Exile*, ed. Marc Robinson (Boston: Faber and Faber, 1994), pp. 140–141.

82. "Della pace e della guerra," *GL*, 12 April 1935; *Scritti dell'esilio*, II, p. 137.

83. "Contro lo Stato," *GL*, 21 September 1934; *Scritti dell'esilio*, II, pp. 42–45.

84. Ibid., pp. 43–45.

85. Santi Fedele, *Storia della Concentrazione Antifascista* (Milan: Feltrinelli, 1976).

86. *GL*, no. 9, July 1930; AGL, sezione IV, fascicolo 2, sottofascicolo 1, inserto 2, no. 5.

87. "Il Patto di novembre della Concentrazione Antifascista," *QGL*, no. 5 (De-

cember 1932): 73–74. Also published in the official organ of the Antifascist Concentration, *La Libertà*, 17 November 1932. The original of this document, with Rosselli's handwritten notes and marginalia, can be found in AGL, sezione III, fascicolo 2, no. 54.

88. "Proposta di Unificazione," *QGL*, no. 11 (June 1934): 93–98; on the collapse of the Concentrazione Antifascista, see the same issue, pp. 89–92.

89. "Proposta di Unificazione," *QGL*, no. 11 (June 1934): 95–98.

90. "1935," *QGL*, no. 12 (January 1935): 3.

91. Emilio Lussu, "Orientamenti," *QGL*, no. 10 (February 1934): 58–72. On the relationship between GL and the PSI, see Santi Fedele, "Giellisti e Socialisti dalla fondazione di GL (1929) alla politica dei Fronti Popolari," in Francovich, *Giustizia e Libertà nella lotta antifascista*, pp. 303–322; Joel Blatt, "Carlo Rosselli's Socialism," in *Italian Socialism: Between Politics and History* ed. Spencer Di Scala (Amherst: University of Massachusetts Press, 1996), pp. 80–99.

92. Fedele, "Giellisti e Socialisti," p. 321.

93. Letter to the Central Committee of the Concentrazione Antifascista, 1 December 1931; AGL, sezione III, fascicolo 2, no. 9.

94. AGL, sezione I, fascicolo 1, sottofascicolo 115, inserti 1, 2.

95. Aldo Agosti, "Il PCI di fronte al movimento di GL," in Francovich, *Giustizia e Libertà nella lotta antifascista*, pp. 331–363.

96. Resolution adopted by PCI, published in *Lo Stato Operaio* 4, no. 3 (March 1930): 195.

97. "Le 'loro' prigioni: A proposito di due libri e di numerose pubblicazioni," signed simply "J," *Lo Stato Operaio* 4, no. 4 (April 1930): 275–279.

98. Ruggero Grieco, "Il processo di fascistizzazione della socialdemocrazia italiana: Le 'originalità' di un programma," *Lo Stato Operaio* 4, no. 8 (August 1930): 294.

99. Palmiro Togliatti, "A che punto siamo," quoted in Agosti, "Il PCI di fronte al movimento di GL," p. 336.

100. Ibid.

101. "Agli Operai," *Giustizia e Libertà*, no. 24 (March 1931): 8–11. Originals can be found in the AGL, sezione IV, fascicolo 2, sottofascicolo 1, inserto 4, documento 2. Partially reprinted in *Scritti dell'esilio*, I, pp. 26–32.

102. Luigi Longo, *Gli inganni e le menzogne di Giustizia e Libertà* (Paris: PCd'I, 1931).

103. "Agli Operai," *Scritti dell'esilio*, I, p. 30. On the curious relationship between Bolshevik Russia and fascist Italy, see Joseph Clavitt Clark, *Russia and Italy Against Hitler: The Bolshevik-Fascist Rapprochement of the 1930s* (New York: Greenwood Press, 1991). The Italian communists were sensitive to this criticism; see "Alcuni problemi a proposito dei quali bisogna essere molto chiaro," *Lo Stato Operaio* 4, nos. 11–12 (November-December 1930): 768–771.

104. "Agli Operai," *Scritti dell'esilio*, I, p. 31.

105. Ibid., pp. 31–32; emphasis in the original.

106. Giorgio Amendola, "Con il proletariato o contro il proletariato?" *Lo Stato Operaio* 5, no. 6 (June 1931): 310.

107. "Risposta a Giorgio Amendola," *QGL*, no. 1 (January 1932): 37.

108. Ibid., p. 40.

109. "Ercoli" (Palmiro Togliatti), "Sul movimento di Giustizia e Libertà," *Lo Stato Operaio* 5, no. 9 (September 1931): 463–473; "E. R." (Togliatti), "Il programma di Giustizia e Libertà," 6, no. 3 (March 1932): 87–96; Ruggero Grieco, "Il programma agrario di Giustizia e Libertà," 6, no. 4 (April 1932): 157–165; Ruggero Grieco, "Il nostro programma contadino e i suoi critici," 6, no. 6 (June 1932): 302–316; Ruggero Grieco, "Ancora sul programma agrario di Giustizia e Libertà," 6, no. 11 (November 1932): 669–677.

110. "Ercoli," "Sul movimento di Giustizia e Libertà," pp. 464–468.

111. Palmiro Togliatti, "I parasitti della cultura," *Ordine Nuovo* 1, no. 3 (15 May 1919): 1.

112. "Ercoli," "Sul movimento di Giustizia e Libertà," p. 472. In another essay, Togliatti had written, "Rosselli is dissident fascism"; see "Caldara e gli altri," in Palmiro Togliatti, *Opere*, 4 vols., ed. Ernesto Ragionieri (Rome: Riuniti, 1967–1979), vol. 2, p. 392.

113. *Epistolario familiare*, p. 516.

114. Aldo Agosti, *Rodolfo Morandi: Il pensiero e l'azione politica* (Bari: Laterza, 1971), p. 159.

115. Simona Lunadei Girolami, "Partito comunista e classe operaia a Torino," *Annali della Fondazione Einaudi*, vol. 4 (Turin: Fondazione Luigi Einaudi, 1970), p. 180.

116. "Il programma rivoluzionario di Giustizia e Libertà," *QGL*, no. 1 (January 1932): 1–8.

117. "E. R.," "Il programma di Giustizia e Libertà," *Lo Stato Operaio* 6, no. 3 (March 1932): 87–89.

118. Ruggero Grieco, "Il programma agrario di Giustizia e Libertà," *Lo Stato Operaio*, 6, no. 4 (April 1932): 157–165; "Il nostro programma contadino e i suoi critici," 6, no. 6 (June 1932): 302–310; "Ancora sul programma agrario di Giustizia e Libertà," 6, no. 11 (November 1932): 669–677.

119. When after the Second World War, the new government embarked on a massive program to redistribute land in the south, this possibility is precisely what happened; see Paul Ginsborg, *A History of Contemporary Italy: Society and Politics, 1943–1986* (London: Penguin, 1990), pp. 210–253.

120. "Corporazione e rivoluzione," *QGL*, no. 10 (February 1934): 10n1.

121. Ibid., p. 86.

122. "Libera Russia," *Noi Giovani* 1, no. 4 (24 March 1917): 1.

123. "Note sulla Russia," *QGL*, no. 2 (March 1932): 103.

124. Frank Rosengarten, *Silvio Trentin dall'interventismo alla Resistenza* (Milan: Feltrinelli, 1977), p. 131.
125. Zeffiro Ciuffoletti, "Carlo Rosselli, il mito della rivoluzione e il comunismo," *Il Ponte* 48, no. 5 (May 1992): 186–203.
126. "Note sulla Russia," p. 104.
127. Vit., "Realtà russe e 'ideali' giellisti," *Lo Stato Operaio* 9, no. 1 (January 1935): 77.
128. Aldo Agosti, "Il PCI di fronte al movimento di GL," in Francovich, *Giustizia e Libertà nella lotta antifascista*, p. 352.
129. "Il congresso contro la guerra," *GL* (18 October 1935): 1.
130. "Alla direzione dei partiti e movimenti alla discussione per l'unità d'azione," 5 December 1935; "Lettera di GL al PCI," 5 December 1935; both in the AGL, sezione III, fascicolo 2, nn40,41; "Lettera del CC di GL," Archivio del Partito Comunista (Rome), 1427, pp. 39–45.
131. Carlo Rosselli letter of 1 May 1935 to Di Vittorio, Archivio del Partito Comunista, (Rome), 1397, p. 7.
132. Mario Signorino, "Quei trotskisti di G.L.," *L'Astrolabio* 5, no. 25 (18 June 1967): 30.
133. "Incontro con Trotzski," *GL* (25 June 1934): 1.
134. Ibid.
135. James D. Wilkinson, *The Intellectual Resistance in Europe* (Cambridge, Mass.: Harvard University Press, 1981), p. 21; the police report is in ACS, Ministero Interno, Direzione Generale Pubblica Sicurezza, Divisione Polizia Politica, busta 142, fascicolo K/106 "Movimento intellettuale internazionale antifascista."
136. The fascist police confiscated a copy of the letter, dated 12 May 1934 and signed by Rosselli, Lussu, and Tarchiani, that announced the publication of *GL* as a weekly to the antifascist exile community; ACS, Busta 4221, fascicolo 3.
137. *Epistolario familiare*, p. 519.
138. After Rosselli's death in 1937, this was changed to "Movimento di Unificazione Socialista," reflecting the changed ideology of the movement. Annual subscription rates were 25 francs for France and its colonies, and 50 francs in other countries. The first editorial and administrative office was located at 8 Rue Jolivet in the 14th arrondissement; later the newspaper would move to 21, Rue Val-de-Grâce in the 5th arrondissement.
139. The twelve *Quaderni* were printed in two series, the first six from January 1932 to March 1933, with a gray cover; and a second series from June 1933 until January 1935, with a red cover. They are conserved in the AGL in Florence and were reprinted as *Quaderni di Giustizia e Libertà*, with a foreword by Alessandro Galante Garrone and an Introduction by Alberto Tar-

chiani (Turin: Bottega d'Erasmo, 1959 and 1975). The best study on the subject is Santi Fedele, *E verrà un'altra Italia: Politica e cultura nei "Quaderni di Giustizia e Libertà"* (Milan: Franco Angeli, 1992).

140. AGL, sezione III, fascicolo I, documento 12.

141. "I *Quaderni di Giustizia e Libertà*," in *Scritti dell'esilio*, I, p. 199.

142. "Italia e Europa," *QGL*, no. 7 (June 1933): 7.

143. Renzo De Felice, *Storia degli ebrei italiani sotto il fascismo*, 4th ed. (Turin: Einaudi, 1993), pp. 419–427.

144. For the tragic story of the Ovazza family, see Alexander Stille, *Benevolence and Betrayal: Five Italian Jewish Families Under Fascism*, (New York: Summit Books, 1991), pp. 19–89.

145. Susan Zuccotti, *The Italians and the Holocaust* (New York: Basic Books, 1987), pp. 255–259. On the relationship between Rosselli and Modgliani, see Ariane Landuyt, "Rosselli e Modigliani: due 'socialismi' a confronto," in Francovich, *Giustizia e Libertà nella lotta antifascista*, pp. 99–111.

146. The episode is recounted in Stille, *Benevolence and Betrayal*, p. 99, and Zuccotti, *Italians and the Holocaust*, p. 28.

147. Sion Segre Amar, "Sui 'fatti' di Torino del 1934," *Gli ebrei in Italia durante il fascismo: Quaderni del Centro di Documentazione Ebraica Contemporanea* 2 (March 1962): 126.

148. Alberto Cavaglion, quoted in *The Italian Refuge: Rescue of Jews During the Holocaust*, ed. Ivo Herzen (Washington, D.C.: Catholic University Press, 1989), p. 91.

149. The episode was recounted (with elaborate and false details) in the two most anti-Semitic fascist newspapers, Roberto Farinacci's *Il regime fascista* and Telesio Interlandi's *Il Tevere*.

150. On the importance of Justice and Liberty in Turin and on the fascist regime's insistent efforts to wipe it out, see Joel Blatt, "The Battle of Turin, 1933–1936: Carlo Rosselli, Giustizia e Libertà, OVRA and the origins of Mussolini's anti-Semitic campaign," *Journal of Modern Italian Studies* 1, 1 (Fall 1995): 22–57.

151. On the Foa family, see Stille, *Benevolence and Betrayal*, pp. 93–165.

152. Meir Michaelis, *Mussolini and the Jews: German-Italian Relations and the Jewish Question in Italy, 1922–1945* (Oxford: Oxford University Press, 1978), pp. 57–80.

153. De Felice, *Storia degli ebrei italiani sotto il fascismo*, p. 147, and Blatt, "The Battle of Turin, 1933–1936," p. 33.

154. OVRA reports of 20 December 1933, ACS, Polizia Politica, Busta 114; 7 June 1936; quoted in Blatt, "The Battle of Turin, 1933–1936," pp. 28, 45.

155. Letter to Harold Laski, 17 September 1933; in Carlo Rosselli, *Dall'esilio: Lettere alla moglie 1929–1937*, ed. Costanzo Casucci (Florence: Passigli, 1997), p. 157.

156. A representative early work was Pietro Montasini, *L'Organisation des antifascistes italiennes à l'étranger* (Paris: Edizioni Giustizia e Libertà, 1929).

157. AGL, sezione VI, Fondo "Mazzini Society" fascicolo 2, Manifesti e memorandum, 1–7.

158. For works in English, see Barbara Spackman, *Fascist Virilities: Rhetoric, Ideology, and Social Fantasy in Italy* (Minneapolis: University of Minnesota Press, 1996); Robin Pickering-Iazzi, ed., *Politics of the Visible: Writing Women, Culture, and Fascism* (Minneapolis: University of Minnesota Press, 1997); idem, *Mothers of Invention: Women, Italian Fascism, Culture* (Minneapolis: University of Minnesota Press, 1995); David S. Horn, *Social Bodies: Science, Reproduction, and Italian Modernity* (Princeton, N.J.: Princeton University Press, 1994); Perry R. Willson, *The Clockwork Factory: Women and Work in Fascist Italy* (New York: Oxford University Press, 1993); Victoria De Grazia, *How Fascism Ruled Women: Italy, 1922–1945* (Berkeley: University of California Press, 1992); Alexander De Grand, "Women Under Italian Fascism," in *The Historical Journal* 19, no. 4 (October 1976): 947–968.

159. The only full-length work in English is Jane Slaughter, *Women of the Italian Resistance, 1943–1945* (Denver, Colo.: Arden Press, 1997); see also Victoria De Grazia, *How Fascism Ruled Women, Italy 1922–1945,* pp. 272–288, and Anna Maria Bruzzone, "Women in the Italian Resistance," in *Our Common History,* ed. Paul Thompson and Natasha Burchhardt (London: Pluto Press, 1983), pp. 272–296. In Italian see Anna Bravo and Anna Maria Bruzzone, *In guerra senza armi: storie di donne, 1940–1945* (Rome: Laterza, 1995); Giovanni De Luna, *Donne in oggetto: L'antifascismo nella società italiana 1922–1939* (Turin: Bollatti Boringhieri, 1995); Miriam Mafai, *Pane nero: donne e vita quotidiana nella Seconda guerra mondiale* (Milan: Mondadori, 1987); Bianca Guidetta Sera, "Donne, violenza, politica, armi: un'esperienze giudiziaria," in *Rivista storia contemporanea* no. 2, 1988; Bianca Guidetta Serra, *Compagne: Testimonianze di participazione politica femminile,* 2 vols. (Turin: Einaudi, 1977); Laura Mariani, *Quelle dell'idee: Storia delle detenute politiche, 1927–1948* (Bari: De Donato, 1982); Mirella Alloisio and Giuliana Beltrami, *Volontarie della libertà* (Milan: Mazzotta, 1981).

160. De Grazia, *How Fascism Ruled Women,* p. 274.

161. The documents of the Special Tribunal are now available thanks to the tireless efforts of Gaetano Arfè and Giuseppe Fiori, two historians and members of Parliament who wrote—and were the first to sign—law n. 291, on 11 October 1990. The figures (which differ slightly) are from De Luna, *La donne in oggetto,* p. 19, and De Grazia, *How Fascism Ruled Women,* p. 274; see also Serra, "Donne, violenza, politica, armi: un'esperienza guidiziaria." For the women brought before the Special Tribunal, see Laura Mariani, *Quelle dell'idea. Storia delle detenute politiche, 1927–1948,* p. 13.

162. See Gaetano Salvemini's obituary of Marion Cave Rosselli, *Il Ponte* 5, no. 11 (November 1949): 1443.

163. Ibid. Franco Bandini speculates (with no supporting evidence other than that both women were of English-Irish descent) that Marion Cave was involved with Violet Gibson's assassination attempt against Mussolini in 1926; *Il cono d'ombra: chi armò la mano degli assassini dei fratelli Rosselli* (Milan: SugarCo, 1990), p. 476n46.

164. Calabresi taught for several years at the University in Exile, part of the New School for Social Research and at Hunter College. From 1947 until her retirement in 1969, she was a clinical psychologist for the U.S. Veterans Administration. Born the same year as Carlo Rosselli, she survived until 1995; her nephew, Guido Calabresi, is a judge and Dean of the Yale Law School.

165. Rosengarten, *Silvio Trentin: dall'interventismo alla Resistenza*, p. 115.

166. Joyce Lussu, *Fronti e frontiere* (Florence: Edizioni U, 1945).

167. Bianca Ceva, *1930: Retroscena di un dramma* (Milan: Ceschina, 1955).

168. Bianca Ceva, "Il processo di 'Giustizia e Libertà' nel 1930–31," in *Fascismo e antifascismo (1918–1936)* (Milan: Feltrinelli, 1976), pp. 246–250.

169. Bianca Ceva, *Tempo dei vivi* (Milan: Ceschina, 1954); she has also edited a volume, *Antologia del Caffè: giornale dell'antifascismo, 1924–1925* (Milan: Lerici, 1961).

170. Barbara Allason, *Memorie di un'antifascista, 1919–1940* (Rome Edizione U, 1945).

171. Their moving and poetic letters have been collected in Ada Gobetti and Piero Gobetti, *Nella tua breve esistenza: Lettere 1918–1926*, ed. Ersilia A. Perona (Turin: Einaudi, 1991).

172. Ada Gobetti, *Camilla Ravera: Una vita in carcere e al confino* (Parma: Guanda, 1969).

173. Ada Gobetti, *Diario partigiano* (Turin: Einaudi, 1996), p. 15.

174. "Il nostro movimento e i partiti," *GL*, no. 10 (September 1930); AGL, sezione IV, fascicolo 2, sottofascicolo 1, inserto 1, no. 3.

175. "Veturio" (Augusto Monti), "Consensi a Tirreno," *QGL*, no. 5 (December 1932): 14–21; "S.D." (Lelio Basso), "Il partito, ma in Italia," *QGL*, no. 7 (June 1933): 105–109.

176. "Pro o contro il partito," *QGL*, no. 8 (August 1933): 5.

177. Ibid.

178. "Essenza del fascismo," AGL, sezione I, fascicolo 4, sottofascicolo 5, p. 9.

179. "Pro o contro il partito," p. 9.

180. Norberto Bobbio, *Ideological Profile of Twentieth-Century Italy*, trans. Lydia G. Cochrane (Princeton, N.J.: Princeton University Press, 1995), p. 144.

181. Carlo Levi, *Christ Stopped at Eboli*, trans. Frances Frenaye (New York: Farrar, Straus and Giroux, 1947), pp. 249–253.

182. Garosci, *Vita*, II, p. 8.

183. Rosengarten, *Silvio Trentin dall'interventismo alla Resistenza*, pp. 101–118.

184. See especially Erich Fromm, *Escape From Freedom* (New York: Avon Books, 1969).

185. "Essenza del fascismo," p. 4.

186. "Risposta a Giorgio Amendola," *QGL*, no. 1 (January 1932): 35.

187. Carlo Levi, "Seconda lettera dall'Italia," *QGL*, no. 2 (March 1933): 11.

188. Carlo Levi, *Paura della libertà* (Turin: Einaudi, 1948); *Of Fear and Freedom*, trans. Adolphe Gourevitch (New York: Farrar, Straus: 1950).

189. Emilio Lussu, "Errico Malatesta," *QGL*, no. 5 (December 1932): 37–41.

190. Ferruccio Parri, *Scritti 1915–1975* (Milan: Feltrinelli, 1976), p.179.

191. "Discussione sul Risorgimento," *GL*, 26 April 1935.

192. Stefano Merli, "Il dibattito socialista sotto il fascismo: Lettere di Rodolfo Morandi e Carlo Rosselli," *Rivista Storica del Socialismo* 6, no. 19 (May–August 1963): 341.

193. Piero Gobetti, "Elogio della ghiglottina," *La Rivoluzione Liberale*, 23 November 1922.

194. Nicola Tranfaglia, *Labirinto italiano: il fascismo, antifascismo, gli storici* (Florence: La Nuova Italia, 1989), p. 197.

195. Carlo Rosselli, *Liberal Socialism*, pp. 104, 108.

196. "Un nuovo movimento italiano," AGL, sezione III, fasciscolo I, documento 8; no date; *Scritti dell'esilio*, I, pp. 269–273.

197. "Il programma dell'Opposizione Comunista," *QGL*, no. 4 (September 1932): 49.

198. "La situazione italiana e i compiti del nostro movimento," *QGL*, no. 5 (December 1932): 4.

199. "E. Bianchi" (Carlo Levi), "Sport," *QGL*, no. 10 (February 1934): 46–50.

200. "Italia e Europea," *QGL*, no. 7 (June 1933): 1.

201. Ibid., p. 3.

202. Ibid., pp. 3–4.

203. "Corporazione e rivoluzione," *QGL*, no. 10 (February 1934): 11.

204. "Sincero" (Nicola Chiaromonte), "La morte si chiama fascismo," *QGL*, no. 12 (January 1935): 20–60; on the concept of totalitarianism in Italy, see Abbott Gleason, *Totalitarianism* (New York: Oxford University Press, 1995); on nationalism as a "myth of salvation," see Vladimir Tismaneanu, *Fantasies of Salvation: Democracy, Nationalism, and Myth in Post-Communist Europe* (Princeton, N.J.: Princeton University Press, 1998).

205. "La guerra che torna," *QGL*, no. 9 (November 1933): 1–8; *Scritti dell'esilio*, I, pp. 250–258. A year later, Rosselli quoted Mussolini's speech from atop a tank during military exercises near Florence: "The entire structure of the State, of the party, the very conception of totalitarian politics, the economic directives,

the battle for grain, cannot be explained except as a precise blueprint for war." Benito Mussolini, *Il Popolo d'Italia*, 28 August 1934; now in Mussolini, *Opera Omnia*, ed. Edoardo and Duilio Susmel, 36 vols. (Florence: La Fenice, 1951–1964), vol. XXVI, pp. 306–309. The quote appears in Carlo Rosselli, "L'asino di Buridano: (L'invito a smobilitare)," *GL*, 14 December 1934. It was Mussolini who coined the phrase "War is to man as maternity is to woman."

206. "La guerra che torna," p. 2.

207. Ibid.

208. Ibid., p. 6.

209. "Essenza del fascismo," p. 5; English in the original.

210. "La guerra che torna," p. 8.

211. Ibid.

212. "Fascismo in guerra," *GL* (10 January 1936): 1.

213. "Alfa" (P. Rugginenti), "I socialisti e la guerra," in *Avanti! L'Avvenire del Lavoratore*, 16 December 1933; Pietro Nenni, "Contro l'illusione della guerra rivoluzionaria e per la libertà," ibid., 2 December 1933 and reprinted in *Scritti dell'esilio*, I, pp. 312–316.

214. Carlo Rosselli to Pietro Nenni, 23 December 1933, *Avanti! L'Avvenire del Lavoratore*, 30 December 1933; now in *Scritti dell'esilio*, I, pp. 259–264.

215. "Depravazione e sangue," *GL* (6 July 1934): 1; *Scritti dell'esilio*, II, pp. 21–24.

216. "Come vince il fascismo," *GL* (22 March 1935): 1.

217. "Europeismo o fascismo," *GL* (17 May 1935): 1.

218. "Against the Fascist War! For the Liberating Revolution!" a manifesto signed by the Central Committee of Justice and Liberty (Rosselli, Lussu, Tarchiani), dated Rome, March 1933. AGL, sezione IV, fascicolo 3, sottofascicolo 8.

219. "Essenza del fascismo," p. 4.

220. AGL, sezione IV, fascicolo 3, sottofascicolo 8.

221. See the two police reports (one from the Questura in Rome, the other from the Prefect in Milan) in ACS, CPC, Busta 4421, fascicolo 2.

222. Max Salvadori, "Giellisti e loro amici degli stati uniti durante la seconda guerra mondiale," Francovich, *Giustizia e Libertà nella lotta antifascista*, p. 273.

223. Joel Blatt, "The Battle of Turin, 1933–1936," pp. 26–29.

5. The Tragic Hero

1. Carlo Rosselli, *Liberal Socialism*, ed. Nadia Urbinati and trans. William McCuaig (Princeton, N.J.: Princeton University Press, 1996), p. 6.

2. George Steiner, quoted in Edward Said, "Reflections on Exile," in *Altogether Elsewhere: Writers on Exile*, ed. Marc Robinson (Boston: Faber and Faber, 1994), p. 357.

3. *Epistolario familiare*, p. 413.

4. Ibid., p. 458.

5. "Pericoli dell'esilio," *GL* (16 November 1934): 1; *Scritti dell'esilio*, II, pp. 69–71.

6. Benito Mussolini, "Errori fatali," *Il Popolo d'Italia*, 1 December 1934; reprinted in Mussolini, *Opera Omnia*, ed. Edoardo and Duilio Susmel (Florence: La Fenice, 1951–1964), vol. XXVI, pp. 390–391. The fanatical ideologue Roberto Farinacci also publicized these criticisms in his article "Fessi confessi," *Regime fascista*, 2 December 1934. Rosselli's reply was "A sua Eccellenza," *GL* (7 December 1934): 1.

7. "Discussione sull'esilio," *GL* (1 February 1935): 1.

8. Ibid.

9. *QGL*, no. 9 (November 1933): 100.

10. Ignazio Silone, *Il fascismo: Origini e sviluppo*, trans. Maria Gabriela Canonico (Milan: SugarCo, 1992), pp. 341, 354; originally published as *Der Faschismus: seine Entstehung und seine Entwicklung* (Zurich: Europa Verlag, 1934).

11. The correspondence between Silone and Rosselli is in AGL, sezione I, fascicolo I, sottofascicolo III, inserti 1–4.

12. Irving Howe, Introduction to Ignazio Silone, *Bread and Wine*, trans. Eric Mosbacher (New York: Penguin, 1986), p. v.

13. Ignazio Silone, *Memoriale dal carcere svizzero*, ed. Lamberto Mercuri (Cosenza: Lerici, 1979), p. 34.

14. On the grotesquely fascinating character of Pitigrilli, see *Lettere di una spia: Pitigrilli e l'OVRA*, ed. Domenico Zucàro (Milan: SugarCo, 1977).

15. Manlio Brigalia, *Emilio Lussu e Giustizia e Libertà* (Sassari, Italy: Edizione della Torre, 1976), pp. 111–137.

16. "Magrini" (Aldo Garosci), "Rosselli e la guerra d'Etiopia," *Quaderni Italiani*, II (New York, August 1942): 32–58. Rosselli's essays on the war are conserved in the BNF, FR, cassetta 1, inserto II, nn. 25, 26, 29, 30.

17. "Nuovo crimine?" *GL* (15 February 1935): 1; *Scritti dell'esilio*, II, pp. 120–122.

18. "Perché siamo contro la guerra d'Africa," *GL* (8 March 1935): 1; *Scritti dell'esilio*, II, pp. 123–127.

19. "Come condurre la propaganda contro la guerra d'Africa," *GL*; I. "Essere realisti," 12 April 1935; II. "Argomenti senza presa," 26 April 1935; III. "Il perché di una guerra," 3 May 1935; *Scritti dell'esilio*, II, pp. 140–151; 158–164.

20. Victoria De Grazia, *How Fascism Ruled Women: Italy, 1922–1945* (Berkeley, Calif.: University of California Press, 1992), p. 279.

21. "Essere realisti," *Scritti dell'esilio*, II, p. 143.

22. "Il perché di una guerra," *Scritti dell'esilio*, II, pp. 158–159.

23. Ibid., p. 162.

24. "La guerra d'Africa sarà la rovina economica d'Italia," *GL* (19 July 1935): 1.

25. "La grande illusione: L'Abissinia colonia di popolamento," *GL* (26 July 1935): 1.

26. "Come si presenta la guerra d'Africa," *GL* (2 August 1935): 1.

27. "Specchi per allodole pacifiste," *GL* (23 August 1935): 1; *Scritti dell'esilio*, II, pp. 196–200.

28. "Mussolini e i giovani," *GL* (30 August 1935): 1; *Scritti dell'esilio*, II, pp. 201–205.

29. "Che cosa è stata il convegno di Giustizia e Libertà," *GL* (20 September 1935): 1; *Scritti dell'esilio*, II, pp. 217–221. The Manifesto was published in the 20 September 1935 issue of *GL*.

30. "Fascism is winning in Abyssinia. The predictions of those, us included, who judged that a military campaign of several years would be necessary, are revealed as mistaken." "Realismo," *GL* (10 April 1936): 1; *Scritti dell'esilio*, II, p. 339.

31. "La palla di piombo," *GL* (16 April 1936): 1; *Scritti dell'esilio*, II, pp. 342–344.

32. Garosci, *Vita*, II, p. 146.

33. "Per l'unità dell'antifascismo italiano," *GL* (22 January 1937): 1; now in *Oggi in Spagna, domani in Italia* (Turin: Einaudi, 1967), pp.102–106, and *Scritti dell'esilio*, II, pp. 445–449.

34. "L'Europa si fascistizza. . .," *GL* (10 July 1936): 1; *Scritti dell'esilio*, II, pp. 385–387.

35. Aldo Garosci, "Spagna: il Battaglione Garibaldi," *Il Mondo*, 3 July 1956.

36. For the history of Italian volunteers in the Spanish Civil War, see Sandro Attanasio, *Gli italiani e la guerra di Spagna* (Milan: Mursia, 1974); Aldo Garosci, *Gli intellettuali e la guerra di Spagna* (Turin: Einaudi, 1959); for Rosselli's role, see Garosci's "Rosselli in Spagna," signed with his nom de guerre "Magrini," *Quaderni Italiani*, IV (New York, April 1943): 15–112. In English, see Massimo Mangili-Climpson, *Men of Heart of Red, White and Green: Italian Antifascists in the Spanish Civil War* (New York: Vantage Press, 1985); Margaret Jane Slaughter, "Italian Antifascism: The Italian Volunteers in the Spanish Civil War," Ph.D. diss., University of New Mexico, 1972.

37. Letter of 31 August 1936 to Marion Rosselli; now in *Oggi in Spagna, domani in Italia*, p. 48.

38. The fascist police were aware of Rosselli's trip to Spain, as proved by their report of 26 June 1931. The one-sentence document stated, "It has been reported from Barcelona that the noted *fuoruscito* Carlo Rosselli arrived there yesterday." ACS, CPC, Busta 4221, fascicolo 2. *QGL*, no. 1 (January 1932): 58–78. "Aspetti della crisi spagnola," *QGL*, no. 12 (January 1935): 105–119.

39. "La posta in gioco," *GL* (24 July 1936): 1; *Scritti dell'esilio*, II, pp. 392–394.

40. "Il dovere dei rivoluzionari," *GL* (31 July 1936): 1; *Scritti dell'esilio*, II, pp. 395–398.

41. *Oggi in Spagna, domani in Italia*, p. 21.
42. For an excellent study of fascist Italy's support of Franco, see John F. Coverdale, *Italian Intervention in the Spanish Civil War* (Princeton, N.J.: Princeton University Press, 1975).
43. Mangili-Climpson, *Men of Heart of Red, White and Green*, p. 9.
44. ACS, CPC, busta 4221, fascicolo 4.
45. AGL, sezione I, fascicolo 2, sottofascicolo 5, No. 3; *Oggi in Spagna, domani in Italia*, p. 25.
46. The Column was named after Francisco Ascaso, a Spanish anarchist killed in Barcelona in the early stages of the military uprising against the Republic. Lina Simonetti of Trieste joined the Column soon after its formation. For the important role of women in the Spanish Civil War, see Shirley Mangini, *Memories of Resistance: Women's Voices From the Spanish Civil War* (New Haven, Conn.: Yale University Press, 1995).
47. Garosci, *Vita*, II, p. 180.
48. Ibid., p. 165.
49. In December 1936, Giuliano Viezzoli, who had received a medal of honor for his service in the First World War, sent a letter to the *podestà* (the ancient Roman term used by the fascists for "Mayor") of Trieste, his hometown: "My son Giordano, born in Trieste, fought with a Garibaldian faith in Spain, continued the same struggle for the freedom of peoples in which I believed in fighting the war. The lead of Italian bombs has ended his short life. It is not your victory! It is rather the shame of the decadence of the monarchy that you represent. I return the medal to you; make more bombs with it: with it you accelerate the final reckoning and the hour of the social revolution." Quoted in Franco Fucci, *Ali contro Mussolini: I raid aerei antifascisti degli anni Trenta* (Milan: Mursia, 1978), pp. 132–133. On Viezzoli's death, see *GL*, 9 October 1936.
50. ACS, CPC, busta 4221, fascicolo 4.
51. Published in three segments in *Giustizia e Libertà:* 9 July, 16 July, and 23 August 1936; later reprinted as "Giornale d'un miliziano," in *Oggi in Spagna, domani in Italia*, pp. 27–43; and as "Diario di Spagna," in *Scritti dell'esilio*, II, pp. 399–414.
52. "Giornale d'un miliziano," in *Oggi in Spagna, domani in Italia*, pp. 28–29. See George Orwell's similar experience in his *Homage to Catalonia* (Boston: Beacon Press, 1952), pp. 12–13.
53. "Giornale d'un miliziano," p. 29.
54. Ibid., pp. 30–31.
55. Ibid., p. 32.
56. Ibid., pp. 32–33.
57. On the battle of Monte Pelato, see the accounts of two participants, Garosci,

Vita, II, pp. 183–187, and Umberto Calosso, "La battaglia di Monte Pelato," in *No al fascismo*, ed. Ernesto Rossi (Turin: Einaudi, 1957), pp. 237–253.

58. "Giornale d'un miliziano," *Oggi in Spagna, domani in Italia*, p. 42.

59. Ibid., pp. 47–48.

60. He described the event to Marion in a letter: "The alarm had been given and I climbed atop the trench; I was observing the zone in the early light of dawn when the first bullets began to fly. I felt a very light blow on the right side. No pain. I climbed down into the trench, saw that I was losing a little bit of blood, and brought myself to the infirmary. A very fortunate bullet: superficial entrance and exit, no injury, no pain . . . *I feel that I will return*, as I felt, although I didn't tell you, that the honor of the first bullet (extremely intelligent) would be mine." Letter of 31 August 1936, emphasis in the original; reprinted in *Oggi in Spagna, domani in Italia*, pp. 46–48.

61. Garosci, *Vita*, II, pp. 189–200.

62. Camillo Berneri, "La polemica con Carlo Rosselli," in the collection of his works, *Pietrogrado 1917–Barcellona 1937*, ed. Pier Carlo Masini and Alberto Sorti (Milan: SugarCo, 1964), pp. 161–182. On the relation between Rosselli and the anarchists, see Umberto Marzocchi, "Carlo Rosselli e gli anarchici," in *Giustizia e Libertà nella lotta antifascista*, pp. 399–408.

63. Camillo Berneri, "Difesa dell'anarchismo," *GL* (6 December 1935): 1.

64. Rosselli's reply is quoted in Garosci, *Vita*, II, p. 191.

65. "Catalogna, baluardo della rivoluzione," *GL* (27 November 1936): 1; *Scritti dell'esilio*, II, p. 419.

66. Speech over Radio Barcelona, 13 November 1936; published in *GL* (27 November 1936): 1; now in *Oggi in Spagna, domani in Italia*, pp. 70–75, and *Scritti dell'esilio*, II, pp. 424–428.

67. "L'eroica morte di Antonio Cieri sul fronte di Huesca," *GL* (16 April 1937): 3.

68. "Catalogna, baluardo della rivoluzione," *Scritti dell'esilio*, II, pp. 415–423.

69. Garosci, *Vita*, II, p. 197.

70. "I know that many in France are pessimistic. I remain optimistic. Such a great popular movement cannot be crushed. . ." Letter to Marion Rosselli, 16 September 1936; *Oggi in Spagna, domani in Italia*, p. 51.

71. Ibid., p. 66.

72. Rosselli's proposal was drafted in the form of a letter to the military and political command of the Ascaso Column, 13 November 1936; *Oggi in Spagna, domani in Italia*, p. 67.

73. Rosselli expanded on this theme in "Storia di una importante vittoria mancata," a report sent to the Military Command of the Aragon Front; *Oggi in Spagna, domani in Italia*, pp. 78–90, and *Scritti dell'esilio*, pp. 429–439.

74. "Oggi in Spagna, domani in Italia," speech over Radio Barcelona, 13 November 1936, published in *GL*; now in *Oggi in Spagna, domani in Italia*, pp. 70–75,

and *Scritti dell'esilio,* II, pp. 424–428. The speech can be found even in cyber-space: www2.mir.it/mani/25 aprile/01_25 Aprile.

75. *Oggi in Spagna, domani in Italia,* p. 72.

76. Ibid., p. 74.

77. Aldo Rosselli, *La famiglia Rosselli: una tragedia italiana* (Milan: Bompiani, 1983), pp. 94–99.

78. 17 November 1936, now in the ACS, CPC; quoted in Giordano Bruno Guerri, *Galeazzo Ciano* (Milan: Bompiani, 1979), p. 148.

79. Letter of 1 January 1937, *Oggi in Spagna, domani in Italia,* p. 98.

80. Letter to Alberto Cianca, 16 December 1936; *Oggi in Spagna, domani in Italia,* p. 94. In a letter written the same day to Marion, Rosselli repeated that the new Giacomo Matteotti Battalion would be open to all committed antifascists and that it had to be based on "a serious discipline and organization, excluding every form of sectarianism." Ibid., p. 95.

81. Salvemini to Rosselli, 31 December 1935, AGL; quoted in Vivarelli, "Carlo Rosselli e Gaetano Salvemini," in *Giustizia e Libertà nella lotta antifascista,* p. 95.

82. Quoted in Jasper Ridley, *Mussolini* (New York: St. Martin's Press, 1998), p. 281.

83. Letter to Marion, 16 December 1936, *Oggi in Spagna, domani in Italia,* p. 95.

84. "Sul corso della guerra," *GL* (15 January 1937): 1; *Oggi in Spagna, domani in Italia,* pp. 99–101; *Scritti dell'esilio,* II, pp. 442–444.

85. Letter to Amelia, 11 March 1937. Two months earlier (14 January), Carlo had written to his "nostalgic mommy" (*nostalgica mimmola*); both letters, confiscated by the fascist police, are in ACS, CPC, Busta 4421, fascicolo 4.

86. The last essays on the Spanish Civil War, all in *Giustizia e Libertà* in 1937, were ""Nostra guerra," 12 February; "La Spagna è sola," 19 February; "L'eroica morte di Antonio Cieri sul fronte Huesca," 16 April; "Per una Guadalajara in terra italiana," 23 April; "Guerra e politica in Spagna," 7 May; "Dopo le giornate di Barcellona," 14 May; "Crisi in Spagna," 21 May; and "Mediazione impossibile," 28 May. All are reprinted in *Scritti dell'esilio,* II, pp. 468–545. The essays concerning Europe are "Riflessioni sullo stato d'Europa," 29 January 1936; "La situazione in Italia," 5 February 1937; "La crociata antisovietica," 26 February 1937; and "Alla ricerca di farfalle sotto gli archi di Tito e di Brandeburgo," 11 June 1937, all in *Giustizia e Libertà;* now in *Scritti dell'esilio,* II, pp. 453–457; 463–467; 475–479; 549–554.

87. Speech to volunteers at Argenteuil, France, 10 February 1937; partially printed posthumously in *GL* (18 June 1937): 1; now in *Oggi in Spagna, domani in Italia,* pp. 110–114, and *Scritti dell'esilio,* II, pp. 458–462.

88. *Oggi in Spagna, domani in Italia,* p. 112.

89. Ibid., p. 113.

90. *GL* (30 April 1937): 1.

91. "Portrait de la nouvelle opposition en Italie," *GL* (7 May 1937): 3; signed "Curzio."

92. Mussolini was "noisy, irrational, an improvisor, a demagogue and adventurer, a traitor to the ideals of his youth." Gramsci was "intimate, reserved, rational, austere, the enemy of rhetoric and of all sorts of facility, faithful to the working class in good as well as ill fortune." "Due climi politici: due tipi di umanità," speech of 22 May 1937, published posthumously in *GL* (18 June 1937): 1; now in *Scritti dell'esilio*, II, pp. 543–545. The police report is in ACS, CPC, Busta 4421, fascicolo 4.

93. The five essays were published in the spring of 1937 in *Giustizia e Libertà*, and all were titled "Per l'unificazione politica del proletariato italiano"; they were subtitled I. "Sguardo insieme," 19 March; II. "Un ostacolo da superare," 26 March; III. "Il partito comunista," 9 April; IV. "I partiti socialisti," 23 April 1937; V. "Giustizia e Libertà," 14 May. All except No. II are reprinted in *Scritti dell'esilio*, II, pp. 480–537.

94. "Sguardo insieme," *Scritti dell'esilio*, II, p. 484.

95. In early 1937, there were five major political parties that presented themselves as "the party of the proletariat": Partito Socialista dei Lavoratori Italiani (PSLI), Partito Socialista Italiano (PSI), Partito Comunista d'Italia (PCd'I), Azione Repubblicana Socialista (ARS), and Giustizia e Libertà.

96. "Per l'unificazione politica del proletariato italiano," *Scritti dell'esilio*, II, p. 483.

97. Ibid., p. 484.

98. "Un ostacolo da superare," *GL* (26 March 1937): 1.

99. "Il partito comunista," *Scritti dell'esilio*, II, p. 486.

100. Ibid., pp. 485–490.

101. Ibid., p. 490.

102. "I partiti socialisti," *GL* (23 April 1937): 1; *Scritti dell'esilio*, II, pp. 502–510.

103. For the illustrative conception of socialism—rather than fascism as proposed by Gobetti—as "the autobiography of the nation," see Franco Livorsi, "I socialisti come autobiografia della nazione," *Il Ponte* 58, no. 5 (May 1992): 17–57.

104. "I partiti socialisti," *Scritti dell'esilio*, II, p. 502.

105. Ibid., p. 509.

106. "Giustizia e Libertà," *GL* (14 May 1937): 1; *Scritti dell'esilio*, II, p. 531.

107. Ibid., p. 535

108. Ibid., p. 537

109. "Eroe tutto prosa," *Scritti dell'esilio*, I, p. 268.

110. Franco Bandini, *Il cono d'ombra: chi armò la mano degli assassini dei fratelli Rosselli* (Milan: SugarCo, 1990), pp. 34–39. Bandini's work has been impor-

tant in reconstructing the events surrounding the assassination of the Rosselli brothers, yet it often seems as though the author were more intent on character assassination than historical reconstruction. On the assassination, see Stanislao G. Pugliese, "Death in Exile: The Assassination of Carlo Rosselli," *Journal of Contemporary History* 32, no.3 (July 1997): 305–319.

111. The letter from Carlo to Amelia and Maria Todesco, dated 9 May 1937, was intercepted by the fascist police, copied, and preserved in the ACS, CPC, Busta 4421 fascicolo 4.

112. Aldo Rosselli, *La famiglia Rosselli: una tragedia italiana,* p. 104.

113. ACS, CPC, Busta 4421, fascicolo 4.

114. Gaetano Salvemini, *Carlo and Nello Rosselli: A Memoir* (London: For Intellectual Liberty, 1937), pp. 65–68; idem, "L'assassinio dei fratelli Rosselli," in Rossi, *No al fascismo,* pp. 255–304; idem, "The Rosselli Murders," *The New Republic,* 18 August 1937, p. 50; see also Charles F. Delzell, "The Assassination of Carlo and Nello Rosselli, June 9, 1937: Closing a Chapter of Italian Anti-Fascism," *Italian Quarterly* 28, no. 107 (Winter 1987): 47–64; Pierre Guillen, "La risonanza in Francia dell'azione di Giustizia e Libertà e dell'assassinio dei fratelli Rosselli," in *Giustizia e Libertà nella lotta antifascista,* pp. 239–260.

115. Both the postcard and the note are in the AGL, sezione I, fascicolo 9, sottofascicolo 1.

116. Lussu testified at the trial of General Roatta that "the day of the funerals, the immense boulevard that led to Père Lachaise cemetery was filled with more than 300,000 persons, of all countries. Not only Paris, but all of Europe was present that day." His testimony is reproduced in Mario Roatta, *Il processo Roatta: i documenti* (Rome: Universale De Luigi, 1945), pp. 82–84.

117. The phrase is Salvemini's, "L'assassinio dei fratelli Rosselli," p. 258. Twelve years later (1949), a monument was erected in the forest of Bagnoles-de-l'Orne to mark the site of the assassinations. Carlo Sergio Signori was commissioned to create the work, a stark and poignant design that was, according to the artist Gino Severini, "the first abstract monument in France. The abstraction of the forms expresses a mysterious and moving grandeur that is tied to the tragedy." Amelia Rosselli wrote that "the work [was] extremely noble and significant in its austere simplicity." See Luciano Galmozzo, *Monumenti alla libertà: antifascismo, resistenza e pace nei monumenti italiani dal 1945 al 1985* (Milan: La Pietra, 1986), pp. 41–42.

118. On 12 June, *Il Telegrafo* wrote that the assassination was the result of "suppression" due to the "hatreds among the diverse extremist sects of antifascism." Ansaldo wrote that "Rosselli, who recently had become a communist, had expressed, in private and in public, his approval of the 'suppression' of Berneri. This approval attracted the hatred of the Italian and Catalonian anarchists living in France." The next day the paper insisted that Rosselli "had

fallen almost certainly because of some anarchist vendetta." Quoted in Salvemini, "L'assassinio dei fratelli Rosselli," pp. 258–259n1.

119. Salvemini, *Carlo and Nello Rosselli*, p. 68.

120. Yvon de Begnac, *Palazzo Venezia: storia di un regime* (Rome: La Rocca, 1950), p. 613; quoted in Renzo De Felice, *Mussolini: Il Duce*, v. 2 *Lo stato totalitario* (Turin: Einaudi, 1981), p. 422. De Felice writes (unconvincingly) that there may be an indirect confirmation of Mussolini's innocence in the diary entry of 16 September 1937 of his son-in-law and Foreign Minister, Galeazzo Ciano. Referring to a terrorist attack by the *cagoulards* of 11 September, Ciano writes, "In any event, we are not involved." See Galeazzo Ciano, *Diario, 1937–1938* (Bologna: Cappelli, 1948), p. 37.

121. De Felice, *Mussolini il Duce*, v. 2, *Lo stato totalitario*, pp. 419, 423.

122. Ciano, *Diario, 1937–1938*, p. 256.

123. Marion Rosselli to the Editor, *The New York Times*, 2 October 1944.

124. ACS, CPC, Busta 4421, fascicolo 4. Emphasis added.

125. Foreword to Aldo Rosselli, *La famiglia Rosselli: una tragedia italiana*, p. vi.

126. "Marion Rosselli," *Il Ponte* 5, no. 11 (November 1949): 1443.

127. On the *Cagoule*, see Philippe Bourdel, *Le Cagoule* (Paris: Albin Michel, 1970), and Christian Bernadac, *Dagore: Les cahiers secrets de la Cagoule* (Paris: France Empire Ed., 1977); see also J. R. Tournoux, *L'Histoire Secrete: La Cagoule, le Front Populaire, Vichy, Londres, Deuzieme Bureau l'Algérie Française, L'OAS* (Paris: Plon, 1962), and Douglas Porch, *The French Secret Services: From the Dreyfus Affair to the Gulf War* (New York: Farrar, Straus and Giroux, 1995).

128. Marion's identification of Jakubiez is recounted in Salvemini, "L'assassinio dei fratelli Rosselli," p. 263; the Zanatta episode is in Garosci, *Vita*, II, pp. 147–148.

129. *Matin*, 13 January 1938, quoted in Salvemini, "L'assassinio dei fratelli Rosselli," p. 264.

130. *La France*, 17 September 1942.

131. Salvemini, "L'assassinio dei fratelli Rosselli," p. 265.

132. Ibid., pp. 293–294, p. 1.

133. The document, "Highly Classified" (RISSERVATISSIMA RACCOMAN-DATA) is found in the ACS, CPC, busta 4221, fascicolo 4.

134. Roy Palmer Domenico, *Italian Fascists on Trial, 1943–1948* (Chapell Hill, NC: University of North Carolina Press, 1991), p. x.

135. Clara Conti, *Servizio segreto* (Rome: Donatello De Luigi, 1945), p. 112.

136. Ibid., pp. 22–23. Conti was the secretary of Judge Italo Robino; the two were later married.

137. From the transcript of the High Court of Justice, 12 March 1945; quoted in Conti, *Servisio segreto*, p. 31, and Salvemini, "L'assassinio dei fratelli Rosselli," p. 266.

138. Testimony of Santo Emanuele at the Roatta trial, quoted in Conti, *Servizio segreto,* pp. 257–269; and Salvemini, "L'assassinio dei fratelli Rosselli," pp. 267–269.

139. Roatta, *Il processo Roatta: i documenti,* pp. 12–13.

140. Ibid., p. 26.

141. Salvemini, "L'assassinio dei fratelli Rosselli," pp. 279–286.

142. Roatta, *Il processo Roatta: i documenti,* p. 77.

143. Ibid., pp. 82–117. Calamandrei's speech before the court is partially reprinted in Roatta, *Il processo Roatta;* the entire speech was published as Calamandrei, *Arringhe e discorsi: In memoria di Carlo e Nello Rosselli nel processo dinanzi l'Alta Corte contro Roatta e C.* (Naples: Rispoli, 1945).

144. Roatta, *Il processo Roatta: i documenti,* p. 183.

145. Domenico, *Italian Fascists on Trial, 1943–1948,* pp. 134–139. The Italian penal and judicial system continues to "lose" suspects and prisoners; some of the more imfamous episodes include that of SS officer Herbert Kappler, convicted of his role in the Ardeatine Caves massacre of 24 March 1944 (supposedly spirited away by his diminutive wife in a suitcase), and that of Licio Gelli, leader of the murky P2 Masonic Lodge, who had been tied to shadowy right-wing plots to destabilize the country and who fled in 1998.

146. Alberto Moravia, *Il conformista* (Milan: Bompiani, 1951); perhaps the best psychological profile of the "fascist" mentality; in English, *The Conformist,* trans. Angus Davidson (New York: Farrar, Straus, Young, 1951). Moravia relates his book to the Rosselli assassinations in Enzo Siciliano, *Moravia* (Milan: Longanesi, 1971), p. 89. For an analysis of Bertolucci's film, see Angela Dalle Vacche, *The Body in the Mirror: Shapes of History in Italian Cinema* (Princeton, N.J.: Princeton University Press, 1992), pp. 57–92; Peter Bondanella, *Italian Cinema: From Neorealism to the Present* (New York: Frederick Ungar, 1983), pp. 301–306; Millicent Marcus, *Italian Film in the Light of Neorealism* (Princeton, N.J.: Princeton University Press, 1986), pp. 285–312.

Conclusion

1. "The Foreign Policy of Fascist Italy," the original English copy is in the AGL; translated and edited as "La politica estera fascista" by Costanzo Casucci, *Il Mulino* 33, no. 292 (March-April 1984): 241–261.

2. See especially Giovanni De Luna and Marco Revelli, *Fascismo/Antifascismo: Le idee e le identità* (Florence: La Nuova Italia, 1995); Gian Enrico Rusconi, *Resistenza e postfascismo* (Bologna: Il Mulino, 1995); Pietro Scoppola, *25 aprile: La Liberazione* (Turin: Einaudi, 1995). Much debate was stimulated by Claudio Pavone's *Una guerra civile: saggio storico sulla moralità nella Resistenza* (Turin: Bollati Boringhieri, 1991); see also Renzo De Felice, *Rosso e Nero,*

ed. Pasquale Chessa (Milan: Baldini & Cartoldi, 1995), and De Felice's *Fascismo, antifascismo, nazione* (Rome: Bonacci, 1996). For an excellent study of the historiographical problems of antifascism and the Resistance, see Alberto Aquarone, *Fascismo e antifascismo nella storiografia italiana* (Rome: Edizione della Voce, 1986). For a spirited defense of both Rosselli and the Resistance, see Nicola Tranfaglia, *Labirinto italiano: il fascismo, l'antifascismo, gli storici* (Florence: La Nuova Italia, 1989) and *Un passato scomodo: Fascismo e postfascismo* (Rome: Laterza, 1996); and Paolo Bagnoli, *Rosselli, Gobetti e la rivoluzione democratica* (Florence: La Nuova Italia, 1996). More debate was generated with Ernesto Galli della Loggia, *La morte della patria: La crisi dell'idea di nazione tra Resistenza, antifascismo e Repubblica* (Rome: Laterza, 1996); Enzo Collotti and Lutz Klinkhammer, *Il fascismo e l'Italia in guerra* (Rome: Ediesse, 1996); and Furio Colombo and Vittorio Feltri, *Fascismo/Antifascismo* (Milan: Rizzoli, 1994).

3. Two conferences in particular were fruitful: "Passato e presente della Resistenza. 50 anniversario della Resistenza e della Guerra di liberazione," 1–3 October 1993 in Rome; and "Antifascismi e Resistenze" organized by the Gramsci Institute in Rome, 5–6 October 1995. The proceedings of the latter conference have been published as *Fascismo, antifascismo, democrazia. A cinquant'anni dal 25 aprile* in *Studi Storici* 36, no. 3 (July–September 1995).

4. Palmiro Togliatti, "La lotta per la pace e per la libertà è degna di tutti sacrifici," *Lo Stato Operaio* 11 nos. 5–6 (May–June 1937): 298–306. The same issue commemorated the death of Antonio Gramsci.

5. Gaetano Salvemini, *Carlo and Nello Rosselli: A Memoir* (London: For Intellectual Liberty, 1937), p. 38.

6. Pietro Nenni, *Spagna* (Milan: SugarCo, 1976), p. 160.

7. Emilio Lussu, "Carlo Rosselli," *GL* (25 June 1937): 1.

8. Romain Rolland, "Carlo Rosselli," *L'Humanité*, 18 June 1937, p. 1; the statement by European intellectuals was first printed in *GL*, 25 June 1937, p. 1, and reprinted with the additional signatures of G. O. Griffith, Jacques Lipchitz, G. P. Gooch, and Henri Pollès in the same paper on 2 July 1937, p. 4.

9. Aldo Garosci kindly granted this author an interview at his home in Rome, 23 July 1993.

10. Augusto Monti, *Realtà del Partito d'Azione* (Turin: Einaudi, 1945), p. 41.

11. Aldo Rosselli, *La famiglia Rosselli: una tragedia italiana* (Milan: Bompiani, 1983), pp. 136–153.

12. Roberto Vivarelli, "Il testamento di uno 'storico empirico,'" *Il Ponte* 24, no. 1 (January 1968): 40–50.

13. Gaetano Salvemini, "Marion Rosselli," *Il Ponte* 6, no. 5 (May 1951): 1443; Corrado Tumiati, "Amelia Rosselli scrittrice," *Il Ponte* 12, no. 4 (April 1956): 576–586.

14. John Rosselli was interviewed by the author in San Rocco a Pili (Siena) on 2 July 1993. His works include *Singers of Italian Opera: The History of a Profession* (Cambridge: Cambridge University Press, 1992); *Music and Musicians in Nineteenth-Century Italy* (London: B. T. Batsford, 1991); *The Opera Industry in Italy from Cimarosa to Verdi: The Role of the Impresario* (Cambridge: Cambridge University Press, 1984); *Lord William Bentinck: The Making of a Liberal Imperialist* (Berkeley: University of California Press, 1974); *Lord William Bentinck and the British Occupation of Sicily* (Lanham, Md.: University Press of America, 1956).

15. Giacinto Spagnoletti, ed., *Amelia Rosselli: antologia poetica* (Milan: Garzanti, 1987), pp. 149–163. Other works of her poetry include Amelia Rosselli, *Documento (1966–1973)* (Milan: Garzanti, 1976); Amelia Rosselli, *Sleep: poesie in inglese* (Milan: Garzanti, 1992); and the posthumously published Emmanuela Jandello, ed., *Le poesie* (Milan: Garzanti, 1997).

16. Spagnoletti, *Amelia Rosselli: antologia poetica*, p. 163.

17. "Si uccide la poetessa Amelia Rosselli," *America Oggi* (12 February 1996): 31.

18. Guido Calogero, *Difesa del liberalsocialismo*, ed. Michele Schiavone and Dino Cofrancesco (Milan: Marzorati, 1968), p. 199. In Calogero's version, "liberal-socialism" was one word with no hyphen.

19. Norberto Bobbio, *Ideological Profile of Twentieth-Century Italy*, trans. Lydia G. Cochrane (Princeton, N.J.: Princeton University Press, 1995), p. 155.

20. Giovanni De Luna, *Storia del Partito d'Azione*, 2nd ed. (Milan: Feltrinelli, 1996). "Il programma del Partito d'Azione," *Nuovi Quaderni di Giustizia e Libertà*, no. 4 (November–December 1944).

21. The CLN was composed of five parties: the PLI, the DC, the PSI, the PCI, and the Action Party.

22. Leone Ginzburg, *Scritti*, ed. Domenico Zucàro and Carl Ginzburg (Turin: Einaudi, 1962), p. 34.

23. On the Action Party, see David Ward, *Antifascisms: Cultural Politics in Italy, 1943–1946* (Madison, N.J.: Fairleigh Dickinson University Press, 1996), pp. 124–156; Giovanni De Luna, *Storia del Partito d'Azione*; and John L. Hirsh, "Radical Anti-Fascism: Origins and Politics of the Italian Action Party," Ph.D. diss., University of Wisconsin, 1965.

24. Domenico Settembrini, "The Divided Left: After Fascism, What?" in *Italian Socialism: Between Politics and History*, ed., Spencer Di Scala (Amherst: University of Massachusetts Press, 1996), p. 110.

25. Quoted in Giorgio Bocca, *Storia dell'Italia partigiana* (Milan: Mondadori, 1995), p. 416.

26. Ada Gobetti, *Diario partigiano* (Turin: Einaudi, 1956), p. 414.

27. Winston Churchill was adamant in preventing any leftist government from coming to power in Italy. He applied all the political clout available to save the

monarchy in Italy. In December 1944, representatives of the Resistance met the Allies in Rome; there, the so-called "Protocols of Rome" were signed, which symbolized, in the words of Sandro Pertini, "the subjection of the Resistance to British policy." See Paul Ginsborg, *A History of Contemporary Italy: Society and Politics, 1943–1988* (London: Penguin, 1990), pp. 57–58.

28. Ferruccio Parri, *Scritti 1915–1975* (Milan: Feltrinelli, 1976), p. 179.

29. The *svolta di Salerno* (reversal of Salerno) was Palmiro Togliatti's announcement—on returning to Italy from Moscow in 1944—that the "first order of business" was to defeat the Nazis; accordingly, the PCI would support the Badoglio regime, would not raise the "institutional question" of whether Italy was to be a monarchy or a republic after the war, and would defend the Lateran Accords with the Vatican. The Action Party, instead, refused to support Badoglio, demanded the dissolution of the Lateran Accords, and insisted that Victor Emmanuel III abdicate and that Italy be a democratic republic.

30. Parri's speech was printed in the daily newspaper of the Action Party, *L'Italia Libera,* 25 November 1945; reprinted in Parri, *Scritti 1915–1975,* pp. 195–201; and quoted in James D. Wilkinson, *The Intellectual Resistance in Europe* (Cambridge, Mass.: Harvard University Press, 1981), p. 228.

31. Carlo Levi, *L'orologio* (Turin: Einaudi, 1950); in English, *The Watch,* trans. John Farrar (New York: Farrar, Straus and Young, 1951). For an excellent study of this work, see Ward, *Antifascisms,* pp. 173–191.

32. Vincenzo Caciulli, "Nel nome dei Rosselli: La rinascita del Circolo di Cultura e i primi anni di attività," *Quaderni del Circolo Rosselli* 9, no. 1 (January 1991): 61–73. I am particularly indebted to the Honorable Valdo Spini, Director of the Circolo Rosselli for his kind assistance and gracious hospitality in Florence.

33. Enrico Berlinguer, "Reflections on the Events in Chile," *Marxism Today* 18, no. 2 (February 1974): 39–50; originally in *Rinascita* (12 October 1973): 43; quoted in Frank Cunningham, *Democratic Theory and Socialism* (Cambridge: Cambridge University Press, 1987), p. 290.

34. Ginsborg, *A History of Contemporary Italy,* p. 418.

35. Giovanni Spadolini was also a highly respected intellectual and historian, who died in 1994. Among his many scholarly works, see *Carlo e Nello Rosselli: le radice mazziniane del loro pensiero* (Florence: Passigli, 1990). See the essay by Leo Valiani (another member of GL) on Spadolini's death, "L'erede del Risorgimento," *Il Corriere della Sera,* 5 August 1994.

36. www.fabernet.com/sa/Giustizia/Liberta.htm; e-mail GL@Fabernet.com.

37. Giorgio Amendola, "Per una storia dell'antifascismo," *L'Unità,* 20 July 1975. For English language studies of the historiography of the Resistance, see Charles F. Delzell, "The Italian Anti-Fascist Resistance in Retrospect: Three

Decades of Historiography," *Journal of Modern History* 47 (March 1975): 66–96; Marino Berengo, "Italian Historical Scholarship Since the Fascist Era," *Daedalus* (Spring 1971): 469–484; and Emiliana Noether, "Italy Reviews Her Fascist Past," *American Historical Review* 61 (July 1956): 877–899.

38. Amendola, "Per una storia dell'antifascismo," p. 1.

39. Leo Valiani, "Ma quanti erano gli antifascisti?" interview with Valerio Riva in *L'Espresso,* no. 31 (3 August 1975): 30; ironically, Paolo Spriano paints a rather sympathetic portrait of Rosselli in his official history of the PCI, *Storia del Partito comunista italiano,* 5 vols., particularly in vol. III "I fronti popolari, Stalin, la guerra" (Turin: Einaudi, 1970), especially pp. 212–213.

40. Leo Valiani, "No caro Amendola, Rosselli vide giuste," *L'Espresso,* no. 36 (7 September 1975): 23.

41. Giorgio Amendola, "Con il proletariato o contro il proletariato?" *Lo Stato Operaio* 5, no. 6 (June 1931): 309–318; Rosselli's reply was "Risposta a Giorgio Amendola," *QGL,* no. 1 (January 1932): 33–40. For a study of these essays, see chapter 4.

42. Sandro Pertini, "Amendola, a che punto sei arrivato?" *L'Espresso,* no. 37 (14 September 1975); Ugo La Malfa, "Quando cacciamo via il re," *L'Espresso,* no. 36 (7 September 1975).

43. "The communists responded and a confrontation began—naturally polemical—between the communists and GL . . . Rosselli answered me, criticizing and rejecting my positions, but in a very serious manner." Giorgio Amendola, *Intervista sull'antifascismo* (Bari: Laterza, 1976), p. 69.

44. Costanzo Casucci, former Director of the Archivio Centrale dello Stato and editor of Carlo Rosselli's *Scritti dell'esilio,* 2 vols. (Turin: Einaudi, 1988/1992), and *Dall'esilio: Lettere alla moglie 1929–1937* (Florence: Passigli, 1997); in an interview with the author in Rome, 23 June 1993.

45. Tranfaglia, *Labirinto italiano,* p. 186. Gaetano Arfè has argued that Italian socialism abandoned the Rosselli legacy at tremendous cost, in "Carlo Rosselli nella storia del socialismo italiano," in *Giustizia e Libertà nella lotta antifascista,* pp. 23–48.

46. Giovanni Spadolini (1925–1994) of the Italian Republican Party (PRI) was the first prime minister of postwar Italy who was not a Christian Democrat; Norberto Bobbio has been for many years professor of political philosophy at the University of Turin and a member of Parliament. Among Bobbio's many works, see *Left and Right: The Significance of Political Tradition,* trans. Allan Cameron (Chicago: University of Chicago Press, 1996); *Liberalism and Democracy,* trans. Martin Ryle and Kate Soper (London: Verso, 1990); *Democracy and Dictatorship: The Nature and Limits of State Power,* trans. Peter Kennealy (Minneapolis: University of Minnesota Press, 1989); *Which Socialism? Marxism, Socialism and Democracy,* trans. Roger Griffin (Minneapolis: University

of Minnesota Press, 1987); and especially his Introduction to the reprint of Carlo Rosselli's *Socialismo liberale,* ed. John Rosselli (Turin: Einaudi, 1979). A recent translation of Bobbio's work is the invaluable *Ideological Profile of Twentieth-Century Italy.*

47. The first quote is found in Albert S. Lindemann, *A History of Eureopan Socialism* (New Haven: Yale University Press, 1983), p. 340; the second was recounted to the author by the Honorable Valdo Spini in Florence, 18 January 1998.

48. Salvemini's speech was reprinted as "Carlo e Nello Rosselli," *Il Ponte* 6, no. 5 (May 1951): 451–461, and in *Tornano i Rosselli* (Florence: Circolo di Cultura Politica "Fratelli Rosselli," 1951), pp. 7–17. The graves of the Rosselli brothers are flanked by those of Nello Traquandi, Ernesto Rossi, and Gaetano Salvemini who died in 1957.

49. The "ironist's cage" is the political, linguistic, and philosophical trap that contemporary cultural critics have constructed for themselves as compensation for their failure to forge a valid political program; Michael S. Roth, *The Ironist's Cage: Memory, Trauma, and the Construction of History* (New York: Columbia University Press, 1995).

50. Ira Katznelson, *Liberalism's Crooked Circle* (Princeton, N.J.: Princeton University Press, 1996), p. 43.

Selected Bibliography

Works by Carlo Rosselli

Socialisme libéral, trans. Stefan Priacel. Paris: Librairie Valois, 1930.

Oggi in Spagna, domani in Italia, preface by Gaetano Salvemini. Paris: Edizioni di Giustizia e Libertà, 1938.

Scritti politici e autobiografici, preface by Gaetano Salvemini. Naples: Polis Editrice, 1944.

Socialismo liberale, preface by Gaetano Salvemini. Naples: Polis Editrice, 1944.

Socialismo liberale. Rome: Edizioni U, 1945.

Socialismo liberale. Turin: Einaudi, 1989.

Socialismo liberale. Turin: Einaudi, 1997.

Oggi in Spagna, domani in Italia, preface by Gaetano Salvemini, introduction by Aldo Garosci. Turin: Einaudi, 1967.

Opere scelte di Carlo Rosselli: Socialismo liberale, vol. 1, ed. John Rosselli, preface by Aldo Garosci. Turin: Einaudi, 1973.

Epistolario familiare: Carlo, Nello Rosselli e la madre (1914–1937), ed. and preface by Zeffiro Ciuffoletti, introduction by Leo Valiani. Milan: SugarCo, 1979; reprinted as *I Rosselli: Epistolario familiare.* Milan: Mondadori, 1997.

Socialismo liberale, ed. John Rosselli, introduction by Norberto Bobbio. Turin: Einaudi, 1979.

Carlo Rosselli: Scritti politici, ed. Zeffiro Ciuffoletti and Paolo Bagnoli. Naples: Giuda, 1988.

Scritti dell'esilio, I, *Giustizia e Libertà e la Concentrazione Antifascista (1929–1934),* ed. Costanzo Cassucci. Turin: Einaudi, 1988. (Volume II, tome I of *Opere scelte di Carlo Rosselli*).

Socialismo liberal, trans. Diego Abad de Santillán. Madrid: Pablo Iglesias, 1991.

Scritti dell'esilio, II, *Dallo scogliamento della Concentrazione Antifascista alla guerra di Spagna (1934–1937),* ed. Costanzo Casucci. Turin: Einaudi, 1992. (Volume II, tome II of *Opere scelte di Carlo Rosselli*).

Liberal Socialism, ed. and introduction by Nadia Urbinati, trans. William McCuaig. Princeton, N.J.: Princeton University Press, 1994.

Dall'esilio: Lettere alla moglie 1929–1937, ed. Costanzo Casucci. Florence: Passigli, 1997.

Politica e affetti familiare: Lettere di Amelia, Carlo e Nello Rosselli a Guglielmo, Leo e Nina Ferrero e Gina Lombroso Ferrero (1917–1943), ed. Marina Calloni and Lorella Cedroni. Milan: Feltrinelli, 1997.

Journals, Newspapers, Reviews

Avanti!, Istituto Socialista di Studi Storici (Florence).

Critica Sociale, ISRT.

Giustizia e Libertà, ISRT.

La Libertà, (Concentrazione Antifascista), ISRT.

Non Mollare!, ISRT.

Quaderni di Giustizia e Libertà, ISRT.

Il Quarto Stato, INSMLI.

La Riforma Sociale, Biblioteca Nazionale Firenze.

La Rivoluzione Liberale, Centro Gobetti, Turin.

Lo Stato Operaio, ISRT.

Archives

Archivio Centrale dello Stato, Rome.

Archivio Giustizia e Libertà, ISRT, Florence.

Cassellario Politico Centrale, in ACS, Rome.

Centro Gobetti, Turin.

Fondo Rosselli, Biblioteca Nazionale Firenze, Florence.

Istituto Nazionale per la Storia del Movimento di Liberazione in Italia, Milan.

Istituto Storico della Resistenza in Toscana, Florence.

Memoirs

Allason, Barbara. *Memorie di un'antifascista*. Rome: Edizione U, 1946.

Bauer, Riccardo. *Quello che ho fatto: Trent'anni di lotte e di ricordi*. Bari: Laterza, 1987.

Calamandrei, Piero. *Diario 1939–1945*, ed. Giorio Agosti. Florence: La Nuova Italia, 1982.

———. *In memoria di Carlo e Nello Rosselli nel processo dinanzi l'Alta Corte contro Roatta e Co.* Naples: Rispoli, 1945.

Ceva, Bianca. *1930: Retroscena di un dramma*. Milan: Ceschina, 1955.

Gentili, Dino, ed. *Italia ignorata*. Naples: La Città Libera, 1943.

Giua, Michele. *Ricordi di un ex-detenuto politico: 1935–1943*. Turin: Einaudi, 1945.

Giussani, Enrico. *Vita e pensiero di Carlo Rosselli*. Milan: Partito d'Azione, 1944.

Levi, Alessandro. *Ricordi dei fratelli Rosselli*. Florence: La Nuova Italia, 1947.

Lussu, Emilio. *La catena: dalle leggi eccezionali alle isole*. Paris: Edizioni di Giustizia e Libertà, 1929.

———. *Essere a sinistra: democrazia, autonomia e socialismo in cinquant'anni di lotte*. Milan: Mazzotta, 1976.

———. *Per l'Italia dall'esilio,* ed. Manlio Brigaglia. Cagliari: Edizioni della Torre, 1976.

———. *Road to Exile: The Story of a Sardinian Patriot,* trans. Mrs. Graham Rawson, with a preface by Wickham Steed. New York: Covici & Friede, 1936; first published as *Marcia su Roma*. Paris: Casa Editrice Critica, 1933; reprinted as *An Autobiographical Acount by a Leading Sardinian Republican Politician of Resistance to Fascism in Sardinia from 1919–1930,* trans. Roy W. Davis. New York: Edward Mellen Press, 1992.

Montagnana, Mario. *Ricordi di un militante*. Milan: Feltrinelli, 1947.

Montasini, Pietro. *L'Organisation des antifascistes italiennes a l'etranger*. Paris: Edizioni di Giustizia e Libertà, 1929.

Nitti, Francesco Fausto. *Escape: The Personal Narrative of a Political Prisoner Who Was Rescued from Lipari*. New York: Putnam, 1930.

———. *Le nostre prigione e la nostra evasione*. Naples: ESI, 1946.

Rosselli, Aldo. *La famiglia Rosselli: una tragedia italiana*. Milan: Bompiani, 1983.

———. *La mia America e la tua*. Rome: Theoria, 1995.

Rossi, Ernesto. *Un democratico ribelle: cospirazione antifascista, carcere, confino: scritti e testimonianze*. Parma: Guanda, 1975.

———. *Elogio della galera: Lettere 1930–1943,* ed. Manlio Magini. Bari: Laterza, 1968.

———. *Miserie e splendori del confino di polizia: lettere dal Ventotene,* ed. Manlio Magini. Milan: Feltrinelli, 1981.

Salvemini, Gaetano. *Carlo e Nello Rosselli*. Paris: Edizioni di Giustizia e Libertà, 1938.

———. *Memorie di un fuoruscito*. Milan: Feltrinelli, 1960.

Saragat, Giuseppe. *Filippo Turati e Carlo Rosselli*. Rome: PSI, 1944.

Valiani, Leo. *Ricordo dei fratelli Rosselli*. Florence: La Nuova Italia, 1947.